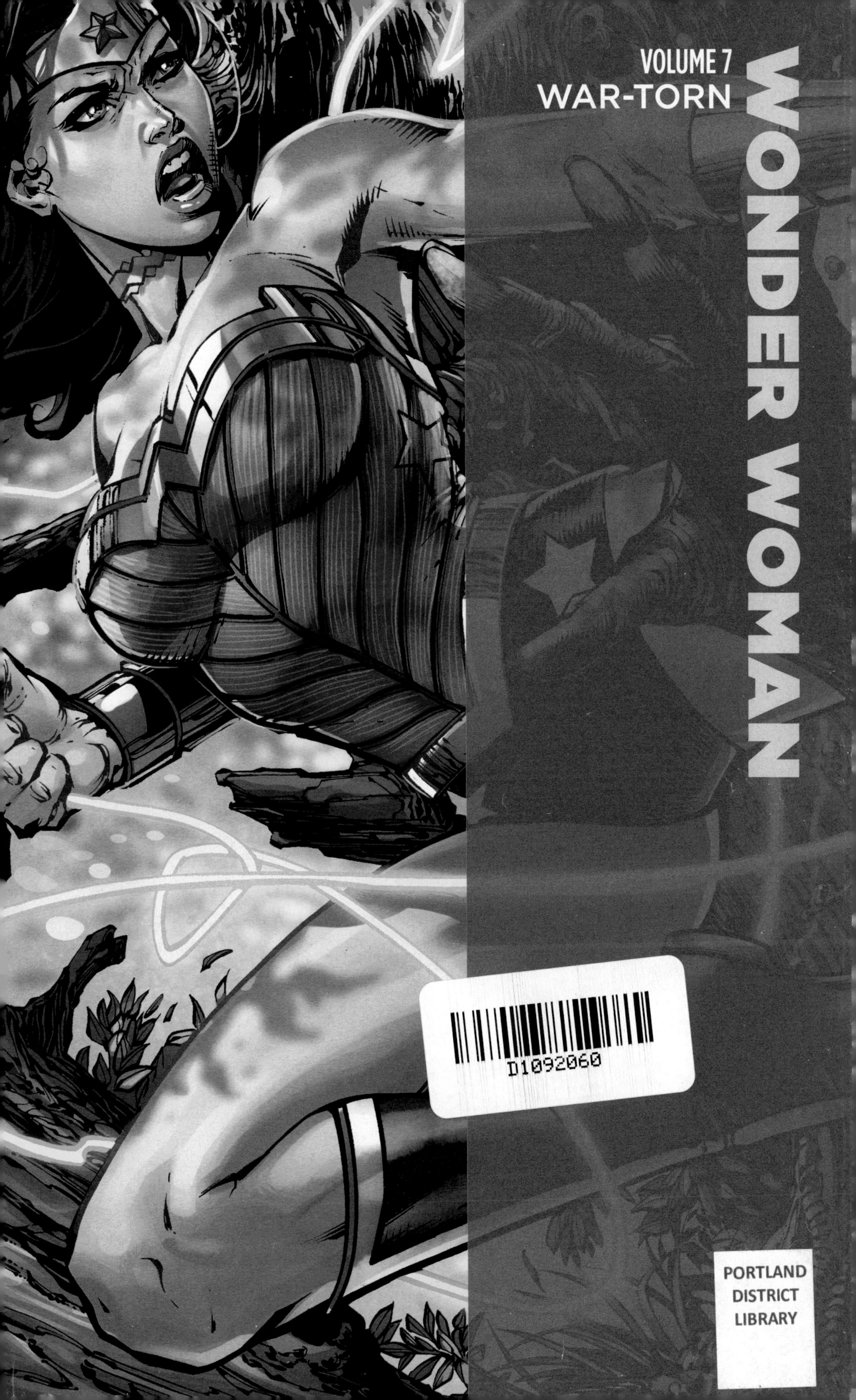
VOLUME 7
WAR-TORN
WONDER WOMAN

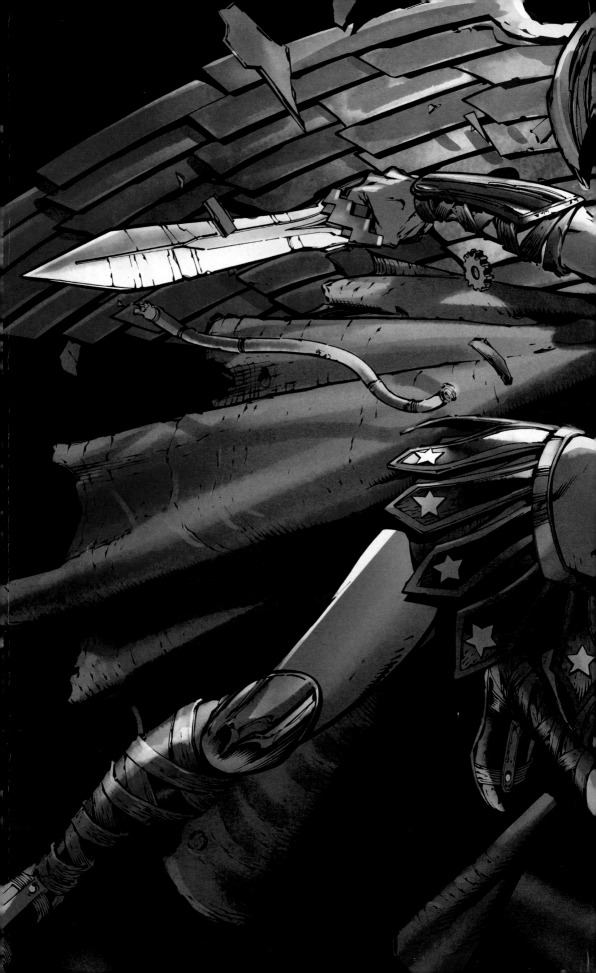

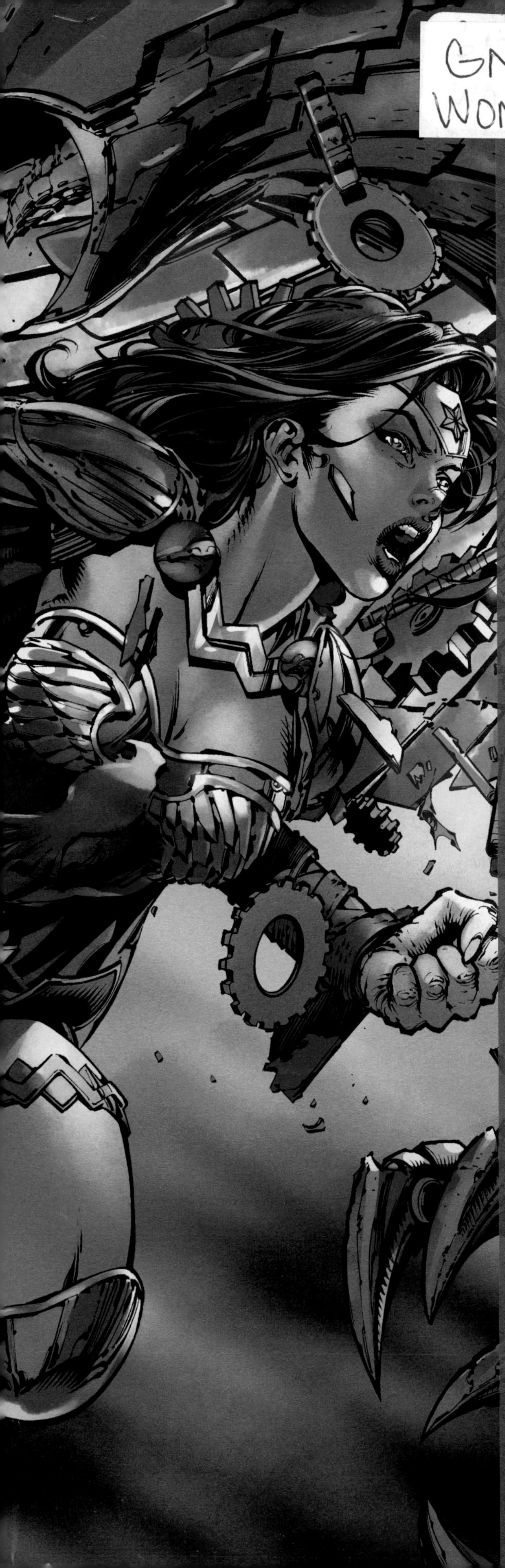

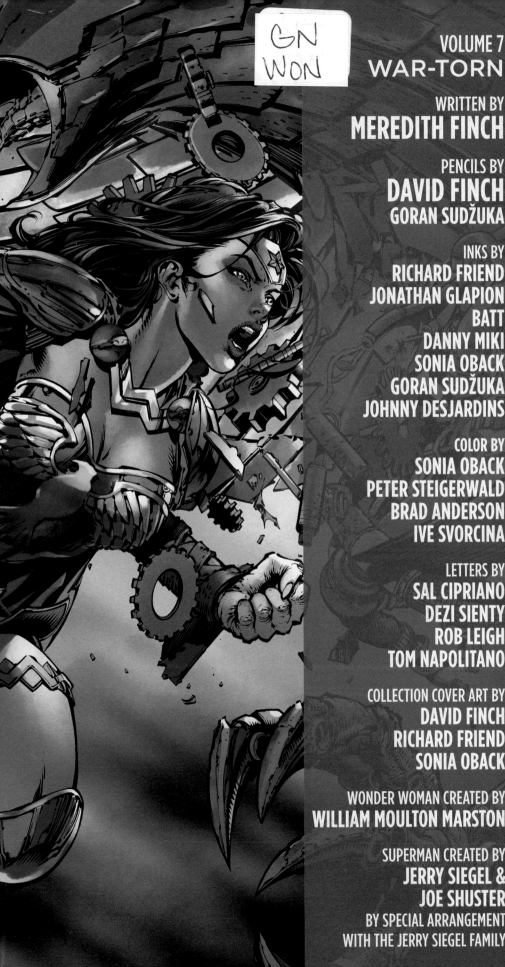

WONDER WOMAN

VOLUME 7
WAR-TORN

WRITTEN BY
MEREDITH FINCH

PENCILS BY
DAVID FINCH
GORAN SUDŽUKA

INKS BY
RICHARD FRIEND
JONATHAN GLAPION
BATT
DANNY MIKI
SONIA OBACK
GORAN SUDŽUKA
JOHNNY DESJARDINS

COLOR BY
SONIA OBACK
PETER STEIGERWALD
BRAD ANDERSON
IVE SVORCINA

LETTERS BY
SAL CIPRIANO
DEZI SIENTY
ROB LEIGH
TOM NAPOLITANO

COLLECTION COVER ART BY
DAVID FINCH
RICHARD FRIEND
SONIA OBACK

WONDER WOMAN CREATED BY
WILLIAM MOULTON MARSTON

SUPERMAN CREATED BY
JERRY SIEGEL &
JOE SHUSTER
BY SPECIAL ARRANGEMENT
WITH THE JERRY SIEGEL FAMILY

MATT IDELSON MIKE COTTON Editor – Original Series
PAUL KAMINSKI Associate Editor – Original Series
DAVID PIÑA Assistant Editor– Original Series
JEB WOODARD Group Editor – Collected Editions
LIZ ERICKSON Editor – Collected Edition
STEVE COOK Design Director – Books
DAMIAN RYLAND Publication Design

BOB HARRAS Senior VP – Editor-in-Chief, DC Comics

DIANE NELSON President
DAN DIDIO and JIM LEE Co-Publishers
GEOFF JOHNS Chief Creative Officer
AMIT DESAI Senior VP – Marketing & Global Franchise Management
NAIRI GARDINER Senior VP – Finance
SAM ADES VP – Digital Marketing
BOBBIE CHASE VP – Talent Development
MARK CHIARELLO Senior VP – Art, Design & Collected Editions
JOHN CUNNINGHAM VP – Content Strategy
ANNE DEPIES VP – Strategy Planning & Reporting
DON FALLETTI VP – Manufacturing Operations
LAWRENCE GANEM VP – Editorial Administration & Talent Relations
ALISON GILL Senior VP – Manufacturing & Operations
HANK KANALZ Senior VP – Editorial Strategy & Administration
JAY KOGAN VP – Legal Affairs
DEREK MADDALENA Senior VP – Sales & Business Development
DAN MIRON VP – Sales Planning & Trade Development
NICK NAPOLITANO VP – Manufacturing Administration
CAROL ROEDER VP – Marketing
EDDIE SCANNELL VP – Mass Account & Digital Sales
SUSAN SHEPPARD VP – Business Affairs
COURTNEY SIMMONS Senior VP – Publicity & Communications
JIM (SKI) SOKOLOWSKI VP – Comic Book Specialty & Newsstand Sales
SANDY YI Senior VP – Global Franchise Management

WONDER WOMAN VOLUME 7: WAR-TORN

Published by DC Comics. Compilation and all new material Copyright © 2016 DC Comics. All Rights Reserved.

Originally published in single magazine form in WONDER WOMAN 36-40,
WONDER WOMAN ANNUAL 1 © 2014, 2015 DC Comics. All Rights Reserved.
All characters, their distinctive likenesses and related elements featured in this publication
are trademarks of DC Comics. The stories, characters and incidents featured in this publication
are entirely fictional. DC Comics does not read or accept unsolicited ideas, stories or artwork.

DC Comics, 2900 West Alameda Ave., Burbank, CA 91505
Printed by RR Donnelley, Salem, VA, USA. 4/15/16. First Printing
ISBN: 978-1-4012-6163-4

Library of Congress Cataloguing in Publication Data is available

PEFC Certified

Printed on paper from
sustainably managed
forests and controlled
sources

PEFC/29-31-75   www.pefc.org

T 112251

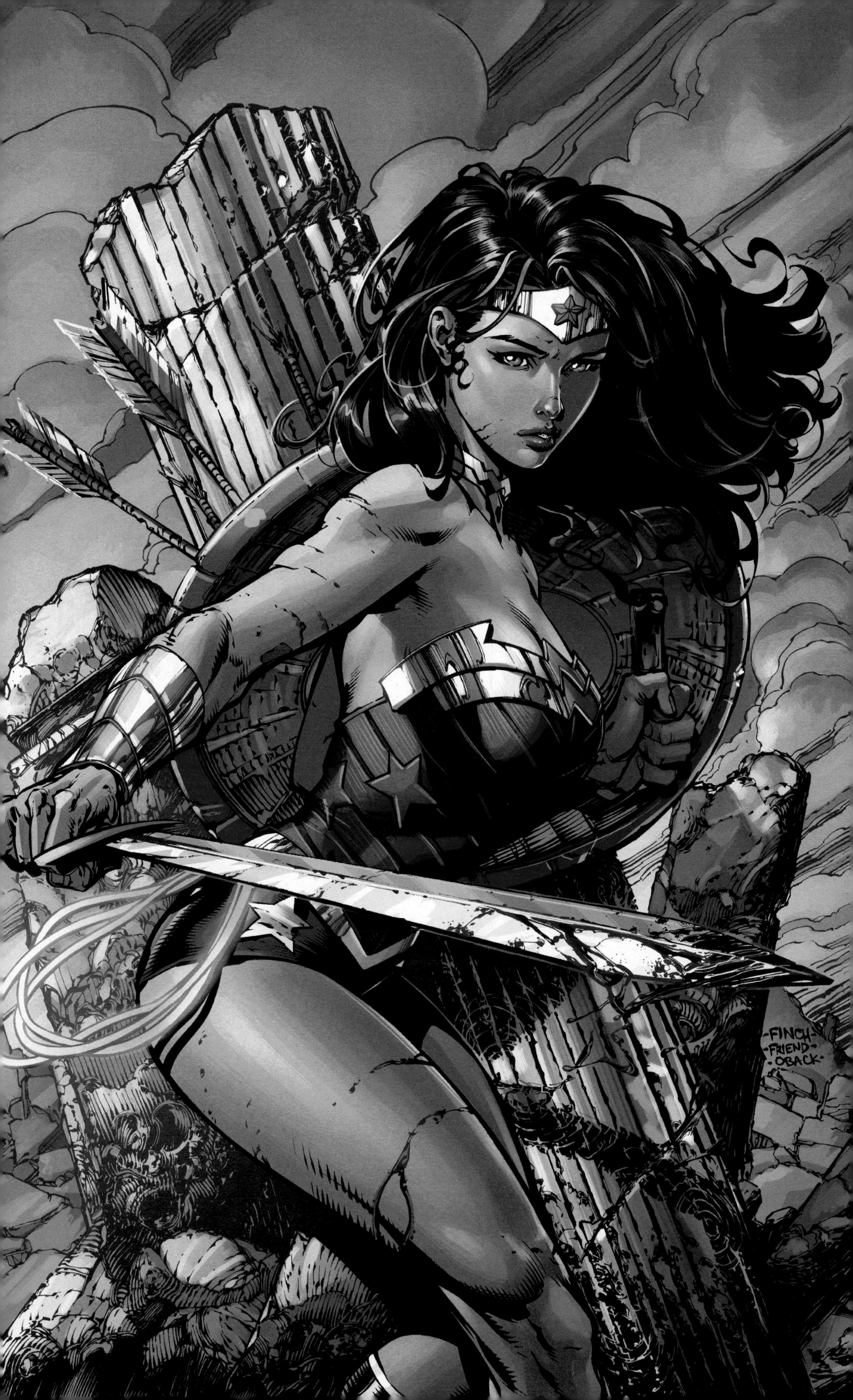
-FINCH-
-FRIEND-
-OBACK-

WAR-TORN CHAPTER 1

MEREDITH FINCH writer **DAVID FINCH** penciller **RICHARD FRIEND** inker **SONIA OBACK** colorist **SAL CIPRIANO** letterer cover by **FINCH, FRIEND** and **OBACK**

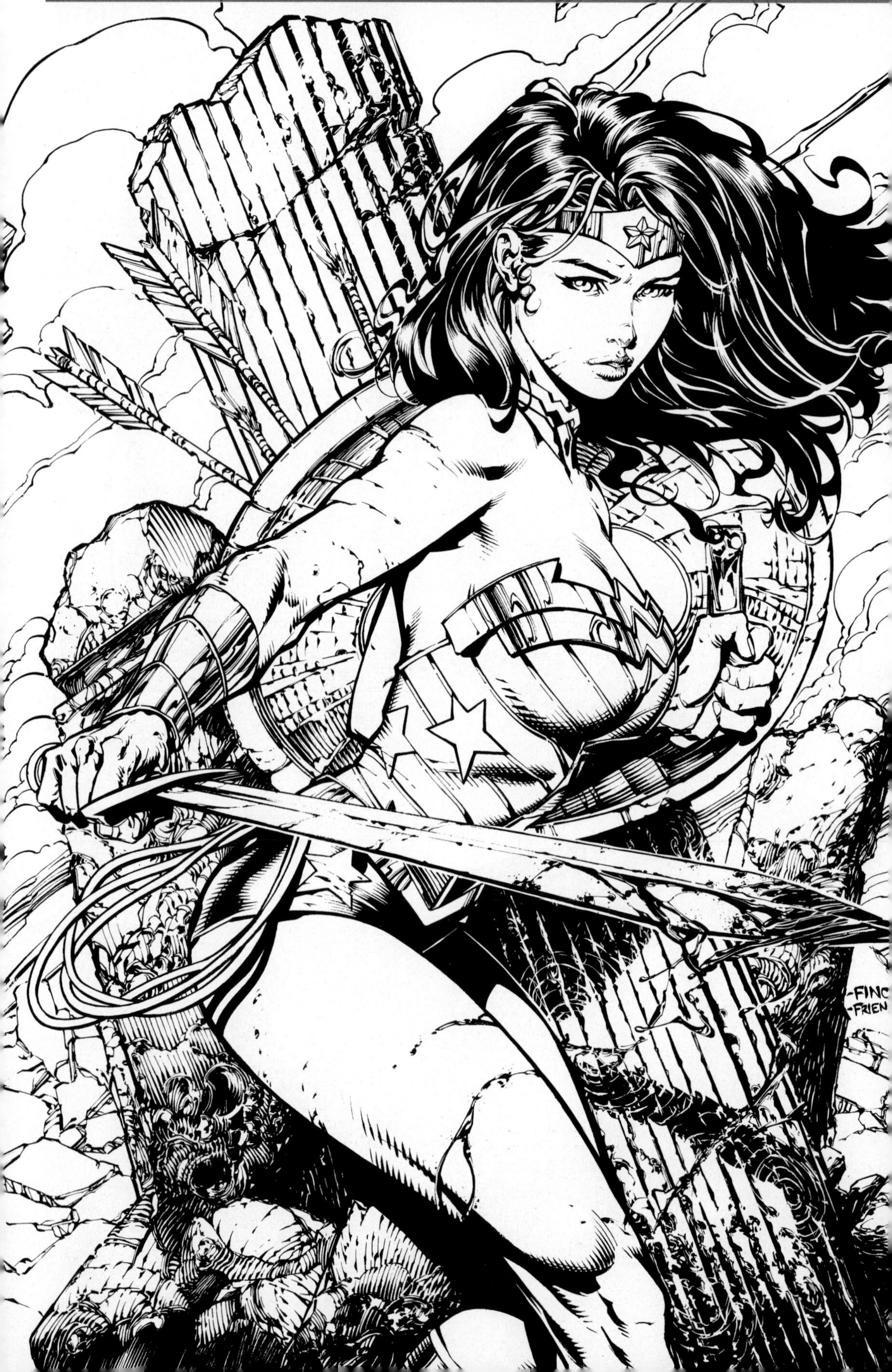

-FINC
-FRIEN

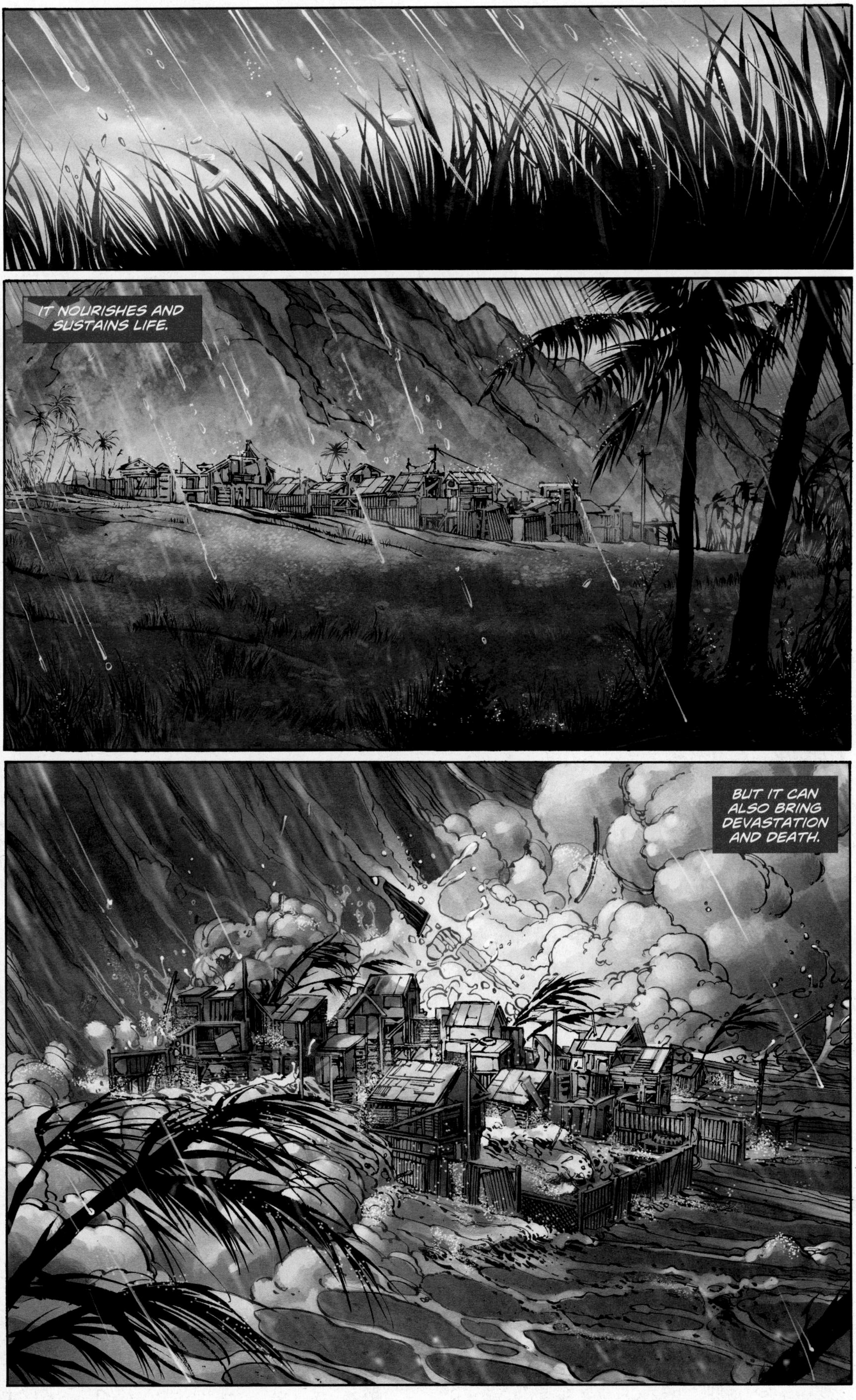
IT NOURISHES AND SUSTAINS LIFE.
BUT IT CAN ALSO BRING DEVASTATION AND DEATH.

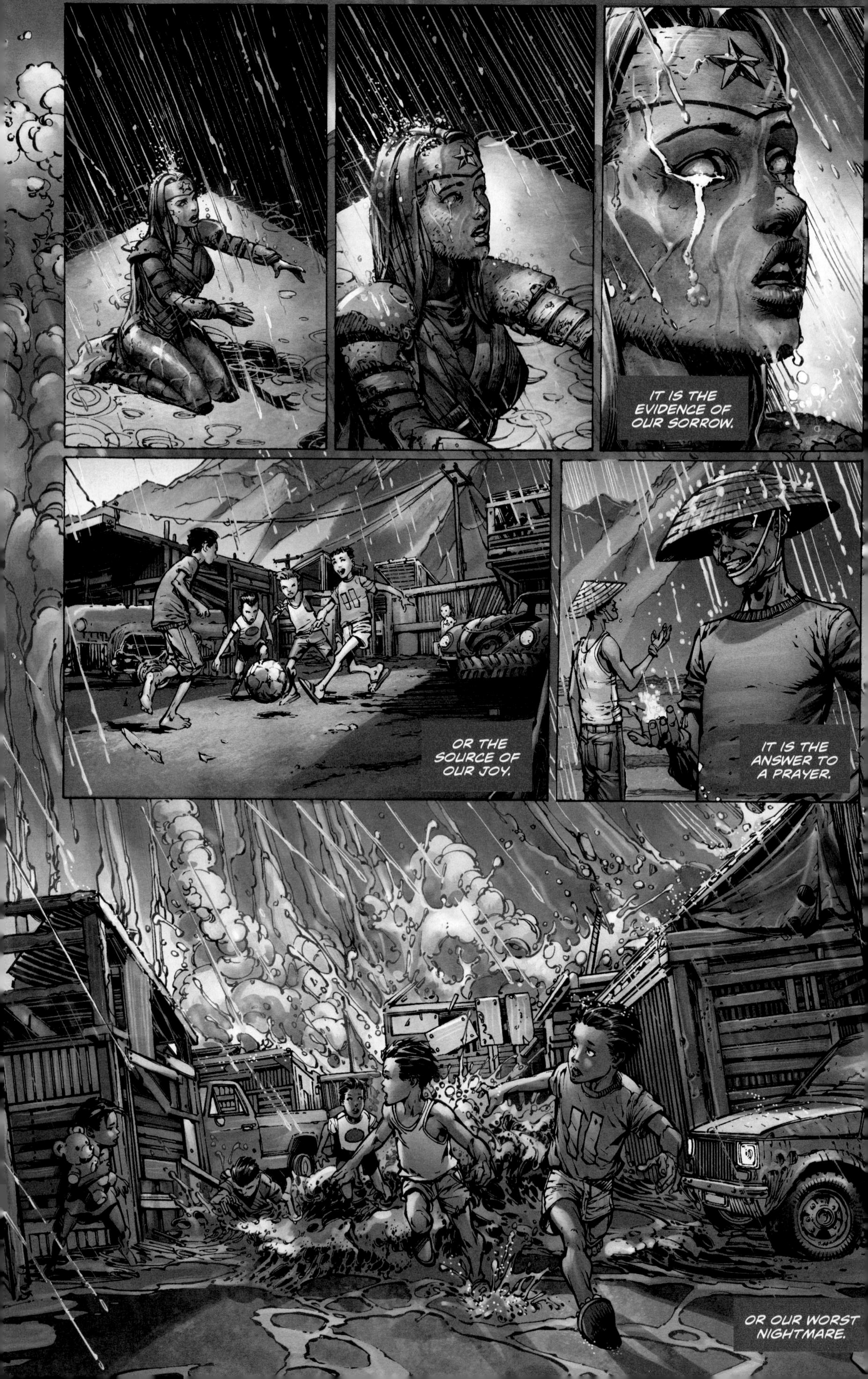
IT IS THE EVIDENCE OF OUR SORROW.
OR THE SOURCE OF OUR JOY.
IT IS THE ANSWER TO A PRAYER.
OR OUR WORST NIGHTMARE.

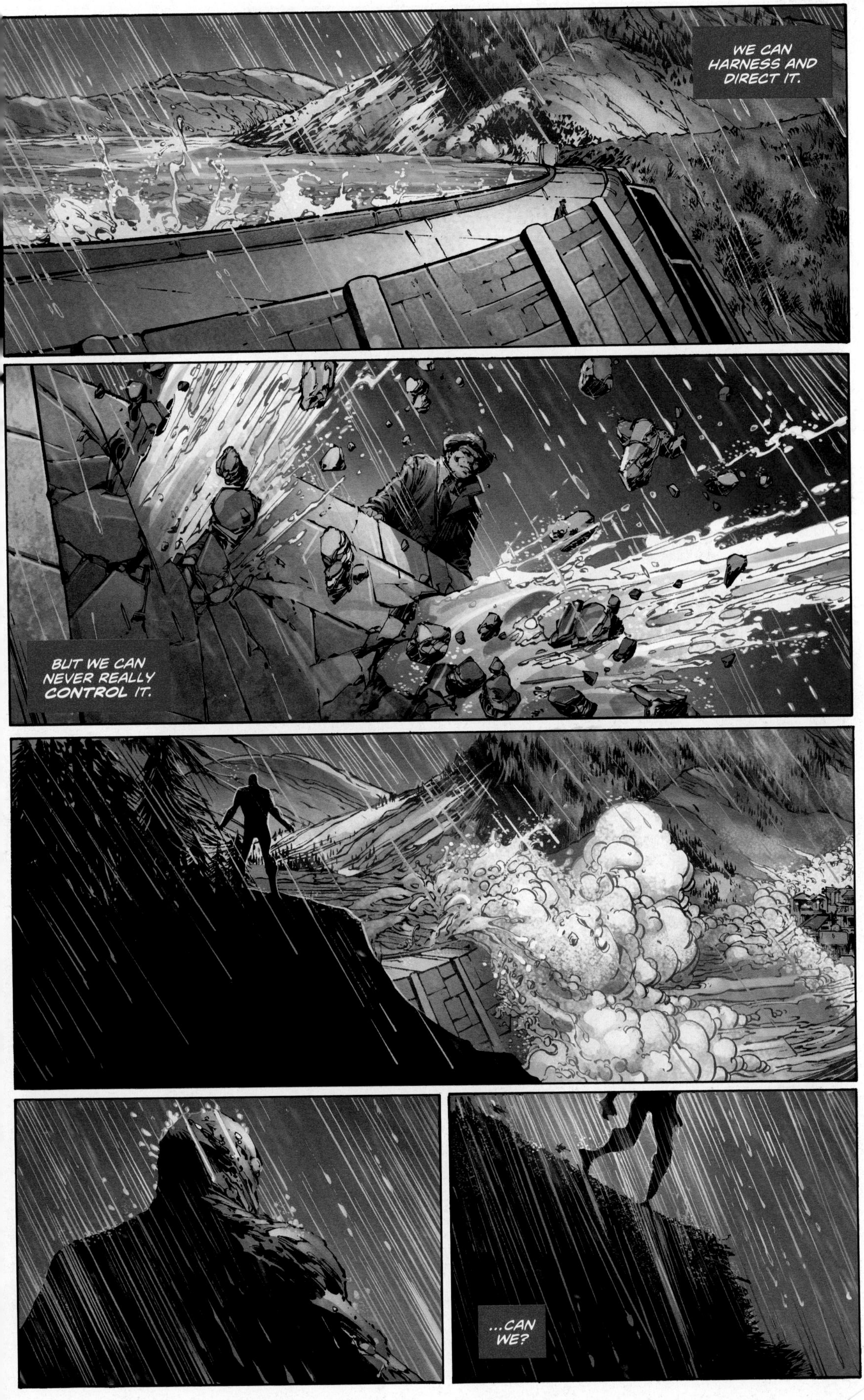
WE CAN HARNESS AND DIRECT IT.
BUT WE CAN NEVER REALLY CONTROL IT.
...CAN WE?

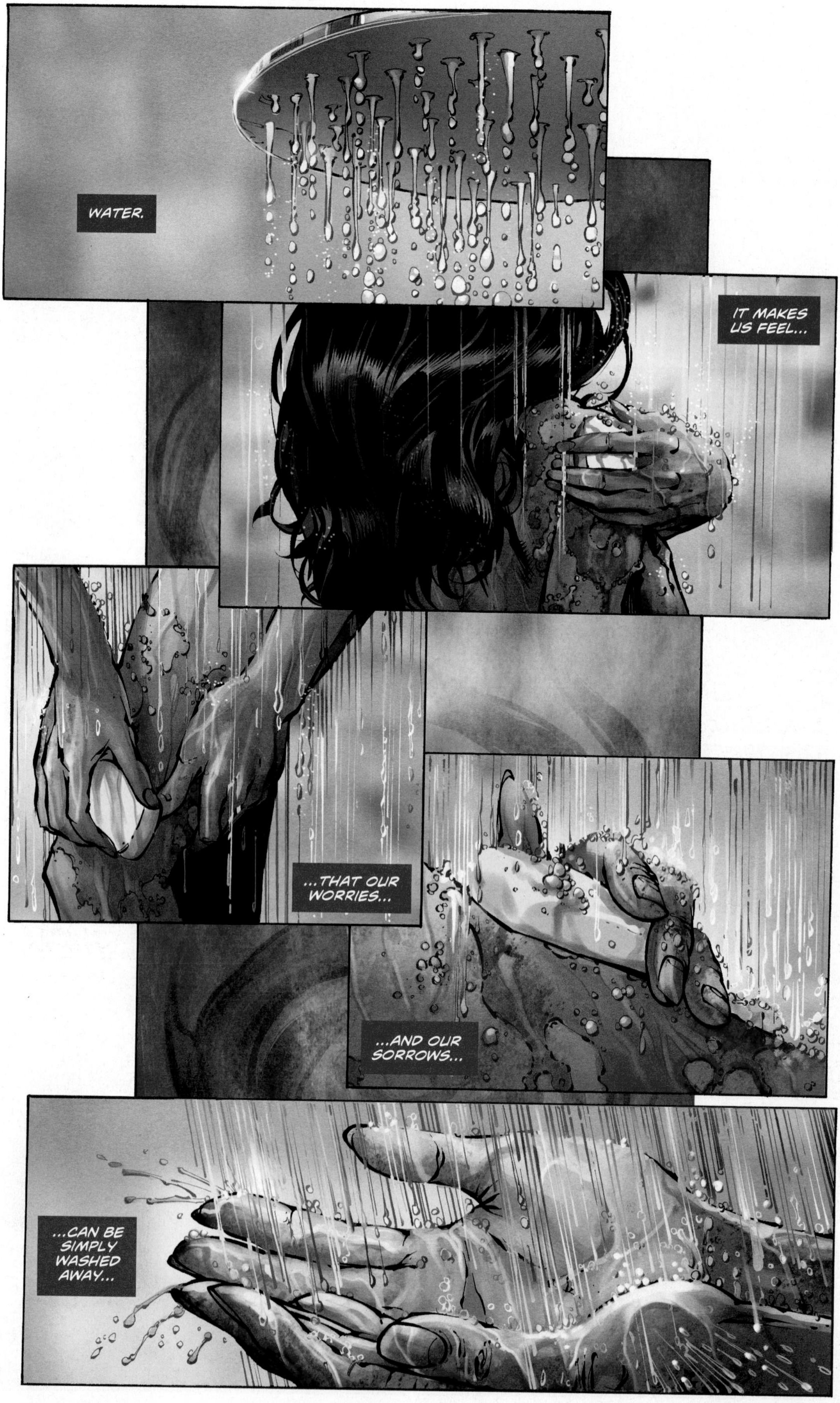
WATER.
IT MAKES US FEEL...
...THAT OUR WORRIES...
...AND OUR SORROWS...
...CAN BE SIMPLY WASHED AWAY...

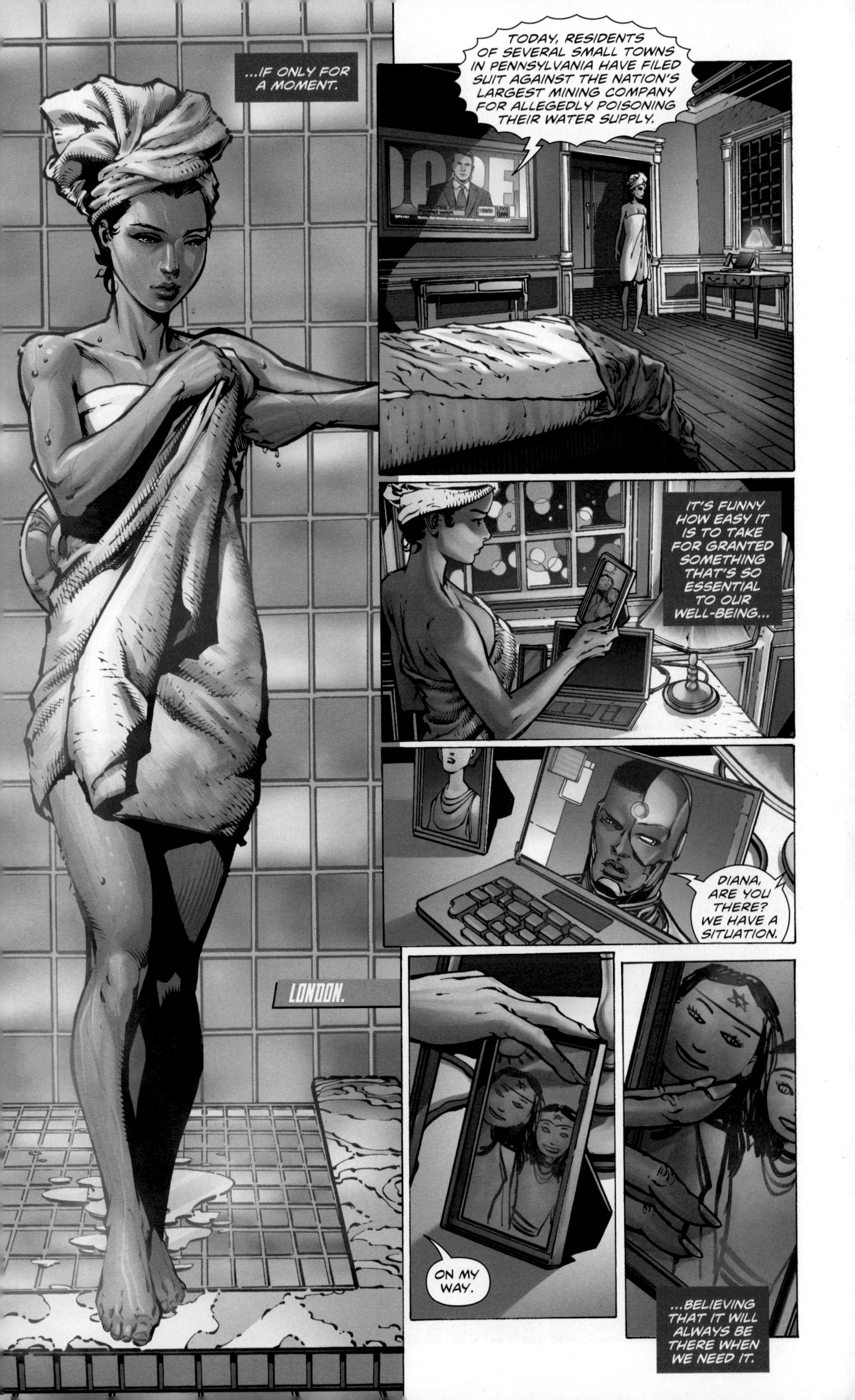
...IF ONLY FOR A MOMENT.
LONDON.
TODAY, RESIDENTS OF SEVERAL SMALL TOWNS IN PENNSYLVANIA HAVE FILED SUIT AGAINST THE NATION'S LARGEST MINING COMPANY FOR ALLEGEDLY POISONING THEIR WATER SUPPLY.
IT'S FUNNY HOW EASY IT IS TO TAKE FOR GRANTED SOMETHING THAT'S SO ESSENTIAL TO OUR WELL-BEING...
DIANA, ARE YOU THERE? WE HAVE A SITUATION.
ON MY WAY.
...BELIEVING THAT IT WILL ALWAYS BE THERE WHEN WE NEED IT.

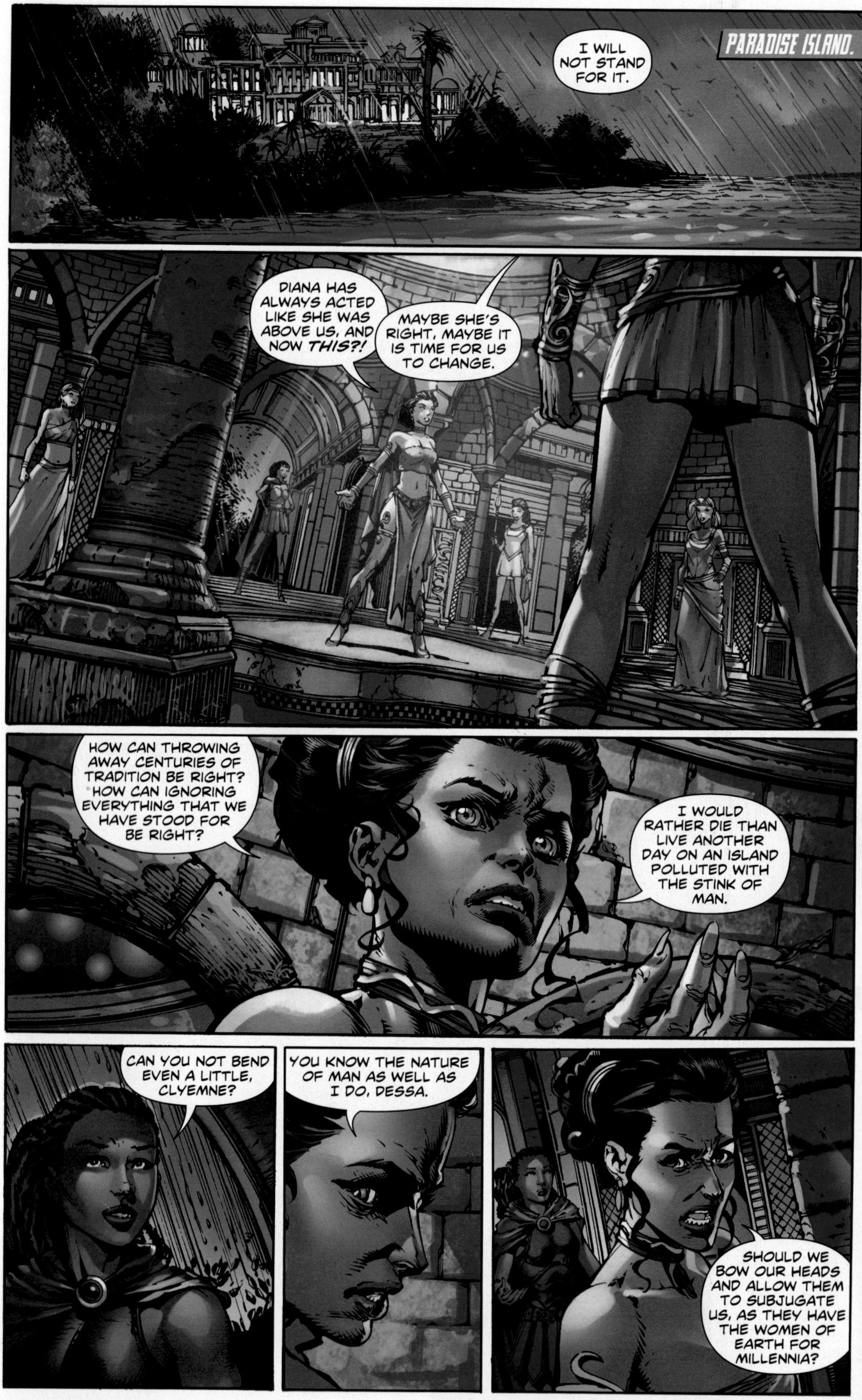
PARADISE ISLAND.
I WILL NOT STAND FOR IT.
DIANA HAS ALWAYS ACTED LIKE SHE WAS ABOVE US, AND NOW THIS?!
MAYBE SHE'S RIGHT, MAYBE IT IS TIME FOR US TO CHANGE.
HOW CAN THROWING AWAY CENTURIES OF TRADITION BE RIGHT? HOW CAN IGNORING EVERYTHING THAT WE HAVE STOOD FOR BE RIGHT?
I WOULD RATHER DIE THAN LIVE ANOTHER DAY ON AN ISLAND POLLUTED WITH THE STINK OF MAN.
CAN YOU NOT BEND EVEN A LITTLE, CLYEMNE?
YOU KNOW THE NATURE OF MAN AS WELL AS I DO, DESSA.
SHOULD WE BOW OUR HEADS AND ALLOW THEM TO SUBJUGATE US, AS THEY HAVE THE WOMEN OF EARTH FOR MILLENNIA?

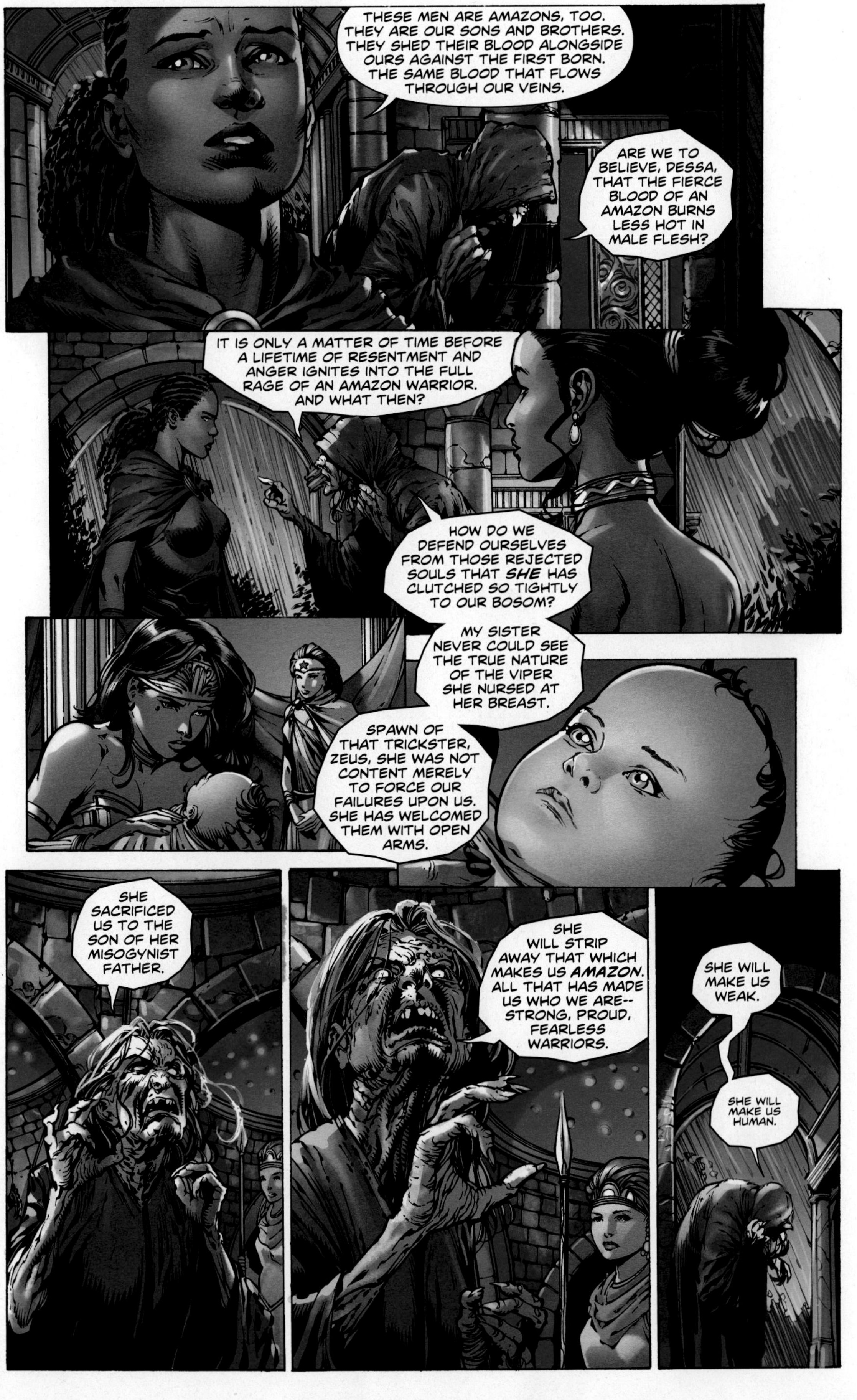
THESE MEN ARE AMAZONS, TOO. THEY ARE OUR SONS AND BROTHERS. THEY SHED THEIR BLOOD ALONGSIDE OURS AGAINST THE FIRST BORN. THE SAME BLOOD THAT FLOWS THROUGH OUR VEINS.
ARE WE TO BELIEVE, DESSA, THAT THE FIERCE BLOOD OF AN AMAZON BURNS LESS HOT IN MALE FLESH?
IT IS ONLY A MATTER OF TIME BEFORE A LIFETIME OF RESENTMENT AND ANGER IGNITES INTO THE FULL RAGE OF AN AMAZON WARRIOR. AND WHAT THEN?
HOW DO WE DEFEND OURSELVES FROM THOSE REJECTED SOULS THAT *SHE* HAS CLUTCHED SO TIGHTLY TO OUR BOSOM?
MY SISTER NEVER COULD SEE THE TRUE NATURE OF THE VIPER SHE NURSED AT HER BREAST.
SPAWN OF THAT TRICKSTER, ZEUS, SHE WAS NOT CONTENT MERELY TO FORCE OUR FAILURES UPON US. SHE HAS WELCOMED THEM WITH OPEN ARMS.
SHE SACRIFICED US TO THE SON OF HER MISOGYNIST FATHER.
SHE WILL STRIP AWAY THAT WHICH MAKES US *AMAZON*. ALL THAT HAS MADE US WHO WE ARE-- STRONG, PROUD, FEARLESS WARRIORS.
SHE WILL MAKE US WEAK.
SHE WILL MAKE US HUMAN.

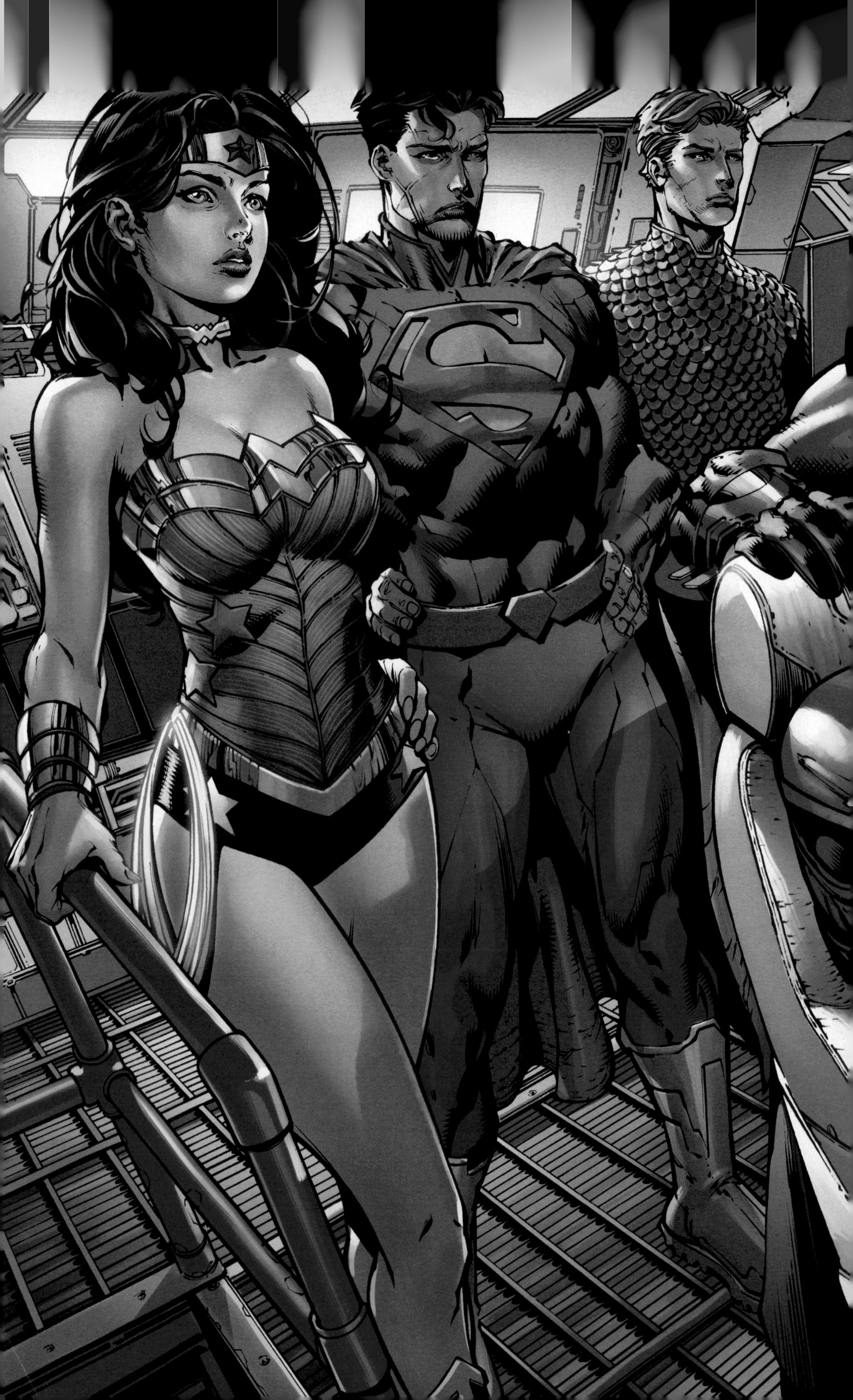

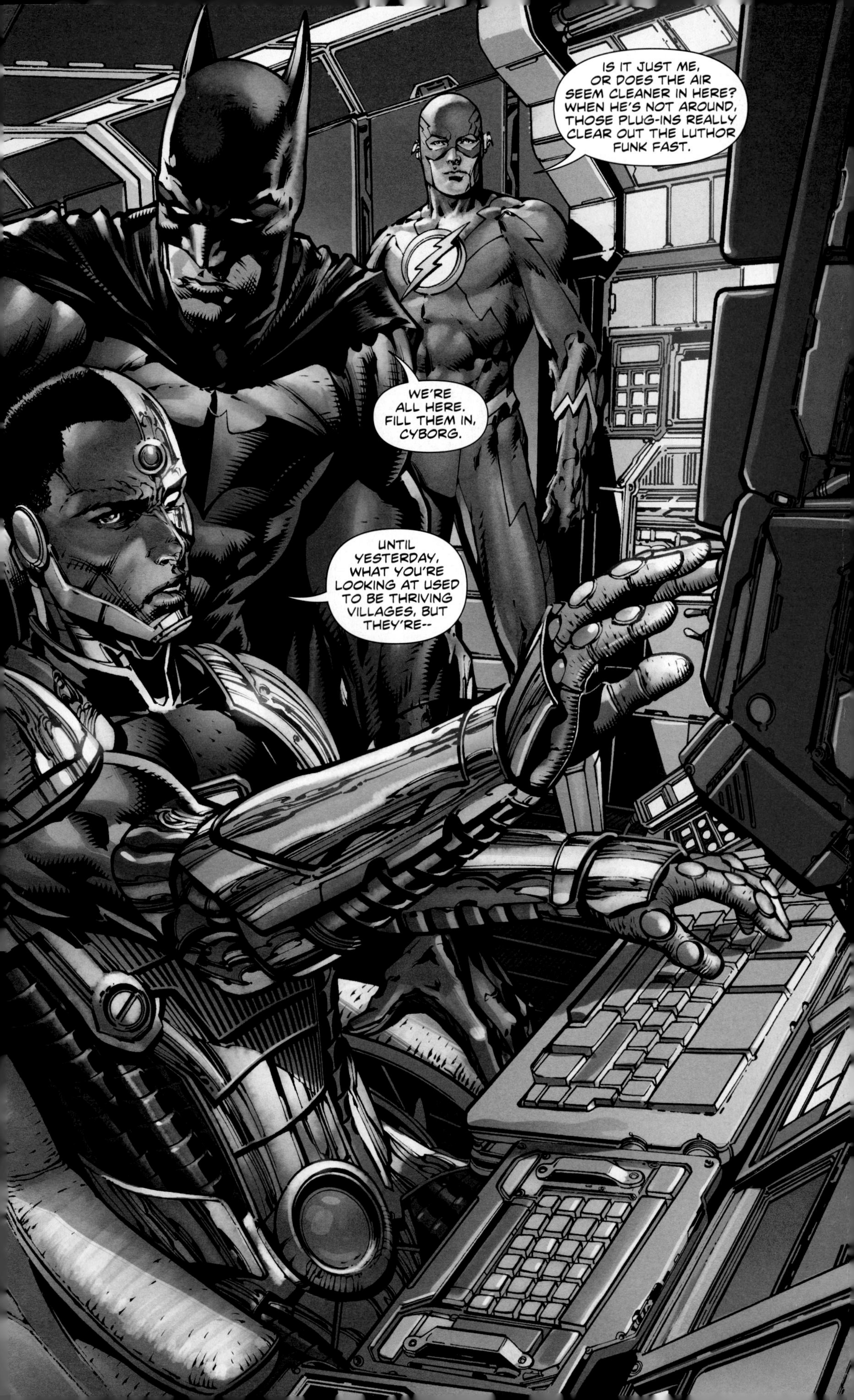
IS IT JUST ME, OR DOES THE AIR SEEM CLEANER IN HERE? WHEN HE'S NOT AROUND, THOSE PLUG-INS REALLY CLEAR OUT THE LUTHOR FUNK FAST.
WE'RE ALL HERE. FILL THEM IN, CYBORG.
UNTIL YESTERDAY, WHAT YOU'RE LOOKING AT USED TO BE THRIVING VILLAGES, BUT THEY'RE--

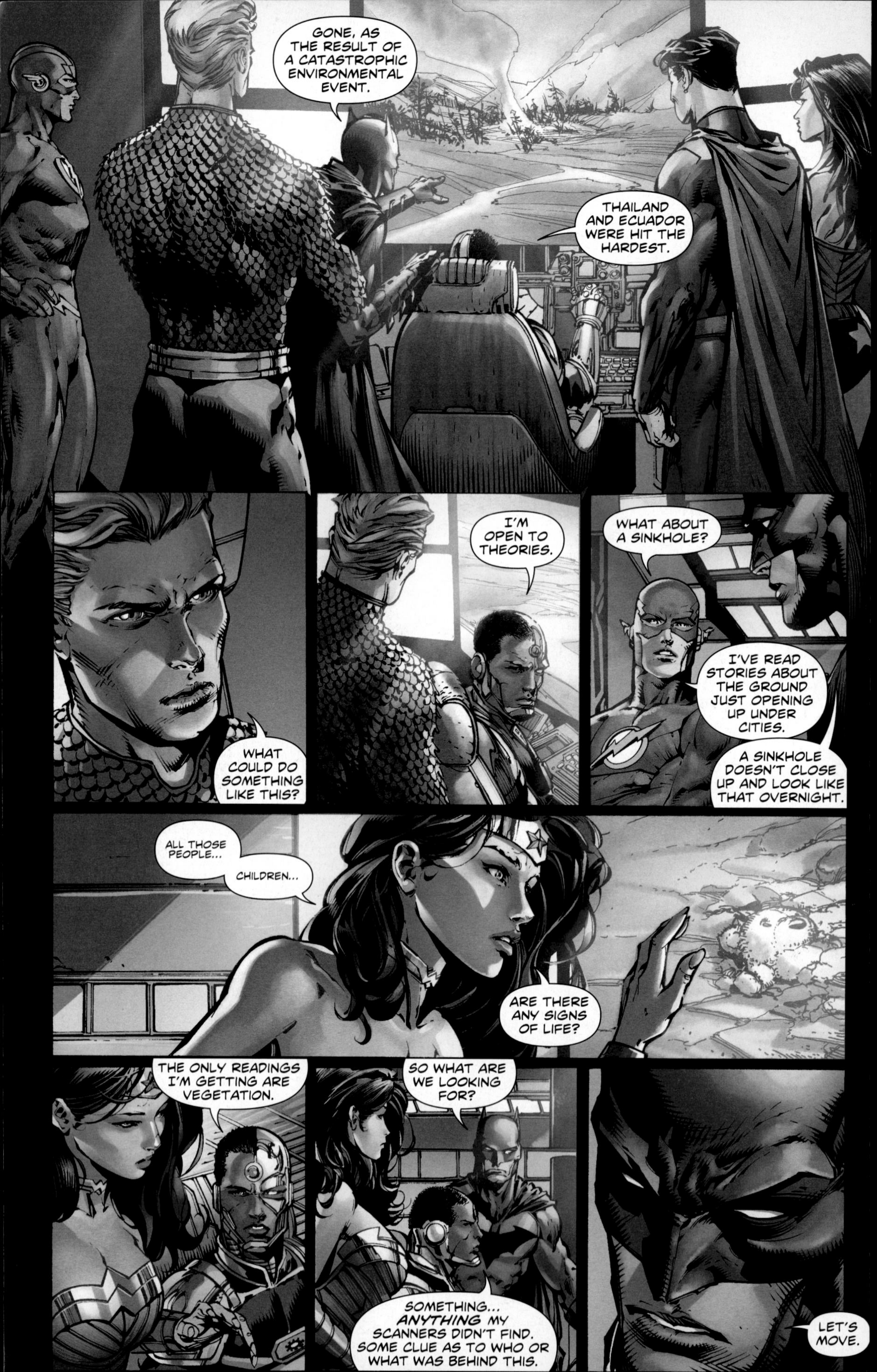
GONE, AS THE RESULT OF A CATASTROPHIC ENVIRONMENTAL EVENT.
THAILAND AND ECUADOR WERE HIT THE HARDEST.
WHAT COULD DO SOMETHING LIKE THIS?
I'M OPEN TO THEORIES.
WHAT ABOUT A SINKHOLE?
I'VE READ STORIES ABOUT THE GROUND JUST OPENING UP UNDER CITIES.
A SINKHOLE DOESN'T CLOSE UP AND LOOK LIKE THAT OVERNIGHT.
ALL THOSE PEOPLE...
CHILDREN...
ARE THERE ANY SIGNS OF LIFE?
THE ONLY READINGS I'M GETTING ARE VEGETATION.
SO WHAT ARE WE LOOKING FOR?
SOMETHING... ANYTHING MY SCANNERS DIDN'T FIND. SOME CLUE AS TO WHO OR WHAT WAS BEHIND THIS.
LET'S MOVE.

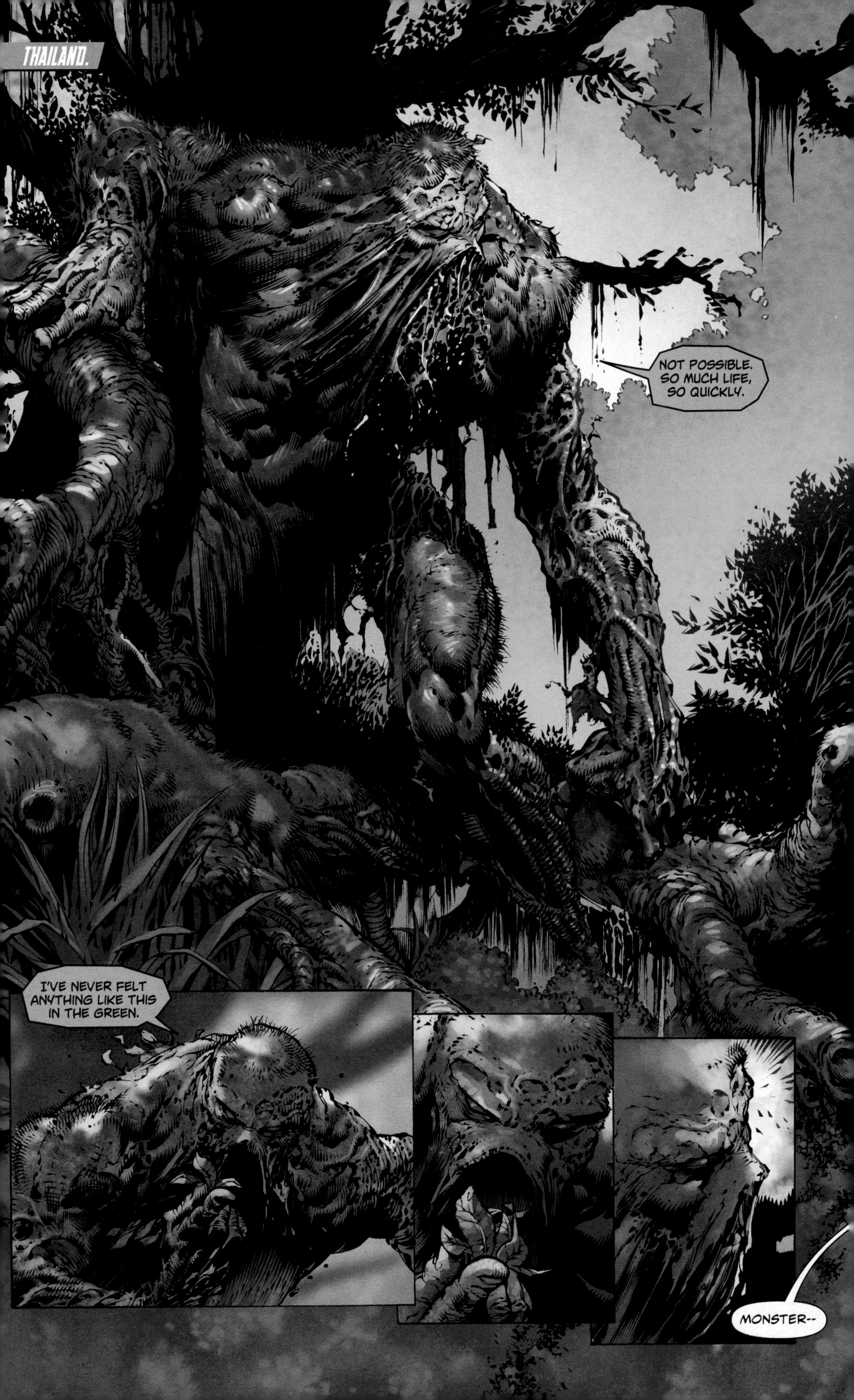
THAILAND.
NOT POSSIBLE. SO MUCH LIFE, SO QUICKLY.
I'VE NEVER FELT ANYTHING LIKE THIS IN THE GREEN.
MONSTER--

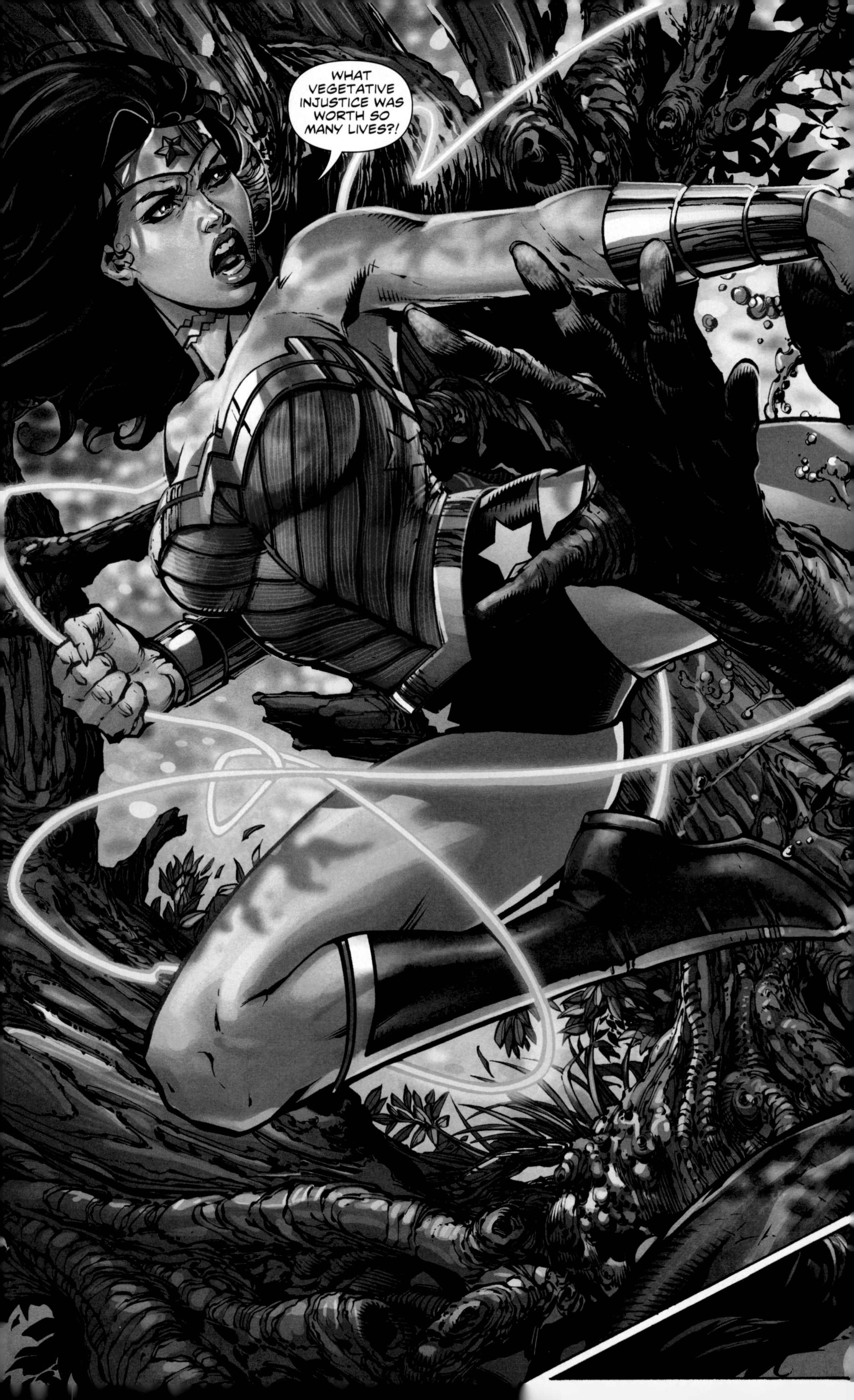
WHAT VEGETATIVE INJUSTICE WAS WORTH SO MANY LIVES?!

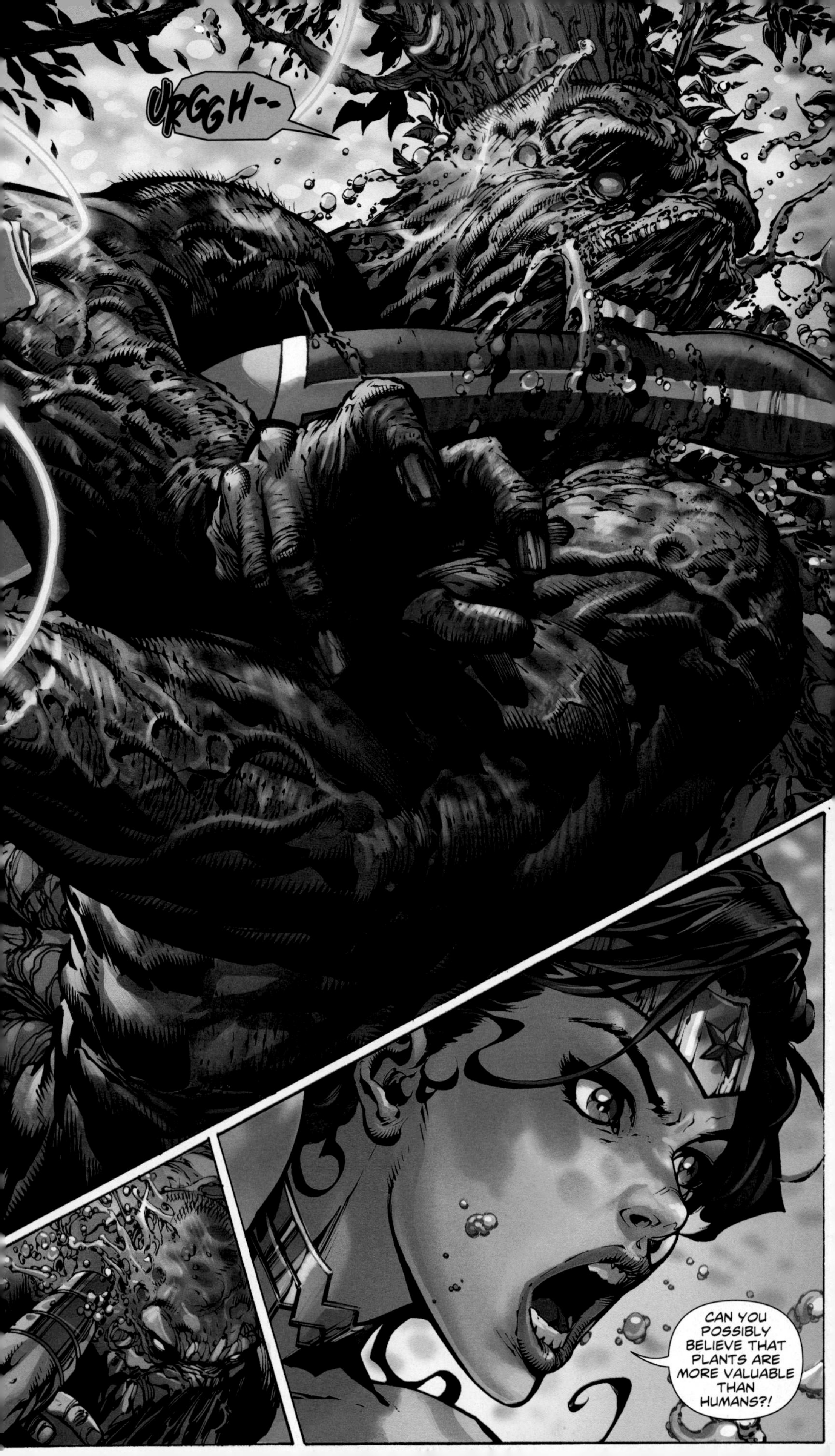
URGGH--
CAN YOU POSSIBLY BELIEVE THAT PLANTS ARE MORE VALUABLE THAN HUMANS?!

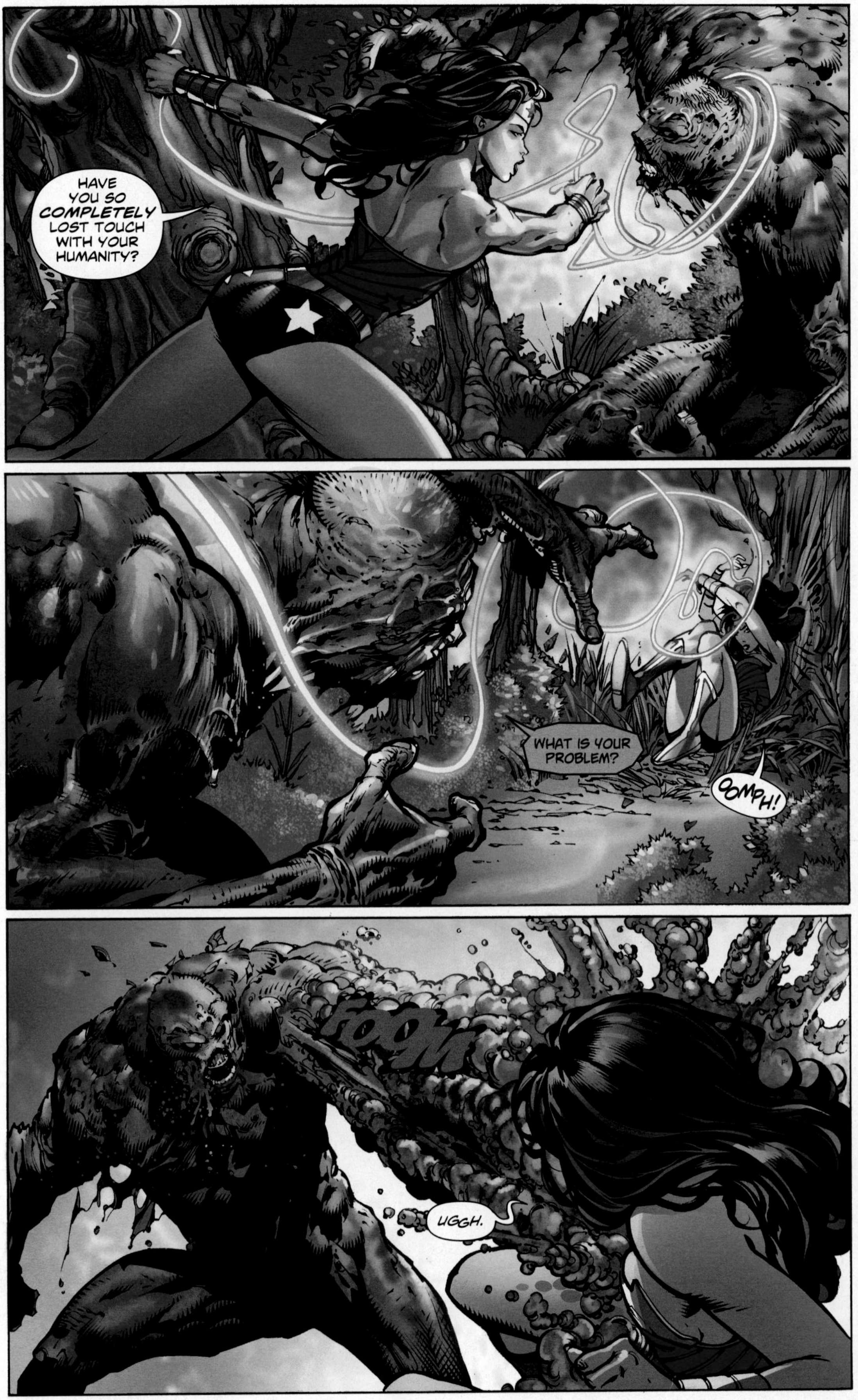
HAVE YOU SO COMPLETELY LOST TOUCH WITH YOUR HUMANITY?
WHAT IS YOUR PROBLEM?
OOMPH!
FOOM
UGGH.

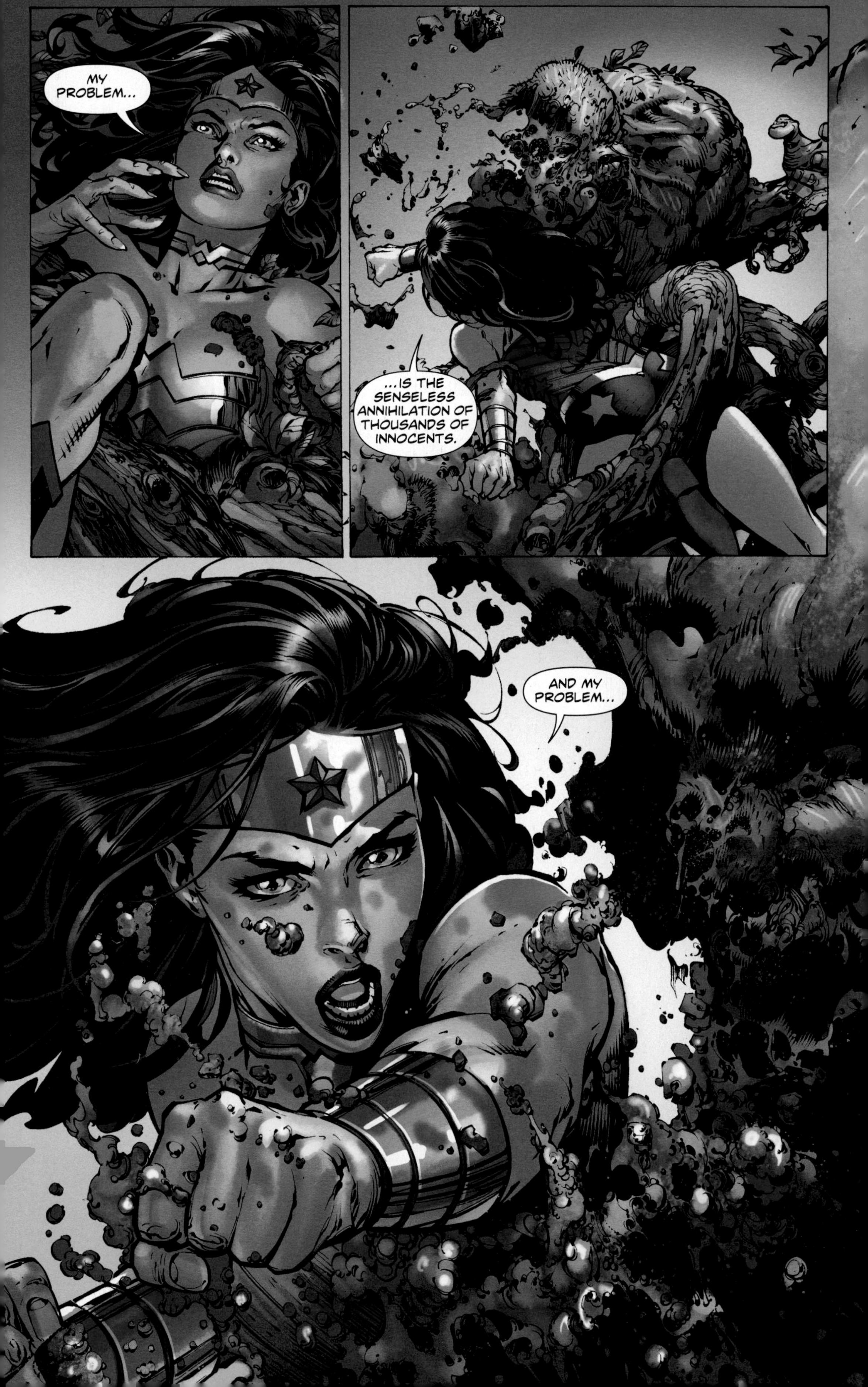
MY PROBLEM...
...IS THE SENSELESS ANNIHILATION OF THOUSANDS OF INNOCENTS.
AND MY PROBLEM...

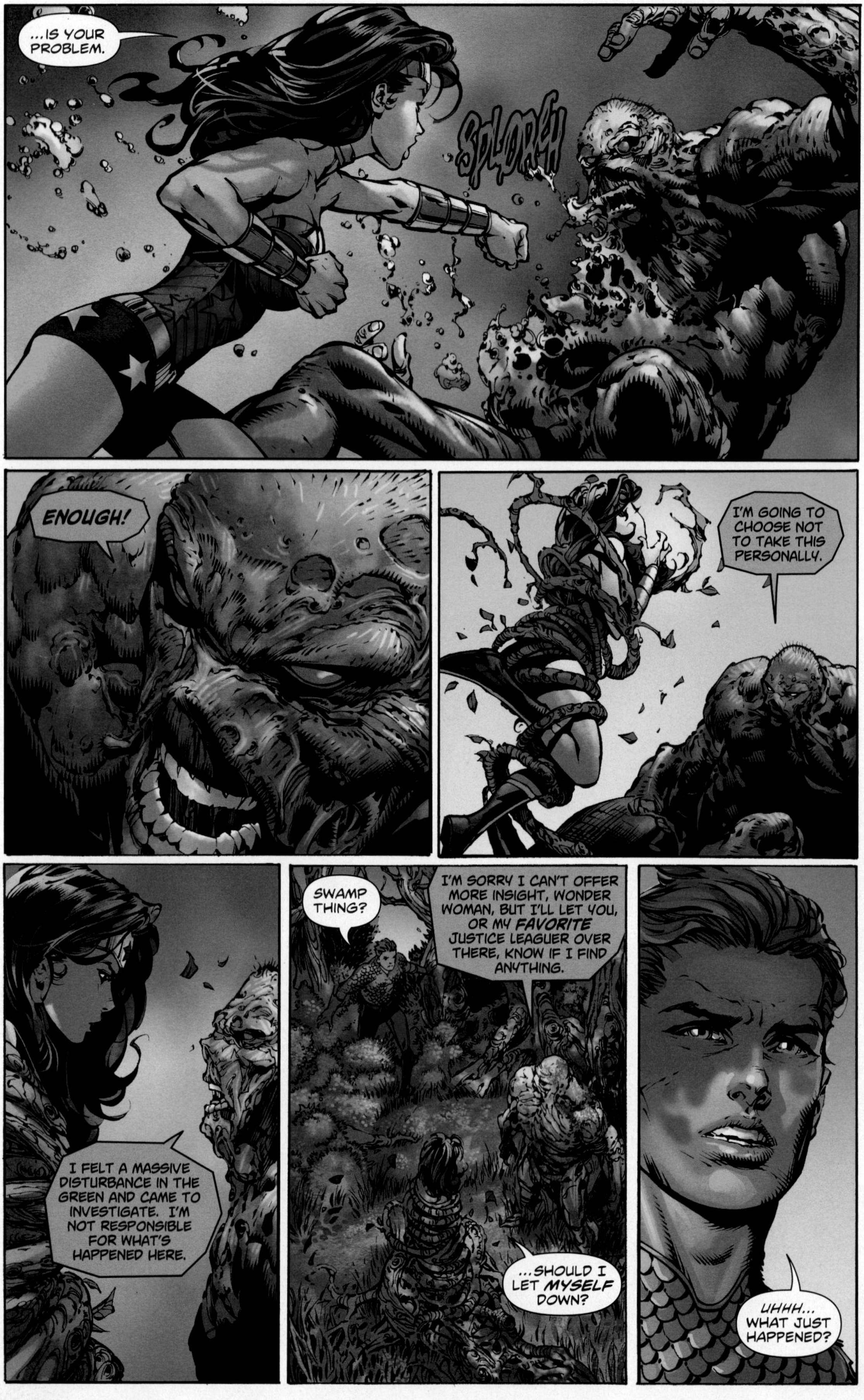
...IS YOUR PROBLEM.
SPLOOSH
ENOUGH!
I'M GOING TO CHOOSE NOT TO TAKE THIS PERSONALLY.
I FELT A MASSIVE DISTURBANCE IN THE GREEN AND CAME TO INVESTIGATE. I'M NOT RESPONSIBLE FOR WHAT'S HAPPENED HERE.
SWAMP THING?
I'M SORRY I CAN'T OFFER MORE INSIGHT, WONDER WOMAN, BUT I'LL LET YOU, OR MY FAVORITE JUSTICE LEAGUER OVER THERE, KNOW IF I FIND ANYTHING.
...SHOULD I LET MYSELF DOWN?
UHHH... WHAT JUST HAPPENED?

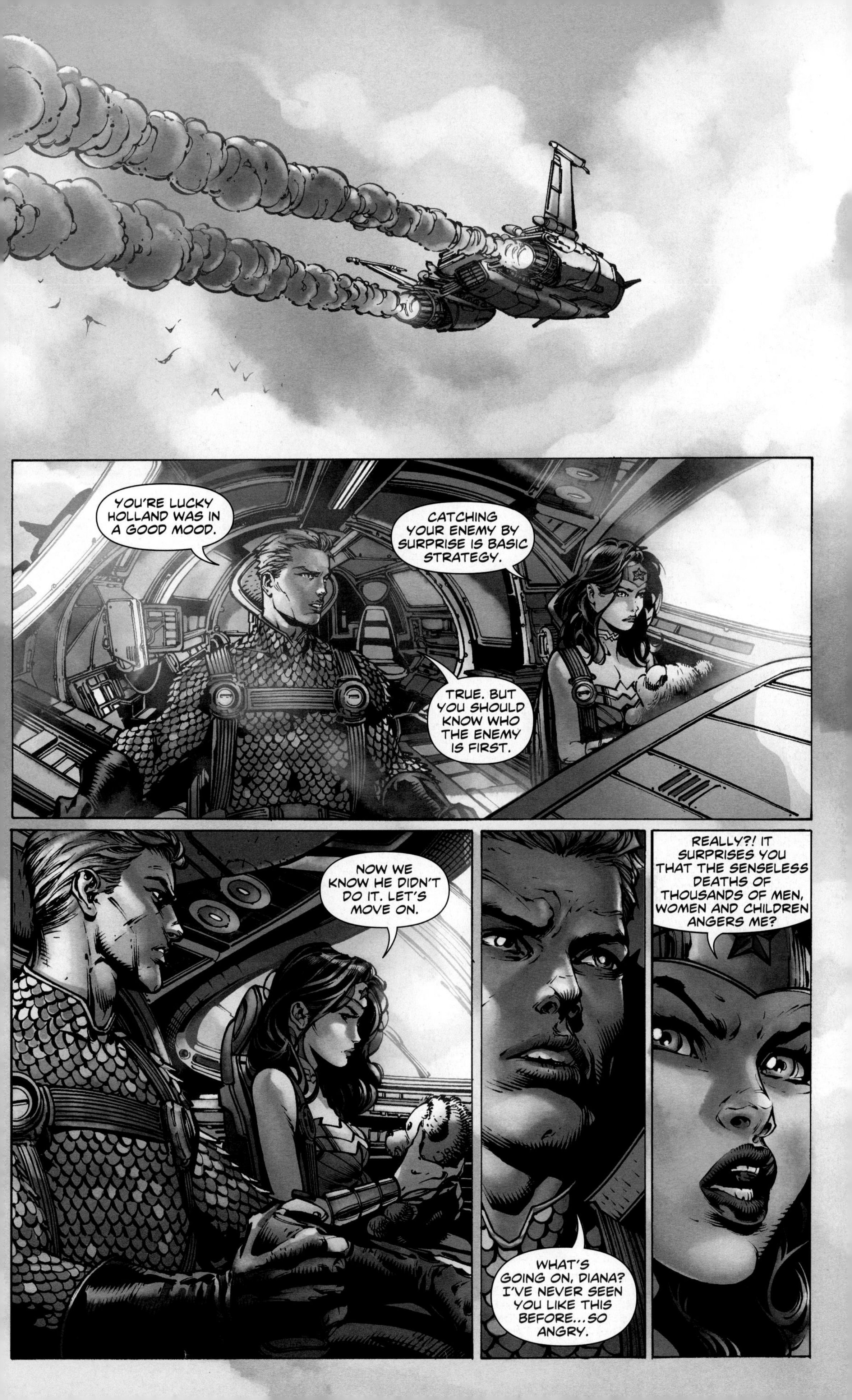
YOU'RE LUCKY HOLLAND WAS IN A GOOD MOOD.
CATCHING YOUR ENEMY BY SURPRISE IS BASIC STRATEGY.
TRUE. BUT YOU SHOULD KNOW WHO THE ENEMY IS FIRST.
NOW WE KNOW HE DIDN'T DO IT. LET'S MOVE ON.
WHAT'S GOING ON, DIANA? I'VE NEVER SEEN YOU LIKE THIS BEFORE...SO ANGRY.
REALLY?! IT SURPRISES YOU THAT THE SENSELESS DEATHS OF THOUSANDS OF MEN, WOMEN AND CHILDREN ANGERS ME?

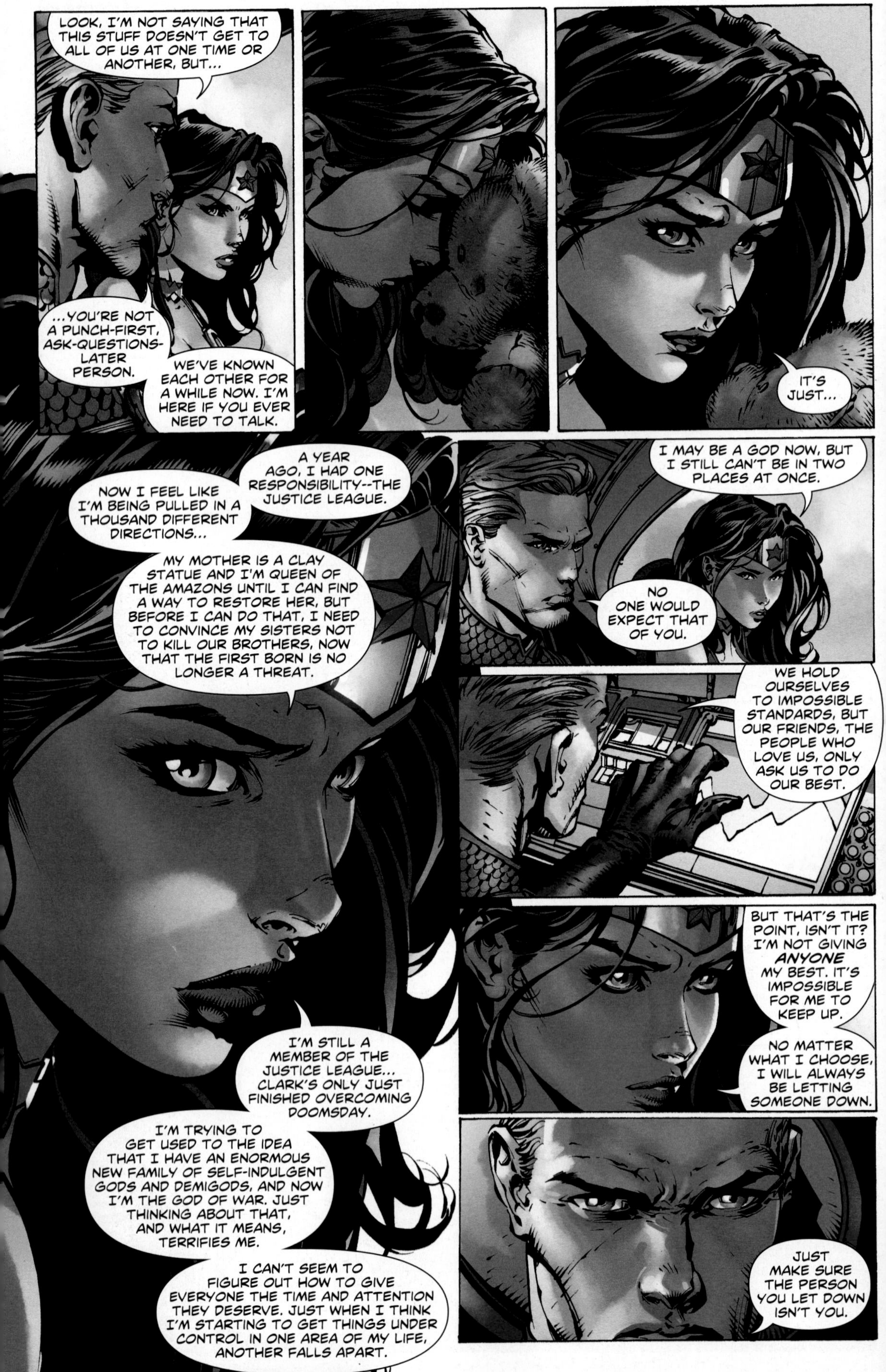
LOOK, I'M NOT SAYING THAT THIS STUFF DOESN'T GET TO ALL OF US AT ONE TIME OR ANOTHER, BUT...
...YOU'RE NOT A PUNCH-FIRST, ASK-QUESTIONS-LATER PERSON.
WE'VE KNOWN EACH OTHER FOR A WHILE NOW. I'M HERE IF YOU EVER NEED TO TALK.
IT'S JUST...
A YEAR AGO, I HAD ONE RESPONSIBILITY--THE JUSTICE LEAGUE.
NOW I FEEL LIKE I'M BEING PULLED IN A THOUSAND DIFFERENT DIRECTIONS...
MY MOTHER IS A CLAY STATUE AND I'M QUEEN OF THE AMAZONS UNTIL I CAN FIND A WAY TO RESTORE HER, BUT BEFORE I CAN DO THAT, I NEED TO CONVINCE MY SISTERS NOT TO KILL OUR BROTHERS, NOW THAT THE FIRST BORN IS NO LONGER A THREAT.
I'M STILL A MEMBER OF THE JUSTICE LEAGUE... CLARK'S ONLY JUST FINISHED OVERCOMING DOOMSDAY.
I'M TRYING TO GET USED TO THE IDEA THAT I HAVE AN ENORMOUS NEW FAMILY OF SELF-INDULGENT GODS AND DEMIGODS, AND NOW I'M THE GOD OF WAR. JUST THINKING ABOUT THAT, AND WHAT IT MEANS, TERRIFIES ME.
I CAN'T SEEM TO FIGURE OUT HOW TO GIVE EVERYONE THE TIME AND ATTENTION THEY DESERVE. JUST WHEN I THINK I'M STARTING TO GET THINGS UNDER CONTROL IN ONE AREA OF MY LIFE, ANOTHER FALLS APART.
I MAY BE A GOD NOW, BUT I STILL CAN'T BE IN TWO PLACES AT ONCE.
NO ONE WOULD EXPECT THAT OF YOU.
WE HOLD OURSELVES TO IMPOSSIBLE STANDARDS, BUT OUR FRIENDS, THE PEOPLE WHO LOVE US, ONLY ASK US TO DO OUR BEST.
BUT THAT'S THE POINT, ISN'T IT? I'M NOT GIVING ANYONE MY BEST. IT'S IMPOSSIBLE FOR ME TO KEEP UP.
NO MATTER WHAT I CHOOSE, I WILL ALWAYS BE LETTING SOMEONE DOWN.
JUST MAKE SURE THE PERSON YOU LET DOWN ISN'T YOU.

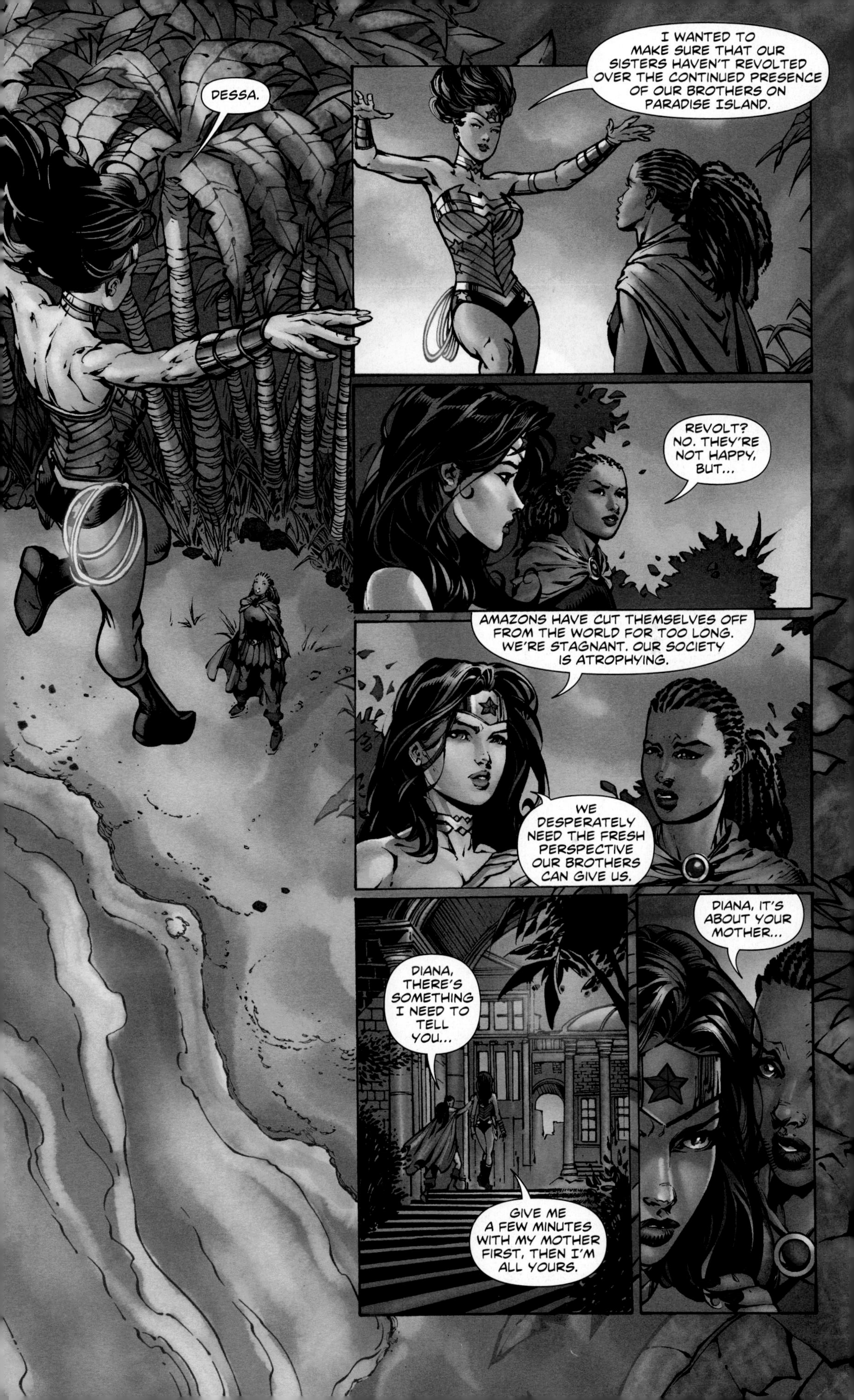
DESSA.
I WANTED TO MAKE SURE THAT OUR SISTERS HAVEN'T REVOLTED OVER THE CONTINUED PRESENCE OF OUR BROTHERS ON PARADISE ISLAND.
REVOLT? NO. THEY'RE NOT HAPPY, BUT...
AMAZONS HAVE CUT THEMSELVES OFF FROM THE WORLD FOR TOO LONG. WE'RE STAGNANT. OUR SOCIETY IS ATROPHYING.
WE DESPERATELY NEED THE FRESH PERSPECTIVE OUR BROTHERS CAN GIVE US.
DIANA, THERE'S SOMETHING I NEED TO TELL YOU...
GIVE ME A FEW MINUTES WITH MY MOTHER FIRST, THEN I'M ALL YOURS.
DIANA, IT'S ABOUT YOUR MOTHER...

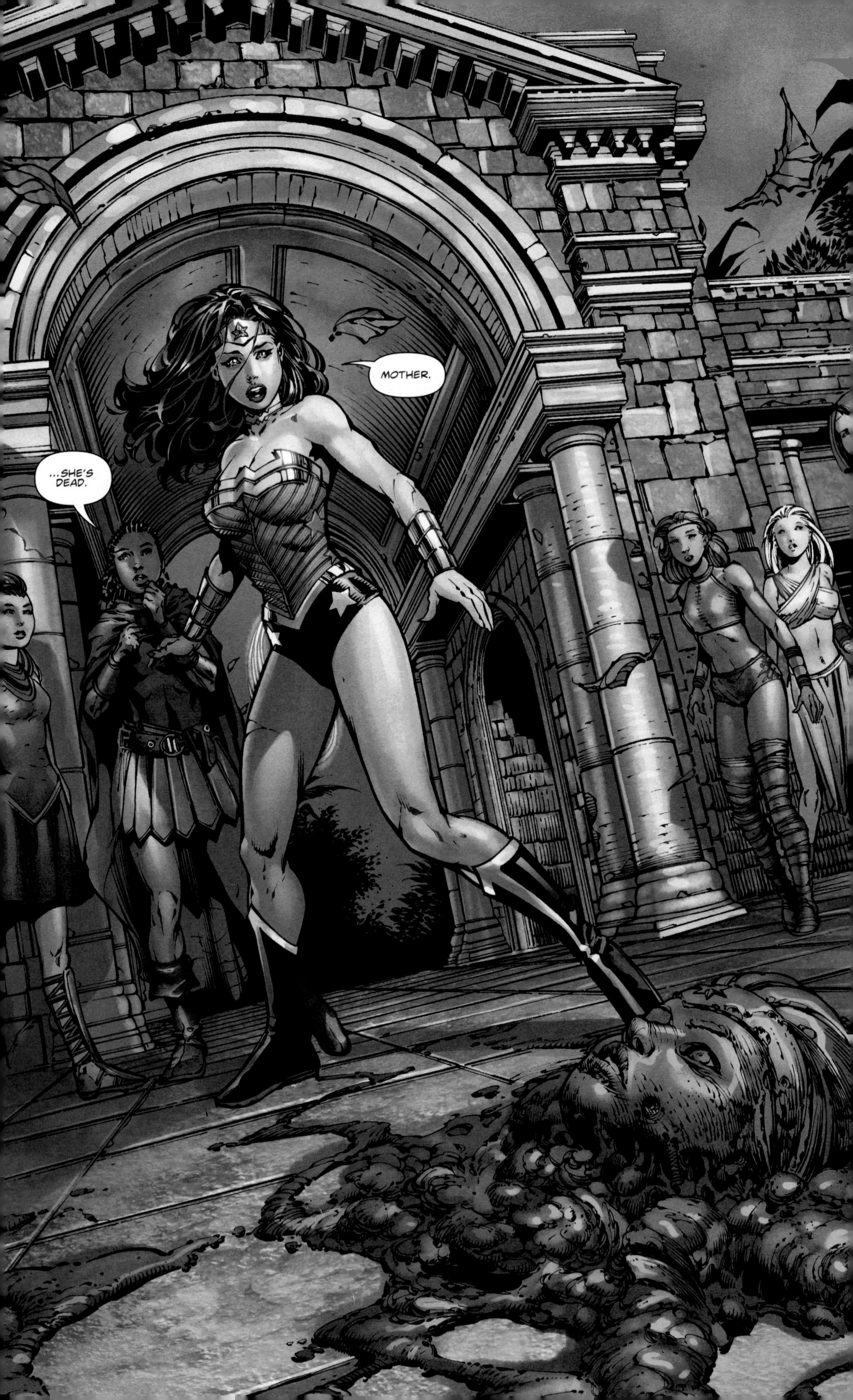
MOTHER.
...SHE'S DEAD.

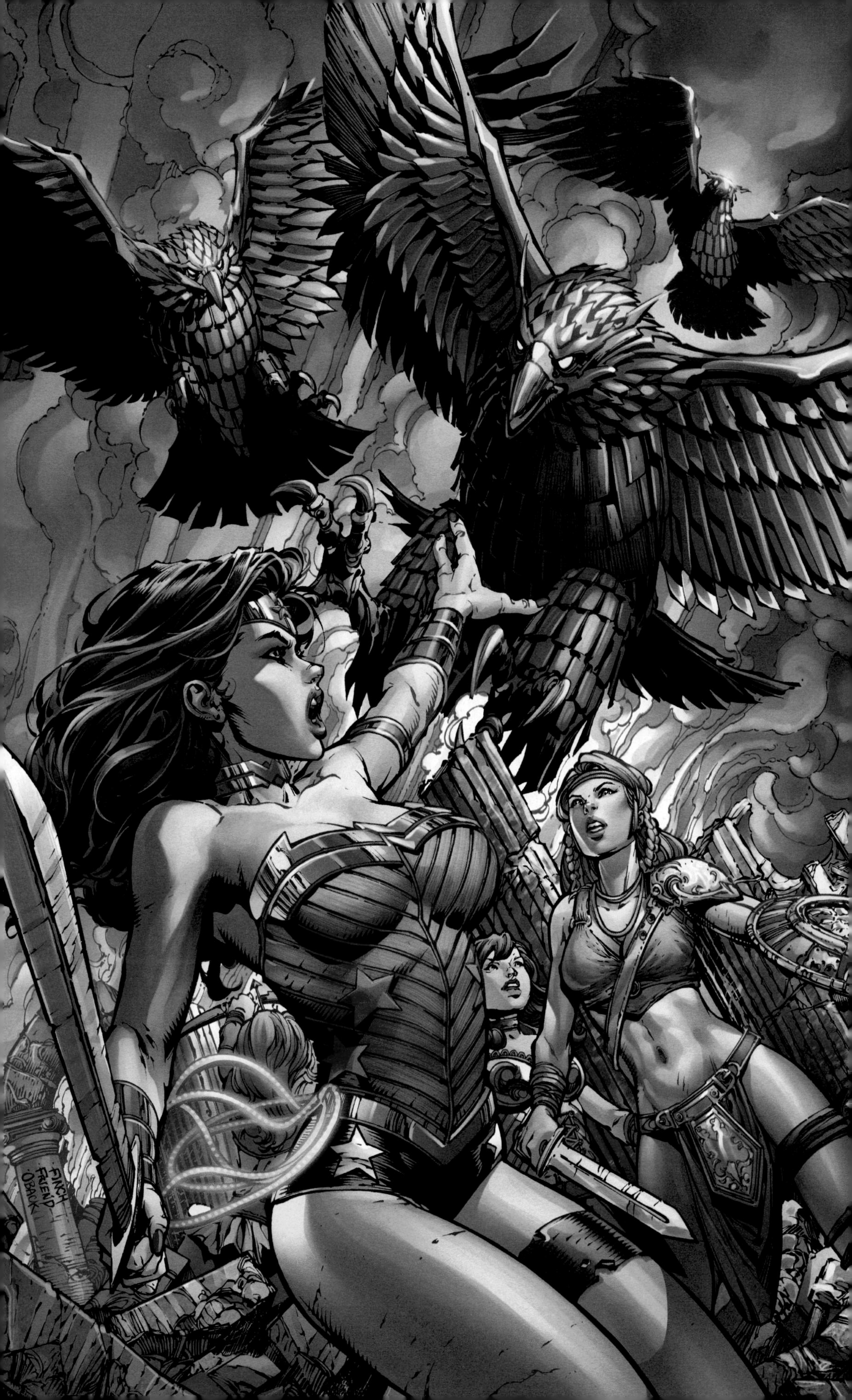
FINCH
FRIEND
O'BACK

WAR-TORN CHAPTER 2

MEREDITH FINCH writer **DAVID FINCH** penciller **RICHARD FRIEND** inker **SONIA OBACK** colorist **DEZI SIENTY** letterer cover by **FINCH, FRIEND** and **OBACK**

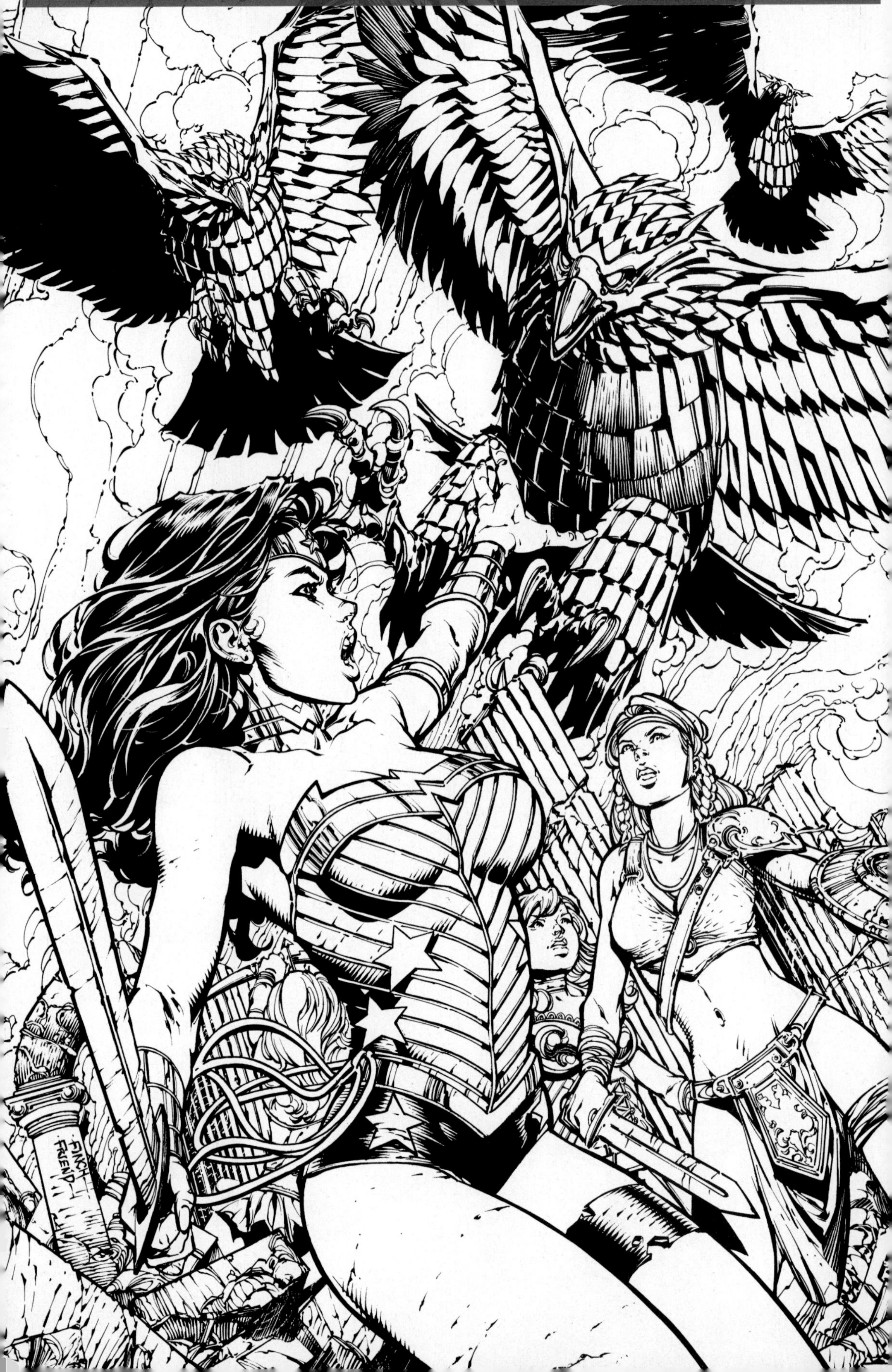
FINCH
FRIEND

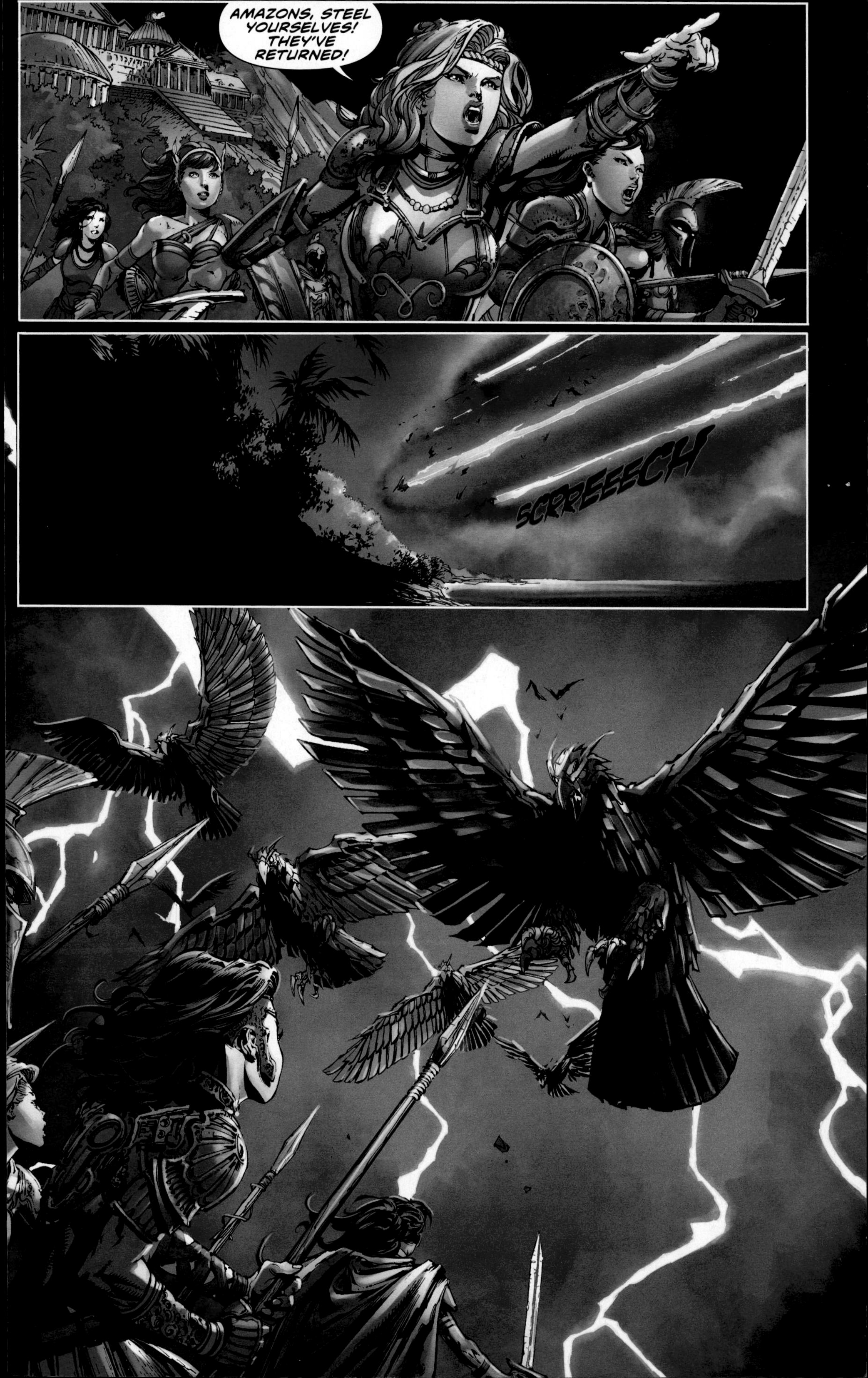
AMAZONS, STEEL YOURSELVES! THEY'VE RETURNED!
SCRREEEECH

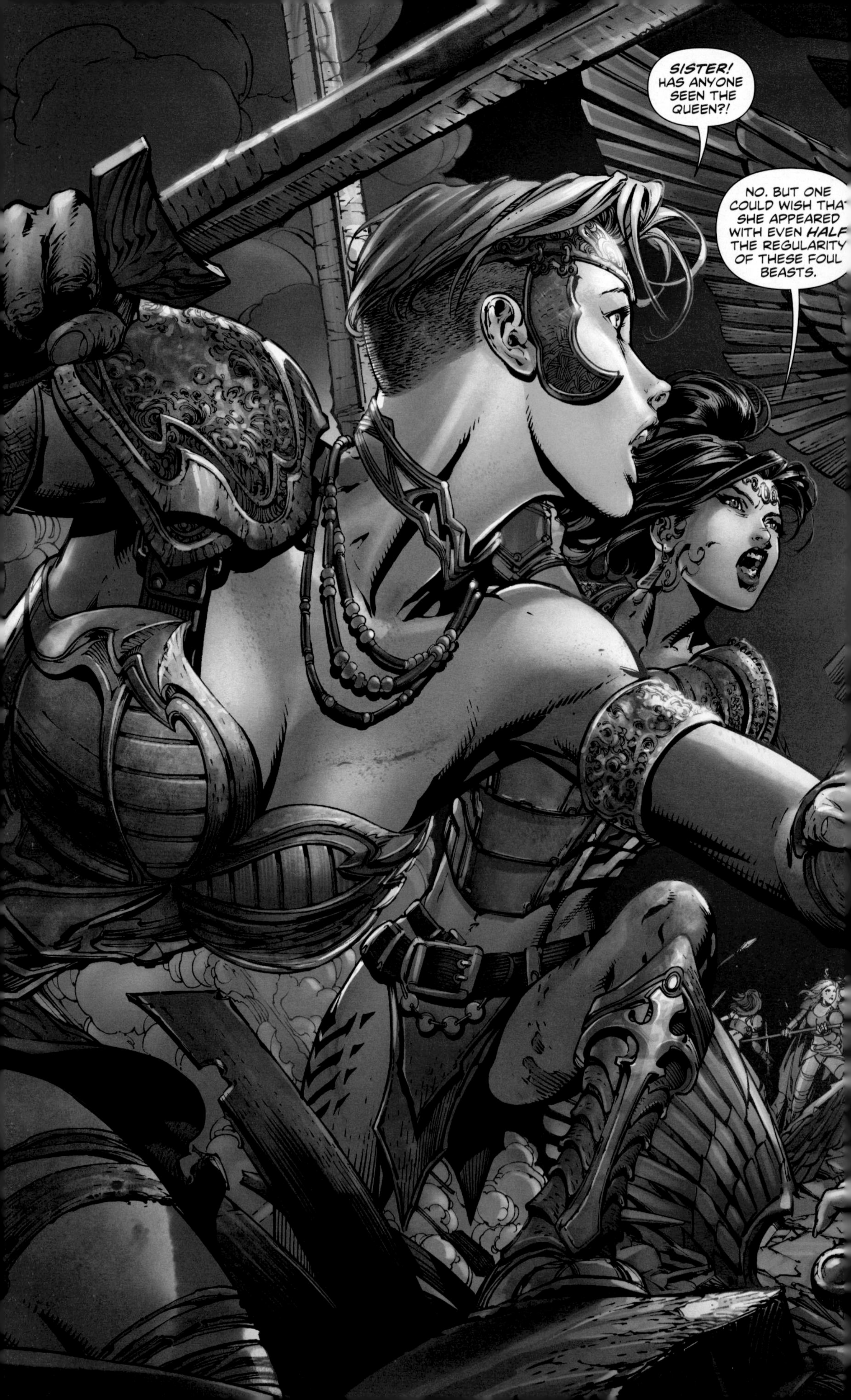
SISTER! HAS ANYONE SEEN THE QUEEN?!
NO. BUT ONE COULD WISH THAT SHE APPEARED WITH EVEN HALF THE REGULARITY OF THESE FOUL BEASTS.

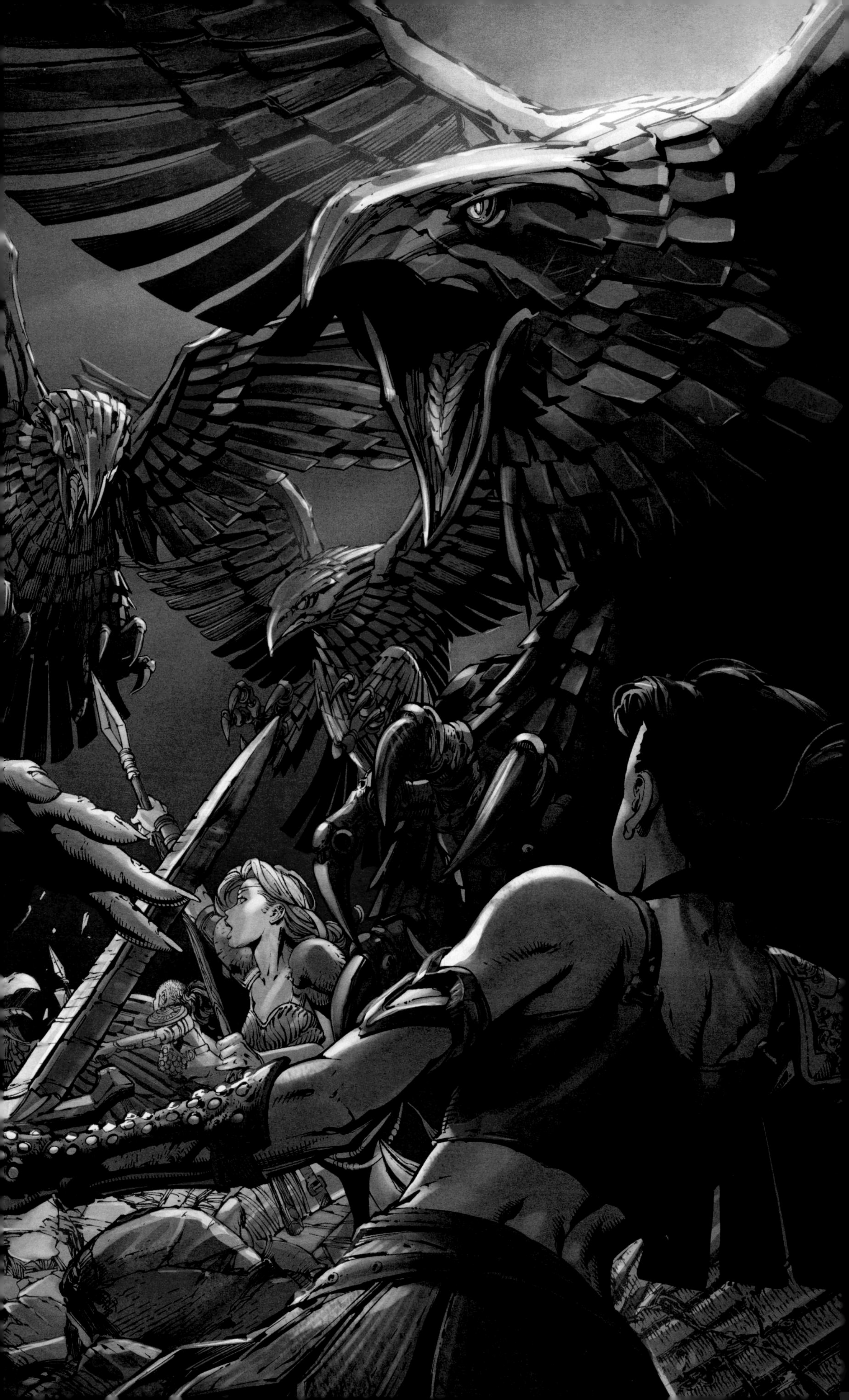

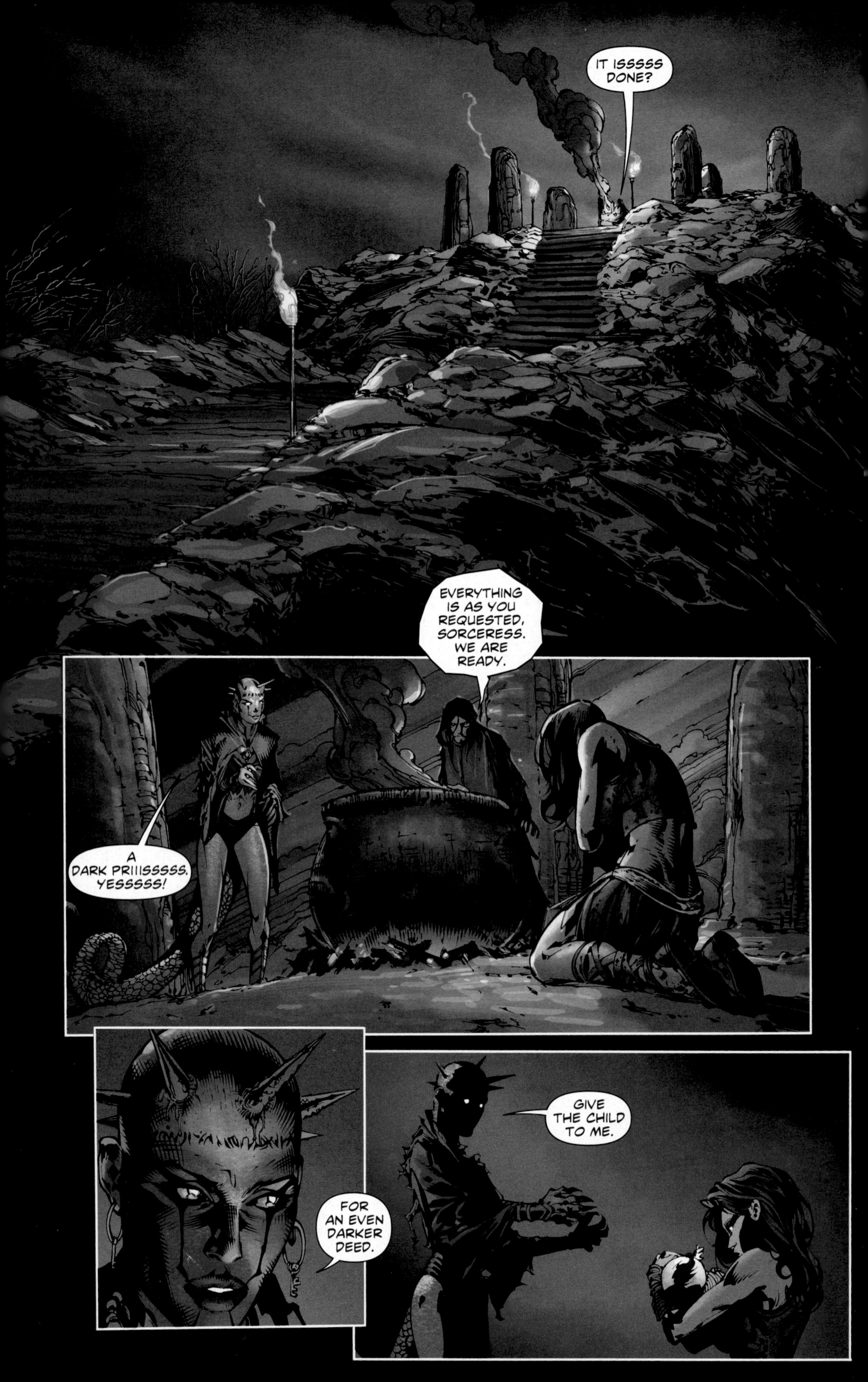
IT ISSSSS DONE?
EVERYTHING IS AS YOU REQUESTED, SORCERESS. WE ARE READY.
A DARK PRIIISSSSS. YESSSSS!
FOR AN EVEN DARKER DEED.
GIVE THE CHILD TO ME.

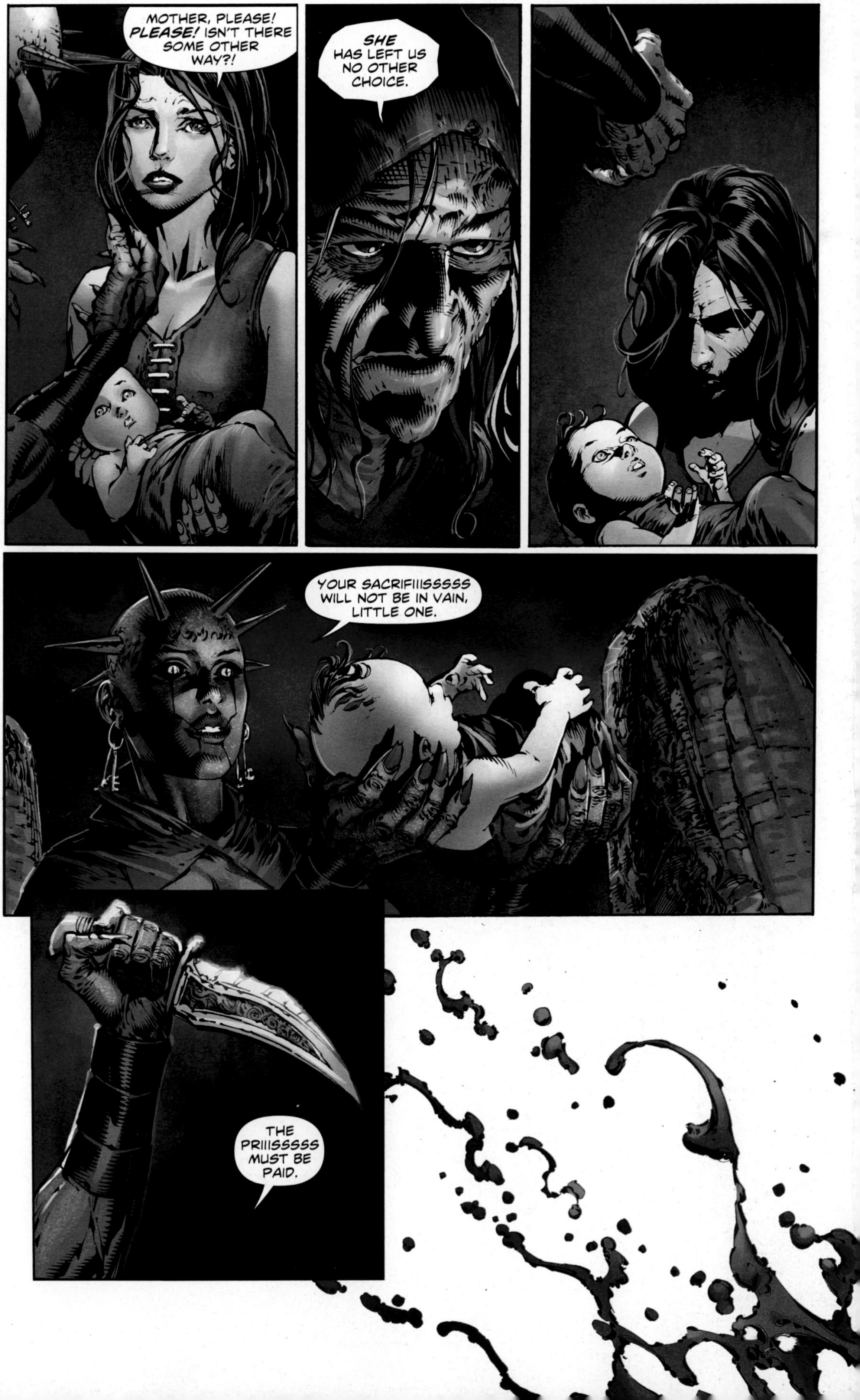
MOTHER, PLEASE! *PLEASE!* ISN'T THERE SOME OTHER WAY?!
SHE HAS LEFT US NO OTHER CHOICE.
YOUR SACRIFIIISSSSS WILL NOT BE IN VAIN, LITTLE ONE.
THE PRIIISSSSS MUST BE PAID.

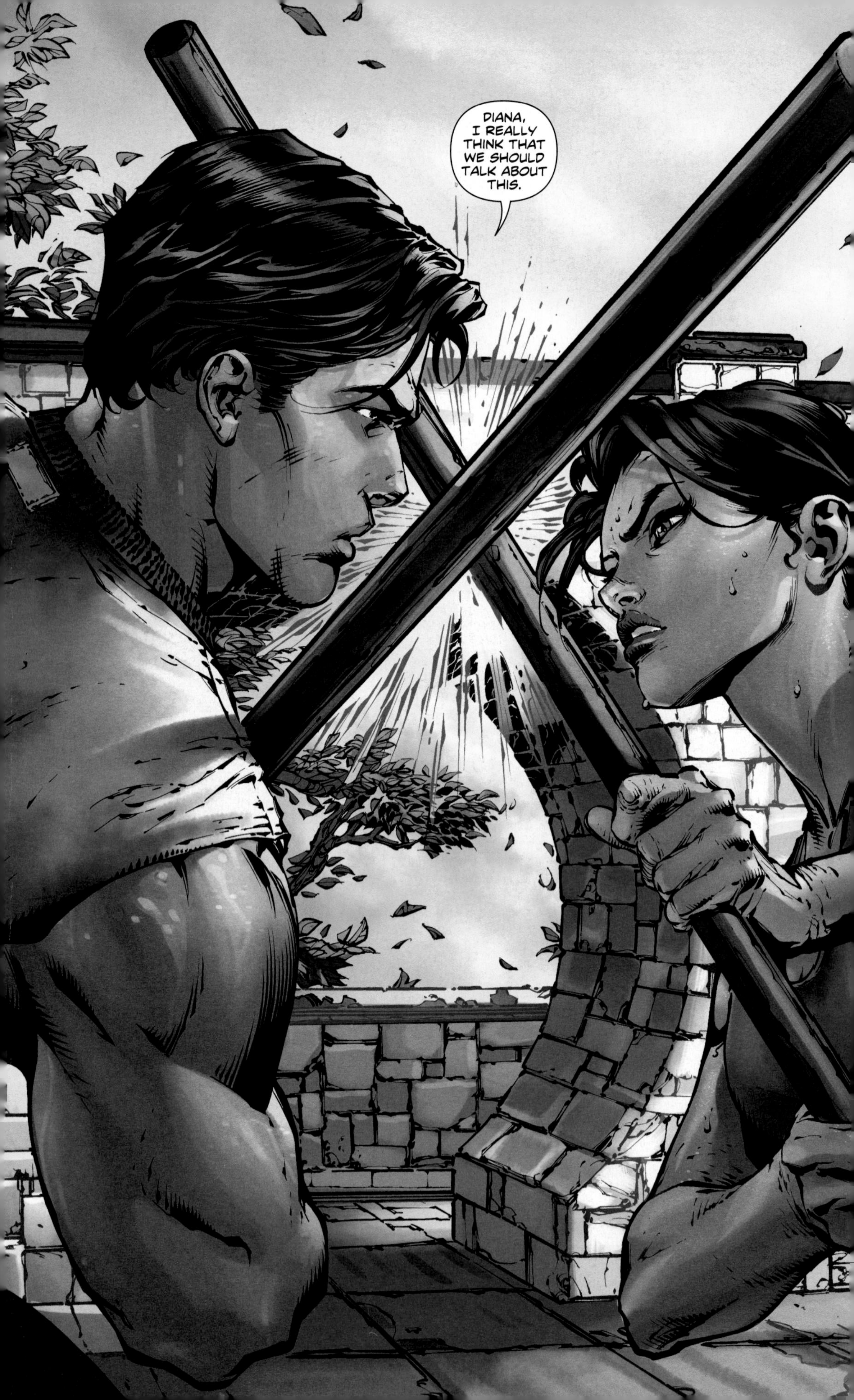
DIANA, I REALLY THINK THAT WE SHOULD TALK ABOUT THIS.

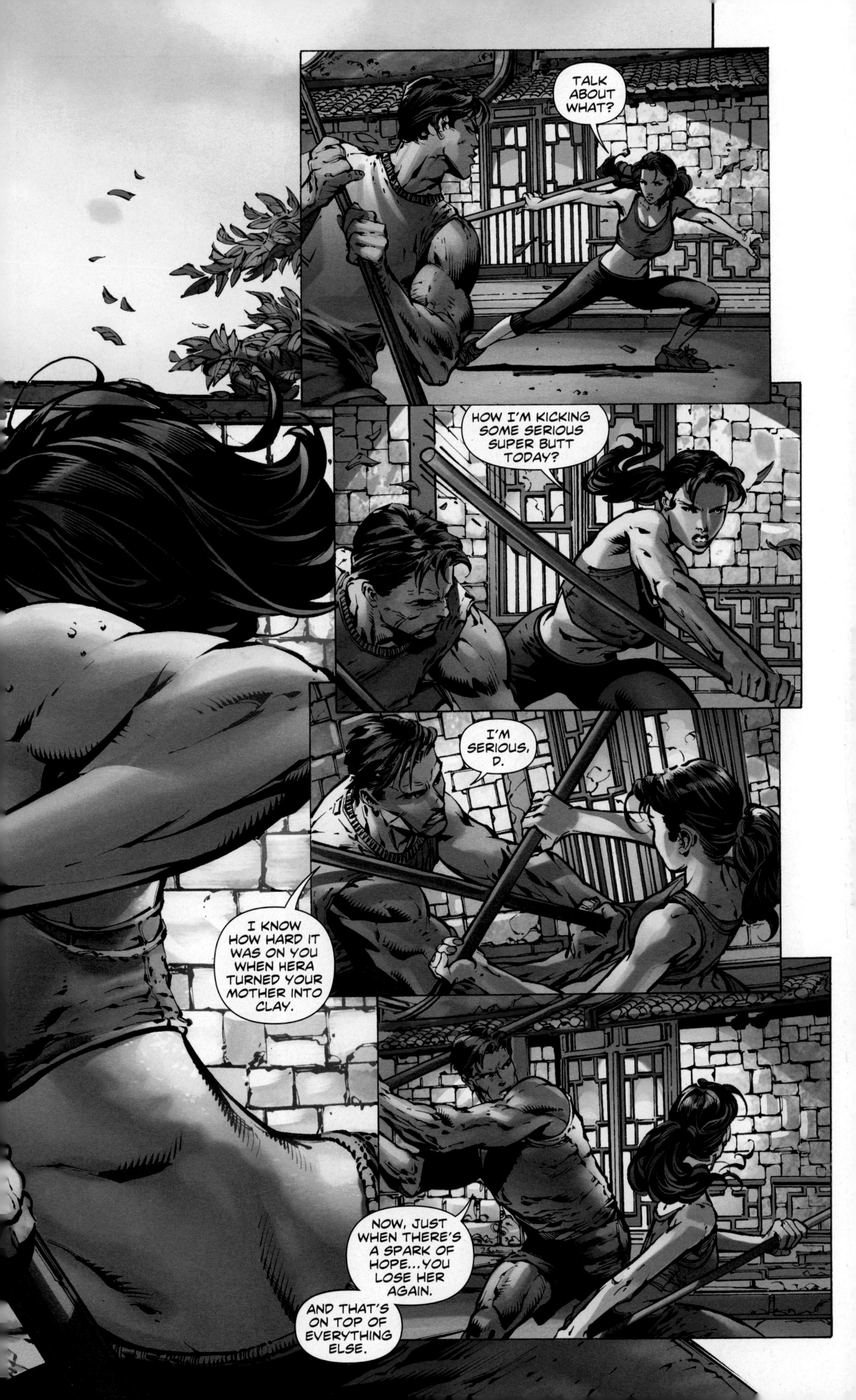
TALK ABOUT WHAT?
HOW I'M KICKING SOME SERIOUS SUPER BUTT TODAY?
I'M SERIOUS, D.
I KNOW HOW HARD IT WAS ON YOU WHEN HERA TURNED YOUR MOTHER INTO CLAY.
NOW, JUST WHEN THERE'S A SPARK OF HOPE...YOU LOSE HER AGAIN.
AND THAT'S ON TOP OF EVERYTHING ELSE.

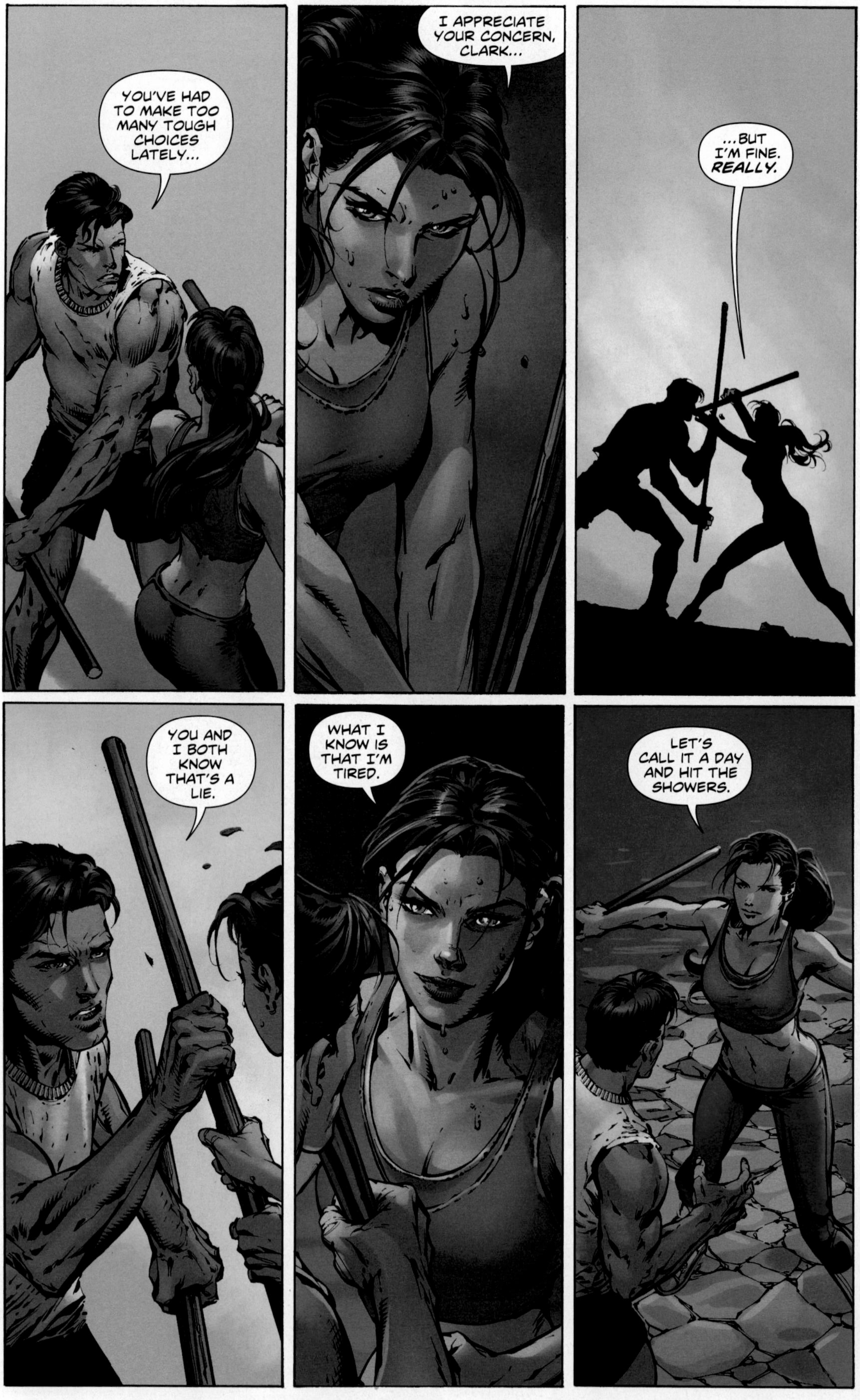
YOU'VE HAD TO MAKE TOO MANY TOUGH CHOICES LATELY...
I APPRECIATE YOUR CONCERN, CLARK...
...BUT I'M FINE. REALLY.
YOU AND I BOTH KNOW THAT'S A LIE.
WHAT I KNOW IS THAT I'M TIRED.
LET'S CALL IT A DAY AND HIT THE SHOWERS.

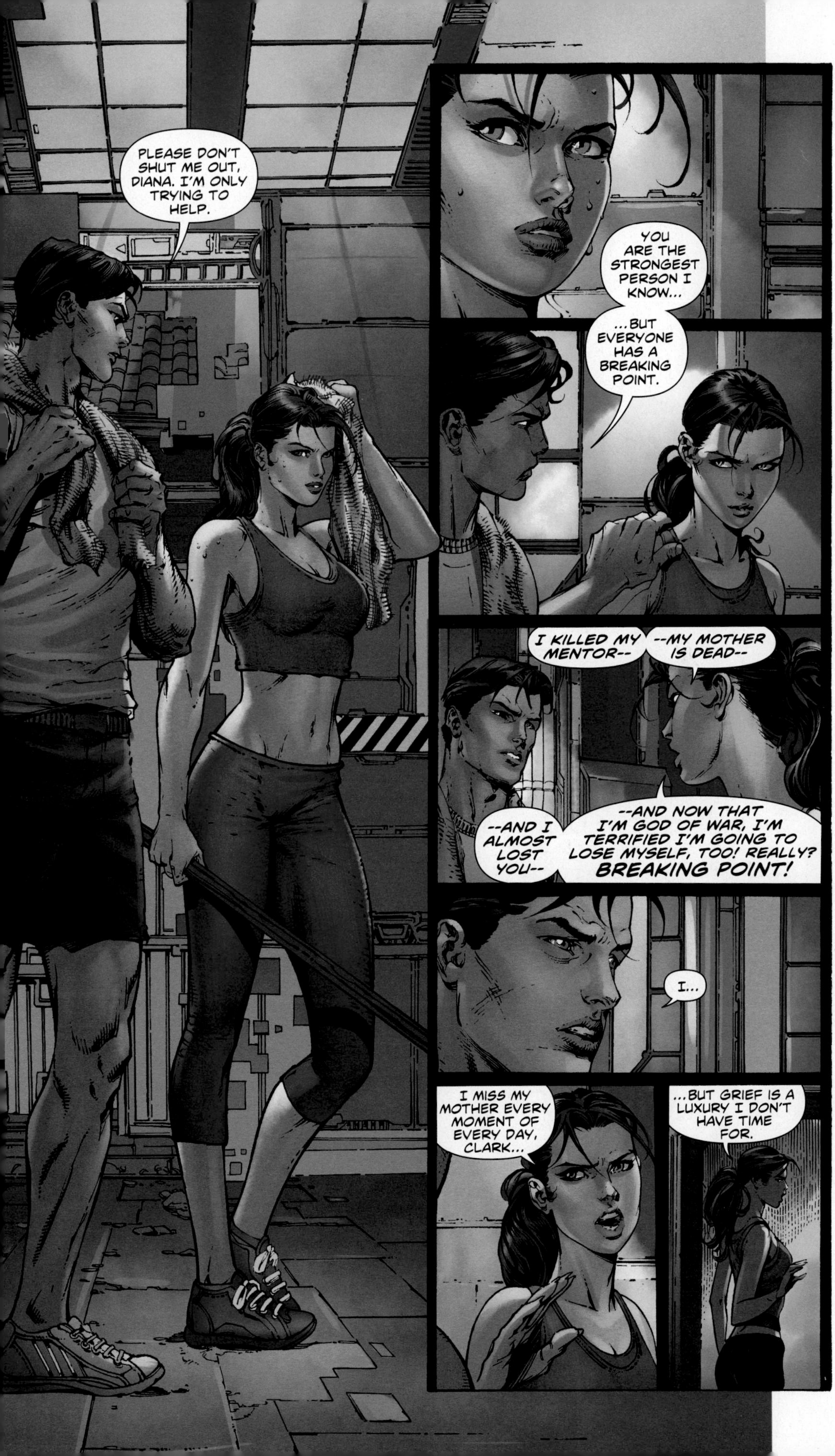
PLEASE DON'T SHUT ME OUT, DIANA. I'M ONLY TRYING TO HELP.
YOU ARE THE STRONGEST PERSON I KNOW...
...BUT EVERYONE HAS A BREAKING POINT.
I KILLED MY MENTOR--
--MY MOTHER IS DEAD--
--AND I ALMOST LOST YOU--
--AND NOW THAT I'M GOD OF WAR, I'M TERRIFIED I'M GOING TO LOSE MYSELF, TOO! REALLY? BREAKING POINT!
I...
I MISS MY MOTHER EVERY MOMENT OF EVERY DAY, CLARK...
...BUT GRIEF IS A LUXURY I DON'T HAVE TIME FOR.

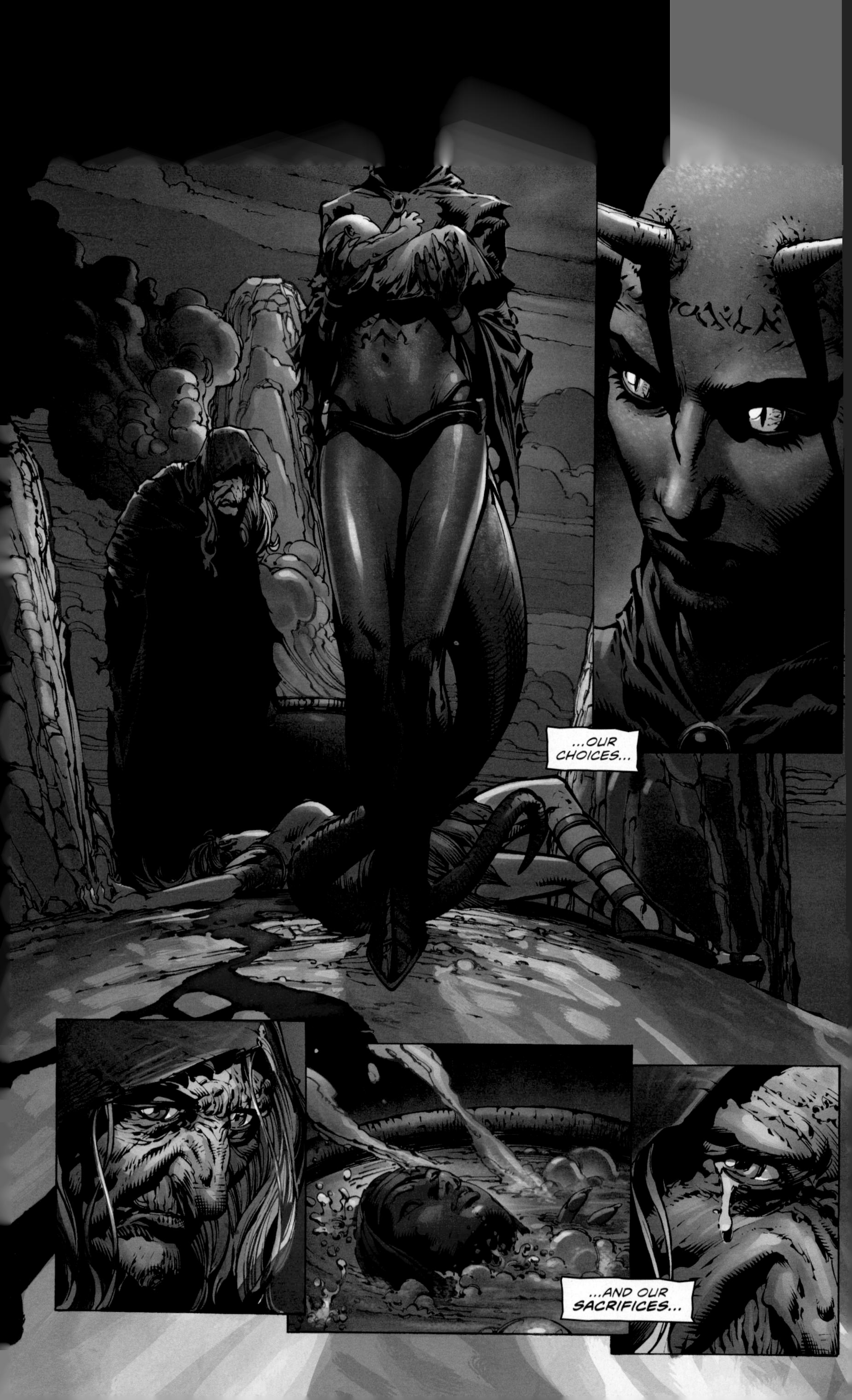
...OUR CHOICES...
...AND OUR SACRIFICES...

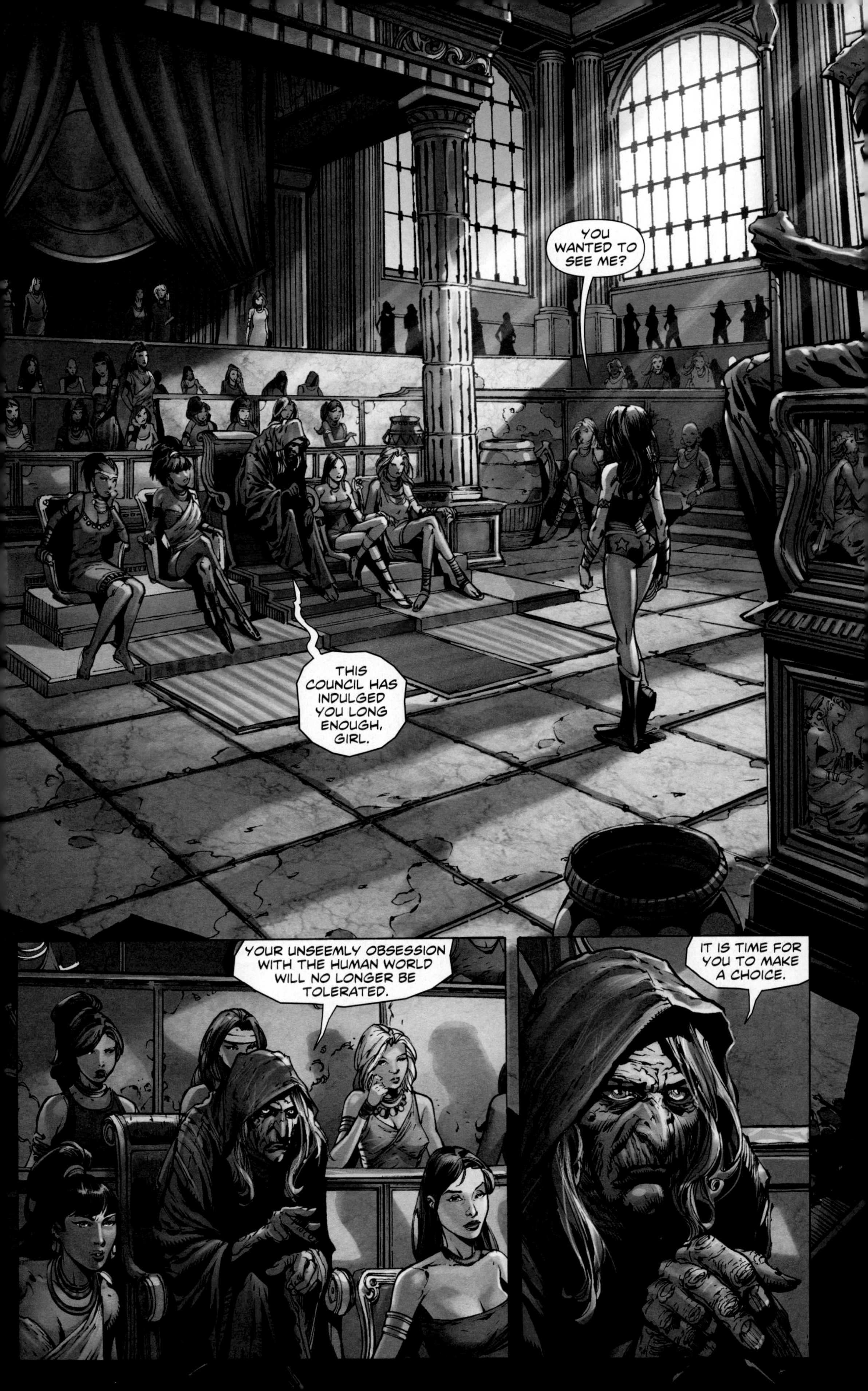
YOU WANTED TO SEE ME?
THIS COUNCIL HAS INDULGED YOU LONG ENOUGH, GIRL.
YOUR UNSEEMLY OBSESSION WITH THE HUMAN WORLD WILL NO LONGER BE TOLERATED.
IT IS TIME FOR YOU TO MAKE A CHOICE.

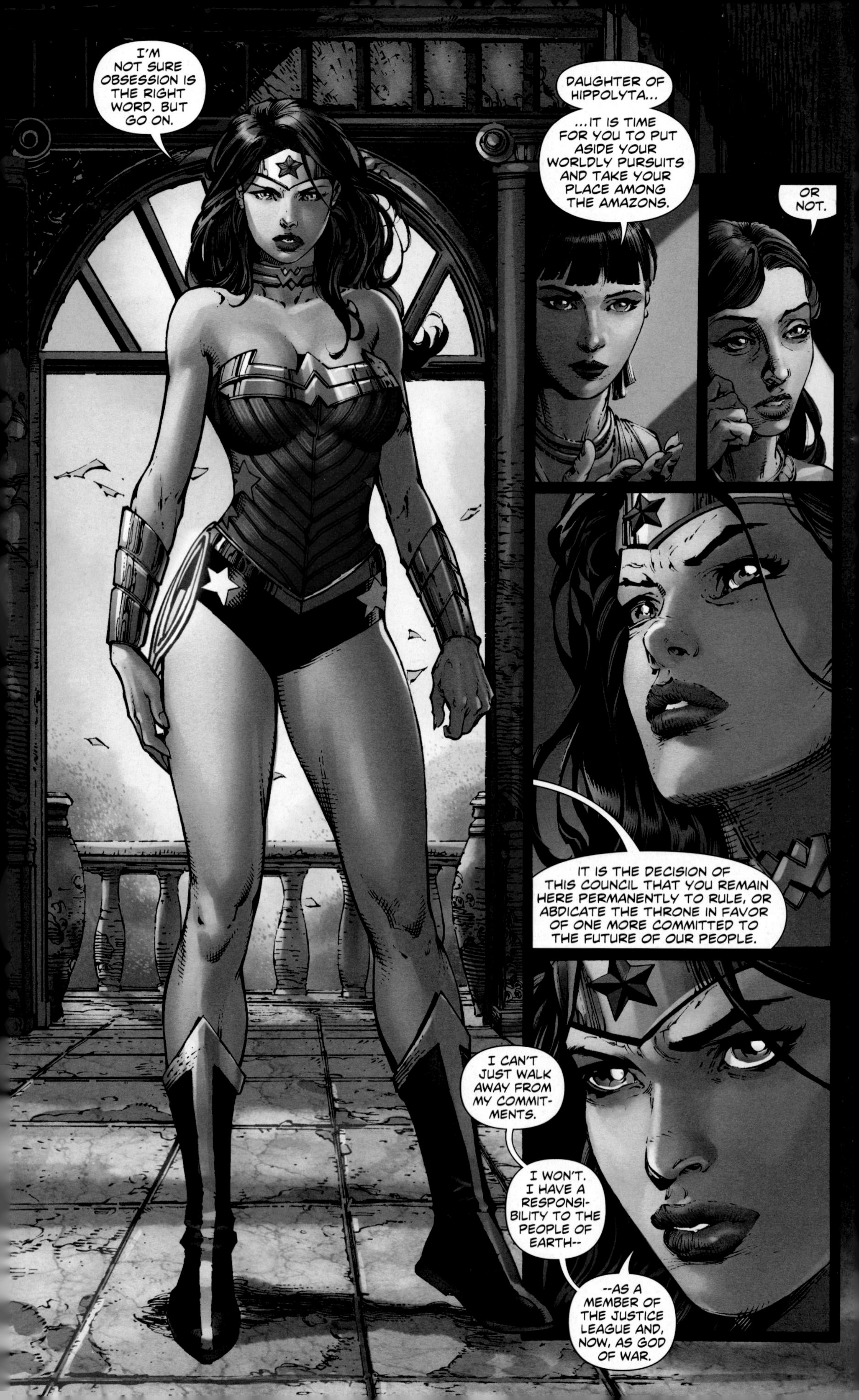
I'M NOT SURE OBSESSION IS THE RIGHT WORD. BUT GO ON.
DAUGHTER OF HIPPOLYTA...
...IT IS TIME FOR YOU TO PUT ASIDE YOUR WORLDLY PURSUITS AND TAKE YOUR PLACE AMONG THE AMAZONS.
OR NOT.
IT IS THE DECISION OF THIS COUNCIL THAT YOU REMAIN HERE PERMANENTLY TO RULE, OR ABDICATE THE THRONE IN FAVOR OF ONE MORE COMMITTED TO THE FUTURE OF OUR PEOPLE.
I CAN'T JUST WALK AWAY FROM MY COMMIT-MENTS.
I WON'T. I HAVE A RESPONSI-BILITY TO THE PEOPLE OF EARTH--
--AS A MEMBER OF THE JUSTICE LEAGUE AND, NOW, AS GOD OF WAR.

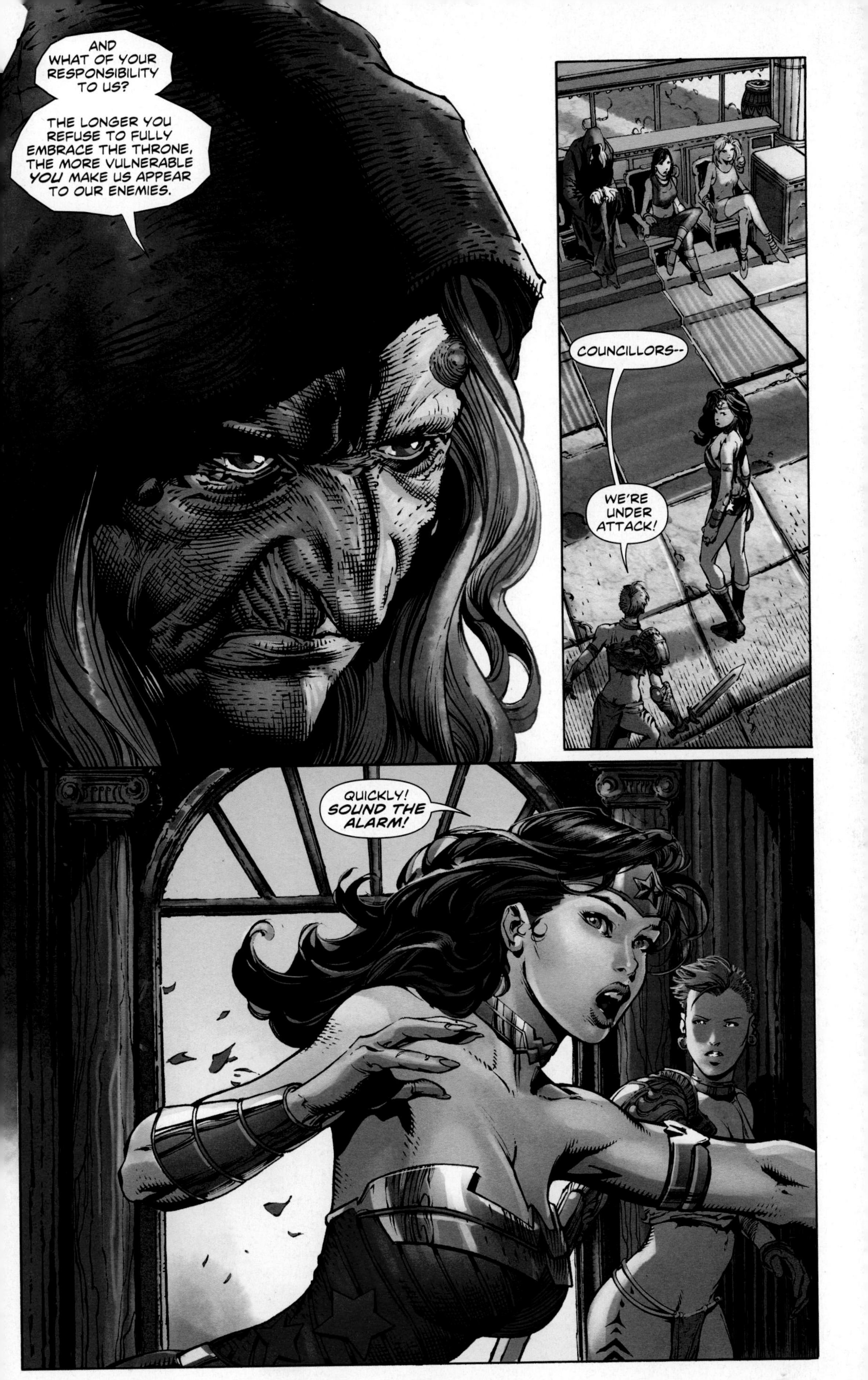
AND WHAT OF YOUR RESPONSIBILITY TO US?
THE LONGER YOU REFUSE TO FULLY EMBRACE THE THRONE, THE MORE VULNERABLE *YOU* MAKE US APPEAR TO OUR ENEMIES.
COUNCILLORS--
WE'RE UNDER ATTACK!
QUICKLY! *SOUND THE ALARM!*

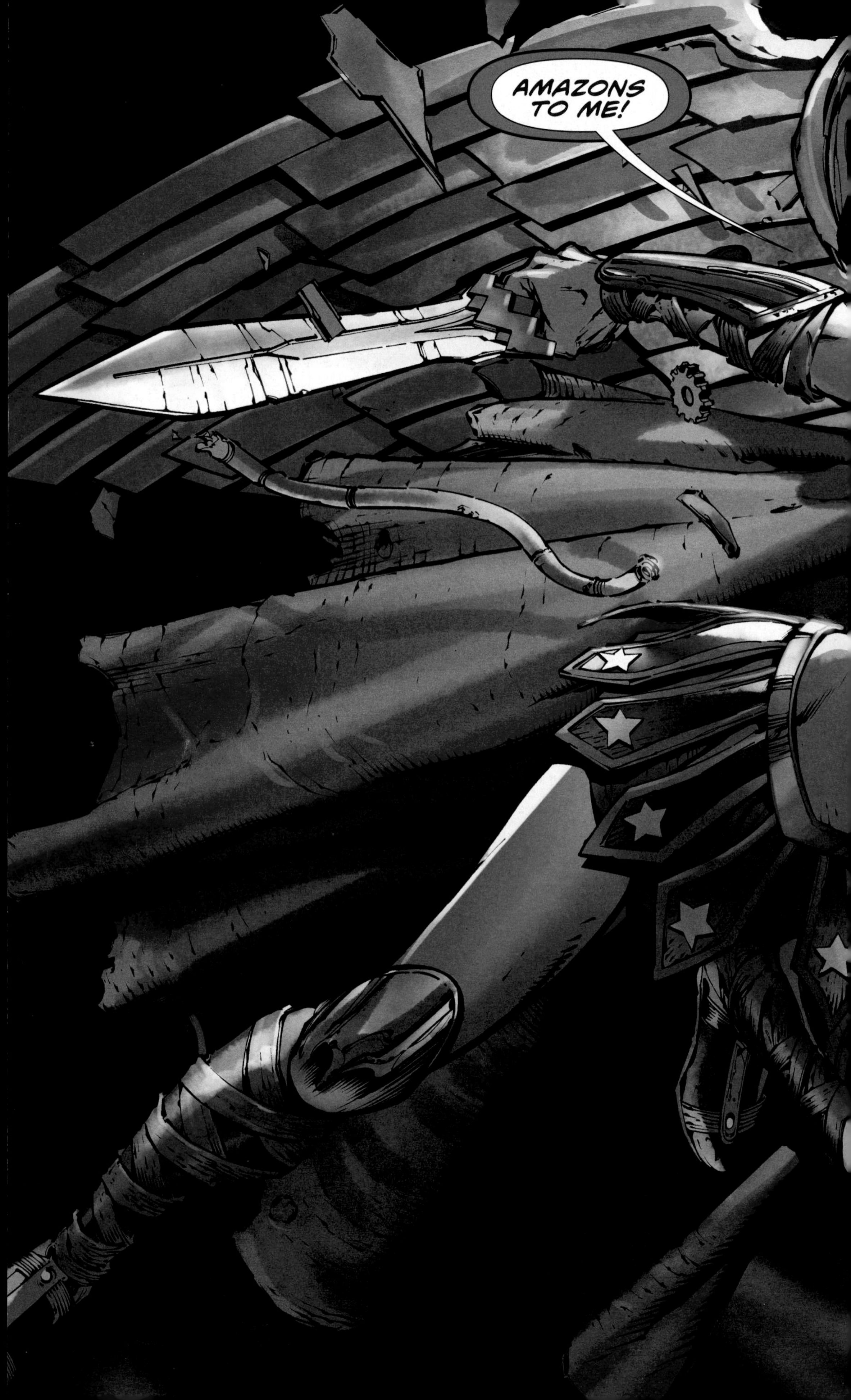
AMAZONS TO ME!

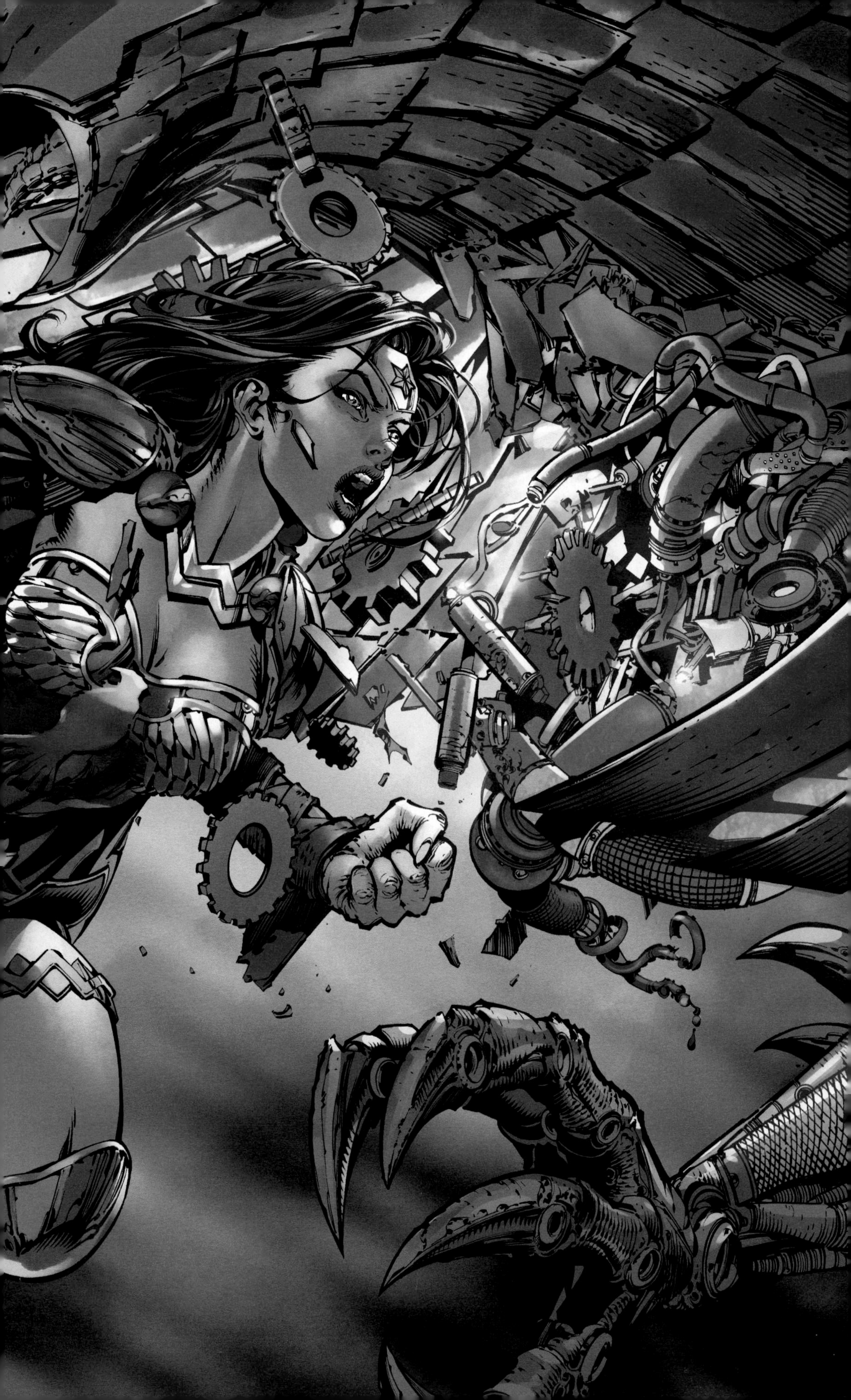

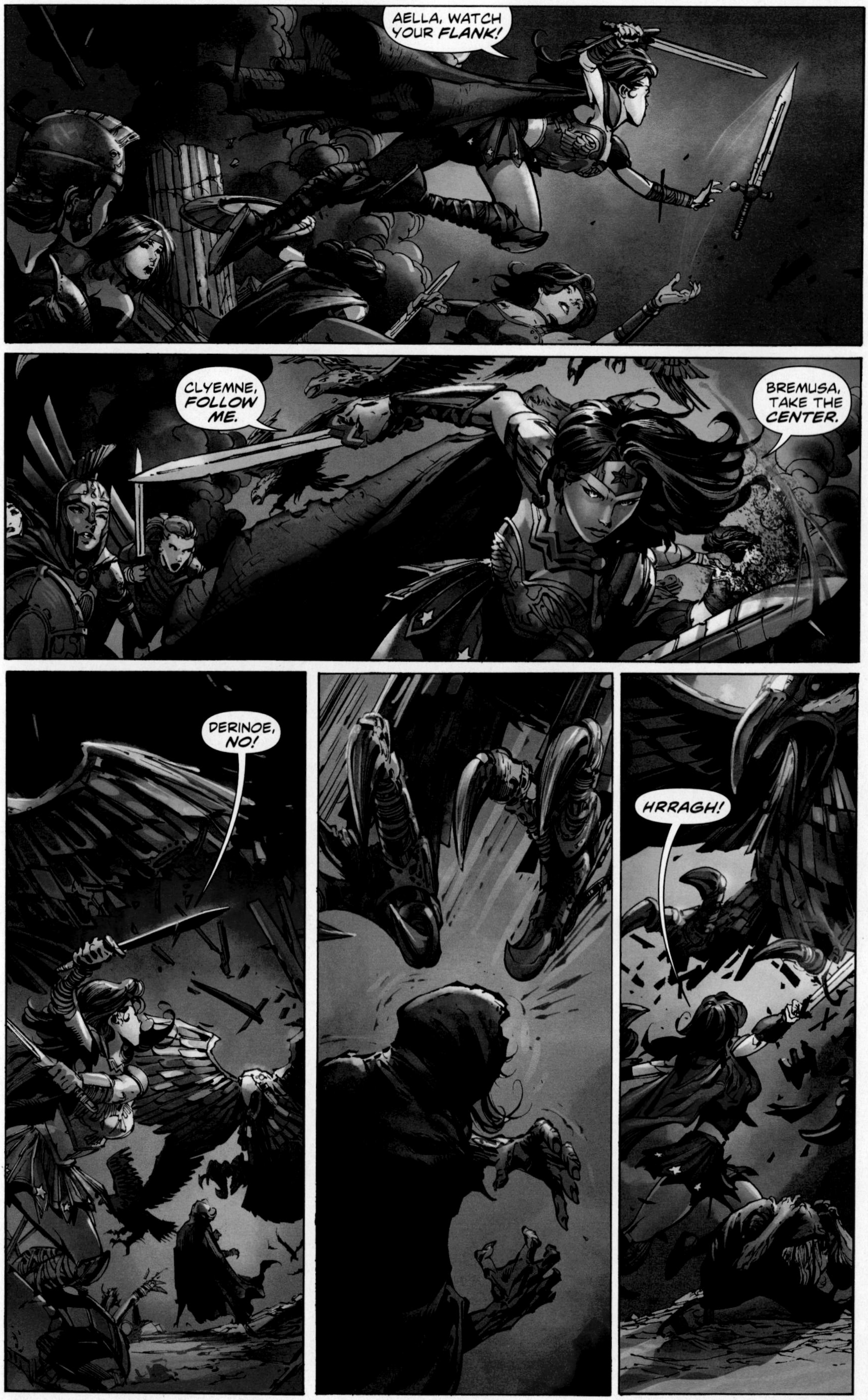
AELLA, WATCH YOUR FLANK!
CLYEMNE, FOLLOW ME.
BREMUSA, TAKE THE CENTER.
DERINOE, NO!
HRRAGH!

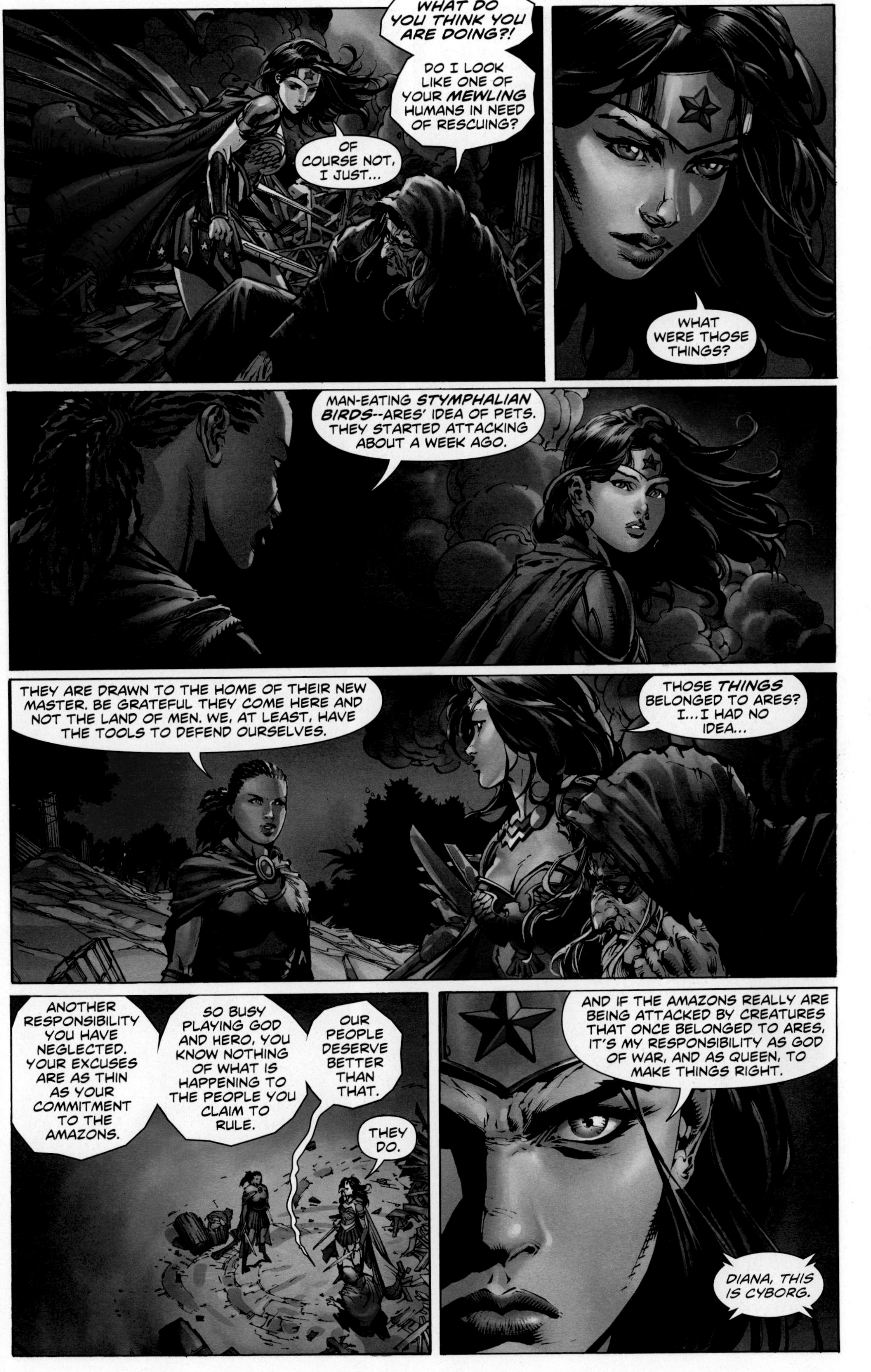
WHAT DO YOU THINK YOU ARE DOING?!
DO I LOOK LIKE ONE OF YOUR MEWLING HUMANS IN NEED OF RESCUING?
OF COURSE NOT, I JUST...
WHAT WERE THOSE THINGS?
MAN-EATING STYMPHALIAN BIRDS--ARES' IDEA OF PETS. THEY STARTED ATTACKING ABOUT A WEEK AGO.
THEY ARE DRAWN TO THE HOME OF THEIR NEW MASTER. BE GRATEFUL THEY COME HERE AND NOT THE LAND OF MEN. WE, AT LEAST, HAVE THE TOOLS TO DEFEND OURSELVES.
THOSE THINGS BELONGED TO ARES? I...I HAD NO IDEA...
ANOTHER RESPONSIBILITY YOU HAVE NEGLECTED. YOUR EXCUSES ARE AS THIN AS YOUR COMMITMENT TO THE AMAZONS.
SO BUSY PLAYING GOD AND HERO, YOU KNOW NOTHING OF WHAT IS HAPPENING TO THE PEOPLE YOU CLAIM TO RULE.
OUR PEOPLE DESERVE BETTER THAN THAT.
THEY DO.
AND IF THE AMAZONS REALLY ARE BEING ATTACKED BY CREATURES THAT ONCE BELONGED TO ARES, IT'S MY RESPONSIBILITY AS GOD OF WAR, AND AS QUEEN, TO MAKE THINGS RIGHT.
DIANA, THIS IS CYBORG.

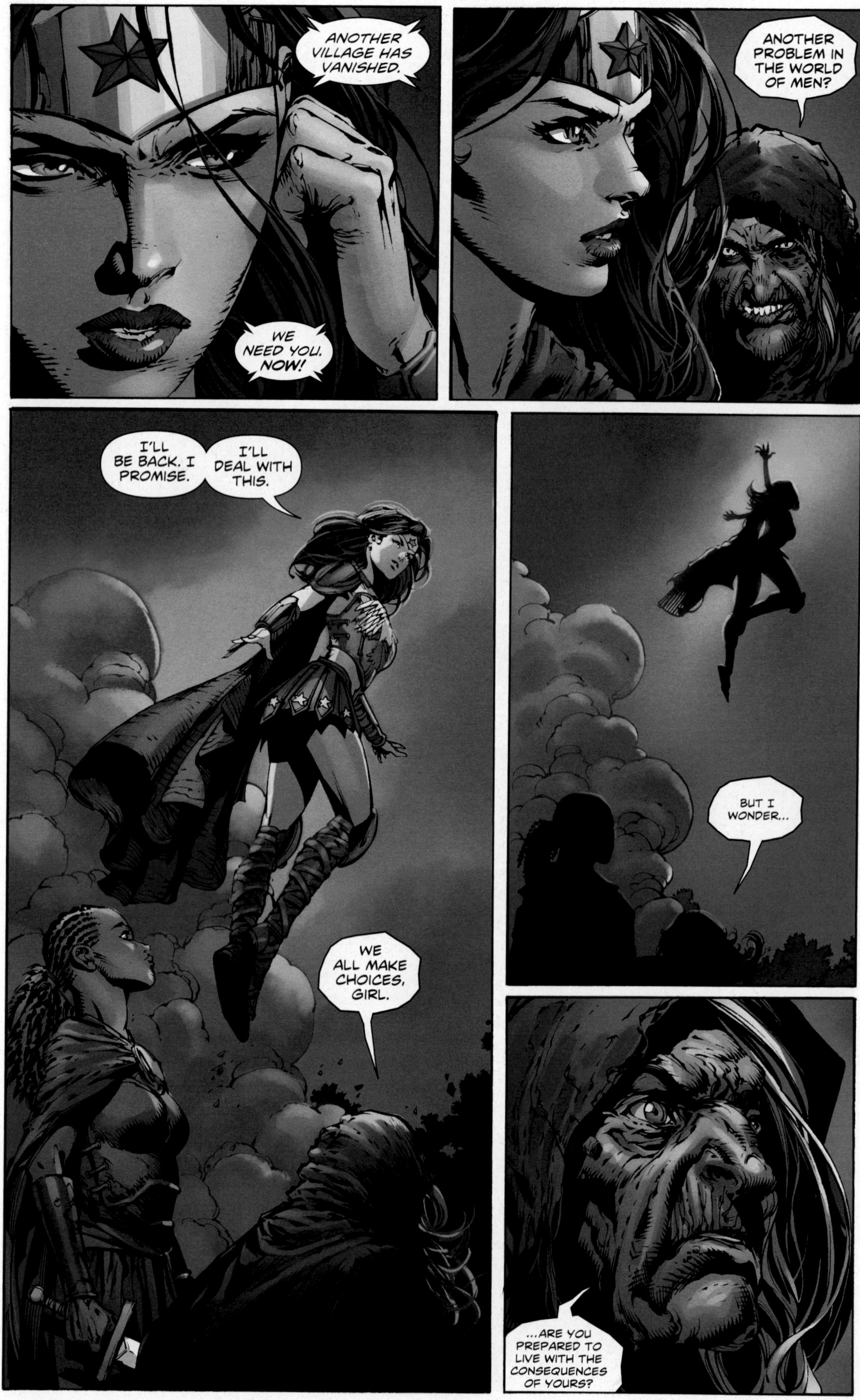
ANOTHER VILLAGE HAS VANISHED.
WE NEED YOU. NOW!
ANOTHER PROBLEM IN THE WORLD OF MEN?
I'LL BE BACK. I PROMISE.
I'LL DEAL WITH THIS.
WE ALL MAKE CHOICES, GIRL.
BUT I WONDER...
...ARE YOU PREPARED TO LIVE WITH THE CONSEQUENCES OF YOURS?

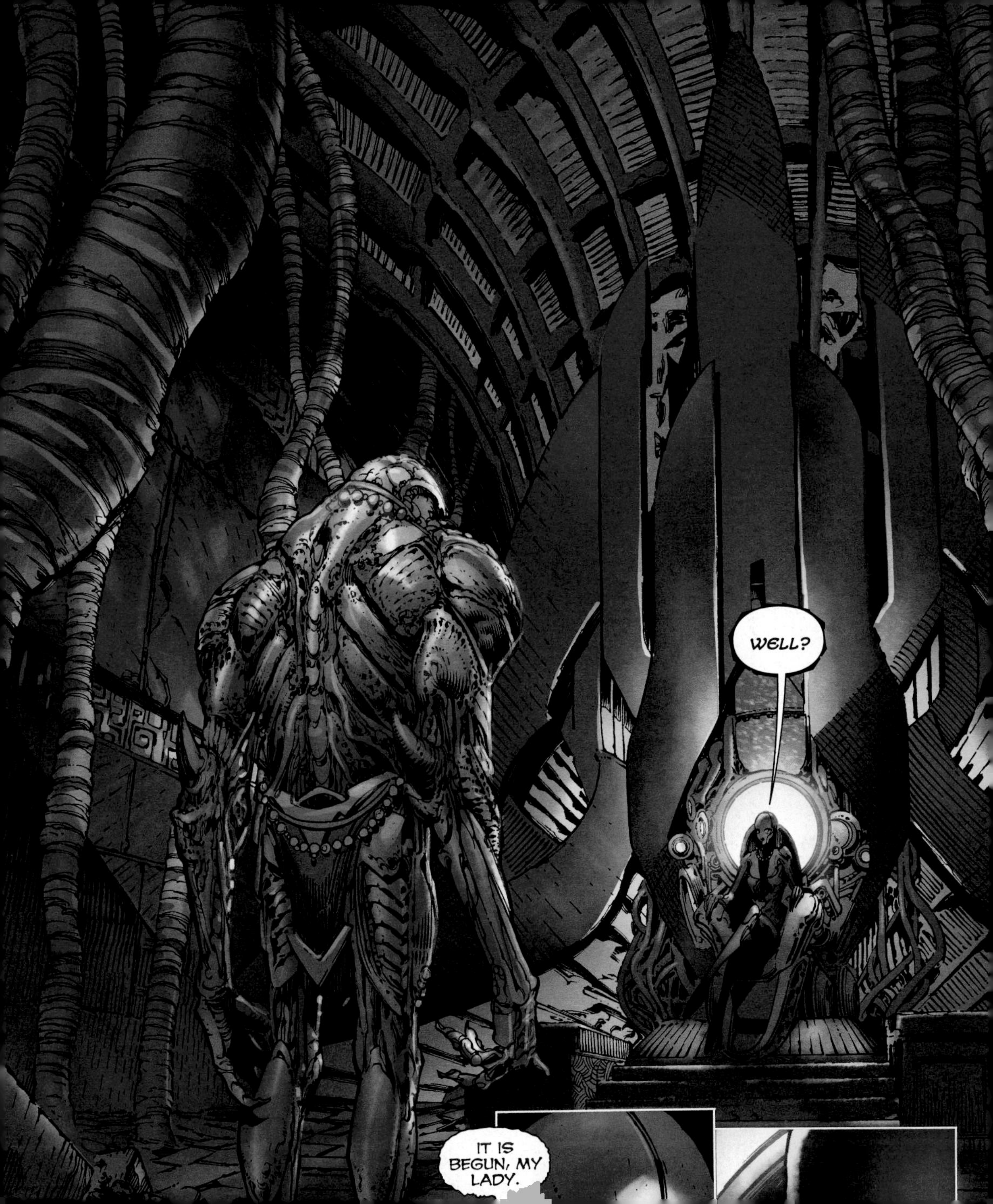
WELL?
IT IS BEGUN, MY LADY.

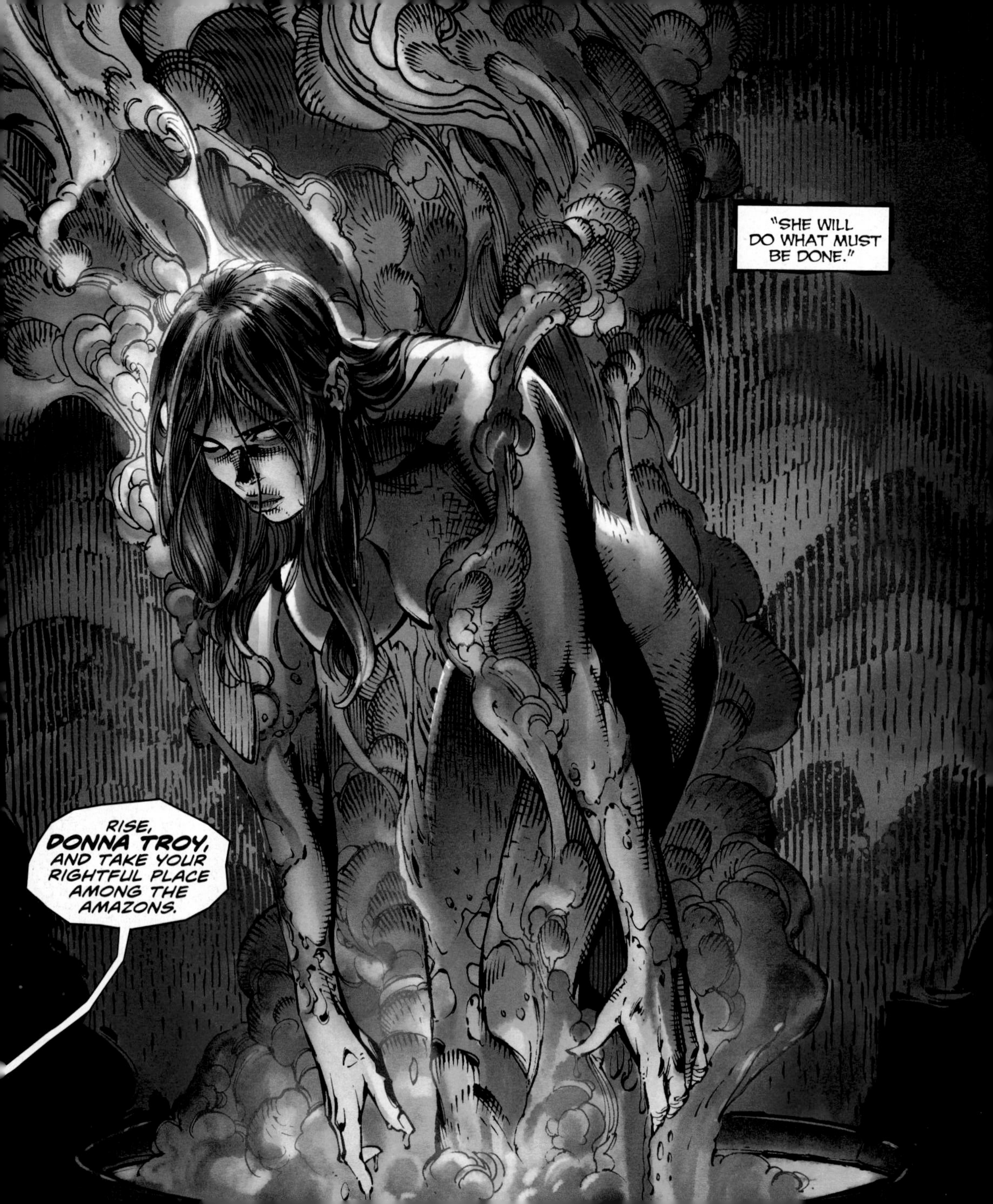
"SHE WILL DO WHAT MUST BE DONE."
RISE, DONNA TROY, AND TAKE YOUR RIGHTFUL PLACE AMONG THE AMAZONS.

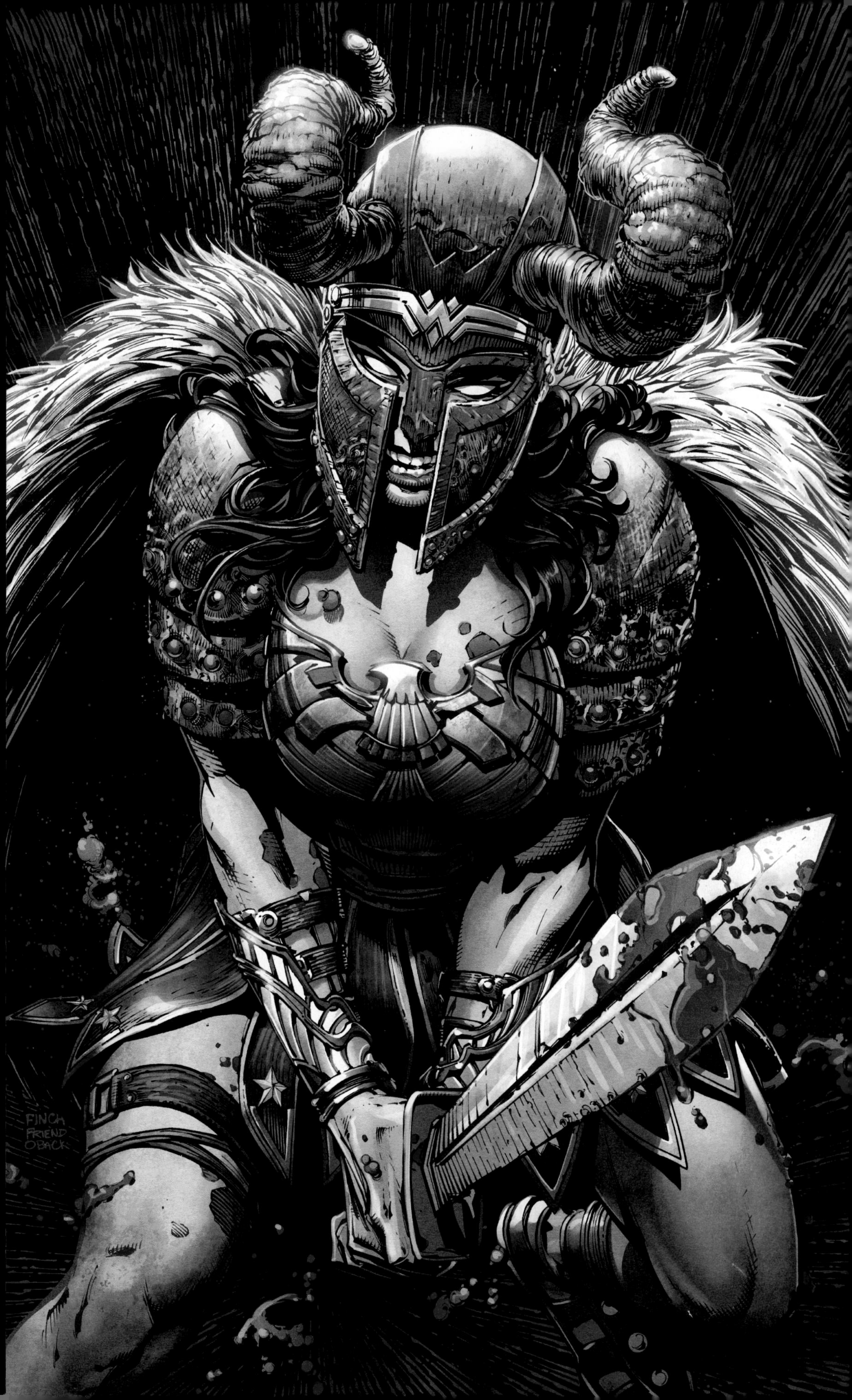
FINCH
FRIEND
OBACK

WAR-TORN CHAPTER 3

MEREDITH FINCH writer DAVID FINCH penciller BATT DANNY MIKI SONIA OBACK inkers SONIA OBACK colorist DEZI SIENTY letterer cover by FINCH, FRIEND and OBACK

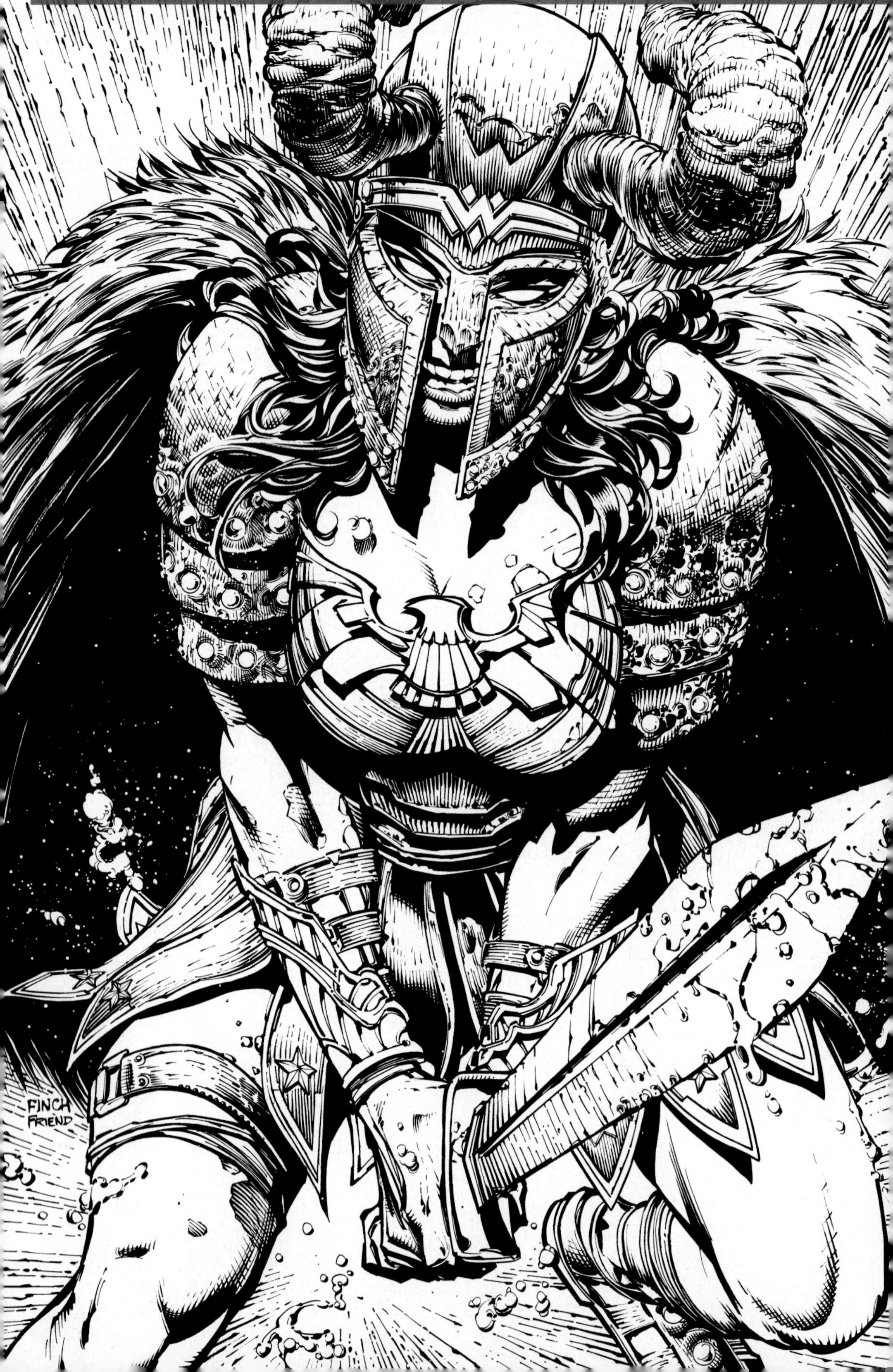
FINCH
FRIEND

GET THOSE
WOUNDED OUT
OF HERE!

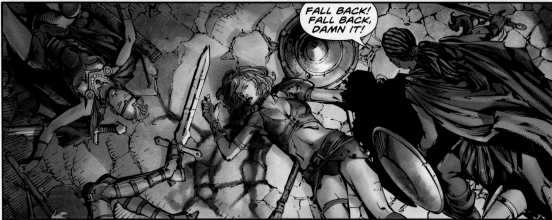

FALL BACK!
FALL BACK,
DAMN IT!

WE'LL COVER
YOU AS LONG AS
WE CAN!

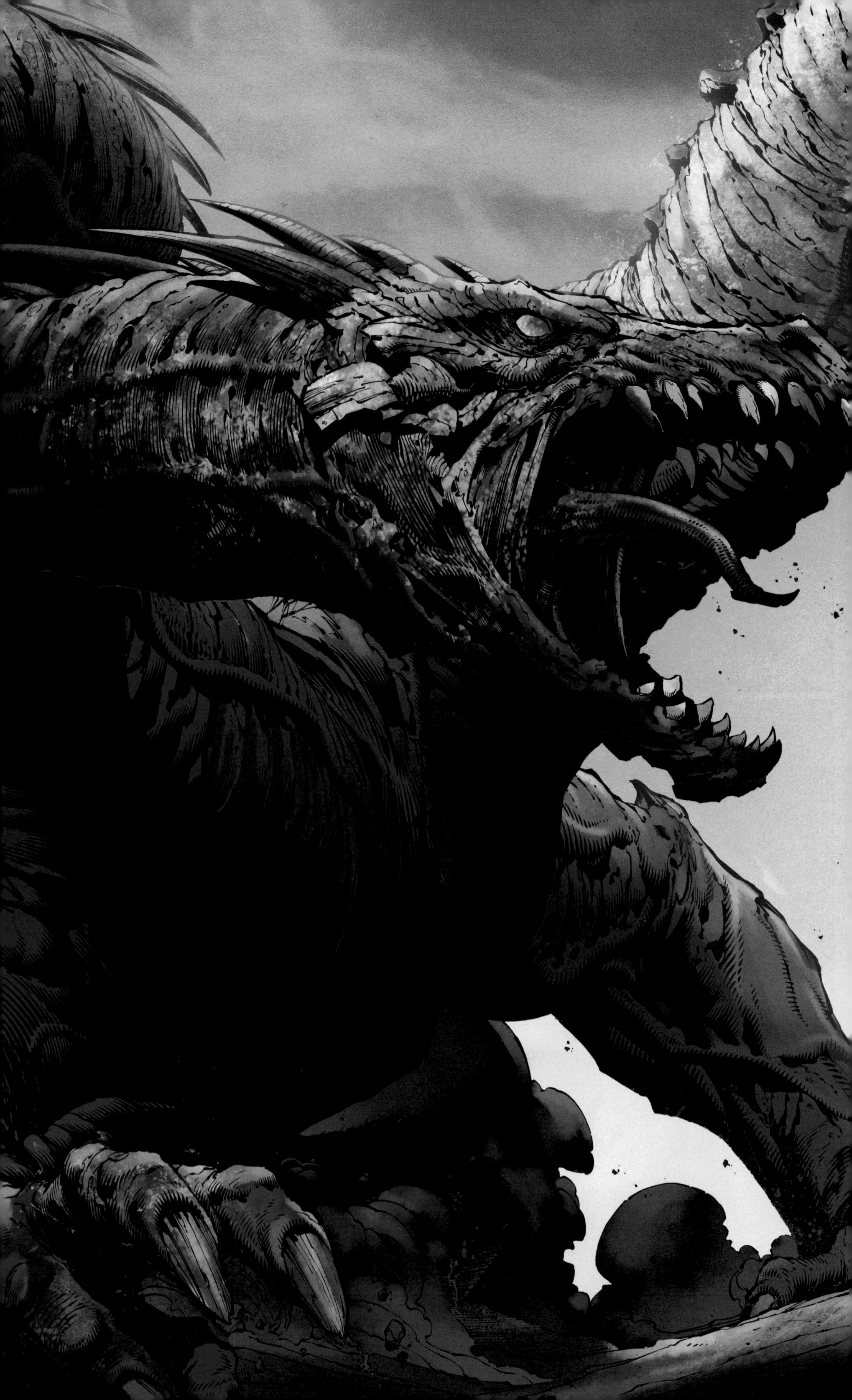

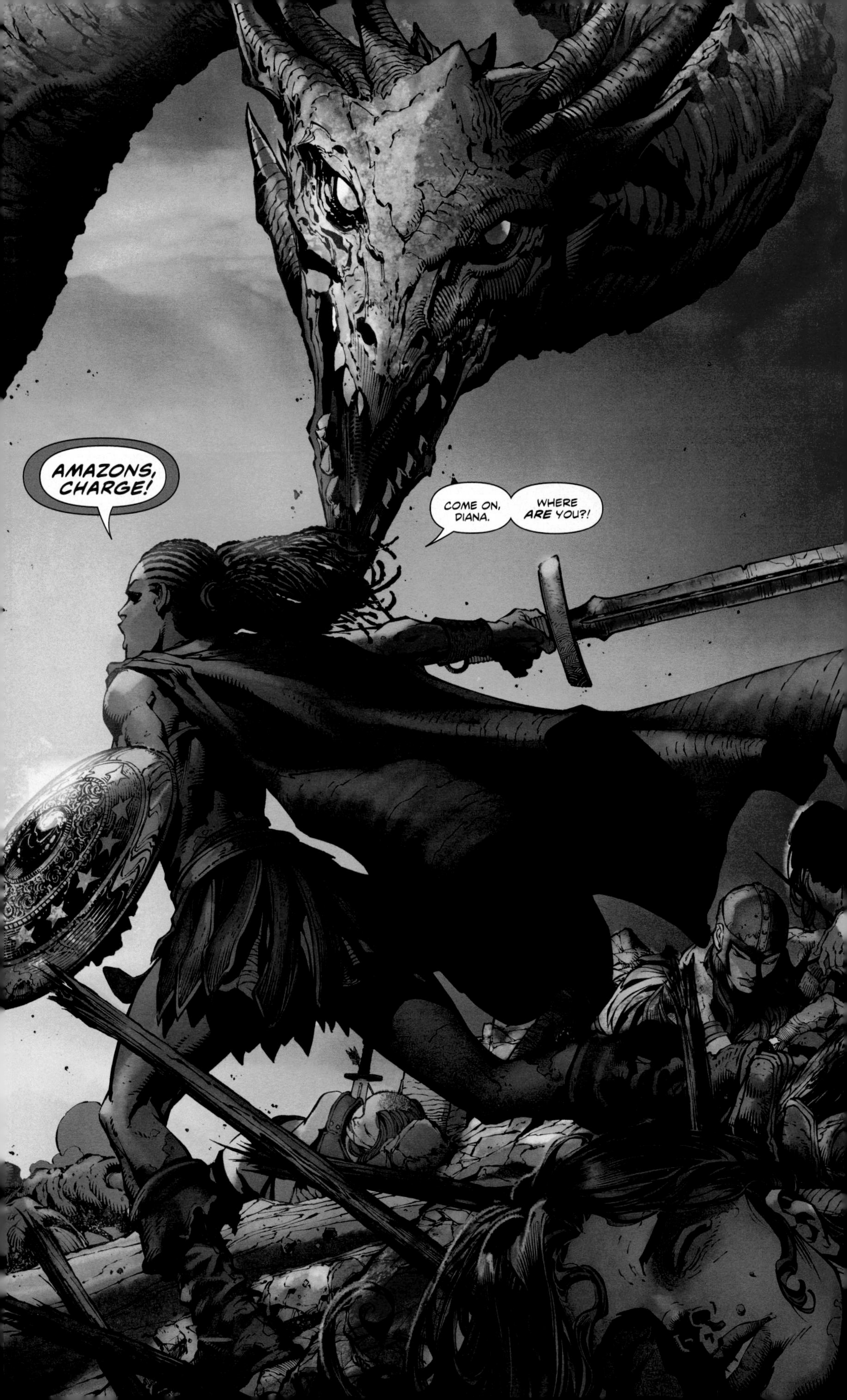
AMAZONS, CHARGE!
COME ON, DIANA.
WHERE ARE YOU?!

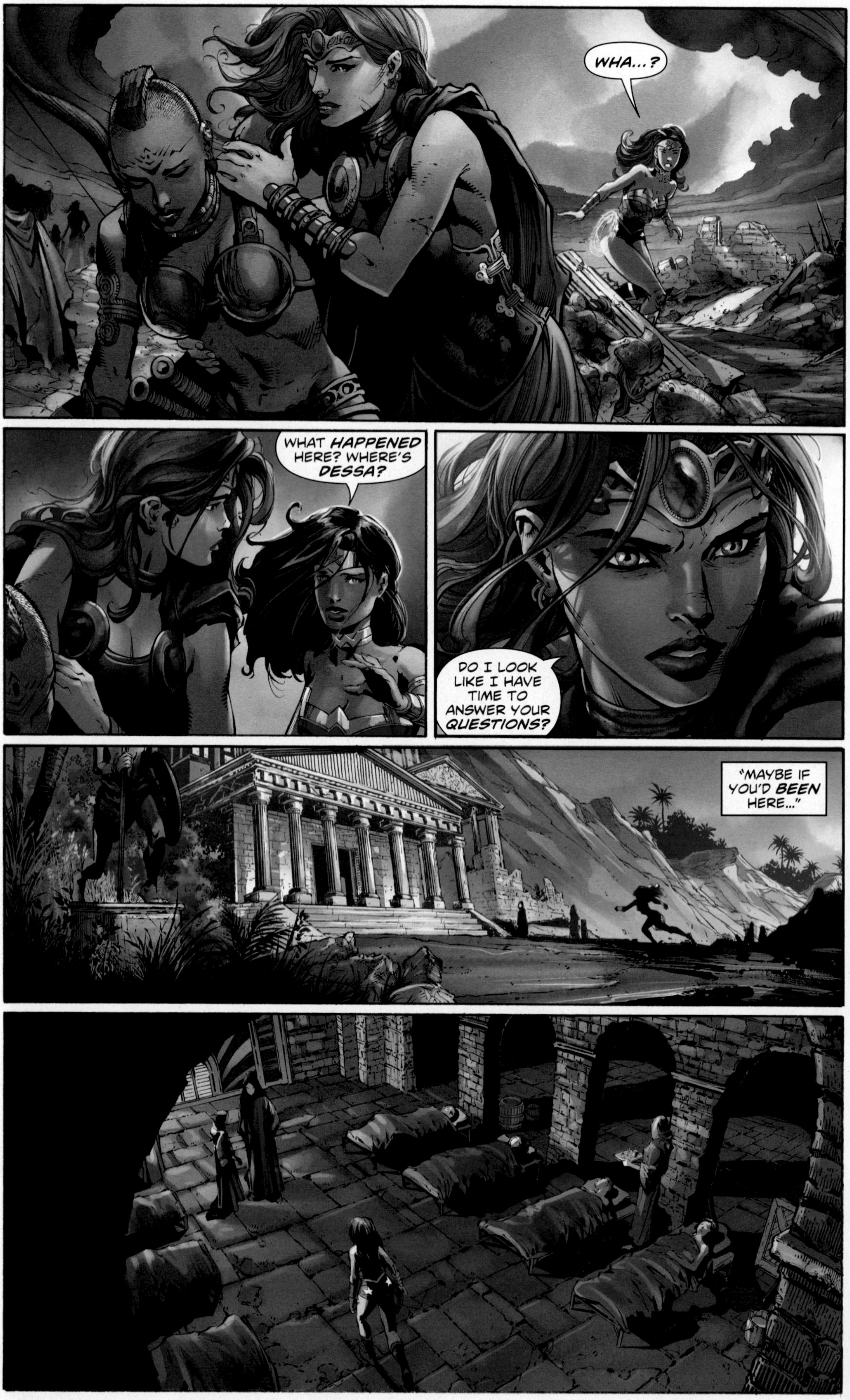
WHA...?
WHAT HAPPENED HERE? WHERE'S DESSA?
DO I LOOK LIKE I HAVE TIME TO ANSWER YOUR QUESTIONS?
"MAYBE IF YOU'D BEEN HERE..."

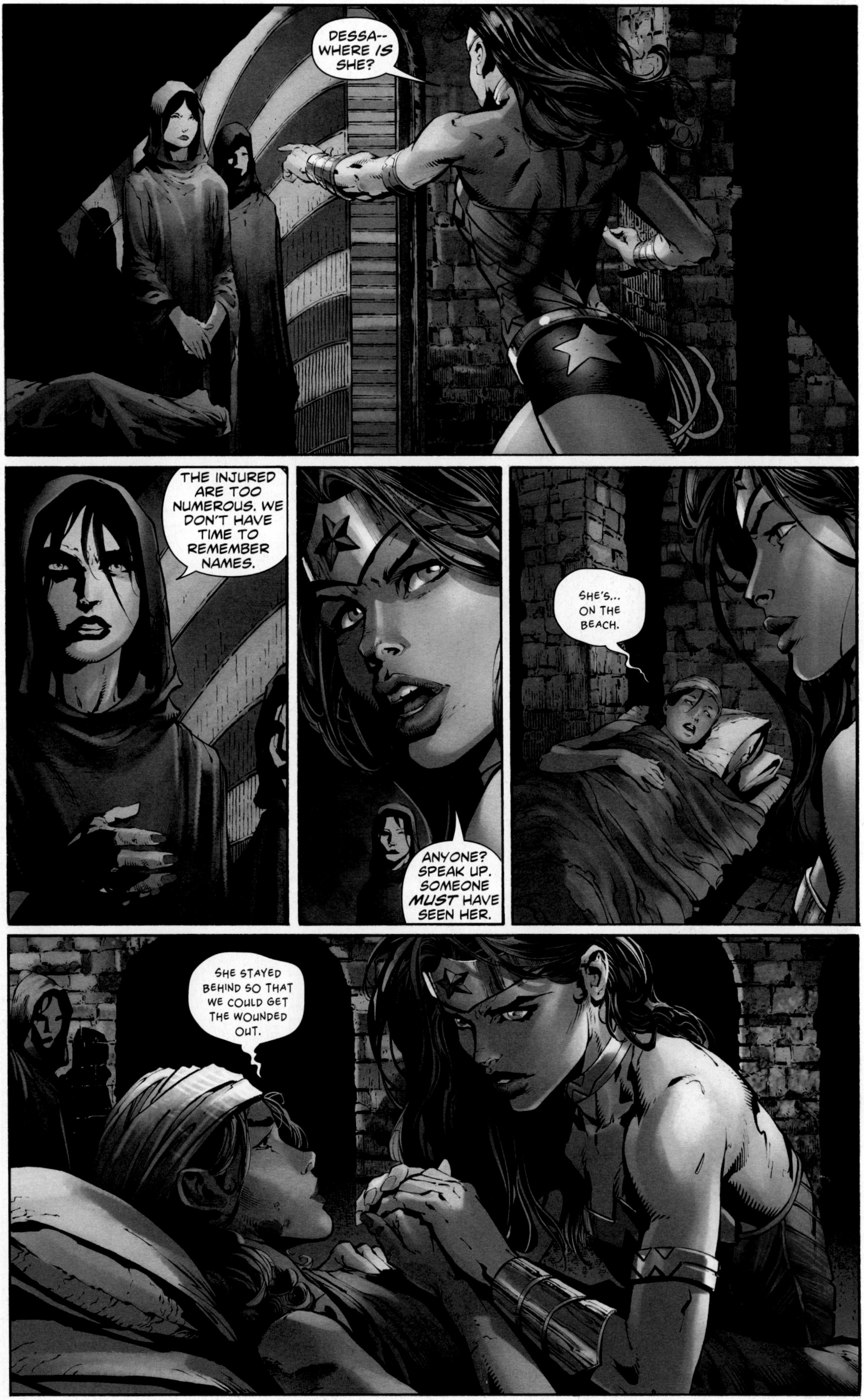
DESSA--
WHERE *IS* SHE?
THE INJURED ARE TOO NUMEROUS. WE DON'T HAVE TIME TO REMEMBER NAMES.
ANYONE? SPEAK UP. SOMEONE *MUST* HAVE SEEN HER.
SHE'S... ON THE BEACH.
SHE STAYED BEHIND SO THAT WE COULD GET THE WOUNDED OUT.

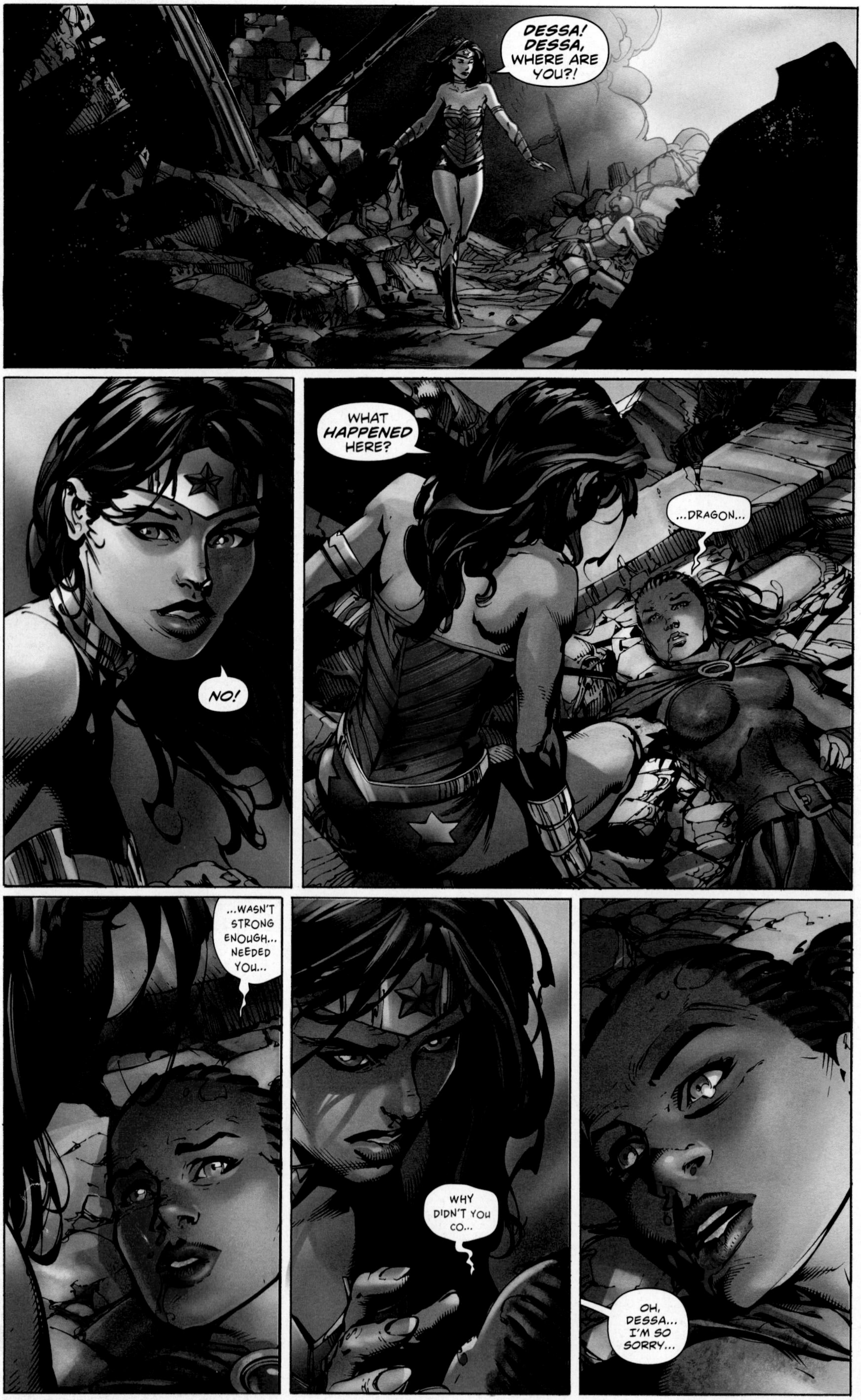
DESSA! DESSA, WHERE ARE YOU?!
NO!
WHAT HAPPENED HERE?
...DRAGON...
...WASN'T STRONG ENOUGH... NEEDED YOU...
WHY DIDN'T YOU CO...
OH, DESSA... I'M SO SORRY...

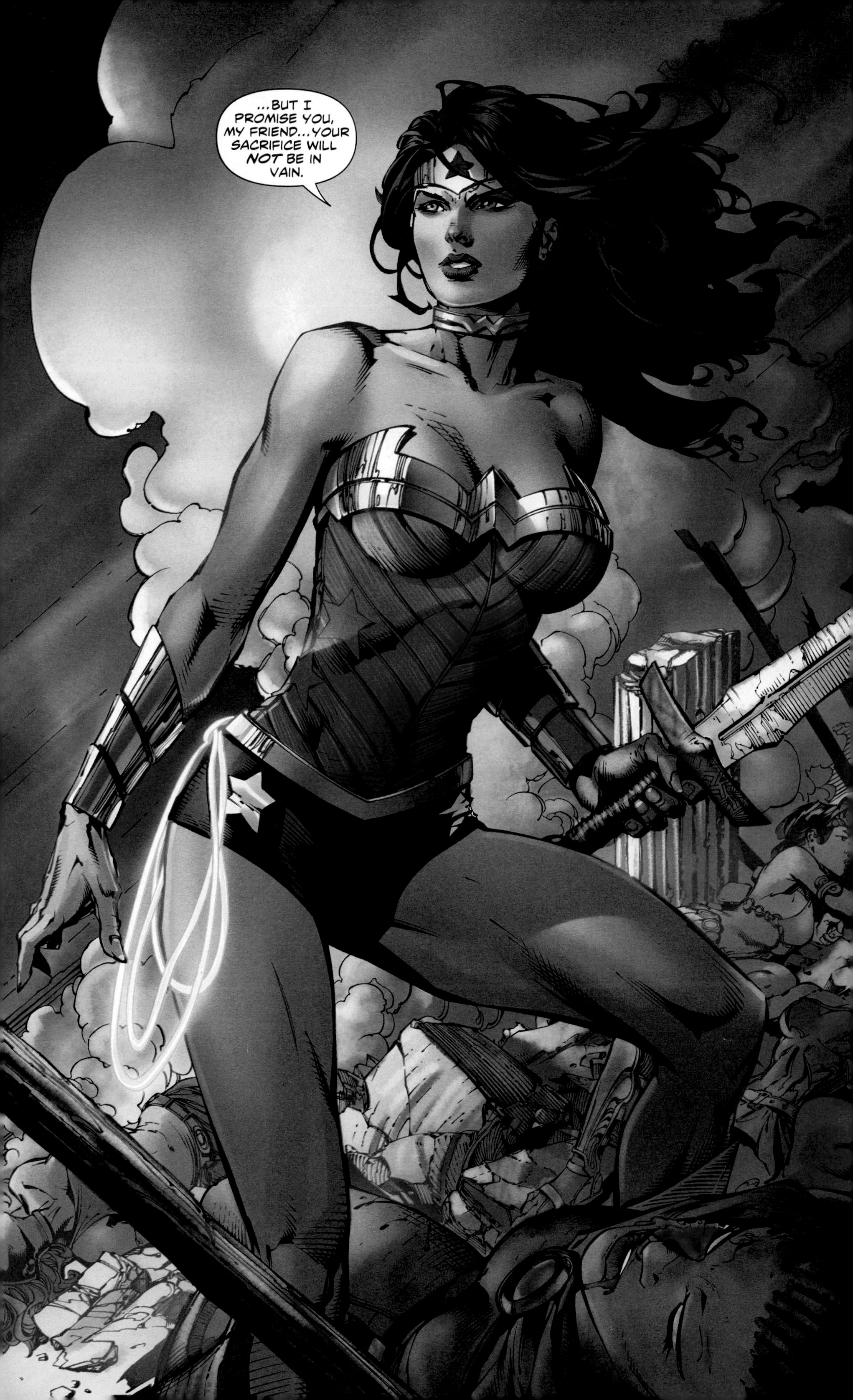
...BUT I PROMISE YOU, MY FRIEND...YOUR SACRIFICE WILL NOT BE IN VAIN.

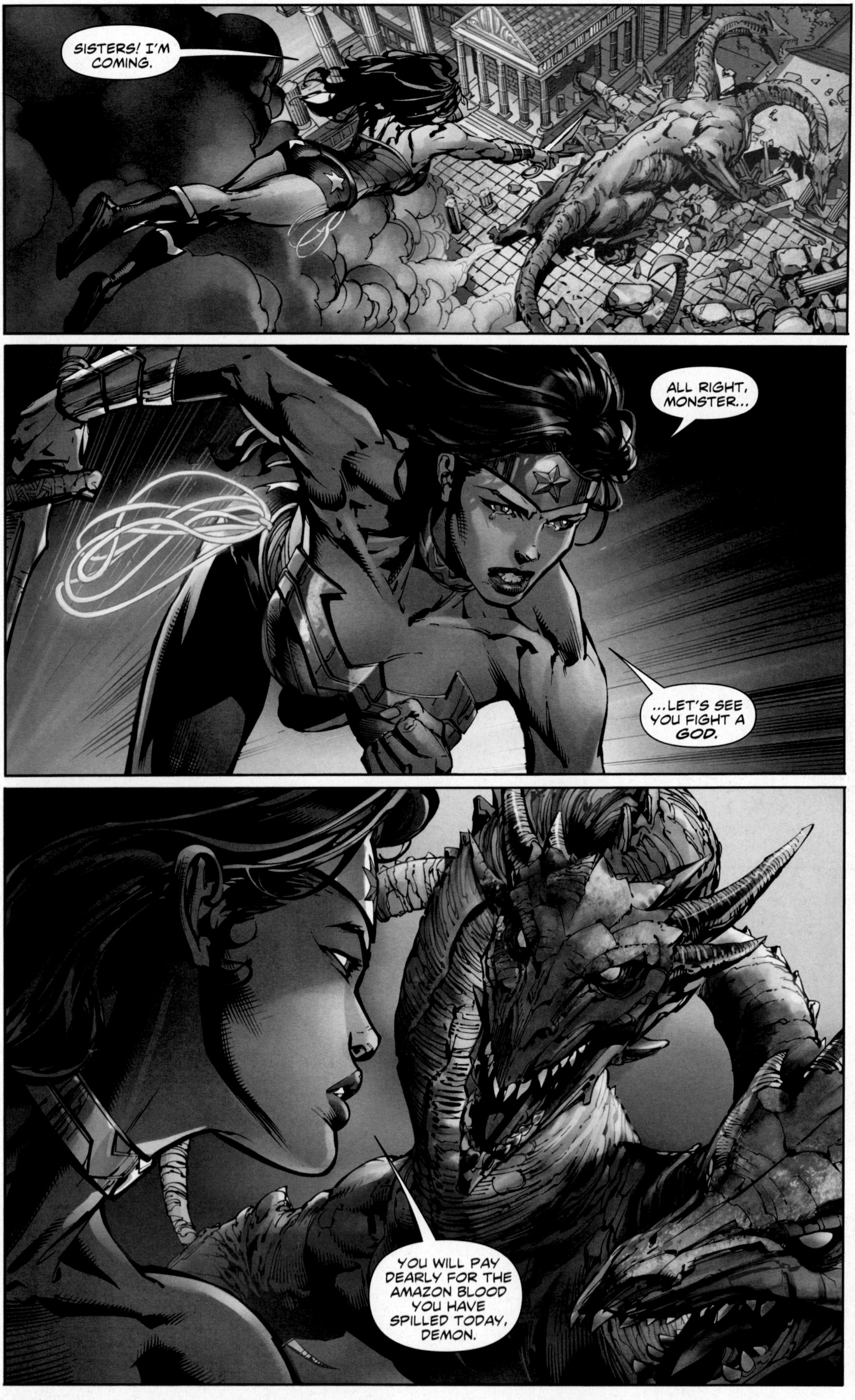
SISTERS! I'M COMING.
ALL RIGHT, MONSTER...
...LET'S SEE YOU FIGHT A GOD.
YOU WILL PAY DEARLY FOR THE AMAZON BLOOD YOU HAVE SPILLED TODAY, DEMON.

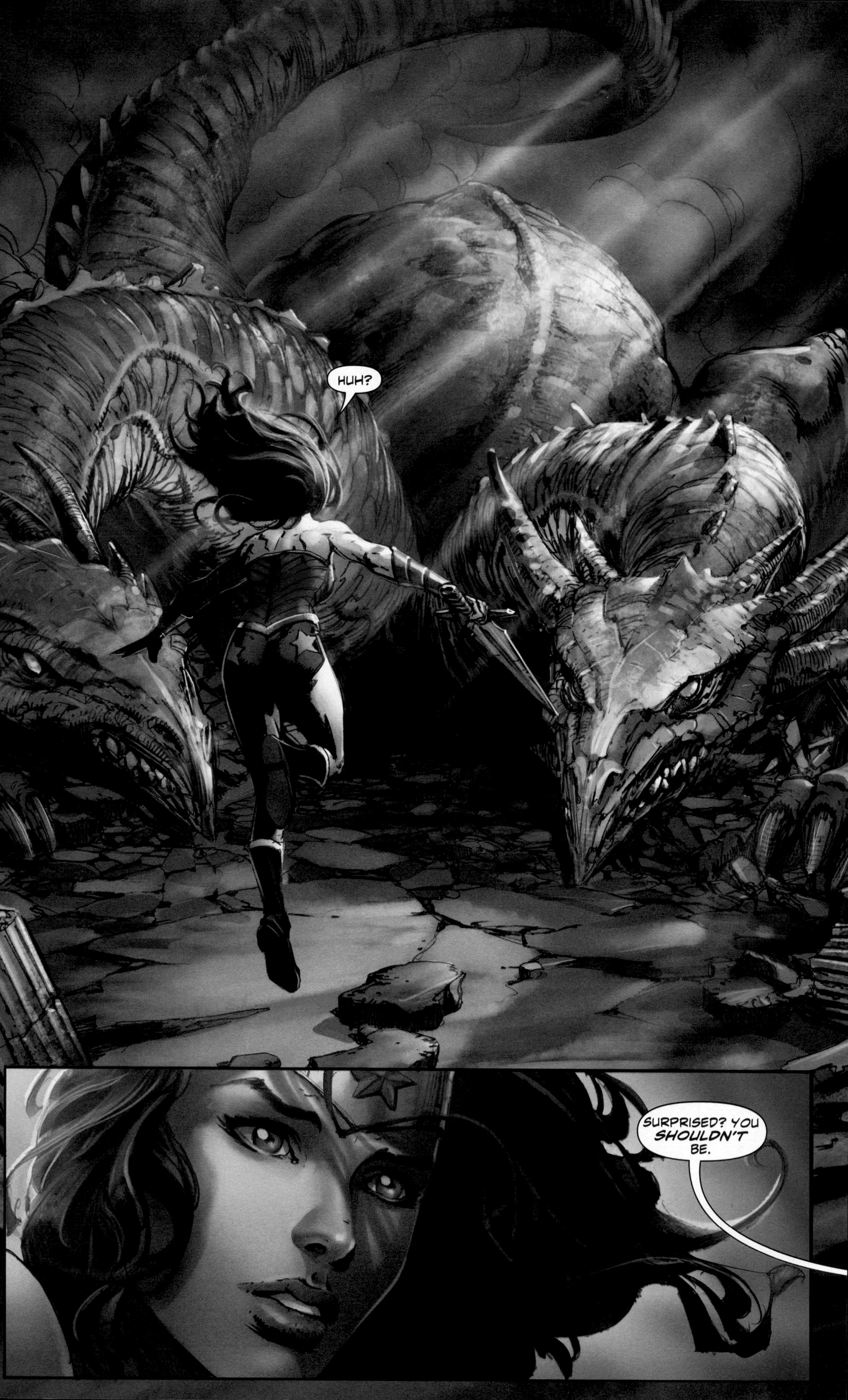
HUH?
SURPRISED? YOU SHOULDN'T BE.

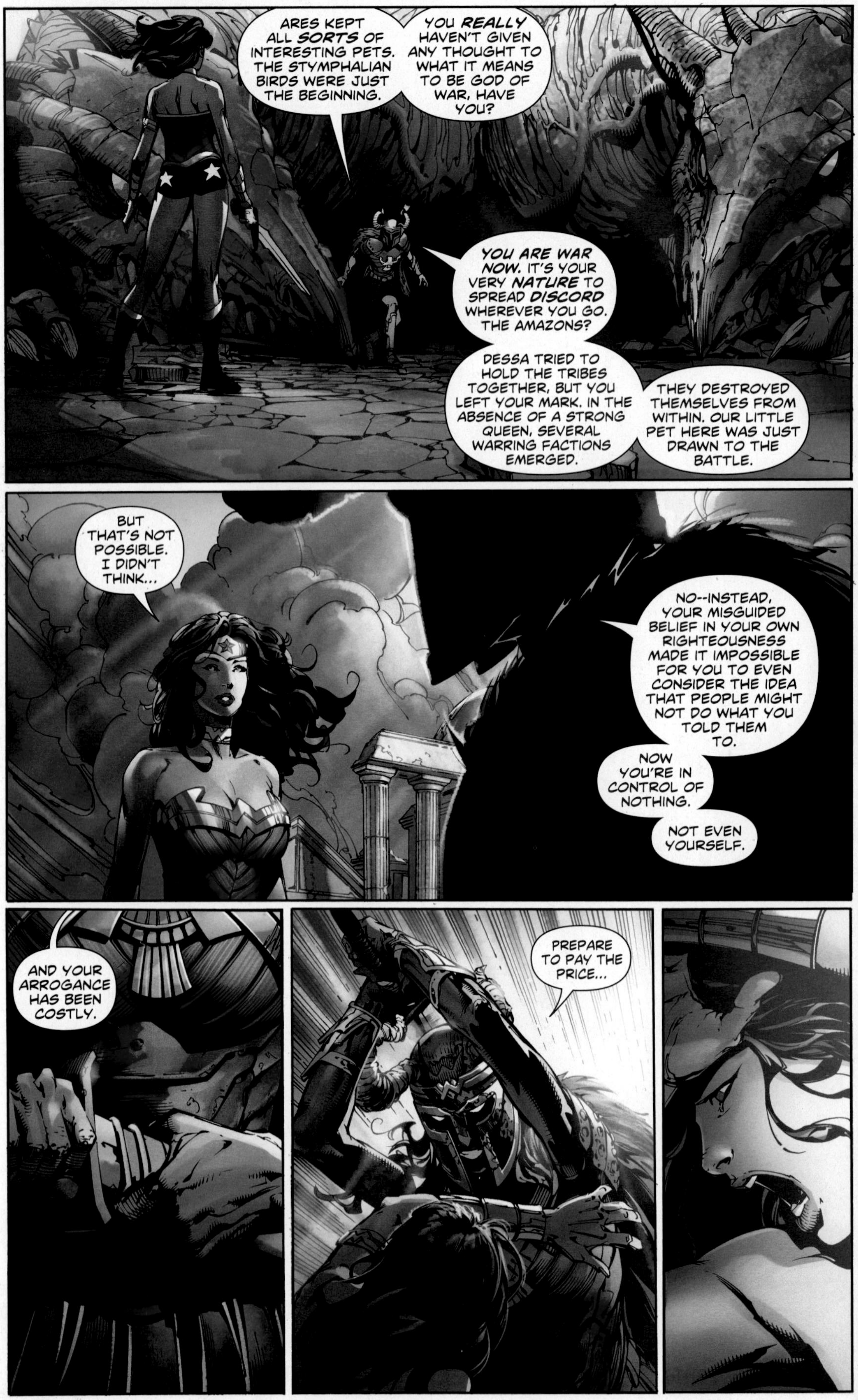
ARES KEPT ALL SORTS OF INTERESTING PETS. THE STYMPHALIAN BIRDS WERE JUST THE BEGINNING.
YOU REALLY HAVEN'T GIVEN ANY THOUGHT TO WHAT IT MEANS TO BE GOD OF WAR, HAVE YOU?
YOU ARE WAR NOW. IT'S YOUR VERY NATURE TO SPREAD DISCORD WHEREVER YOU GO. THE AMAZONS?
DESSA TRIED TO HOLD THE TRIBES TOGETHER, BUT YOU LEFT YOUR MARK. IN THE ABSENCE OF A STRONG QUEEN, SEVERAL WARRING FACTIONS EMERGED.
THEY DESTROYED THEMSELVES FROM WITHIN. OUR LITTLE PET HERE WAS JUST DRAWN TO THE BATTLE.
BUT THAT'S NOT POSSIBLE. I DIDN'T THINK...
NO--INSTEAD, YOUR MISGUIDED BELIEF IN YOUR OWN RIGHTEOUSNESS MADE IT IMPOSSIBLE FOR YOU TO EVEN CONSIDER THE IDEA THAT PEOPLE MIGHT NOT DO WHAT YOU TOLD THEM TO.
NOW YOU'RE IN CONTROL OF NOTHING.
NOT EVEN YOURSELF.
AND YOUR ARROGANCE HAS BEEN COSTLY.
PREPARE TO PAY THE PRICE...

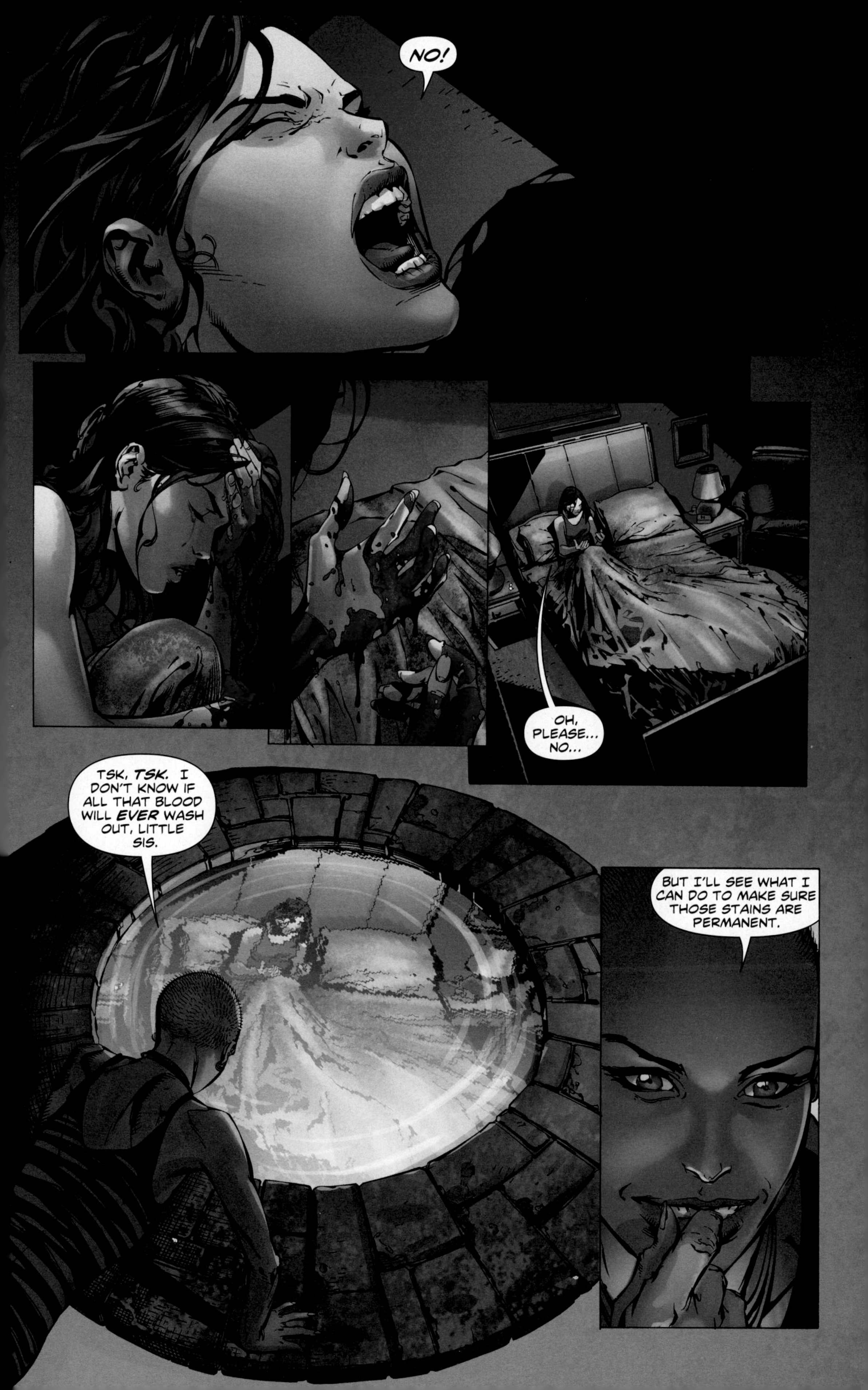
NO!
OH, PLEASE... NO...
TSK, TSK. I DON'T KNOW IF ALL THAT BLOOD WILL EVER WASH OUT, LITTLE SIS.
BUT I'LL SEE WHAT I CAN DO TO MAKE SURE THOSE STAINS ARE PERMANENT.

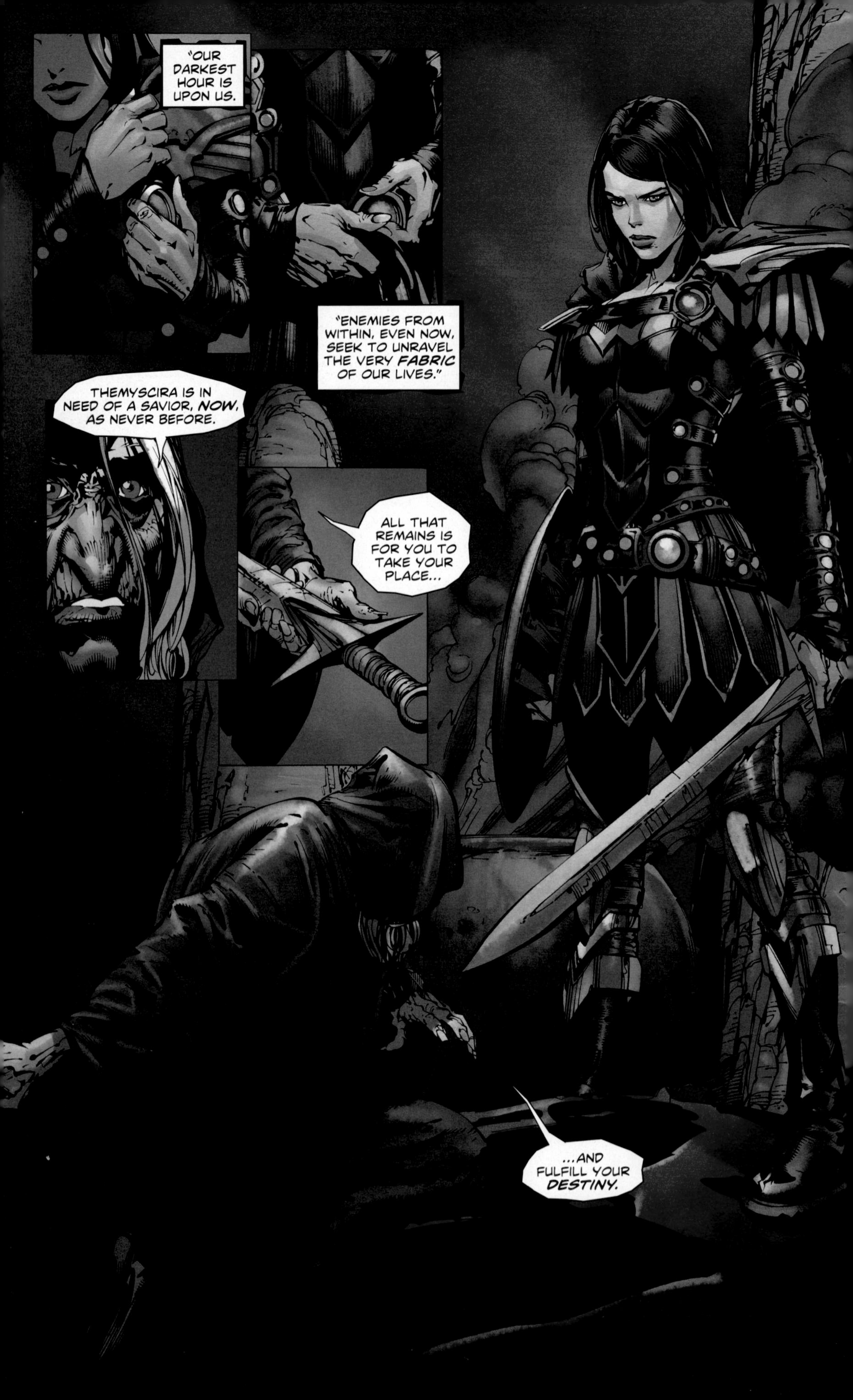
"OUR DARKEST HOUR IS UPON US.
"ENEMIES FROM WITHIN, EVEN NOW, SEEK TO UNRAVEL THE VERY *FABRIC* OF OUR LIVES."
THEMYSCIRA IS IN NEED OF A SAVIOR, *NOW*, AS NEVER BEFORE.
ALL THAT REMAINS IS FOR YOU TO TAKE YOUR PLACE...
...AND FULFILL YOUR *DESTINY*.

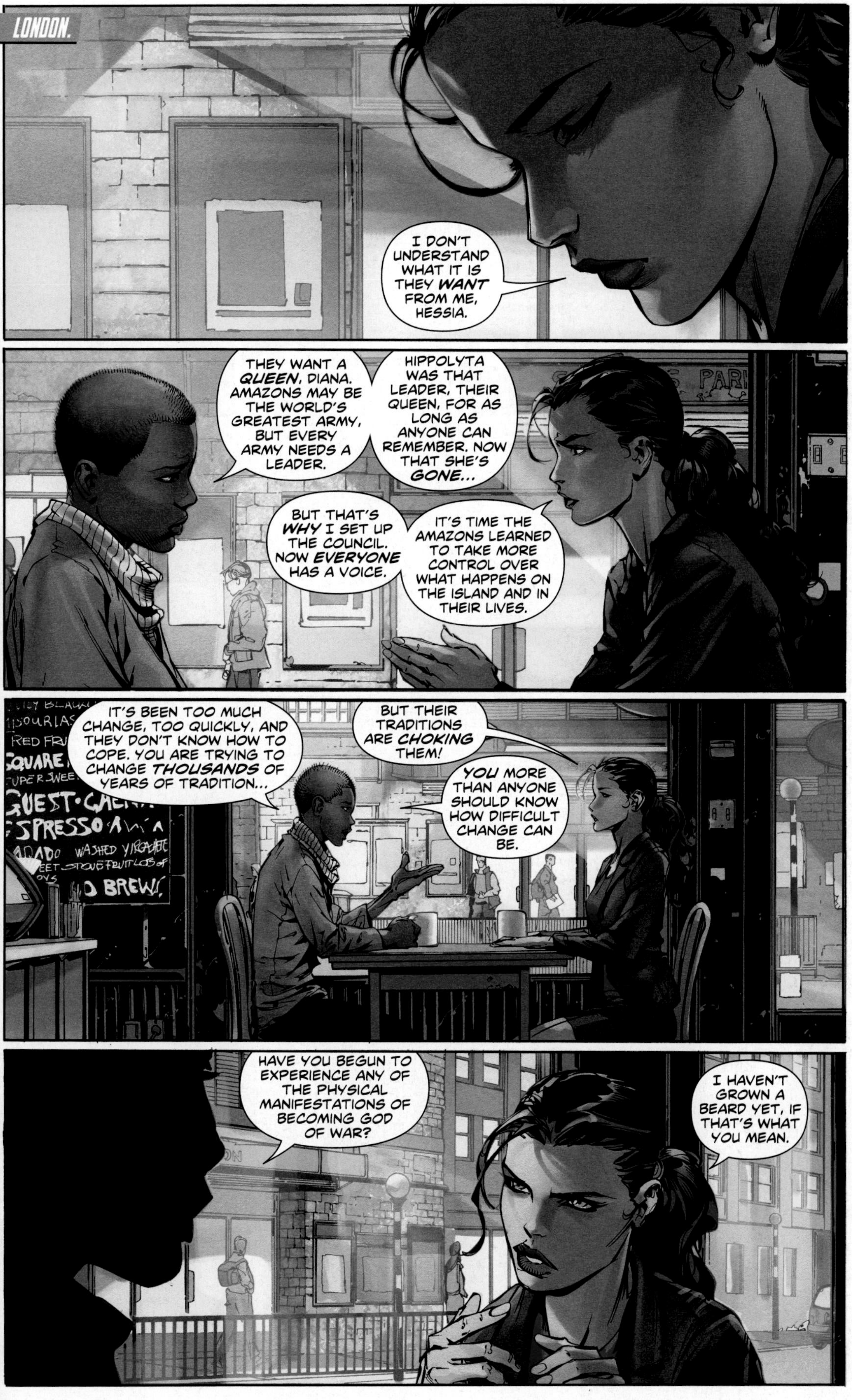
LONDON.
I DON'T UNDERSTAND WHAT IT IS THEY WANT FROM ME, HESSIA.
THEY WANT A QUEEN, DIANA. AMAZONS MAY BE THE WORLD'S GREATEST ARMY, BUT EVERY ARMY NEEDS A LEADER.
HIPPOLYTA WAS THAT LEADER, THEIR QUEEN, FOR AS LONG AS ANYONE CAN REMEMBER. NOW THAT SHE'S GONE...
BUT THAT'S WHY I SET UP THE COUNCIL. NOW EVERYONE HAS A VOICE.
IT'S TIME THE AMAZONS LEARNED TO TAKE MORE CONTROL OVER WHAT HAPPENS ON THE ISLAND AND IN THEIR LIVES.
IT'S BEEN TOO MUCH CHANGE, TOO QUICKLY, AND THEY DON'T KNOW HOW TO COPE. YOU ARE TRYING TO CHANGE THOUSANDS OF YEARS OF TRADITION...
BUT THEIR TRADITIONS ARE CHOKING THEM!
YOU MORE THAN ANYONE SHOULD KNOW HOW DIFFICULT CHANGE CAN BE.
HAVE YOU BEGUN TO EXPERIENCE ANY OF THE PHYSICAL MANIFESTATIONS OF BECOMING GOD OF WAR?
I HAVEN'T GROWN A BEARD YET, IF THAT'S WHAT YOU MEAN.

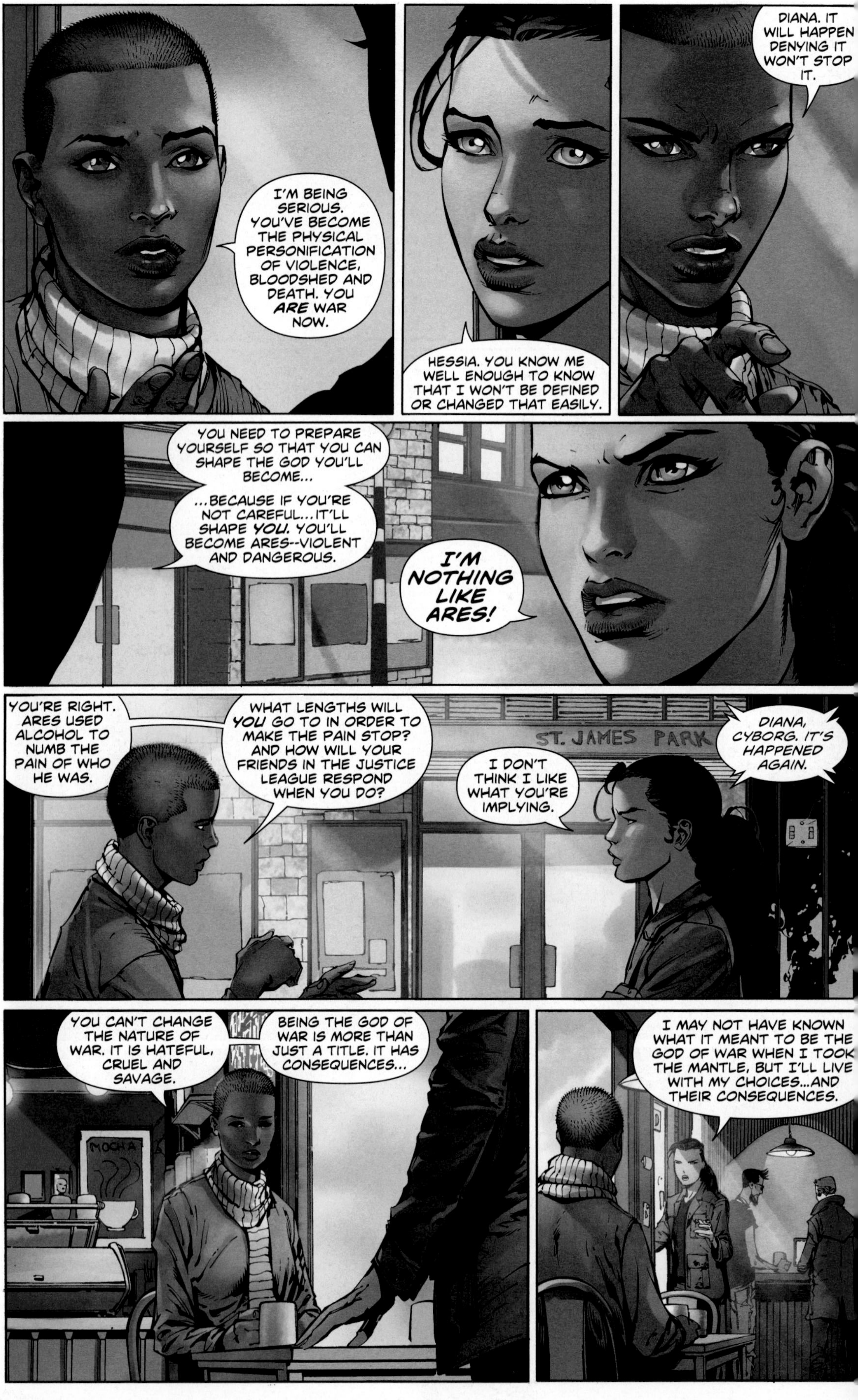

I'M BEING SERIOUS. YOU'VE BECOME THE PHYSICAL PERSONIFICATION OF VIOLENCE, BLOODSHED AND DEATH. YOU *ARE* WAR NOW.
HESSIA. YOU KNOW ME WELL ENOUGH TO KNOW THAT I WON'T BE DEFINED OR CHANGED THAT EASILY.
DIANA. IT WILL HAPPEN DENYING IT WON'T STOP IT.
YOU NEED TO PREPARE YOURSELF SO THAT YOU CAN SHAPE THE GOD YOU'LL BECOME...
...BECAUSE IF YOU'RE NOT CAREFUL...IT'LL SHAPE *YOU*. YOU'LL BECOME ARES--VIOLENT AND DANGEROUS.
I'M NOTHING LIKE ARES!
YOU'RE RIGHT. ARES USED ALCOHOL TO NUMB THE PAIN OF WHO HE WAS.
WHAT LENGTHS WILL *YOU* GO TO IN ORDER TO MAKE THE PAIN STOP? AND HOW WILL YOUR FRIENDS IN THE JUSTICE LEAGUE RESPOND WHEN YOU DO?
ST. JAMES PARK
I DON'T THINK I LIKE WHAT YOU'RE IMPLYING.
DIANA, CYBORG. IT'S HAPPENED AGAIN.
YOU CAN'T CHANGE THE NATURE OF WAR. IT IS HATEFUL, CRUEL AND SAVAGE.
BEING THE GOD OF WAR IS MORE THAN JUST A TITLE. IT HAS CONSEQUENCES...
MOCHA
I MAY NOT HAVE KNOWN WHAT IT MEANT TO BE THE GOD OF WAR WHEN I TOOK THE MANTLE, BUT I'LL LIVE WITH MY CHOICES...AND THEIR CONSEQUENCES.

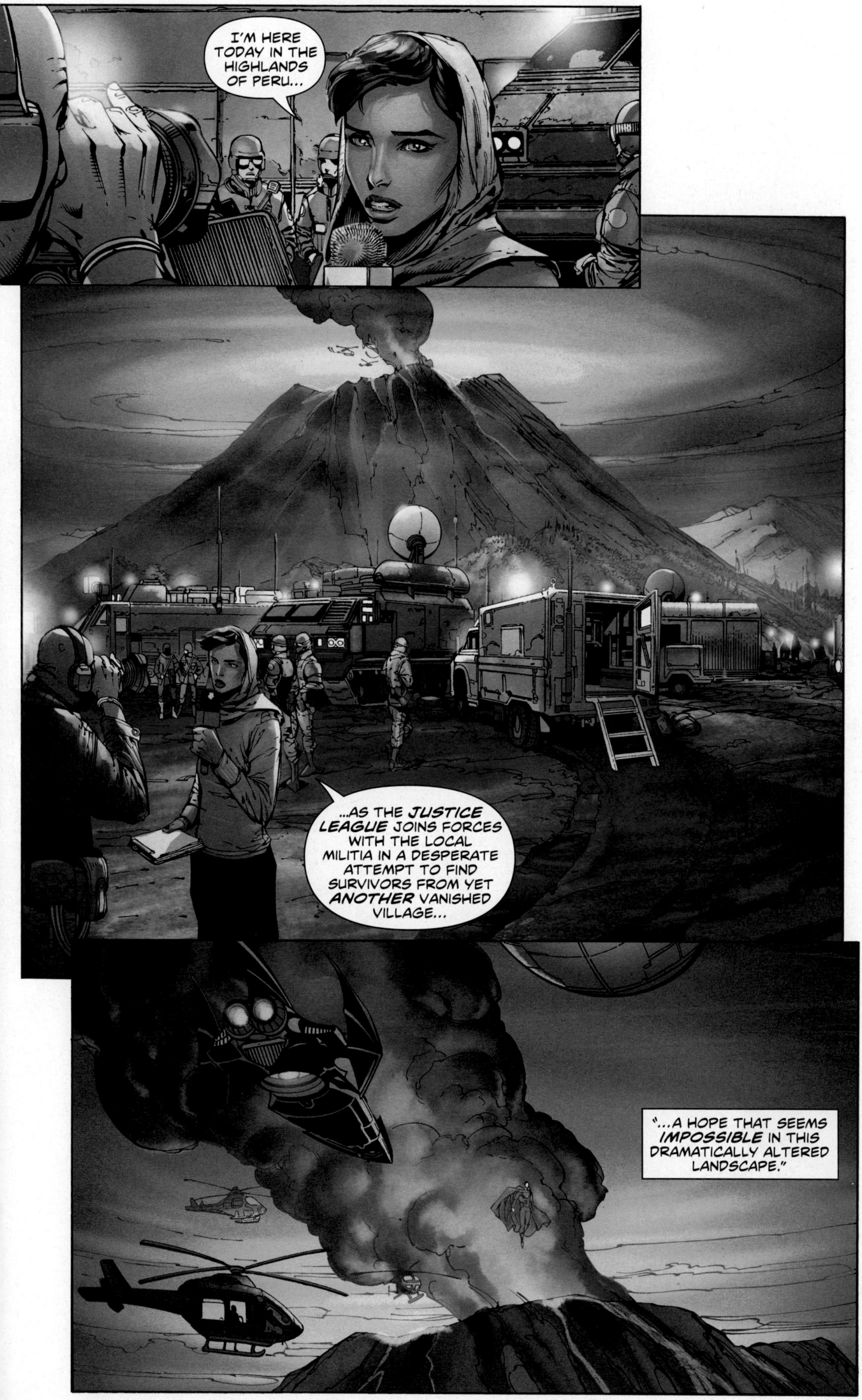
I'M HERE TODAY IN THE HIGHLANDS OF PERU...
...AS THE JUSTICE LEAGUE JOINS FORCES WITH THE LOCAL MILITIA IN A DESPERATE ATTEMPT TO FIND SURVIVORS FROM YET ANOTHER VANISHED VILLAGE...
"...A HOPE THAT SEEMS IMPOSSIBLE IN THIS DRAMATICALLY ALTERED LANDSCAPE."

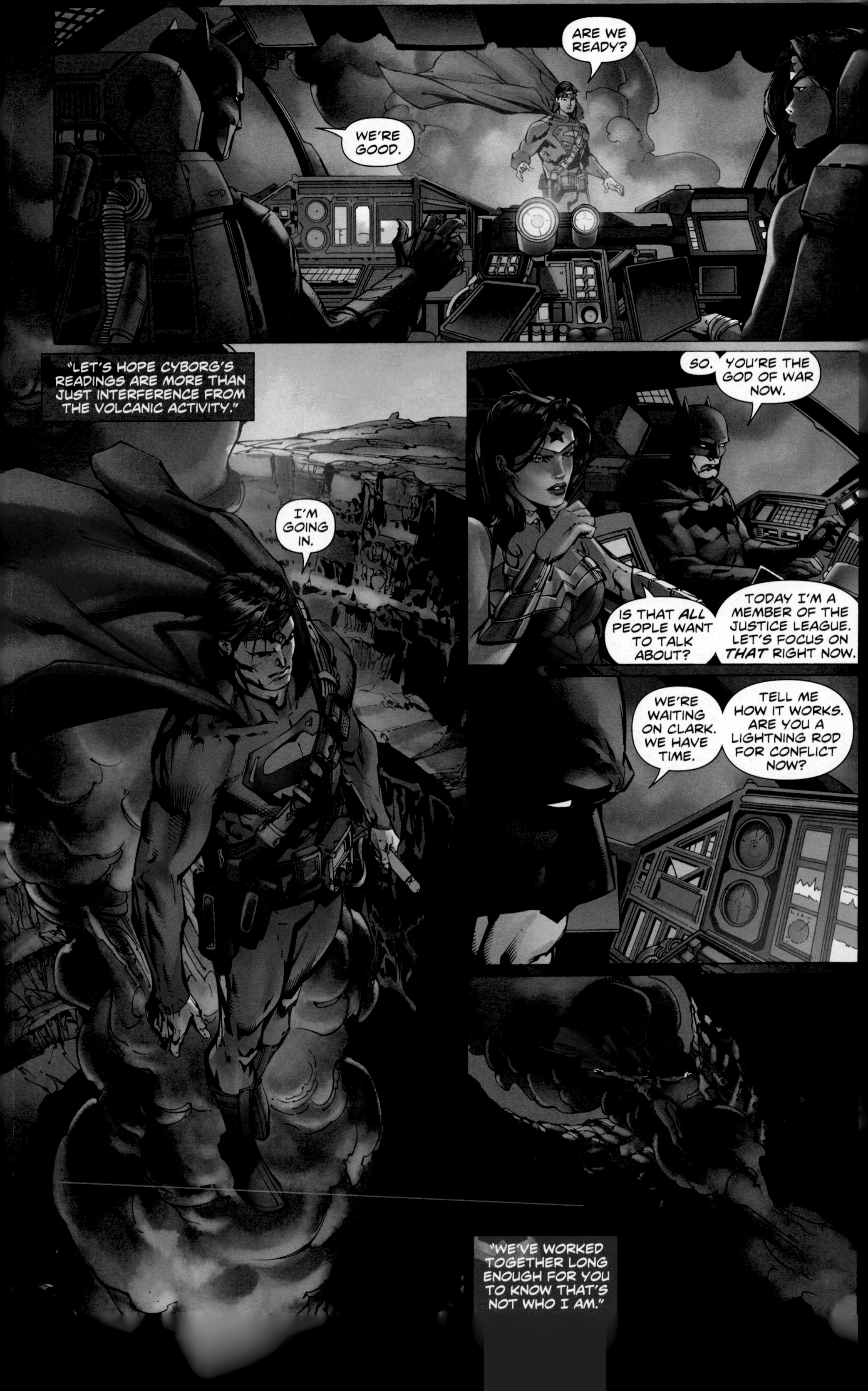
ARE WE READY?
WE'RE GOOD.
"LET'S HOPE CYBORG'S READINGS ARE MORE THAN JUST INTERFERENCE FROM THE VOLCANIC ACTIVITY."
I'M GOING IN.
SO.
YOU'RE THE GOD OF WAR NOW.
IS THAT ALL PEOPLE WANT TO TALK ABOUT?
TODAY I'M A MEMBER OF THE JUSTICE LEAGUE. LET'S FOCUS ON THAT RIGHT NOW.
WE'RE WAITING ON CLARK. WE HAVE TIME.
TELL ME HOW IT WORKS. ARE YOU A LIGHTNING ROD FOR CONFLICT NOW?
"WE'VE WORKED TOGETHER LONG ENOUGH FOR YOU TO KNOW THAT'S NOT WHO I AM."

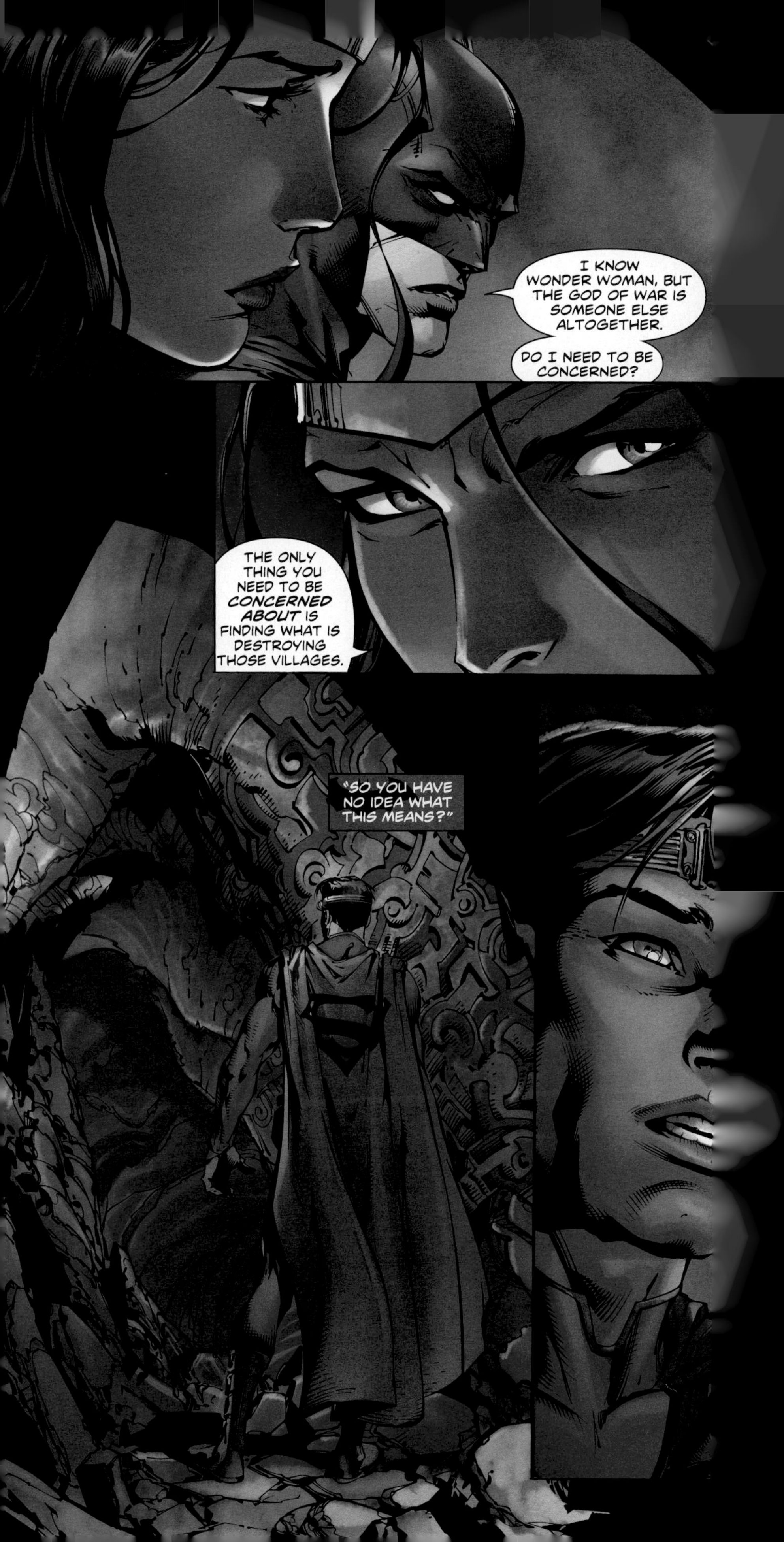
I KNOW WONDER WOMAN, BUT THE GOD OF WAR IS SOMEONE ELSE ALTOGETHER.
DO I NEED TO BE CONCERNED?
THE ONLY THING YOU NEED TO BE CONCERNED ABOUT IS FINDING WHAT IS DESTROYING THOSE VILLAGES.
"SO YOU HAVE NO IDEA WHAT THIS MEANS?"

IT'S TOO DARK DOWN THERE. TURN ON YOUR LIGHTS SO WE CAN SEE.

SORRY ABOUT THAT.

HEY, I'M GETTING A LOT OF BUZZING THROUGH MY COM.

WHOA--!

CLARK! WHAT'S GOING ON DOWN THERE?

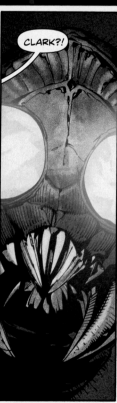

CLARK?!

CLARK!

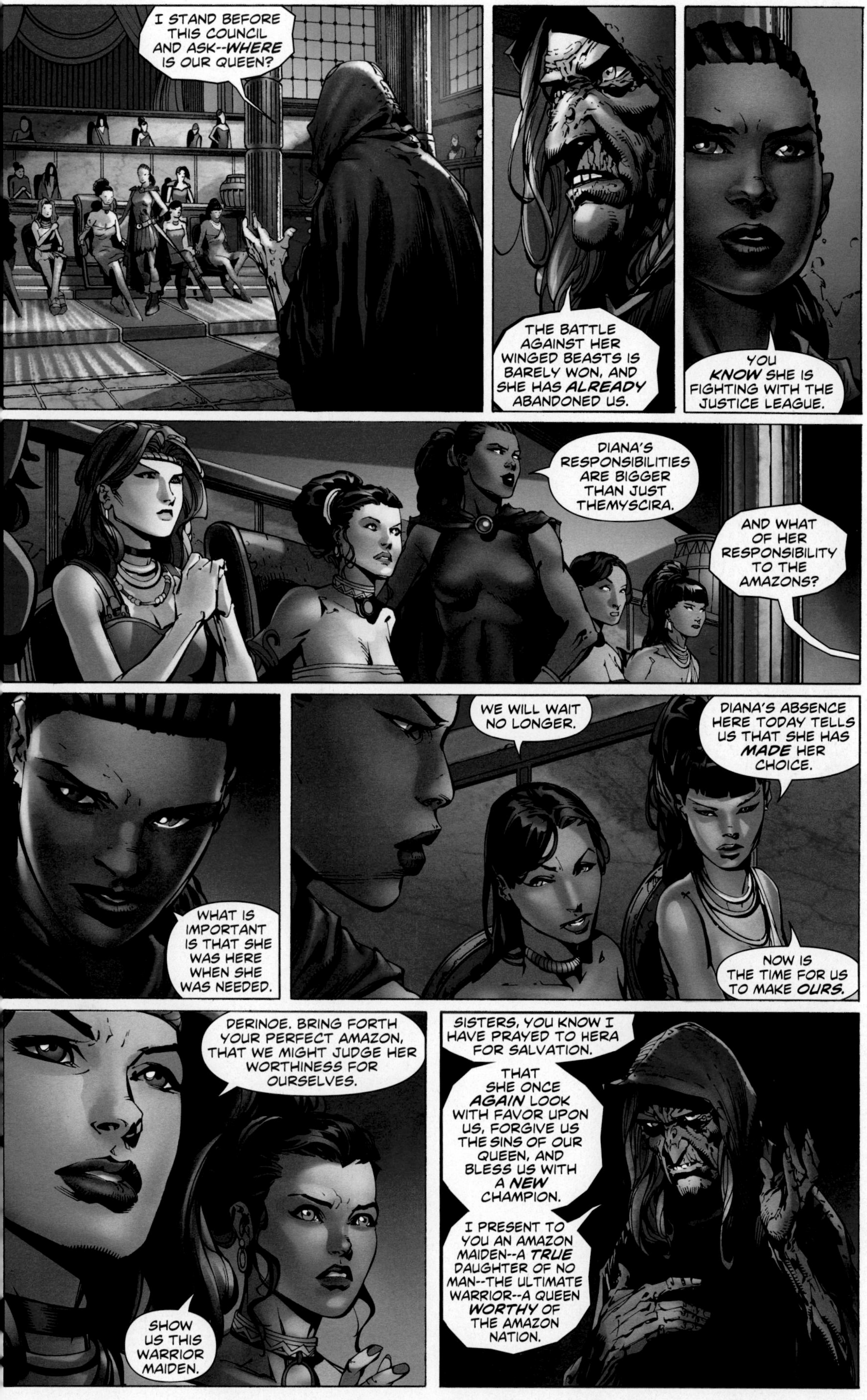
I STAND BEFORE THIS COUNCIL AND ASK--WHERE IS OUR QUEEN?
THE BATTLE AGAINST HER WINGED BEASTS IS BARELY WON, AND SHE HAS ALREADY ABANDONED US.
YOU KNOW SHE IS FIGHTING WITH THE JUSTICE LEAGUE.
DIANA'S RESPONSIBILITIES ARE BIGGER THAN JUST THEMYSCIRA.
AND WHAT OF HER RESPONSIBILITY TO THE AMAZONS?
WHAT IS IMPORTANT IS THAT SHE WAS HERE WHEN SHE WAS NEEDED.
WE WILL WAIT NO LONGER.
DIANA'S ABSENCE HERE TODAY TELLS US THAT SHE HAS MADE HER CHOICE.
NOW IS THE TIME FOR US TO MAKE OURS.
DERINOE. BRING FORTH YOUR PERFECT AMAZON, THAT WE MIGHT JUDGE HER WORTHINESS FOR OURSELVES.
SHOW US THIS WARRIOR MAIDEN.
SISTERS, YOU KNOW I HAVE PRAYED TO HERA FOR SALVATION.
THAT SHE ONCE AGAIN LOOK WITH FAVOR UPON US, FORGIVE US THE SINS OF OUR QUEEN, AND BLESS US WITH A NEW CHAMPION.
I PRESENT TO YOU AN AMAZON MAIDEN--A TRUE DAUGHTER OF NO MAN--THE ULTIMATE WARRIOR--A QUEEN WORTHY OF THE AMAZON NATION.

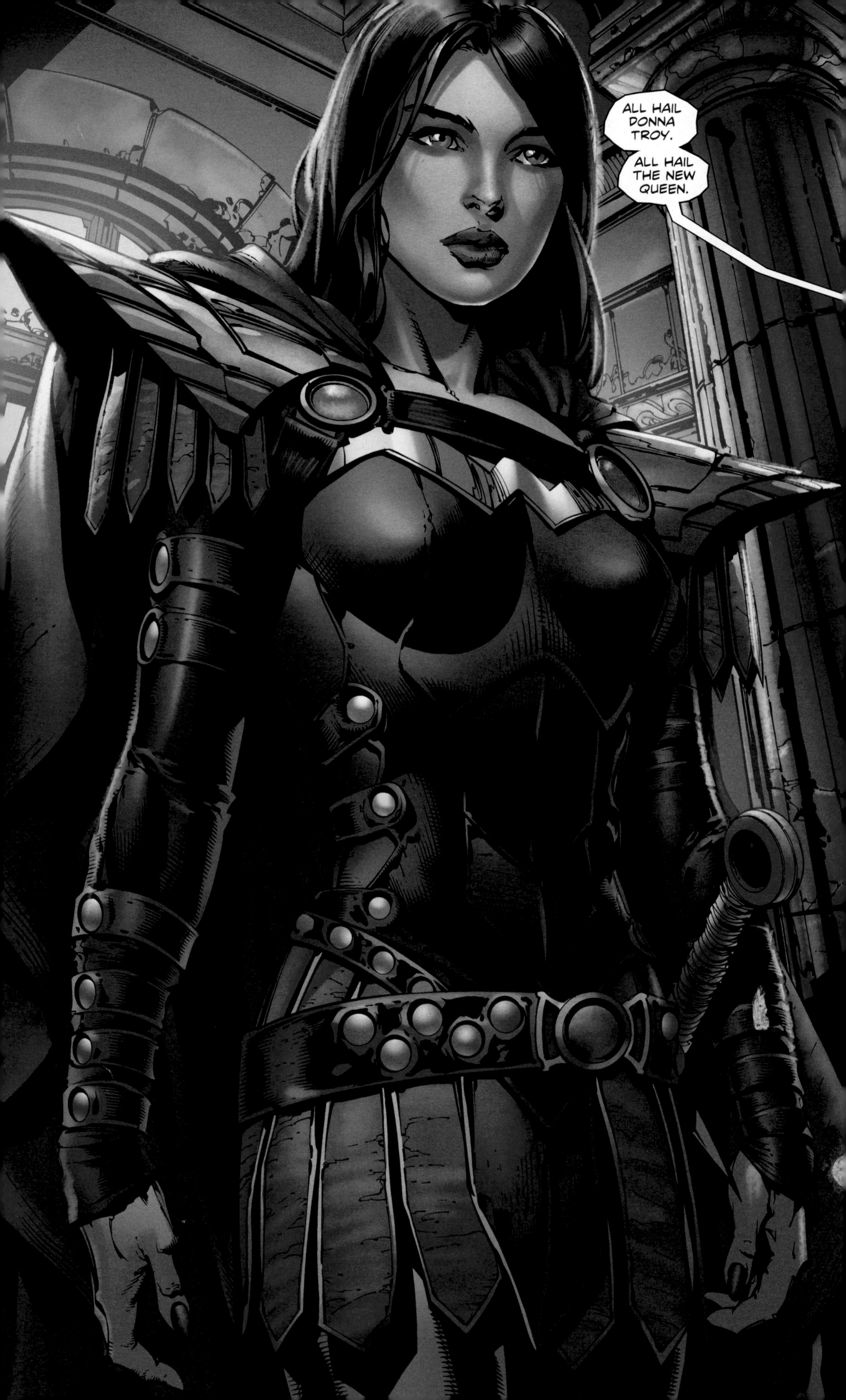
ALL HAIL DONNA TROY.
ALL HAIL THE NEW QUEEN.

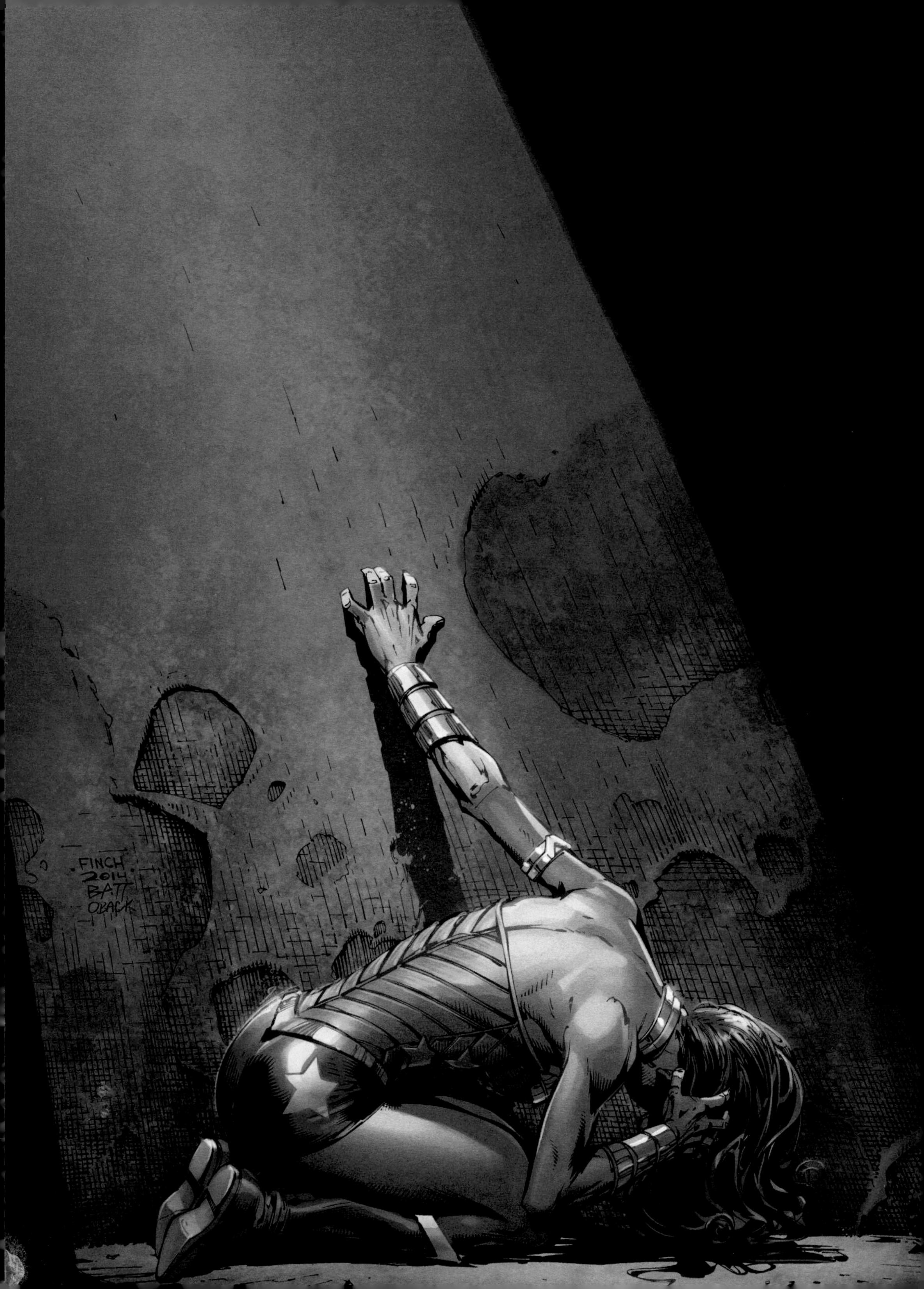
FINCH
2014
BATT
OBACK

WAR-TORN CHAPTER 4

MEREDITH FINCH writer **DAVID FINCH** penciller **JONATHAN GLAPION** inker **SONIA OBACK** colorist **ROB LEIGH** letterer cover by **FINCH, BATT** and **OBACK**

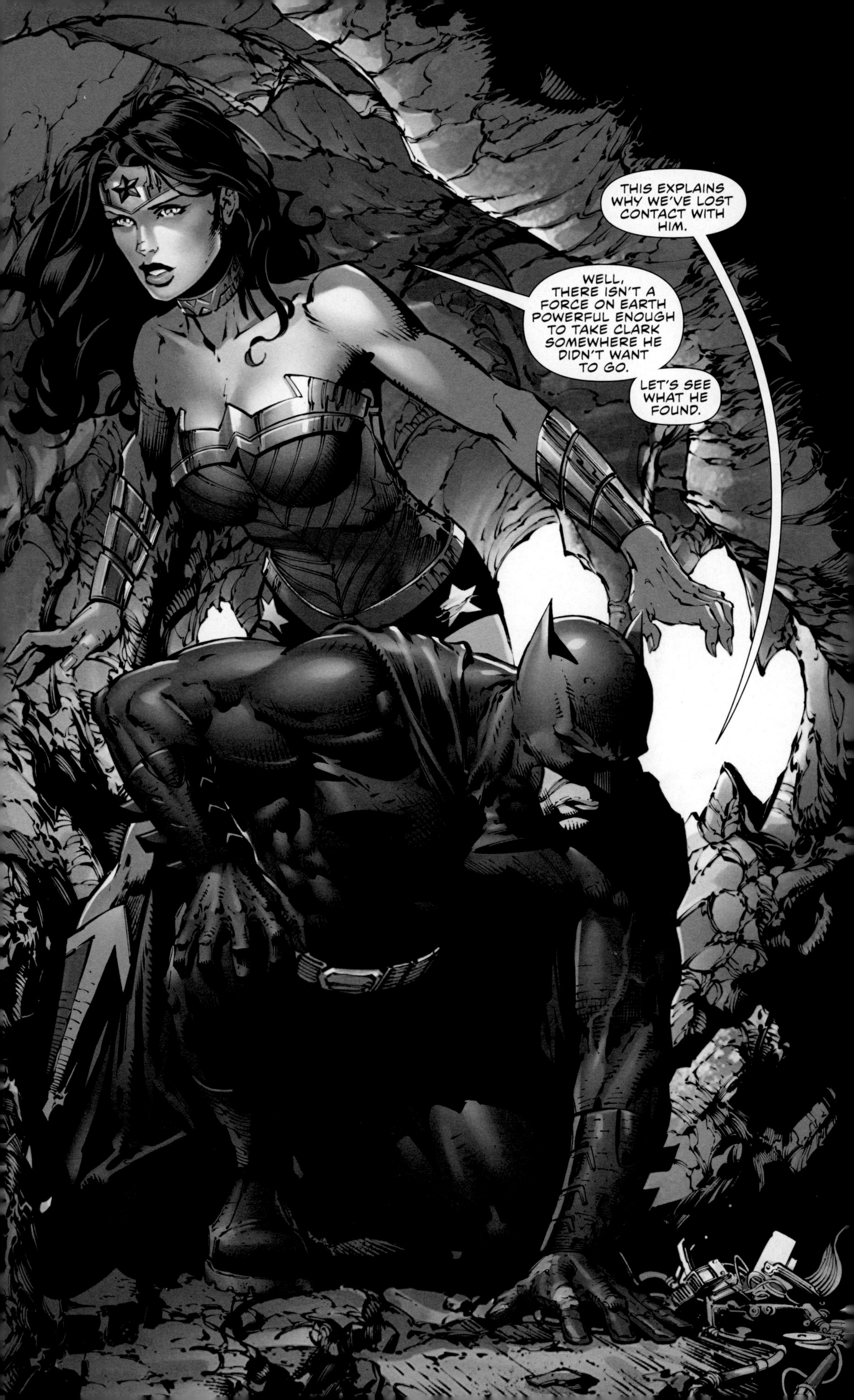
THIS EXPLAINS WHY WE'VE LOST CONTACT WITH HIM.
WELL, THERE ISN'T A FORCE ON EARTH POWERFUL ENOUGH TO TAKE CLARK SOMEWHERE HE DIDN'T WANT TO GO.
LET'S SEE WHAT HE FOUND.

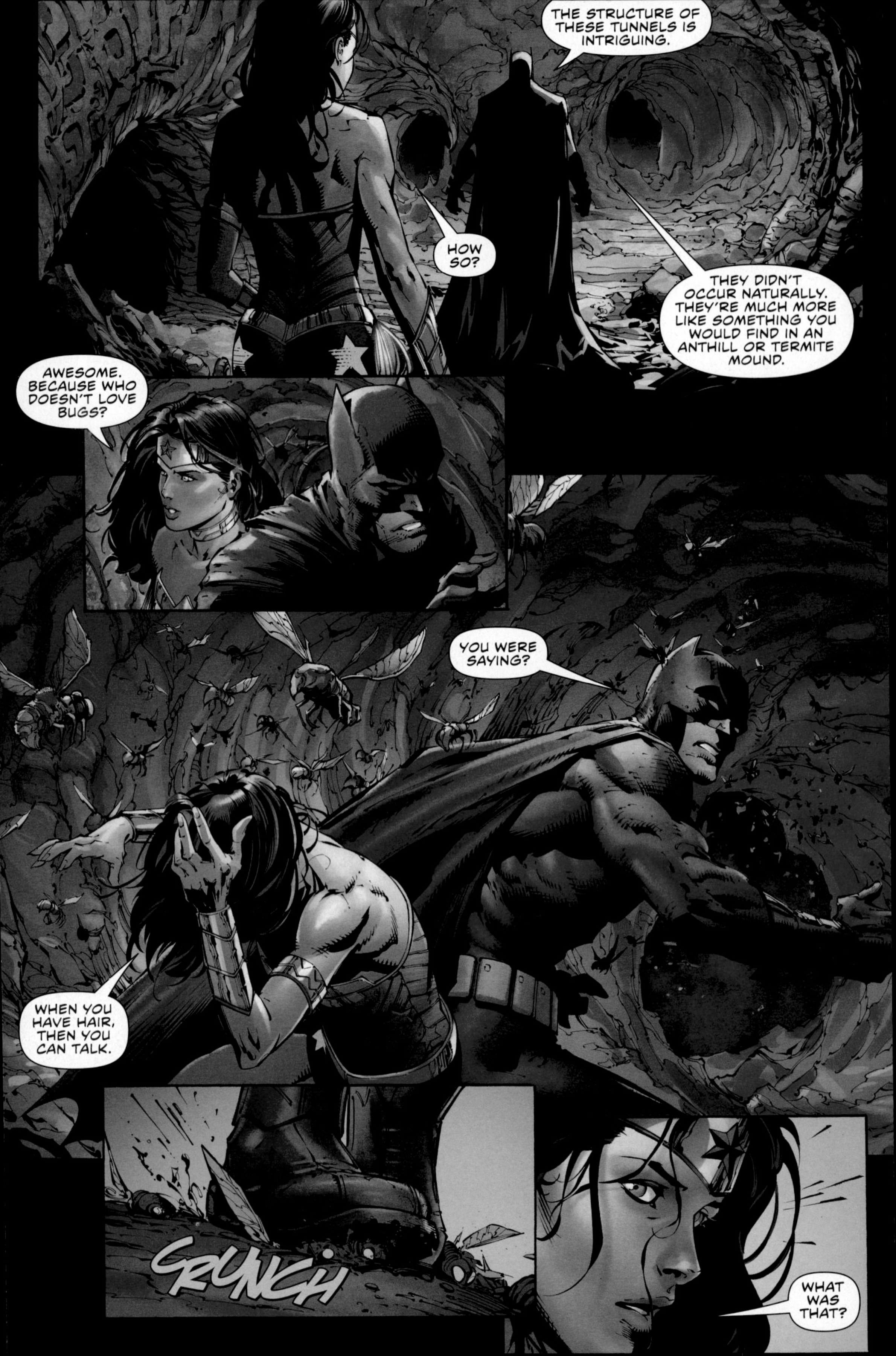
THE STRUCTURE OF THESE TUNNELS IS INTRIGUING.
HOW SO?
THEY DIDN'T OCCUR NATURALLY. THEY'RE MUCH MORE LIKE SOMETHING YOU WOULD FIND IN AN ANTHILL OR TERMITE MOUND.
AWESOME. BECAUSE WHO DOESN'T LOVE BUGS?
YOU WERE SAYING?
WHEN YOU HAVE HAIR, THEN YOU CAN TALK.
CRUNCH
WHAT WAS THAT?

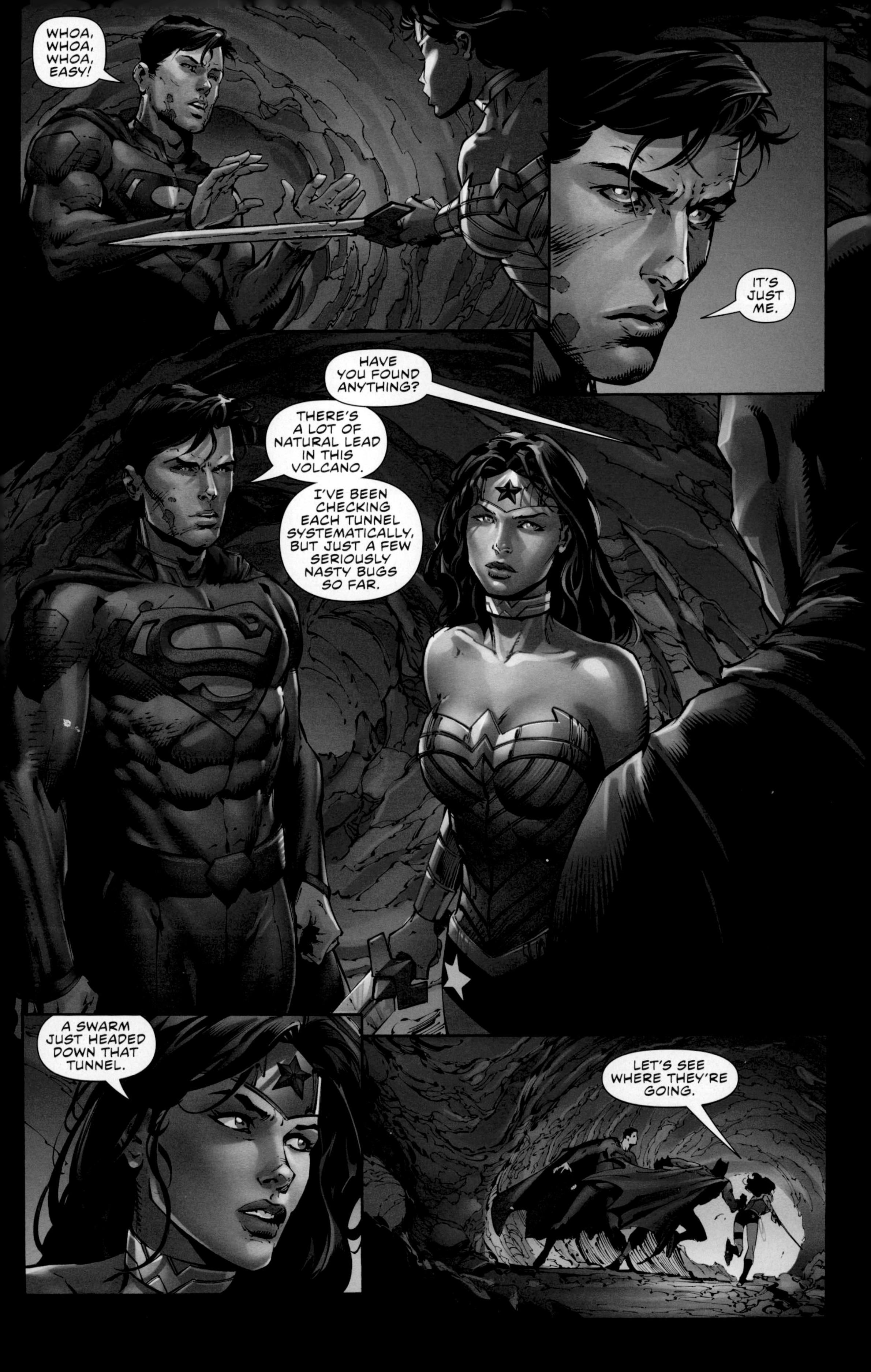
WHOA, WHOA, WHOA, EASY!
IT'S JUST ME.
HAVE YOU FOUND ANYTHING?
THERE'S A LOT OF NATURAL LEAD IN THIS VOLCANO.
I'VE BEEN CHECKING EACH TUNNEL SYSTEMATICALLY, BUT JUST A FEW SERIOUSLY NASTY BUGS SO FAR.
A SWARM JUST HEADED DOWN THAT TUNNEL.
LET'S SEE WHERE THEY'RE GOING.

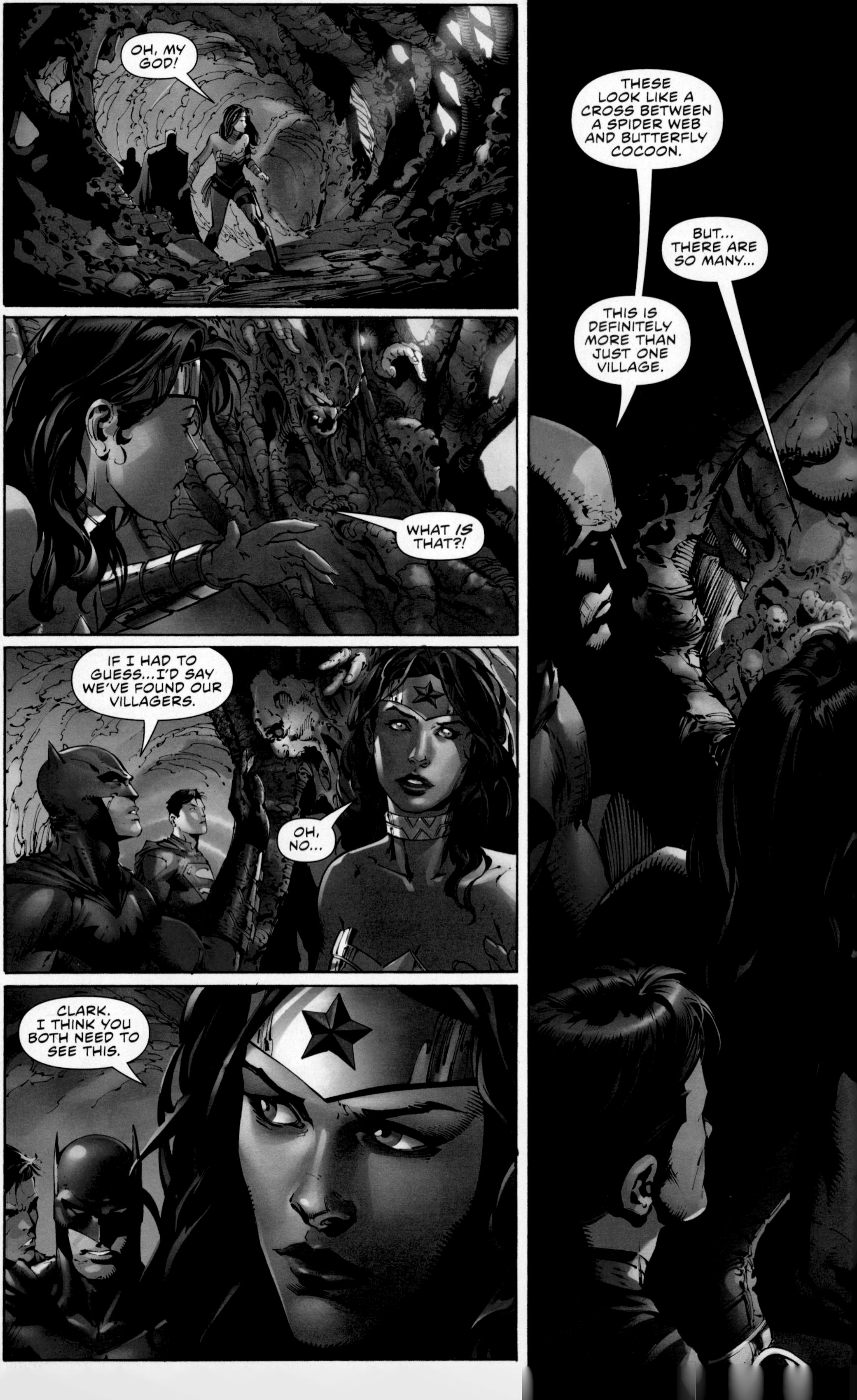
OH, MY GOD!
WHAT *IS* THAT?!
IF I HAD TO GUESS...I'D SAY WE'VE FOUND OUR VILLAGERS.
OH, NO...
CLARK. I THINK YOU BOTH NEED TO SEE THIS.
THESE LOOK LIKE A CROSS BETWEEN A SPIDER WEB AND BUTTERFLY COCOON.
THIS IS DEFINITELY MORE THAN JUST ONE VILLAGE.
BUT... THERE ARE SO MANY...

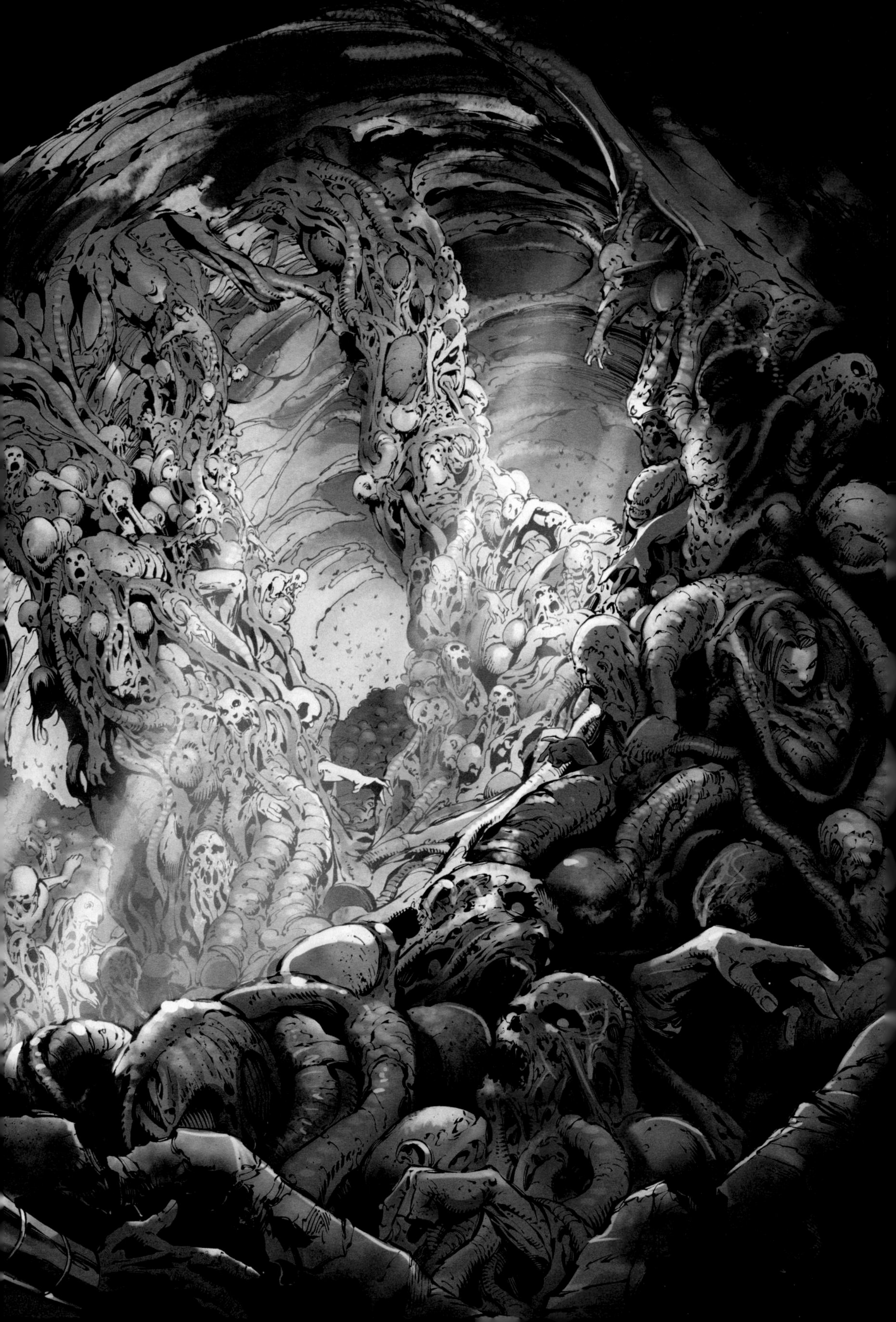

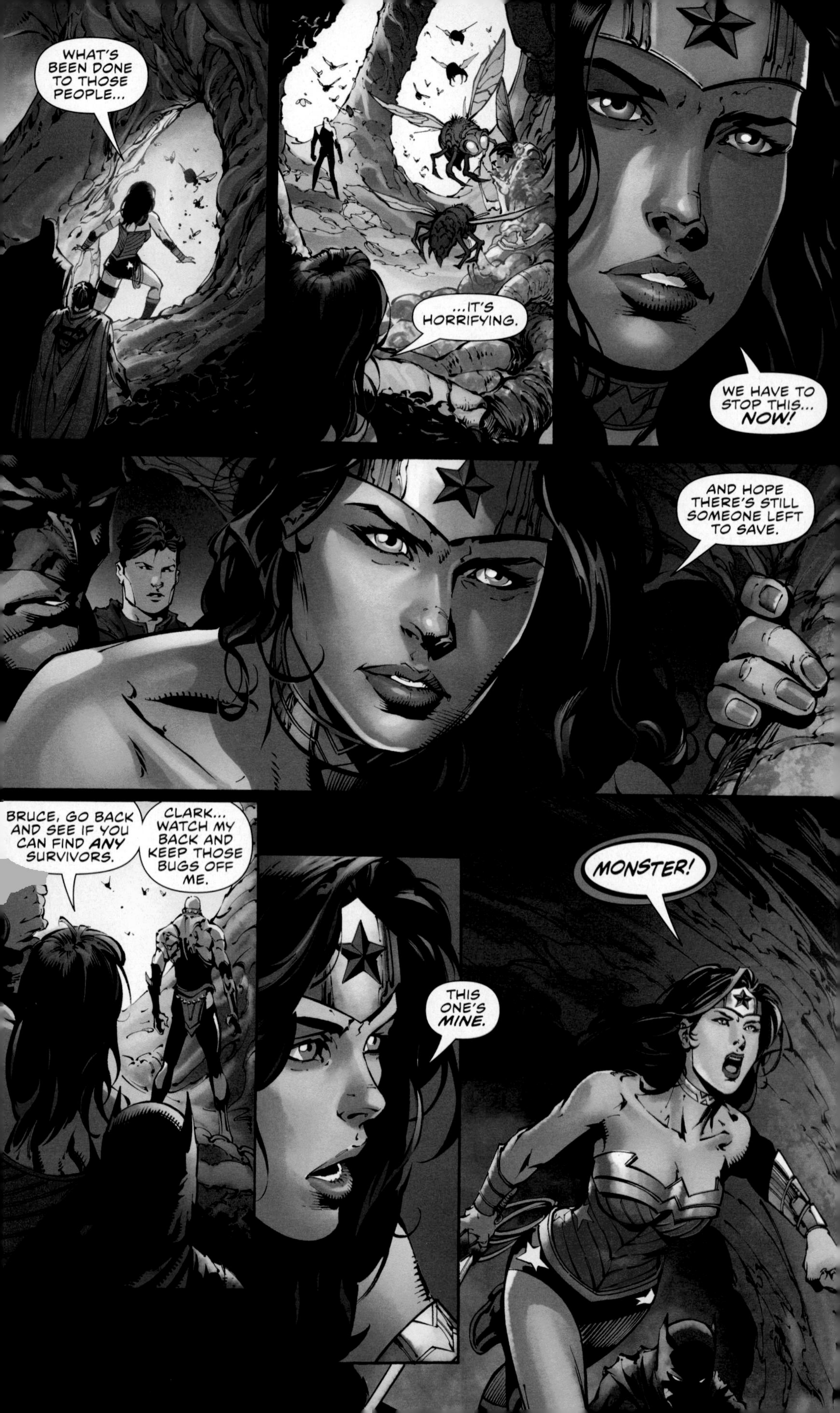
WHAT'S BEEN DONE TO THOSE PEOPLE...
...IT'S HORRIFYING.
WE HAVE TO STOP THIS... NOW!
AND HOPE THERE'S STILL SOMEONE LEFT TO SAVE.
BRUCE, GO BACK AND SEE IF YOU CAN FIND ANY SURVIVORS.
CLARK... WATCH MY BACK AND KEEP THOSE BUGS OFF ME.
THIS ONE'S MINE.
MONSTER!

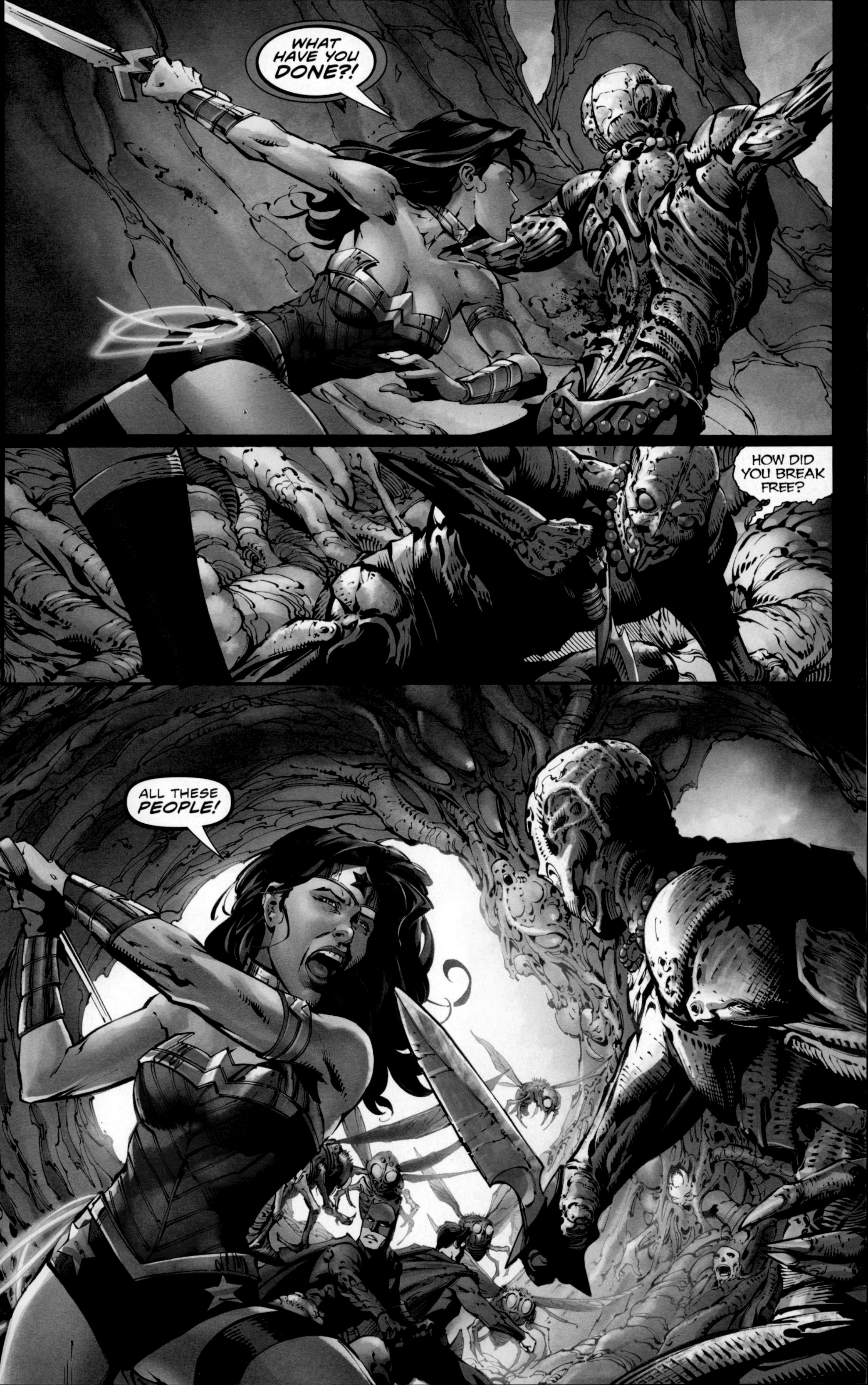
WHAT HAVE YOU DONE?!
HOW DID YOU BREAK FREE?
ALL THESE PEOPLE!

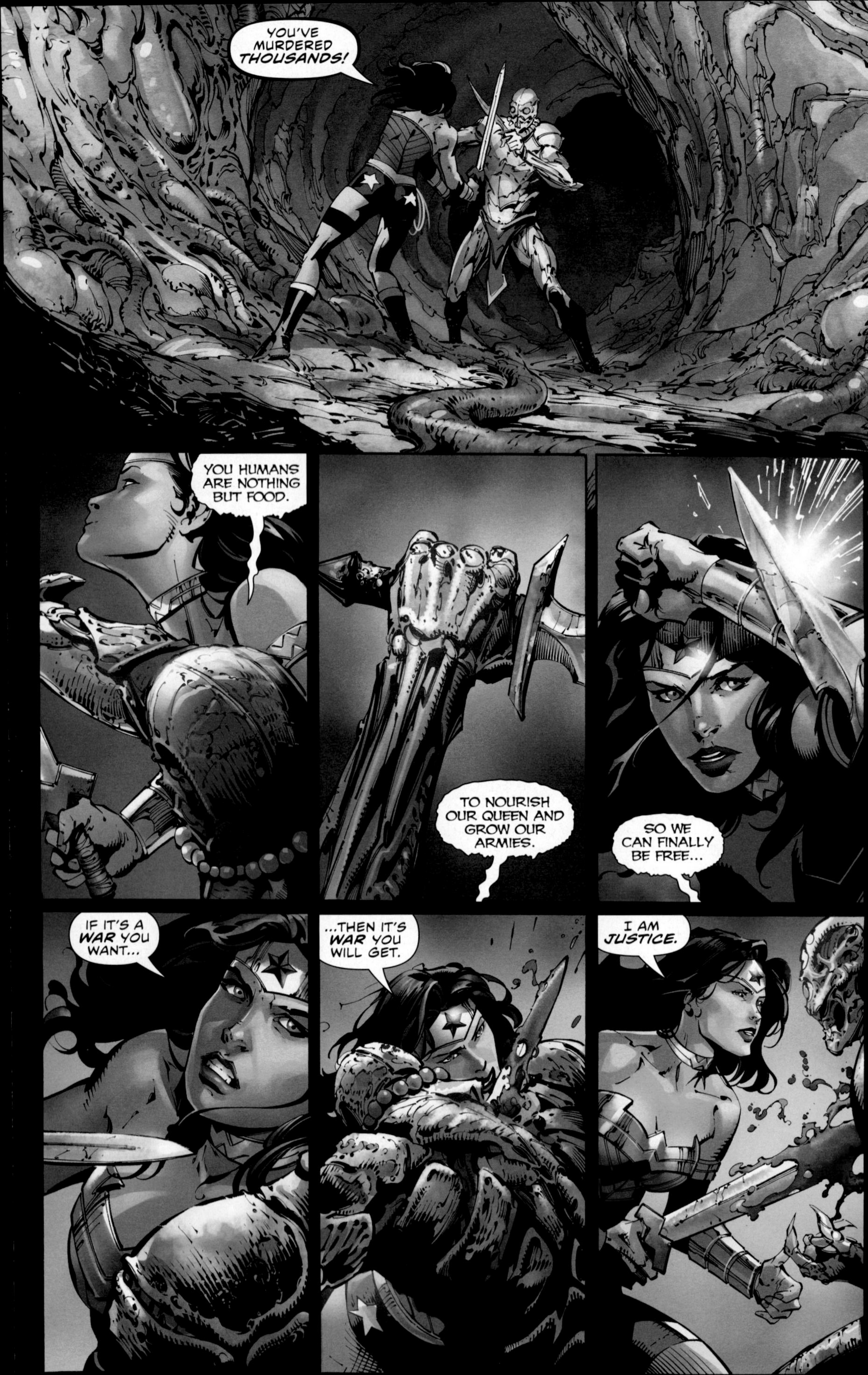
YOU'VE MURDERED THOUSANDS!
YOU HUMANS ARE NOTHING BUT FOOD.
TO NOURISH OUR QUEEN AND GROW OUR ARMIES.
SO WE CAN FINALLY BE FREE...
IF IT'S A WAR YOU WANT...
...THEN IT'S WAR YOU WILL GET.
I AM JUSTICE.

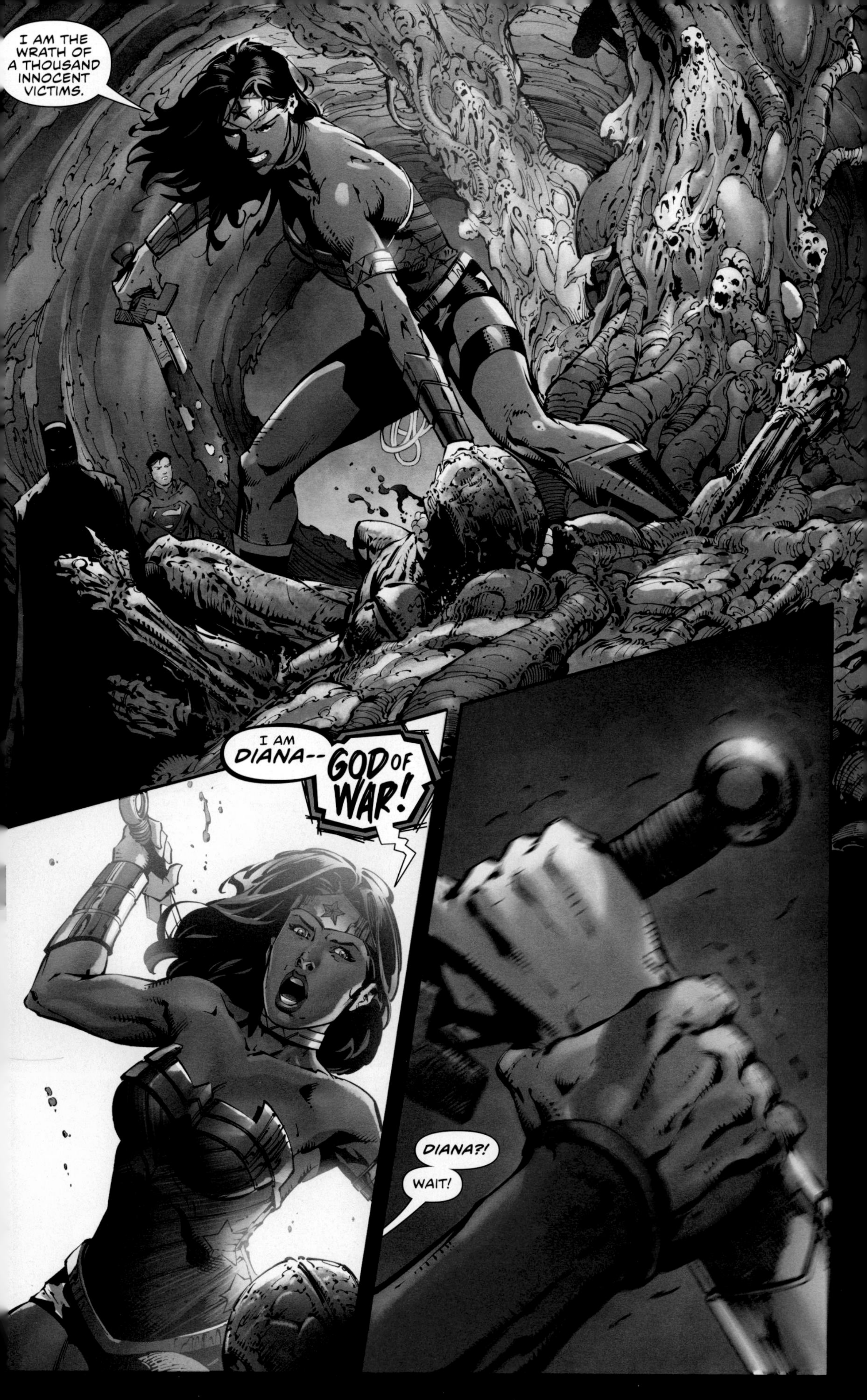
I AM THE WRATH OF A THOUSAND INNOCENT VICTIMS.
I AM DIANA--
GOD OF WAR!
DIANA?!
WAIT!

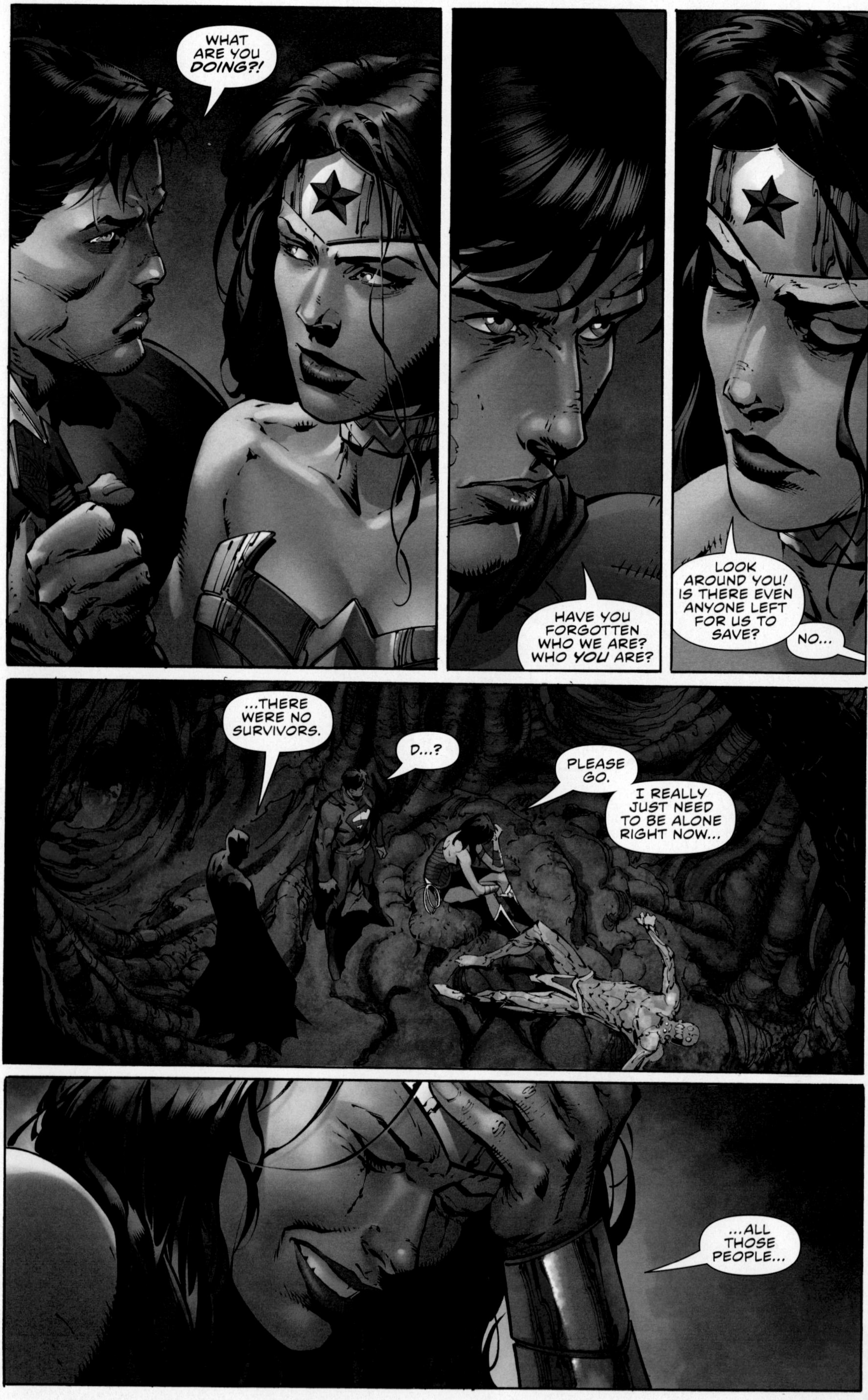
WHAT ARE YOU DOING?!
HAVE YOU FORGOTTEN WHO WE ARE? WHO YOU ARE?
LOOK AROUND YOU! IS THERE EVEN ANYONE LEFT FOR US TO SAVE?
NO...
...THERE WERE NO SURVIVORS.
D...?
PLEASE GO.
I REALLY JUST NEED TO BE ALONE RIGHT NOW...
...ALL THOSE PEOPLE...

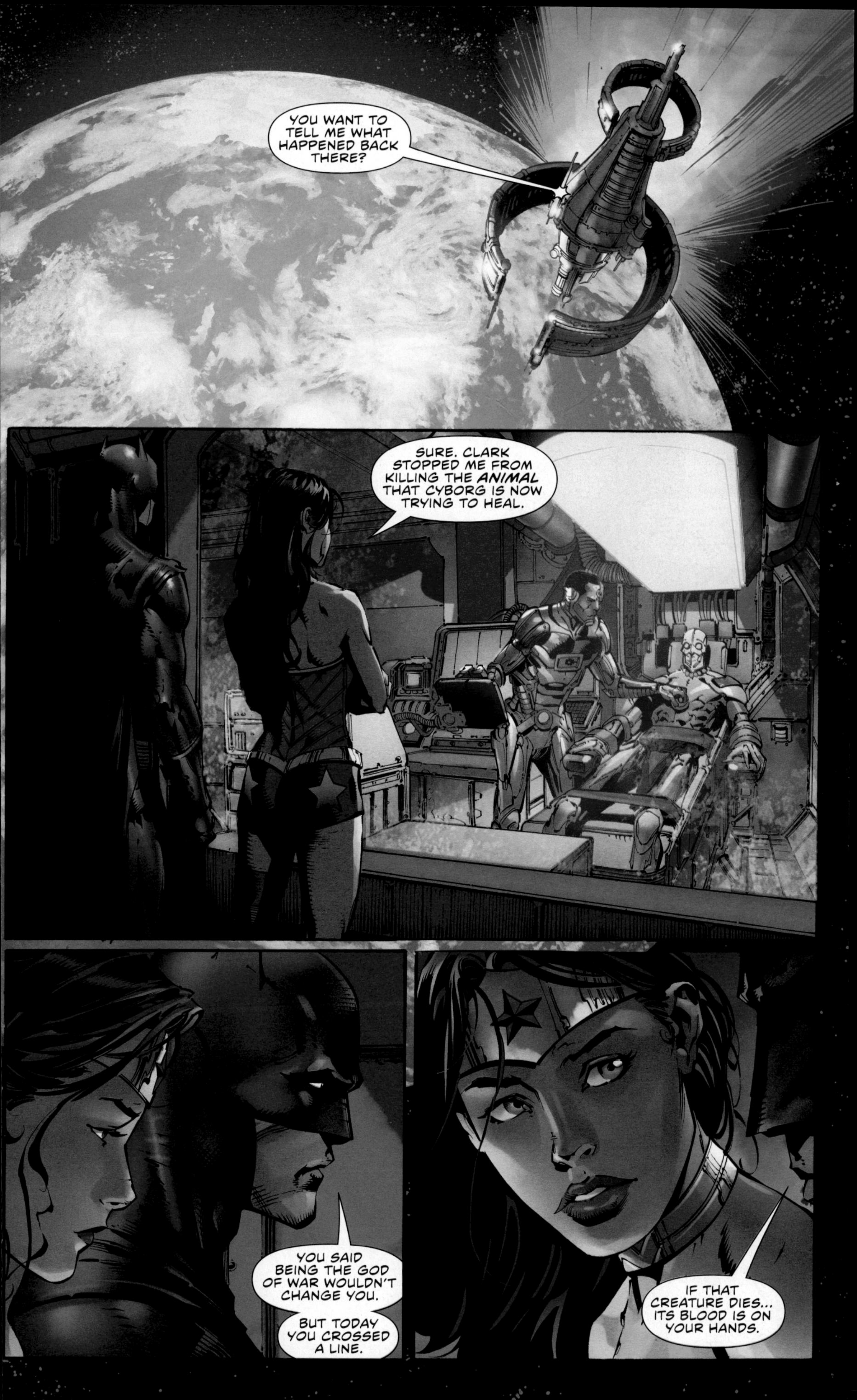
YOU WANT TO TELL ME WHAT HAPPENED BACK THERE?
SURE. CLARK STOPPED ME FROM KILLING THE *ANIMAL* THAT CYBORG IS NOW TRYING TO HEAL.
YOU SAID BEING THE GOD OF WAR WOULDN'T CHANGE YOU.
BUT TODAY YOU CROSSED A LINE.
IF THAT CREATURE DIES... ITS BLOOD IS ON YOUR HANDS.

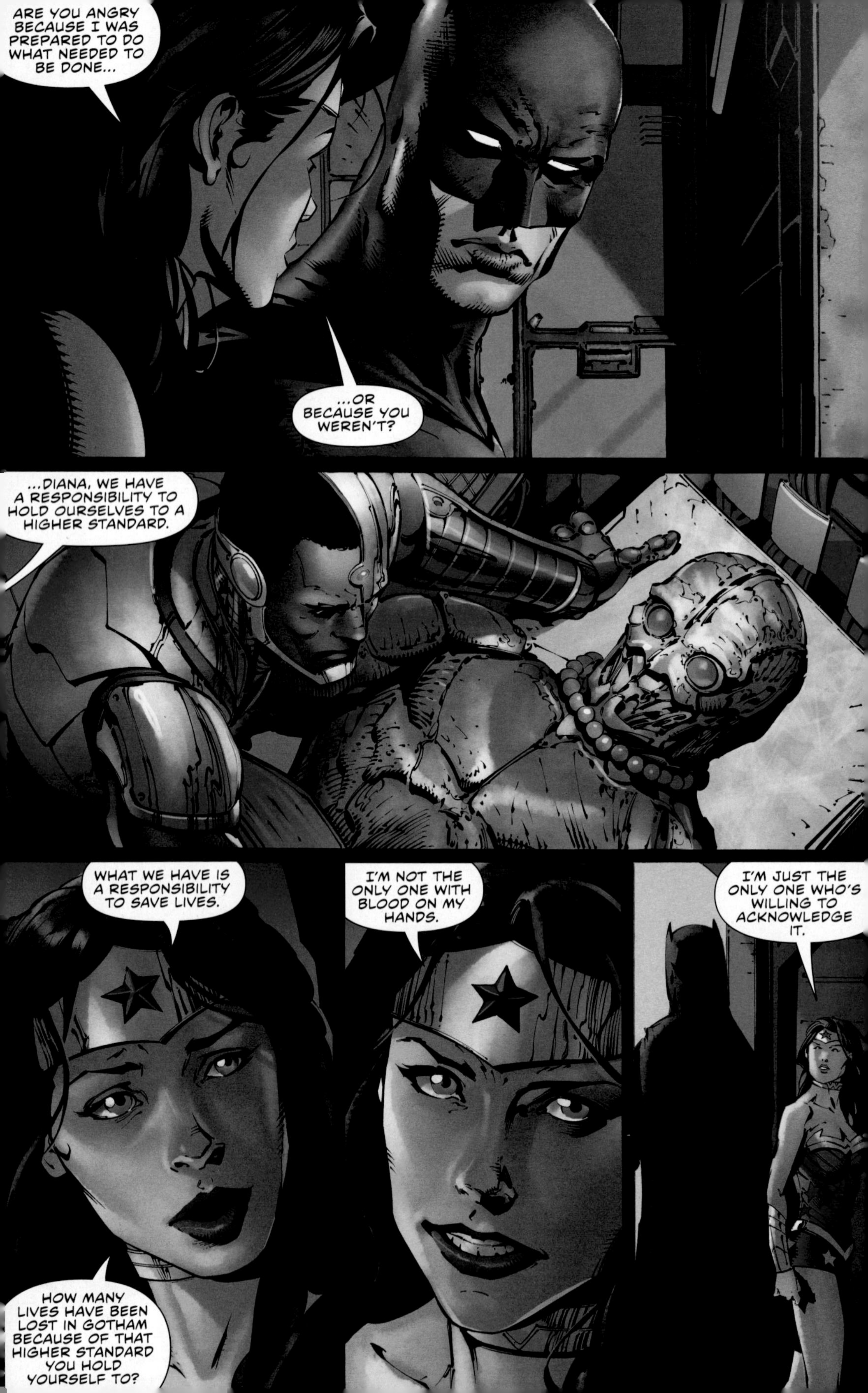
ARE YOU ANGRY BECAUSE I WAS PREPARED TO DO WHAT NEEDED TO BE DONE...
...OR BECAUSE YOU WEREN'T?
...DIANA, WE HAVE A RESPONSIBILITY TO HOLD OURSELVES TO A HIGHER STANDARD.
WHAT WE HAVE IS A RESPONSIBILITY TO SAVE LIVES.
HOW MANY LIVES HAVE BEEN LOST IN GOTHAM BECAUSE OF THAT HIGHER STANDARD YOU HOLD YOURSELF TO?
I'M NOT THE ONLY ONE WITH BLOOD ON MY HANDS.
I'M JUST THE ONLY ONE WHO'S WILLING TO ACKNOWLEDGE IT.

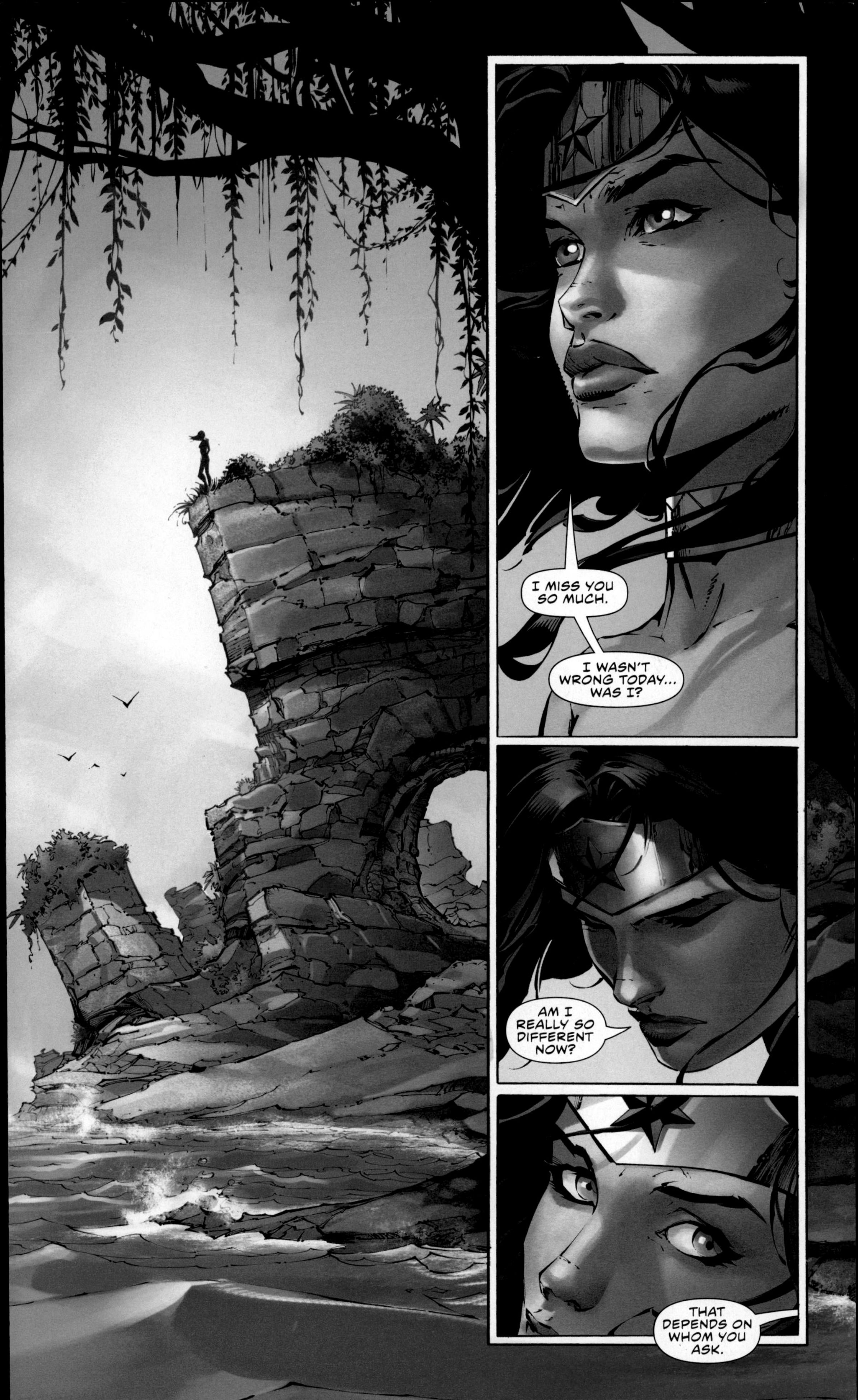
I MISS YOU SO MUCH.
I WASN'T WRONG TODAY... WAS I?
AM I REALLY SO DIFFERENT NOW?
THAT DEPENDS ON WHOM YOU ASK.

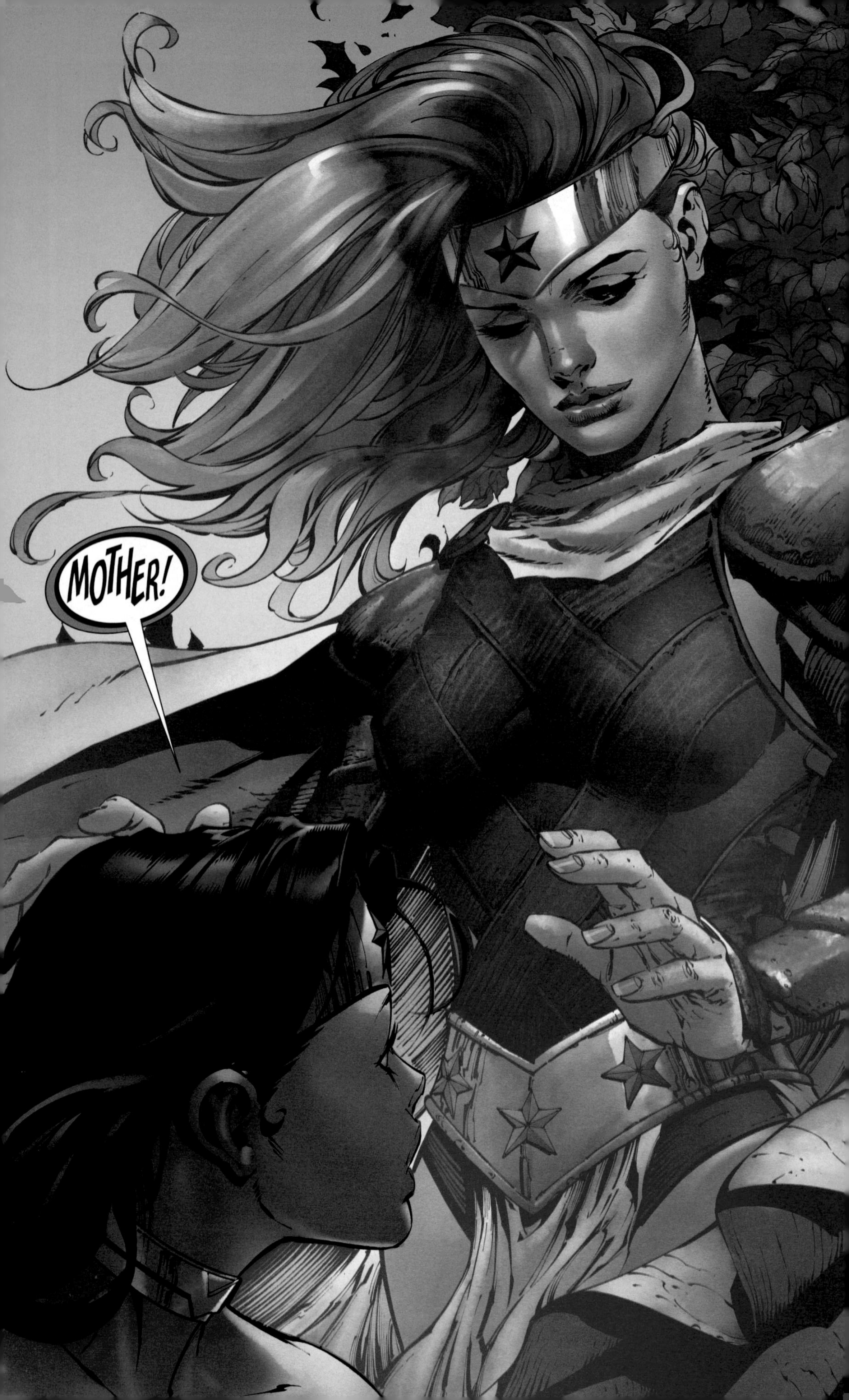
MOTHER!

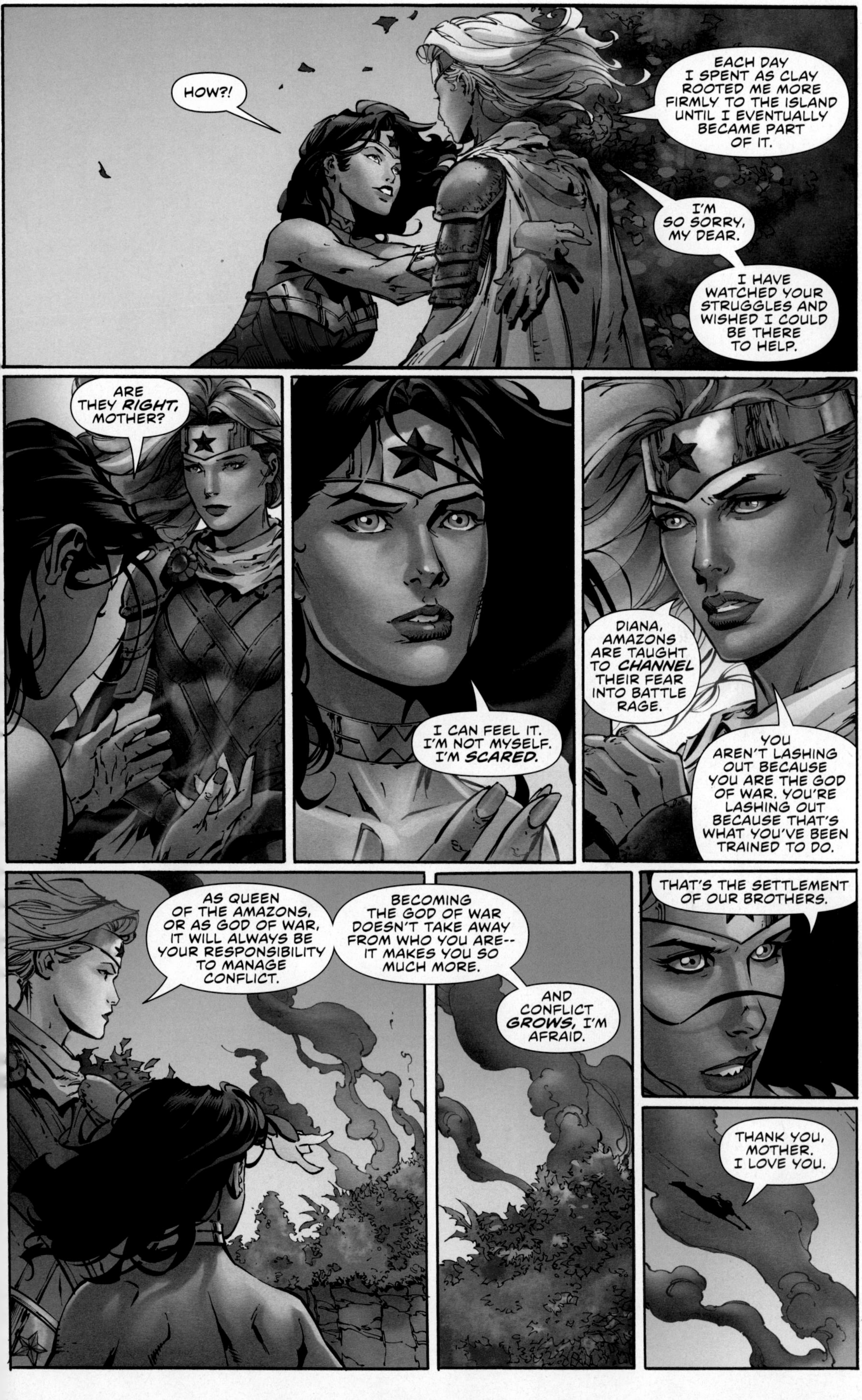
HOW?!
EACH DAY I SPENT AS CLAY ROOTED ME MORE FIRMLY TO THE ISLAND UNTIL I EVENTUALLY BECAME PART OF IT.
I'M SO SORRY, MY DEAR.
I HAVE WATCHED YOUR STRUGGLES AND WISHED I COULD BE THERE TO HELP.
ARE THEY *RIGHT,* MOTHER?
I CAN FEEL IT. I'M NOT MYSELF. I'M *SCARED.*
DIANA, AMAZONS ARE TAUGHT TO *CHANNEL* THEIR FEAR INTO BATTLE RAGE.
YOU AREN'T LASHING OUT BECAUSE YOU ARE THE GOD OF WAR. YOU'RE LASHING OUT BECAUSE THAT'S WHAT YOU'VE BEEN TRAINED TO DO.
AS QUEEN OF THE AMAZONS, OR AS GOD OF WAR, IT WILL ALWAYS BE YOUR RESPONSIBILITY TO MANAGE CONFLICT.
BECOMING THE GOD OF WAR DOESN'T TAKE AWAY FROM WHO YOU ARE-- IT MAKES YOU SO MUCH MORE.
AND CONFLICT *GROWS,* I'M AFRAID.
THAT'S THE SETTLEMENT OF OUR BROTHERS.
THANK YOU, MOTHER. I LOVE YOU.

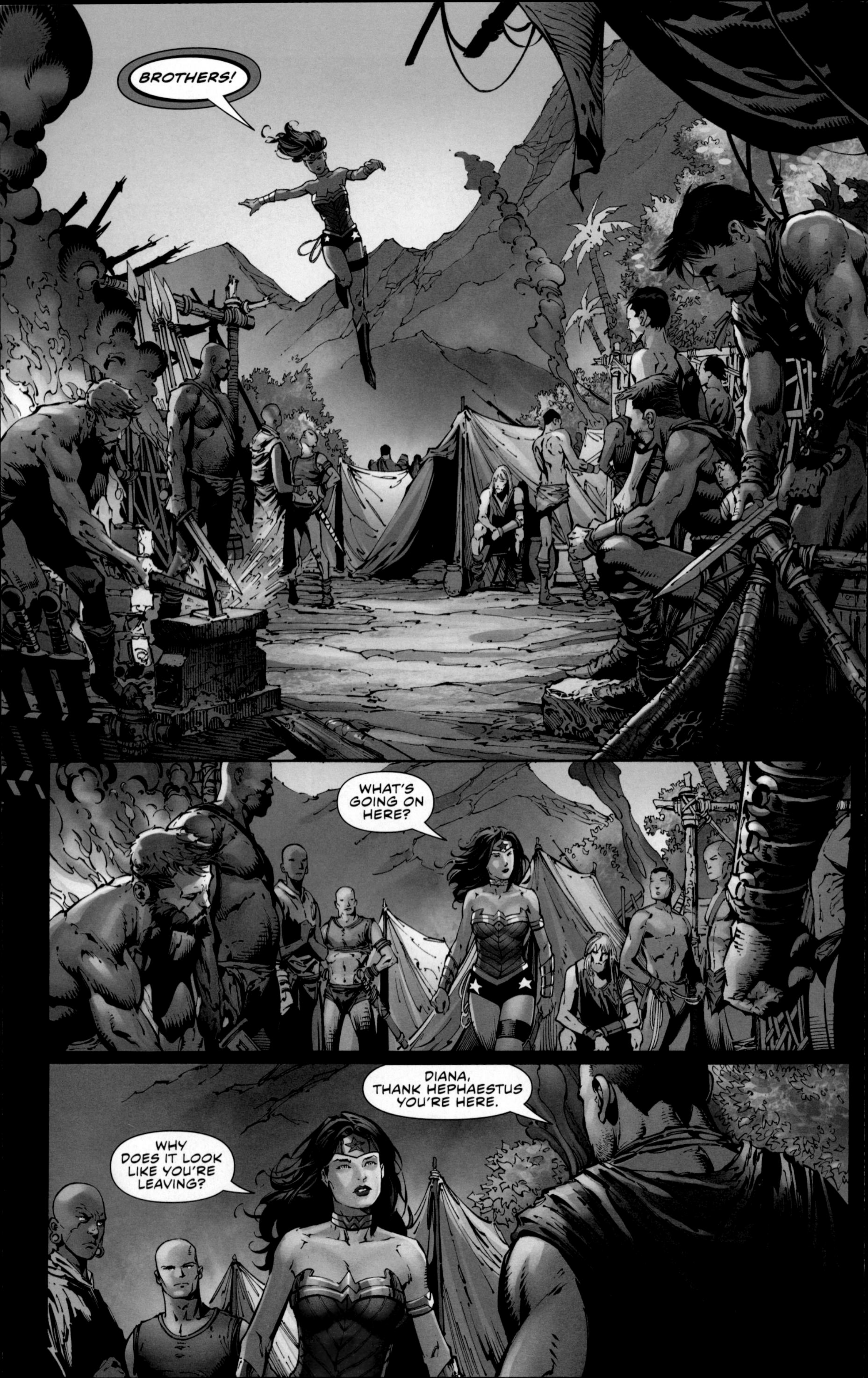
BROTHERS!
WHAT'S GOING ON HERE?
DIANA, THANK HEPHAESTUS YOU'RE HERE.
WHY DOES IT LOOK LIKE YOU'RE LEAVING?

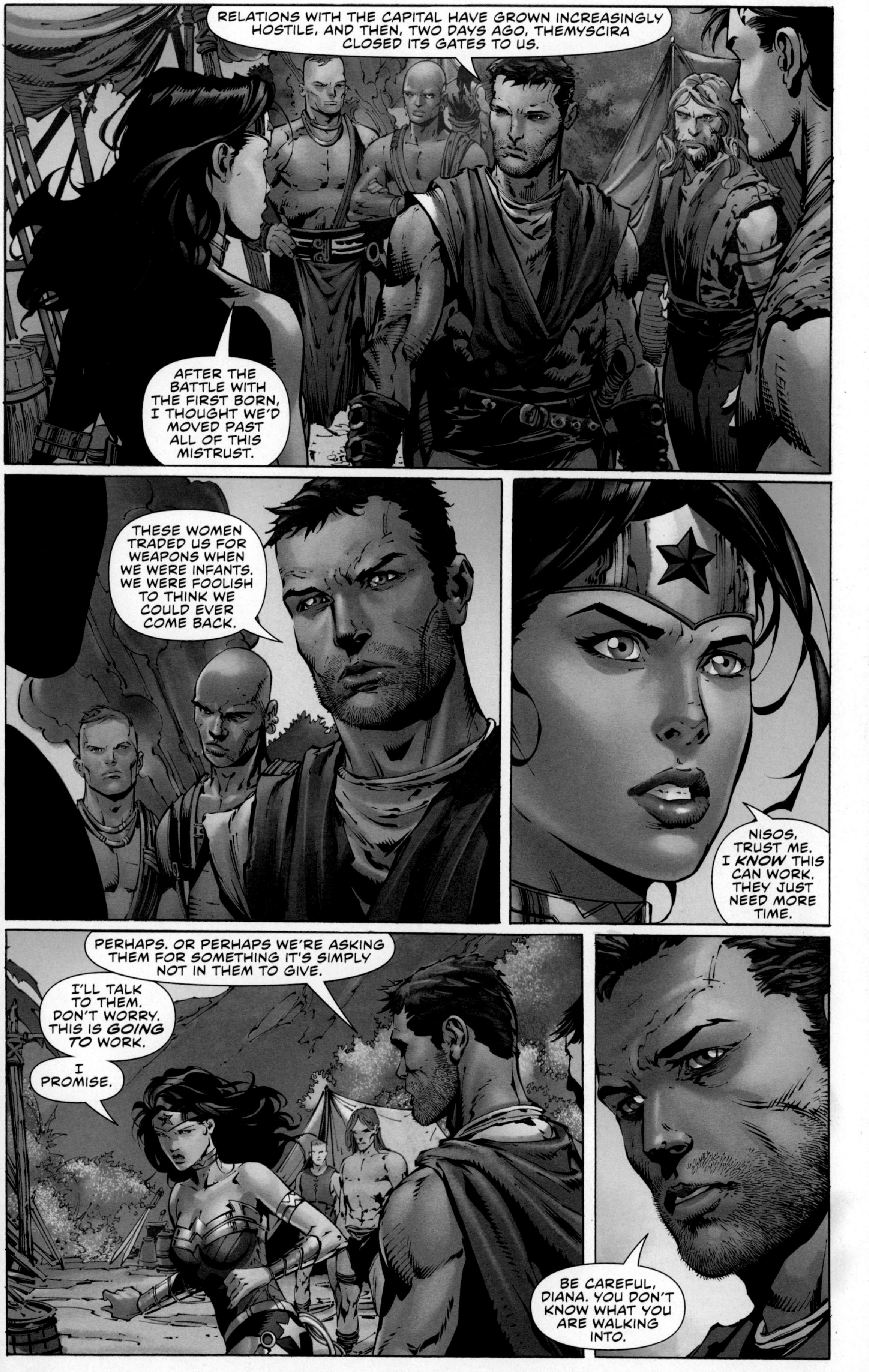
RELATIONS WITH THE CAPITAL HAVE GROWN INCREASINGLY HOSTILE, AND THEN, TWO DAYS AGO, THEMYSCIRA CLOSED ITS GATES TO US.
AFTER THE BATTLE WITH THE FIRST BORN, I THOUGHT WE'D MOVED PAST ALL OF THIS MISTRUST.
THESE WOMEN TRADED US FOR WEAPONS WHEN WE WERE INFANTS. WE WERE FOOLISH TO THINK WE COULD EVER COME BACK.
NISOS, TRUST ME. I *KNOW* THIS CAN WORK. THEY JUST NEED MORE TIME.
PERHAPS. OR PERHAPS WE'RE ASKING THEM FOR SOMETHING IT'S SIMPLY NOT IN THEM TO GIVE.
I'LL TALK TO THEM. DON'T WORRY. THIS IS *GOING TO* WORK.
I PROMISE.
BE CAREFUL, DIANA. YOU DON'T KNOW WHAT YOU ARE WALKING INTO.

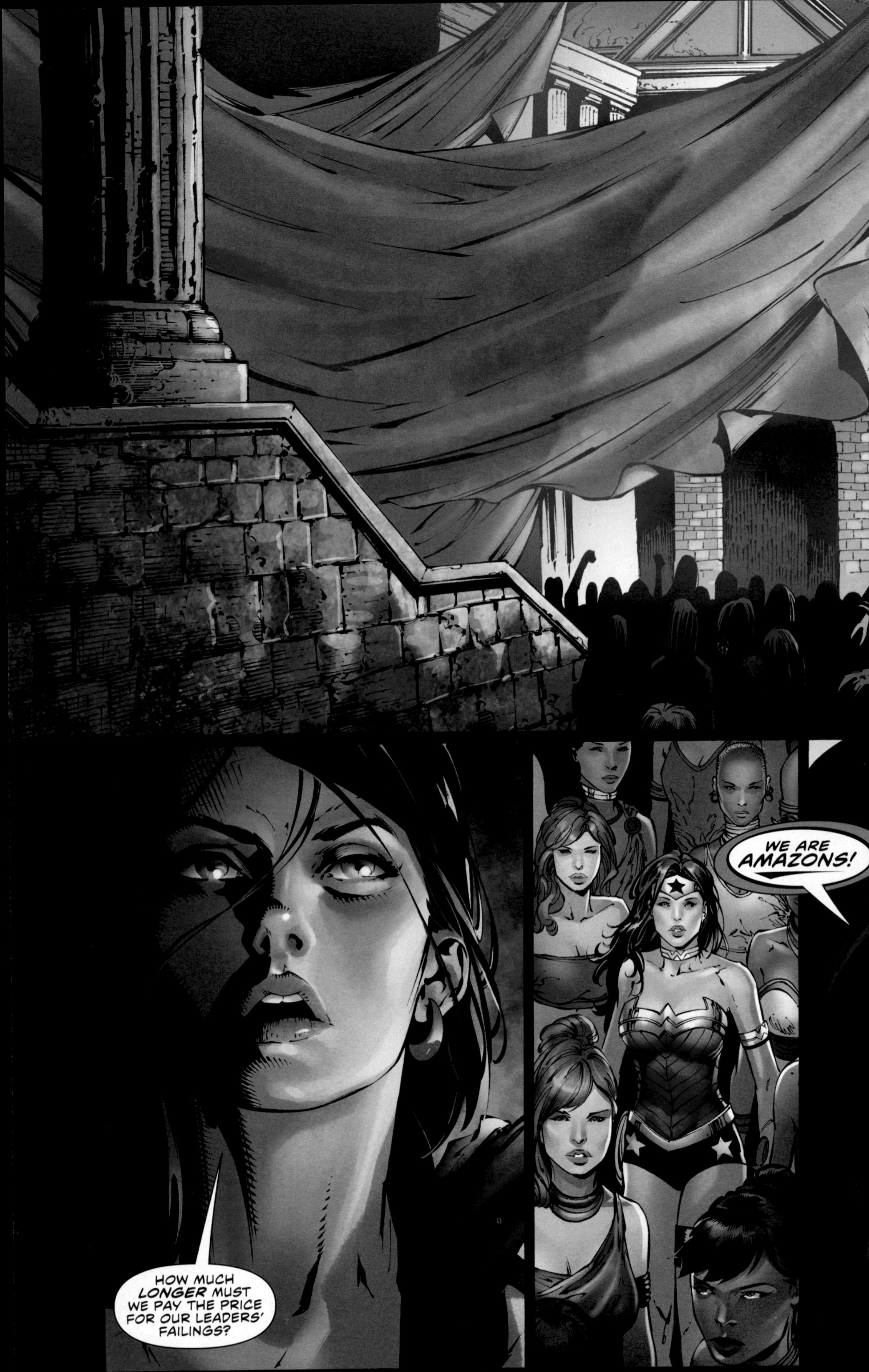
HOW MUCH LONGER MUST WE PAY THE PRICE FOR OUR LEADERS' FAILINGS?
WE ARE AMAZONS!

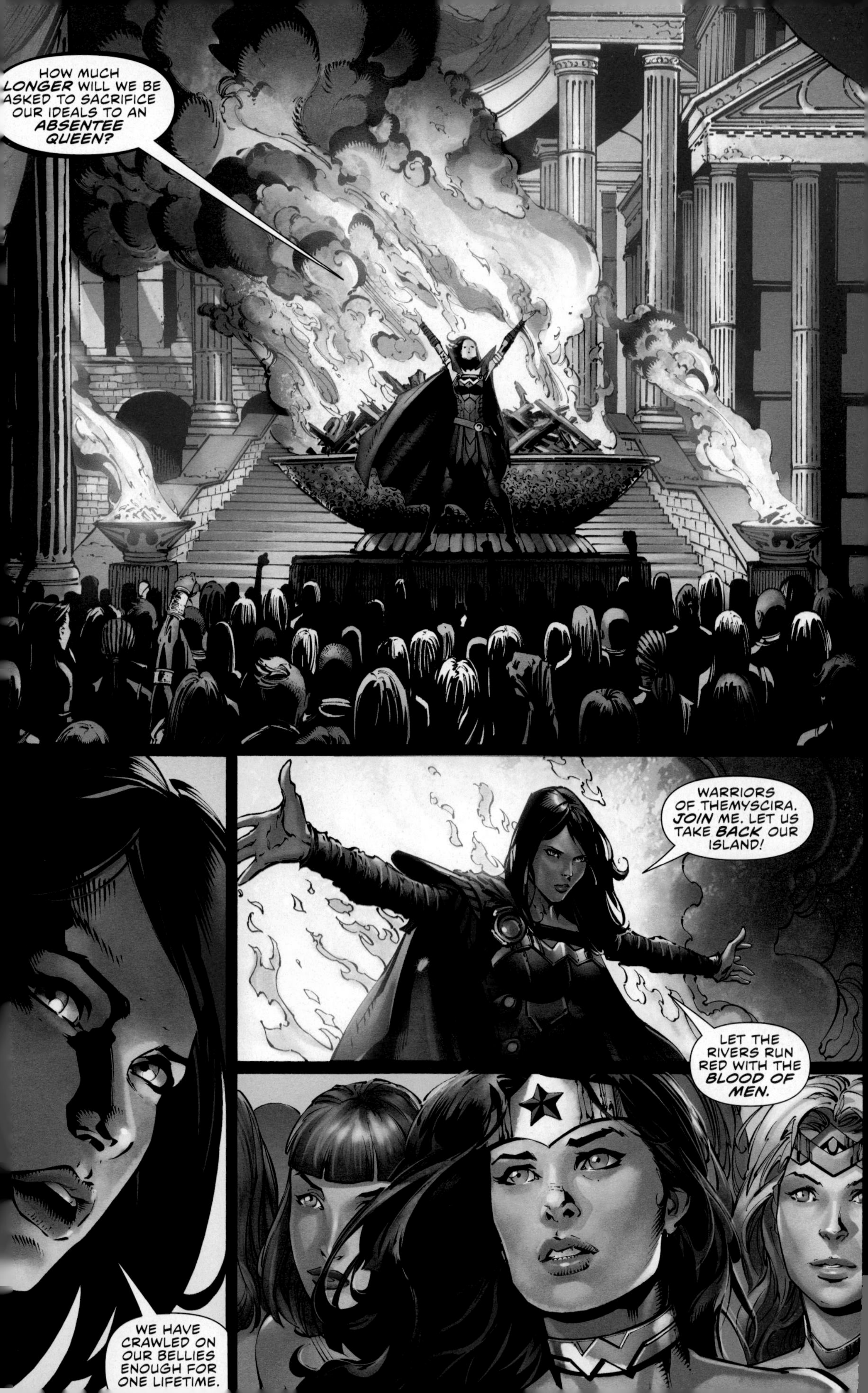

HOW MUCH LONGER WILL WE BE ASKED TO SACRIFICE OUR IDEALS TO AN ABSENTEE QUEEN?
WARRIORS OF THEMYSCIRA. JOIN ME. LET US TAKE BACK OUR ISLAND!
LET THE RIVERS RUN RED WITH THE BLOOD OF MEN.
WE HAVE CRAWLED ON OUR BELLIES ENOUGH FOR ONE LIFETIME.

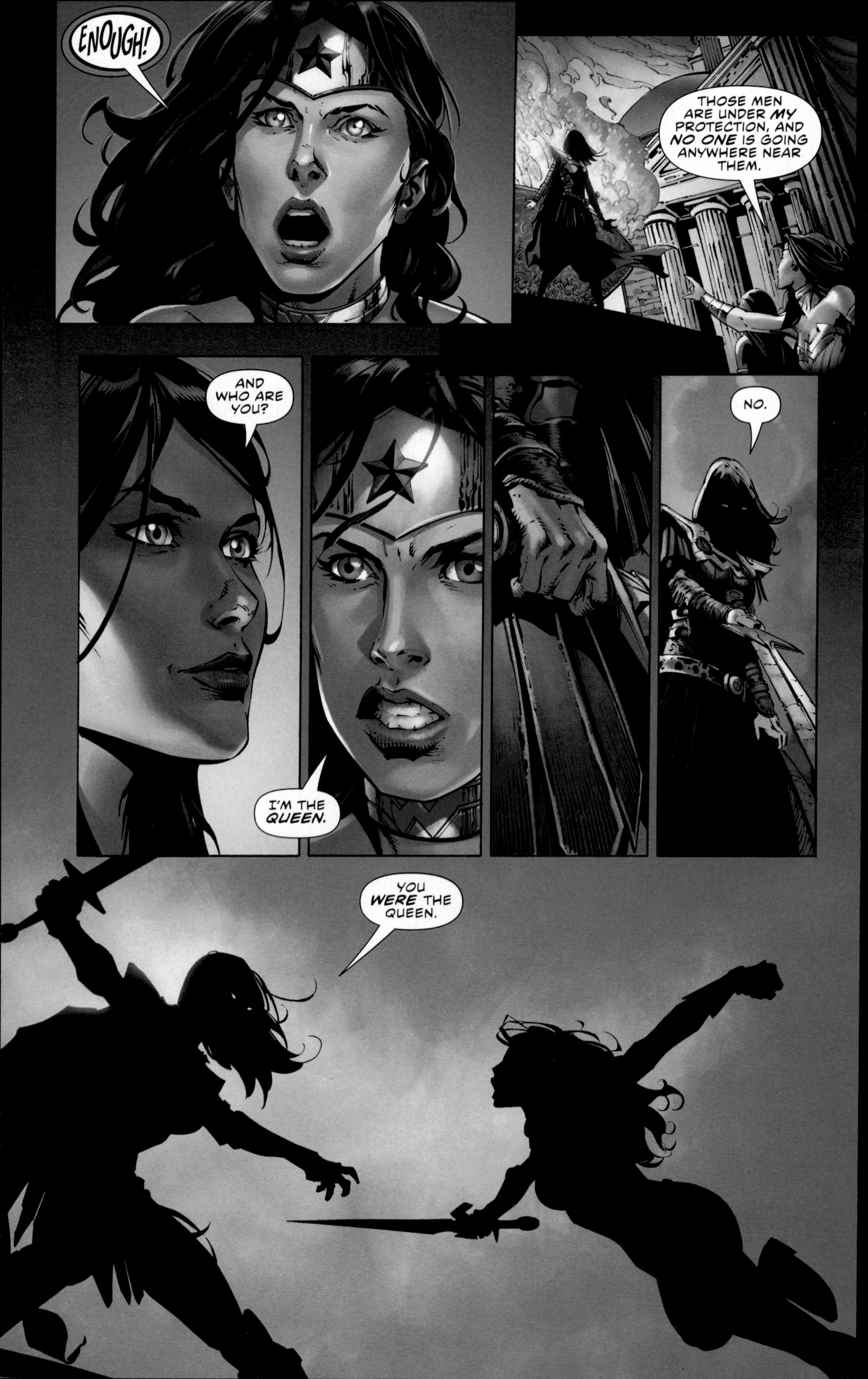

ENOUGH!
THOSE MEN ARE UNDER MY PROTECTION, AND NO ONE IS GOING ANYWHERE NEAR THEM.
AND WHO ARE YOU?
I'M THE QUEEN.
NO.
YOU WERE THE QUEEN.

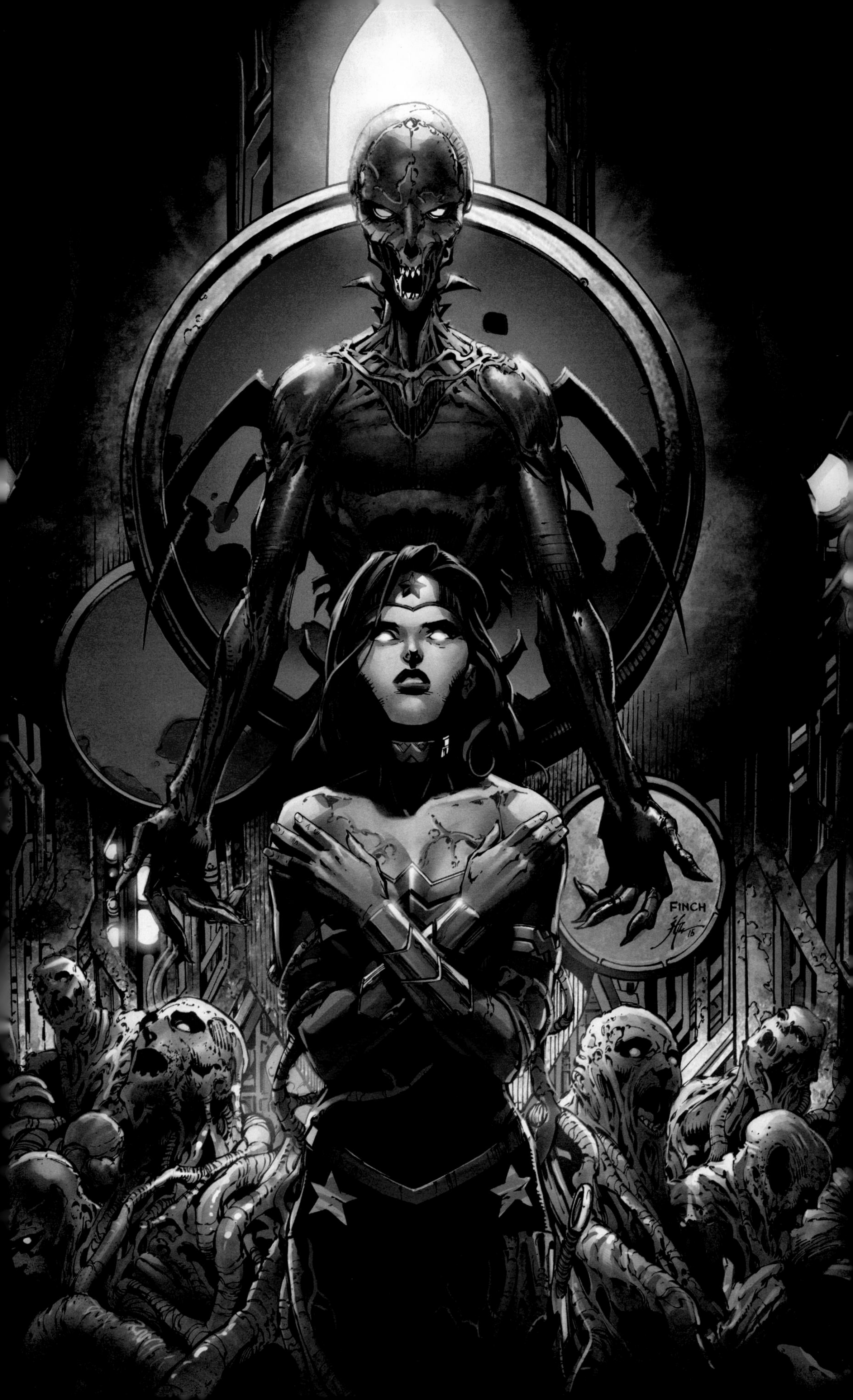
FINCH

WAR-TORN CHAPTER 5

MEREDITH FINCH writer DAVID FINCH penciller JONATHAN GLAPION inker ASPEN MLT'S PETER STEIGERWALD colorist ROB LEIGH letterer cover by FINCH, GLAPION and OBACK

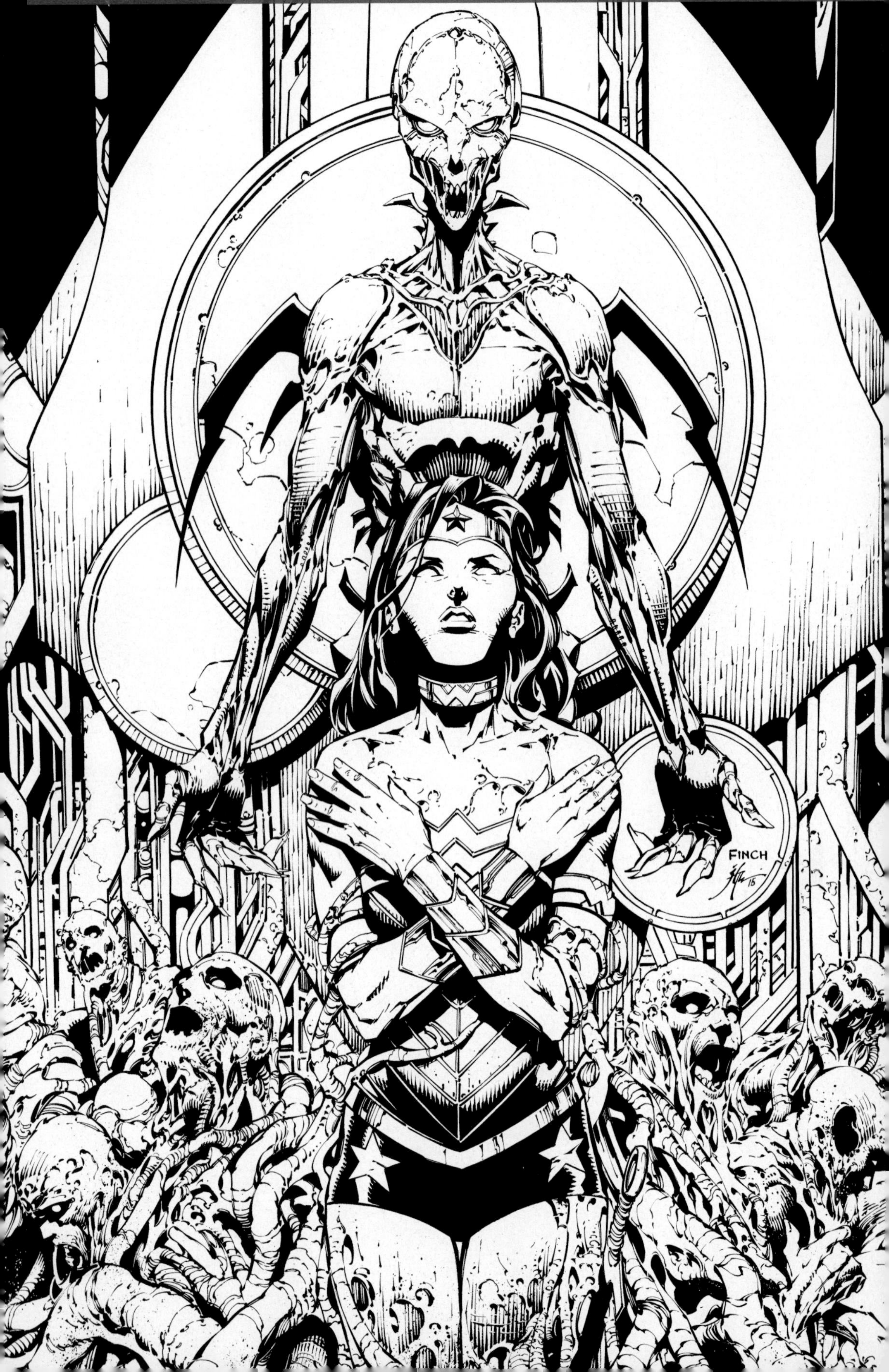
FINCH

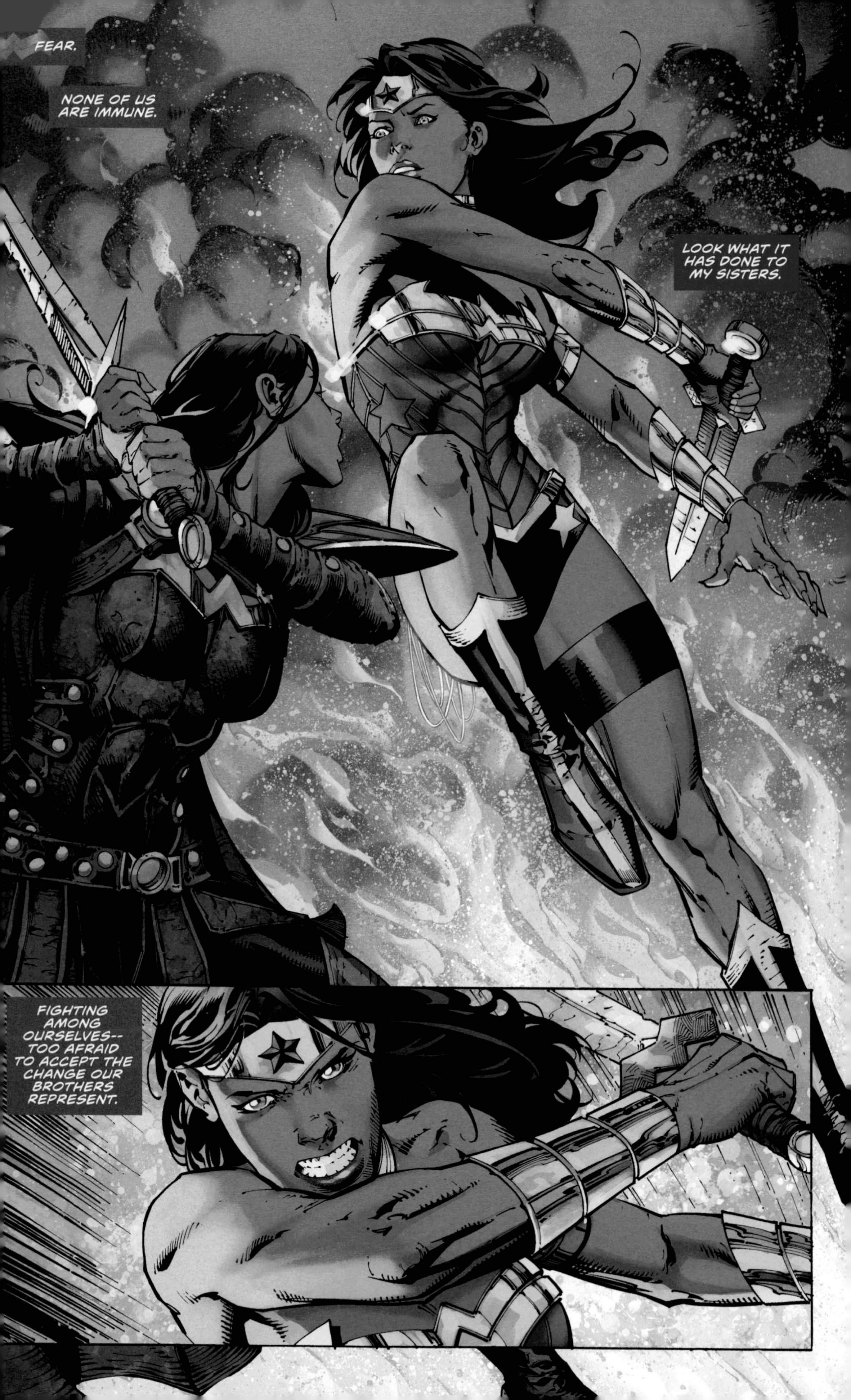
FEAR.
NONE OF US ARE IMMUNE.
LOOK WHAT IT HAS DONE TO MY SISTERS.
FIGHTING AMONG OURSELVES-- TOO AFRAID TO ACCEPT THE CHANGE OUR BROTHERS REPRESENT.

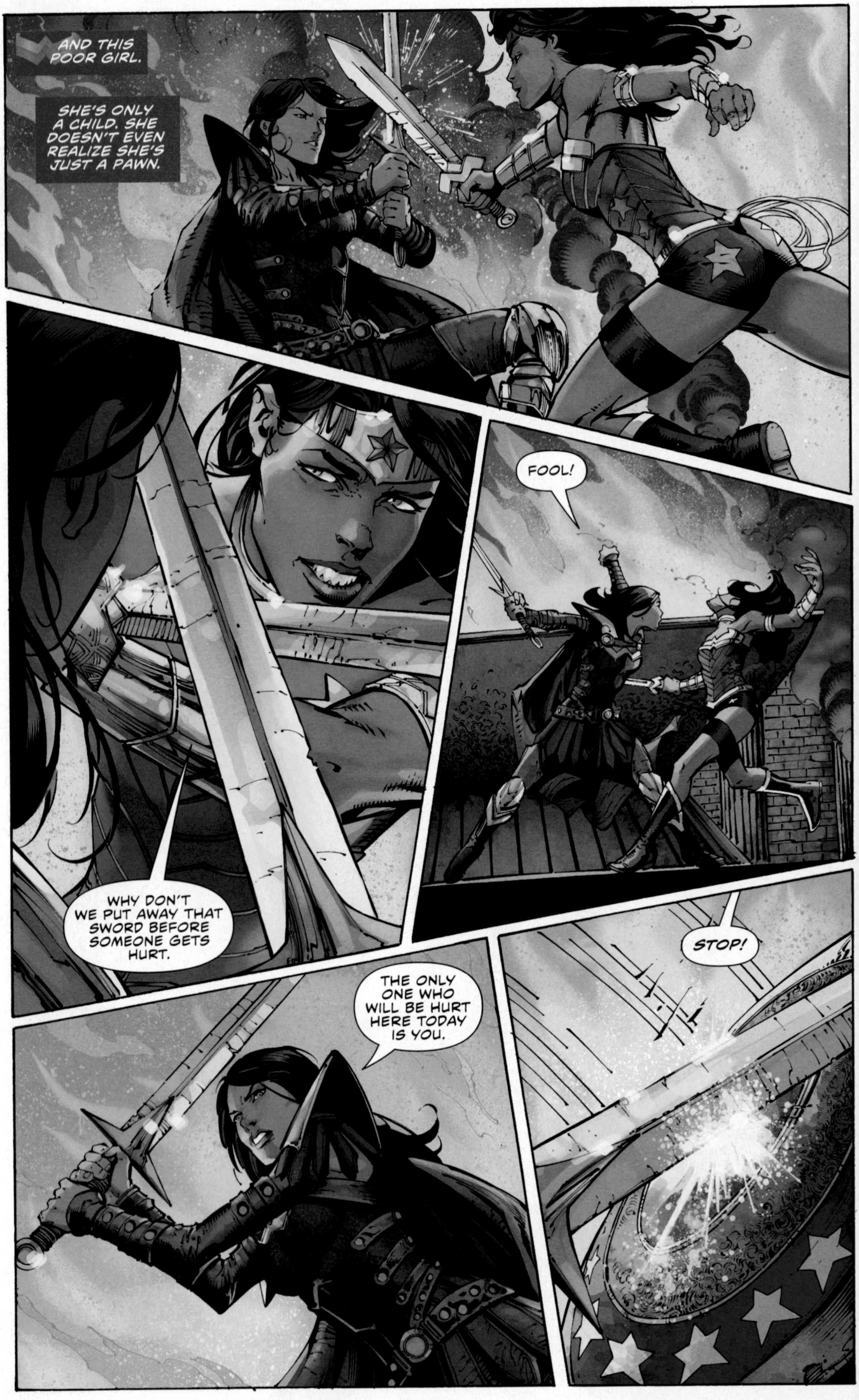
AND THIS POOR GIRL.
SHE'S ONLY A CHILD. SHE DOESN'T EVEN REALIZE SHE'S JUST A PAWN.
WHY DON'T WE PUT AWAY THAT SWORD BEFORE SOMEONE GETS HURT.
FOOL!
THE ONLY ONE WHO WILL BE HURT HERE TODAY IS YOU.
STOP!

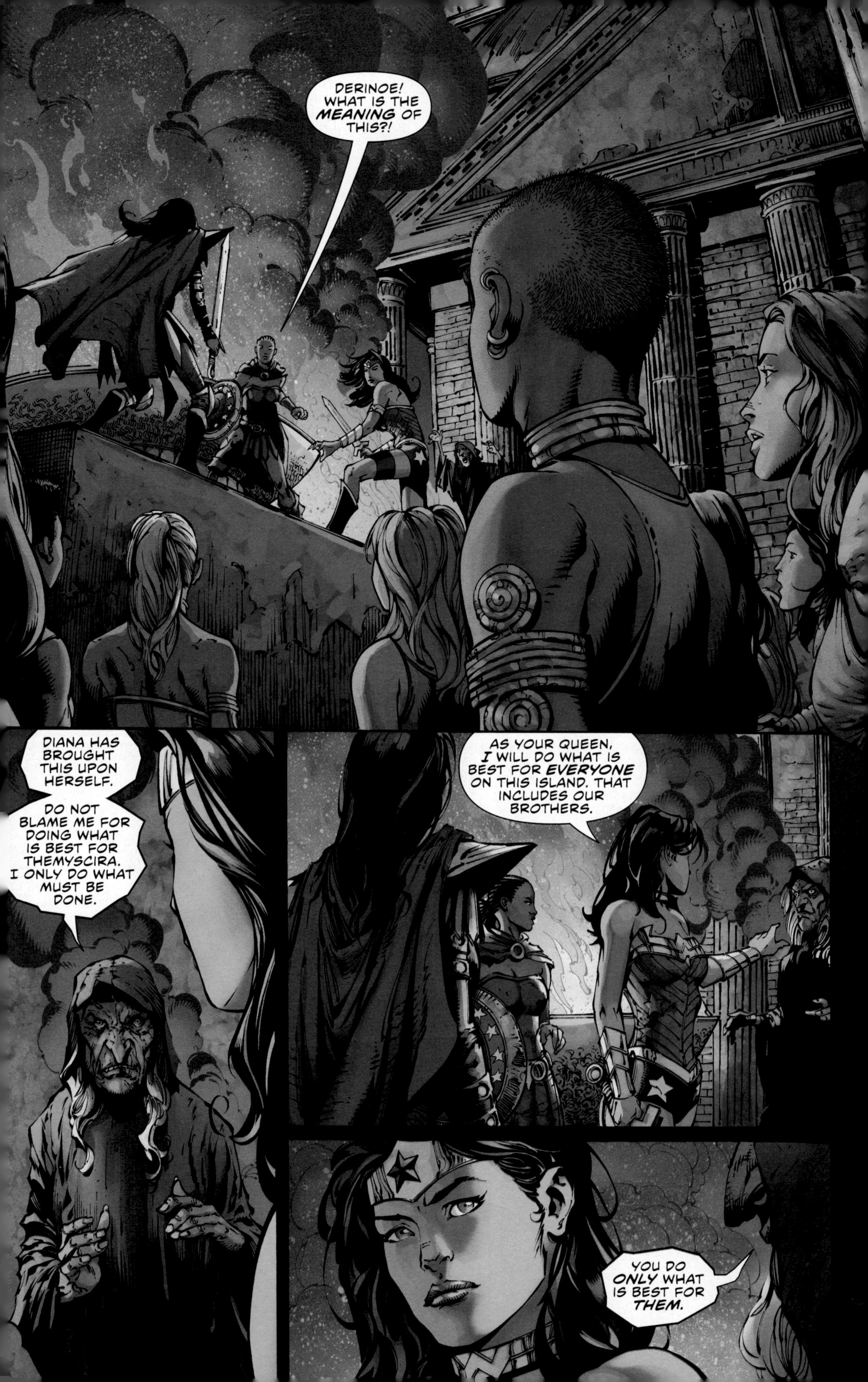

DERINOE! WHAT IS THE MEANING OF THIS?!
DIANA HAS BROUGHT THIS UPON HERSELF.
DO NOT BLAME ME FOR DOING WHAT IS BEST FOR THEMYSCIRA. I ONLY DO WHAT MUST BE DONE.
AS YOUR QUEEN, I WILL DO WHAT IS BEST FOR EVERYONE ON THIS ISLAND. THAT INCLUDES OUR BROTHERS.
YOU DO ONLY WHAT IS BEST FOR THEM.

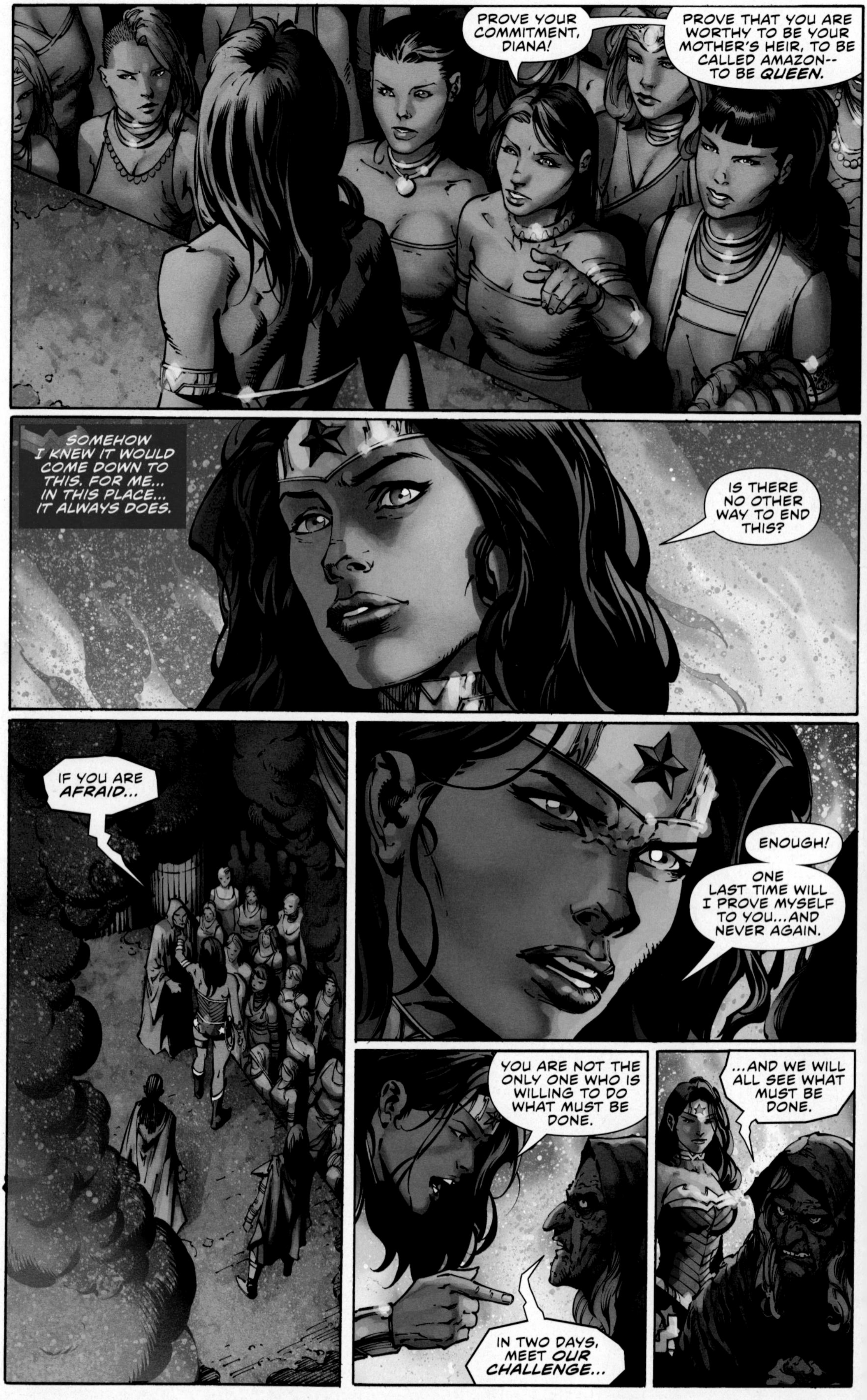
PROVE YOUR COMMITMENT, DIANA!
PROVE THAT YOU ARE WORTHY TO BE YOUR MOTHER'S HEIR, TO BE CALLED AMAZON-- TO BE QUEEN.
SOMEHOW I KNEW IT WOULD COME DOWN TO THIS. FOR ME... IN THIS PLACE... IT ALWAYS DOES.
IS THERE NO OTHER WAY TO END THIS?
IF YOU ARE AFRAID...
ENOUGH!
ONE LAST TIME WILL I PROVE MYSELF TO YOU...AND NEVER AGAIN.
YOU ARE NOT THE ONLY ONE WHO IS WILLING TO DO WHAT MUST BE DONE.
IN TWO DAYS, MEET OUR CHALLENGE...
...AND WE WILL ALL SEE WHAT MUST BE DONE.

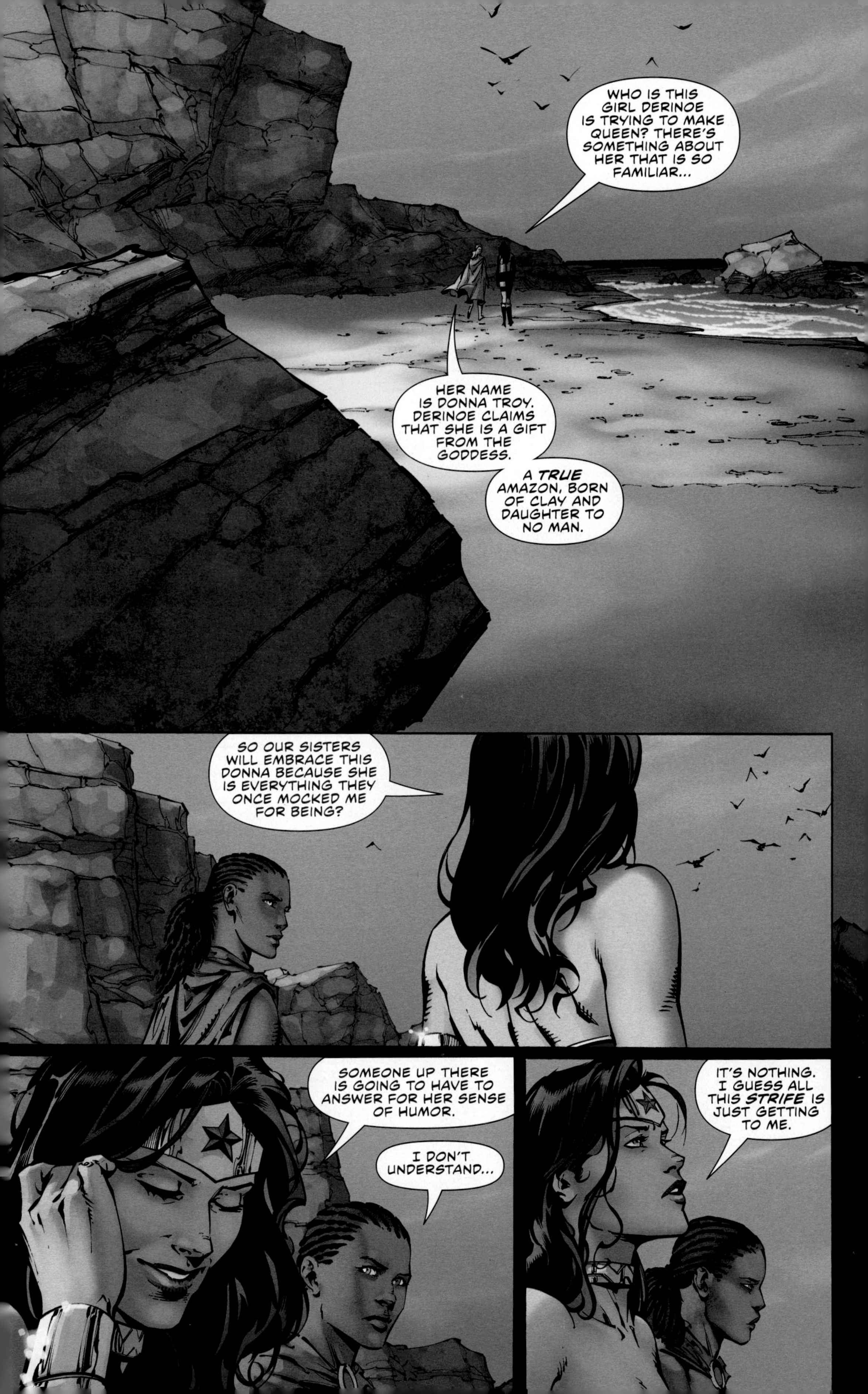
WHO IS THIS GIRL DERINOE IS TRYING TO MAKE QUEEN? THERE'S SOMETHING ABOUT HER THAT IS SO FAMILIAR...
HER NAME IS DONNA TROY. DERINOE CLAIMS THAT SHE IS A GIFT FROM THE GODDESS.
A TRUE AMAZON, BORN OF CLAY AND DAUGHTER TO NO MAN.
SO OUR SISTERS WILL EMBRACE THIS DONNA BECAUSE SHE IS EVERYTHING THEY ONCE MOCKED ME FOR BEING?
SOMEONE UP THERE IS GOING TO HAVE TO ANSWER FOR HER SENSE OF HUMOR.
I DON'T UNDERSTAND...
IT'S NOTHING. I GUESS ALL THIS STRIFE IS JUST GETTING TO ME.

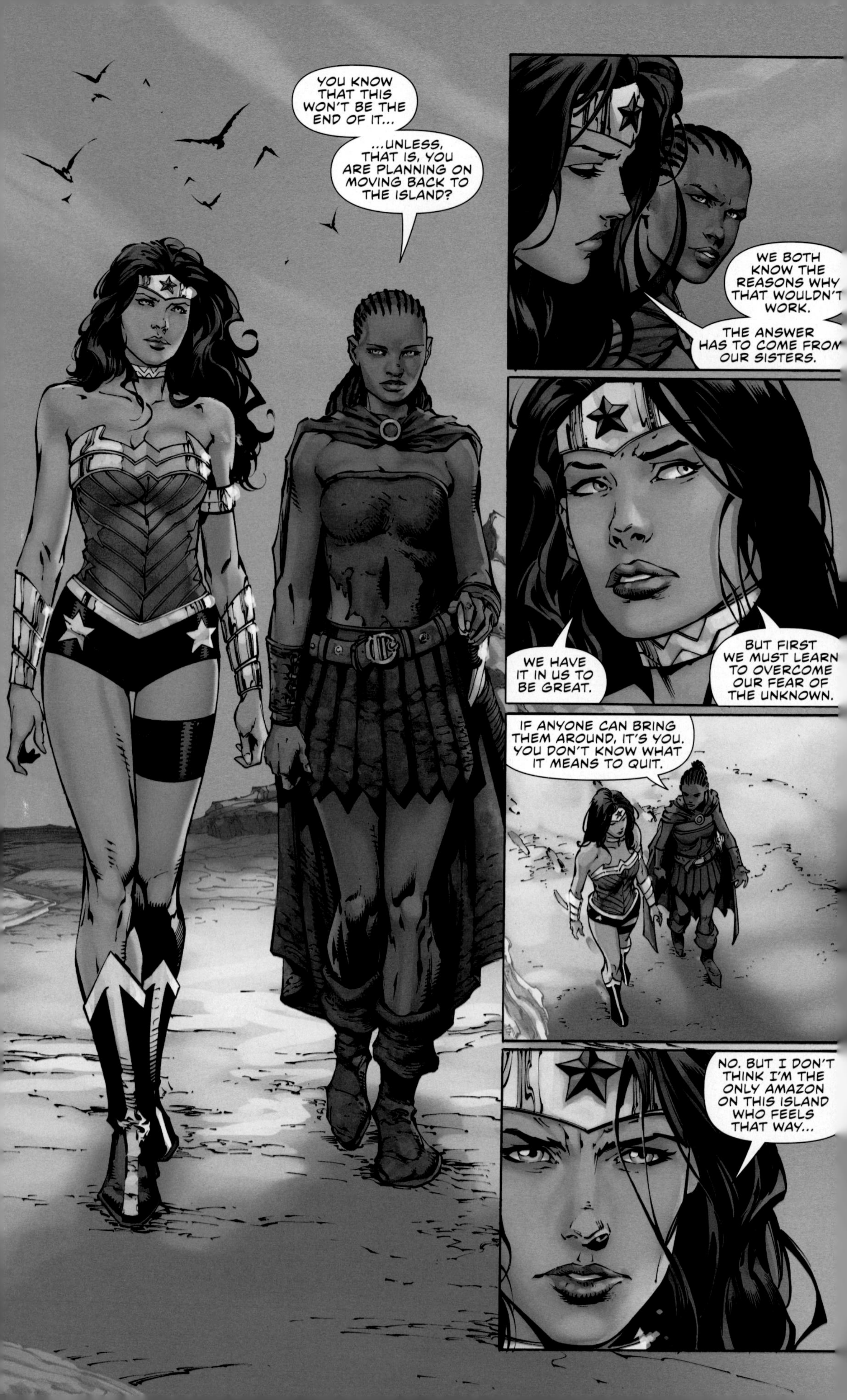
YOU KNOW THAT THIS WON'T BE THE END OF IT...
...UNLESS, THAT IS, YOU ARE PLANNING ON MOVING BACK TO THE ISLAND?
WE BOTH KNOW THE REASONS WHY THAT WOULDN'T WORK.
THE ANSWER HAS TO COME FROM OUR SISTERS.
WE HAVE IT IN US TO BE GREAT.
BUT FIRST WE MUST LEARN TO OVERCOME OUR FEAR OF THE UNKNOWN.
IF ANYONE CAN BRING THEM AROUND, IT'S YOU. YOU DON'T KNOW WHAT IT MEANS TO QUIT.
NO. BUT I DON'T THINK I'M THE ONLY AMAZON ON THIS ISLAND WHO FEELS THAT WAY...

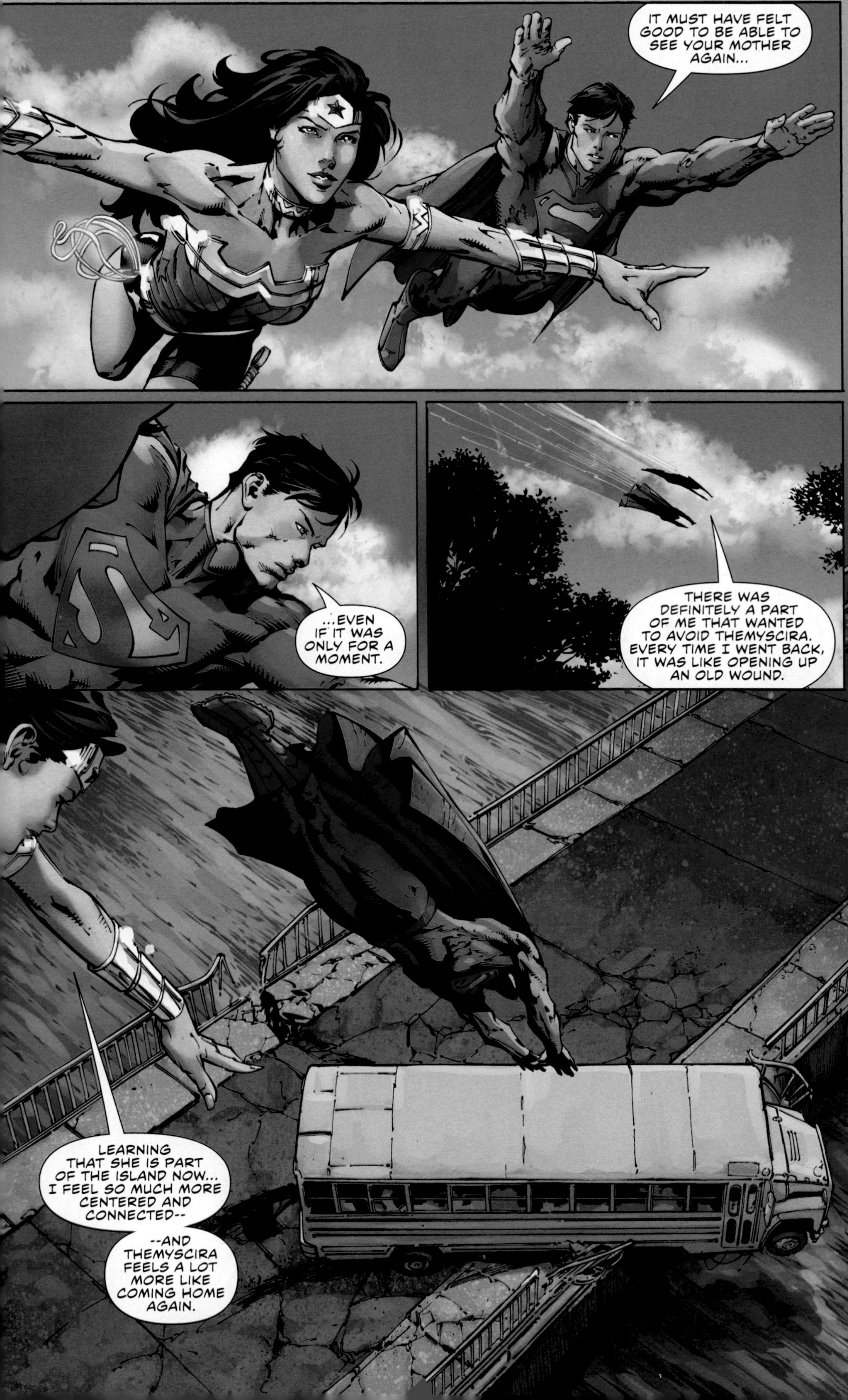
IT MUST HAVE FELT GOOD TO BE ABLE TO SEE YOUR MOTHER AGAIN...
...EVEN IF IT WAS ONLY FOR A MOMENT.
THERE WAS DEFINITELY A PART OF ME THAT WANTED TO AVOID THEMYSCIRA. EVERY TIME I WENT BACK, IT WAS LIKE OPENING UP AN OLD WOUND.
LEARNING THAT SHE IS PART OF THE ISLAND NOW... I FEEL SO MUCH MORE CENTERED AND CONNECTED--
--AND THEMYSCIRA FEELS A LOT MORE LIKE COMING HOME AGAIN.

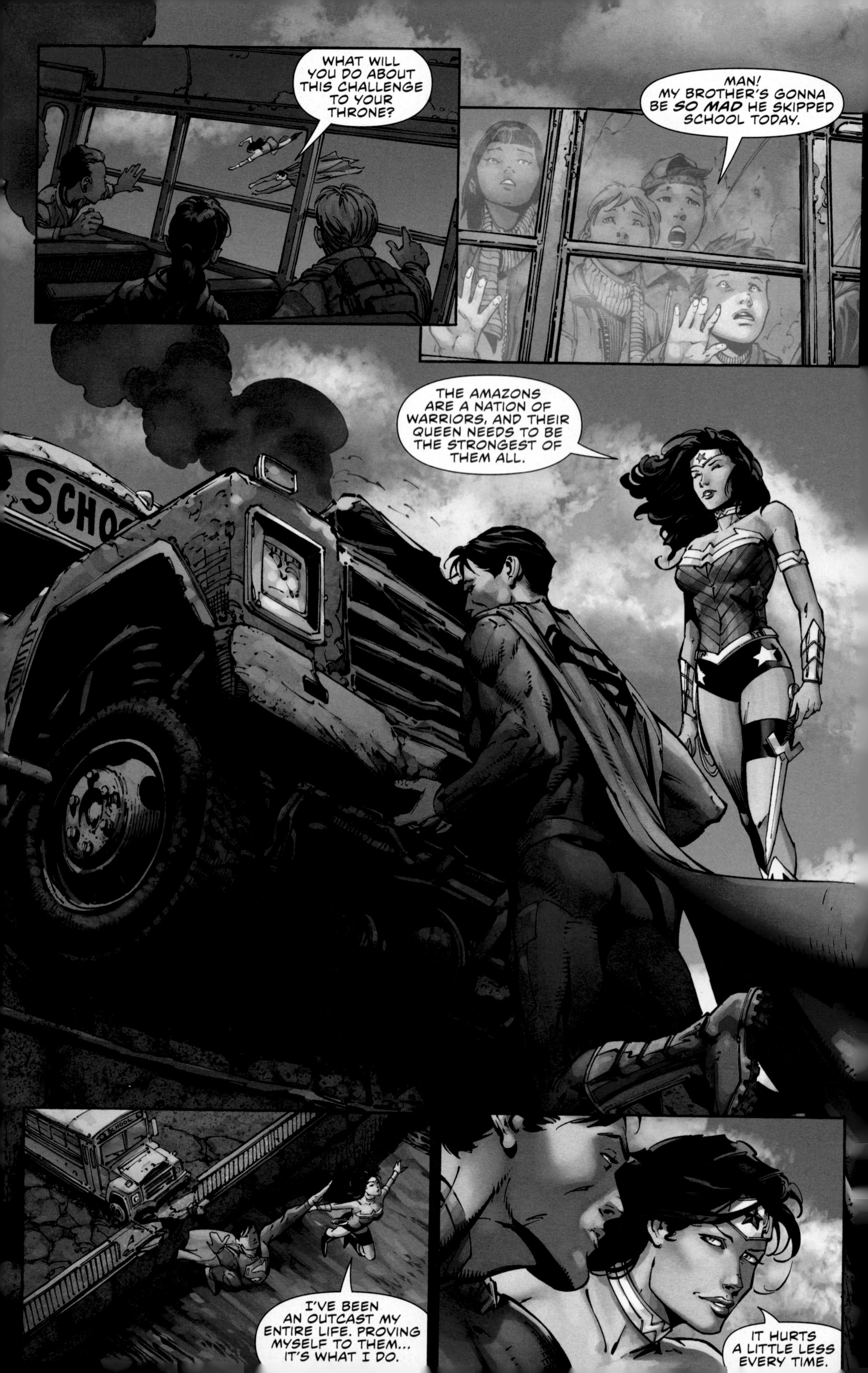
WHAT WILL YOU DO ABOUT THIS CHALLENGE TO YOUR THRONE?
MAN! MY BROTHER'S GONNA BE SO MAD HE SKIPPED SCHOOL TODAY.
THE AMAZONS ARE A NATION OF WARRIORS, AND THEIR QUEEN NEEDS TO BE THE STRONGEST OF THEM ALL.
SCHOOL
I'VE BEEN AN OUTCAST MY ENTIRE LIFE. PROVING MYSELF TO THEM... IT'S WHAT I DO.
IT HURTS A LITTLE LESS EVERY TIME.

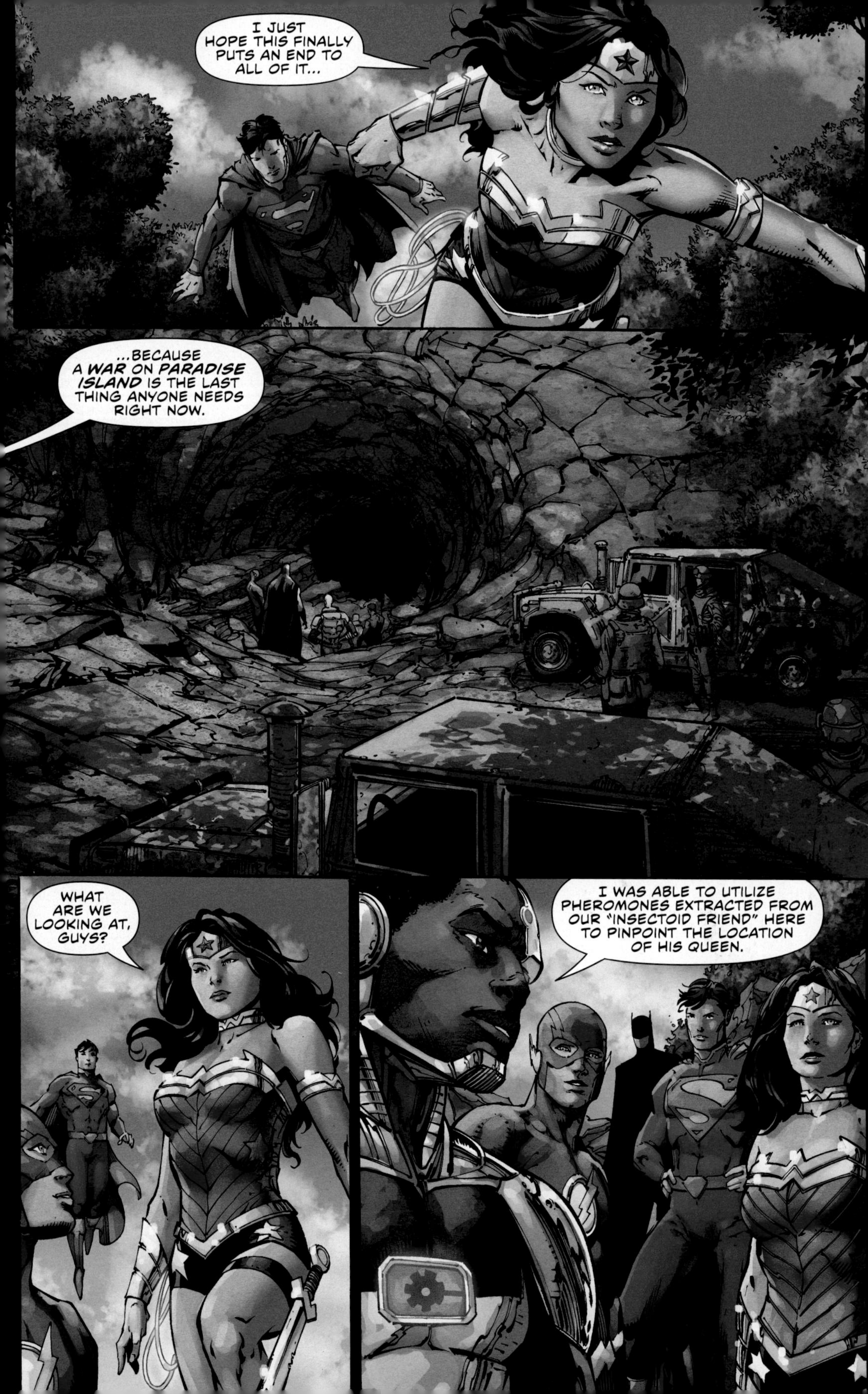
I JUST HOPE THIS FINALLY PUTS AN END TO ALL OF IT...
...BECAUSE A WAR ON PARADISE ISLAND IS THE LAST THING ANYONE NEEDS RIGHT NOW.
WHAT ARE WE LOOKING AT, GUYS?
I WAS ABLE TO UTILIZE PHEROMONES EXTRACTED FROM OUR "INSECTOID FRIEND" HERE TO PINPOINT THE LOCATION OF HIS QUEEN.

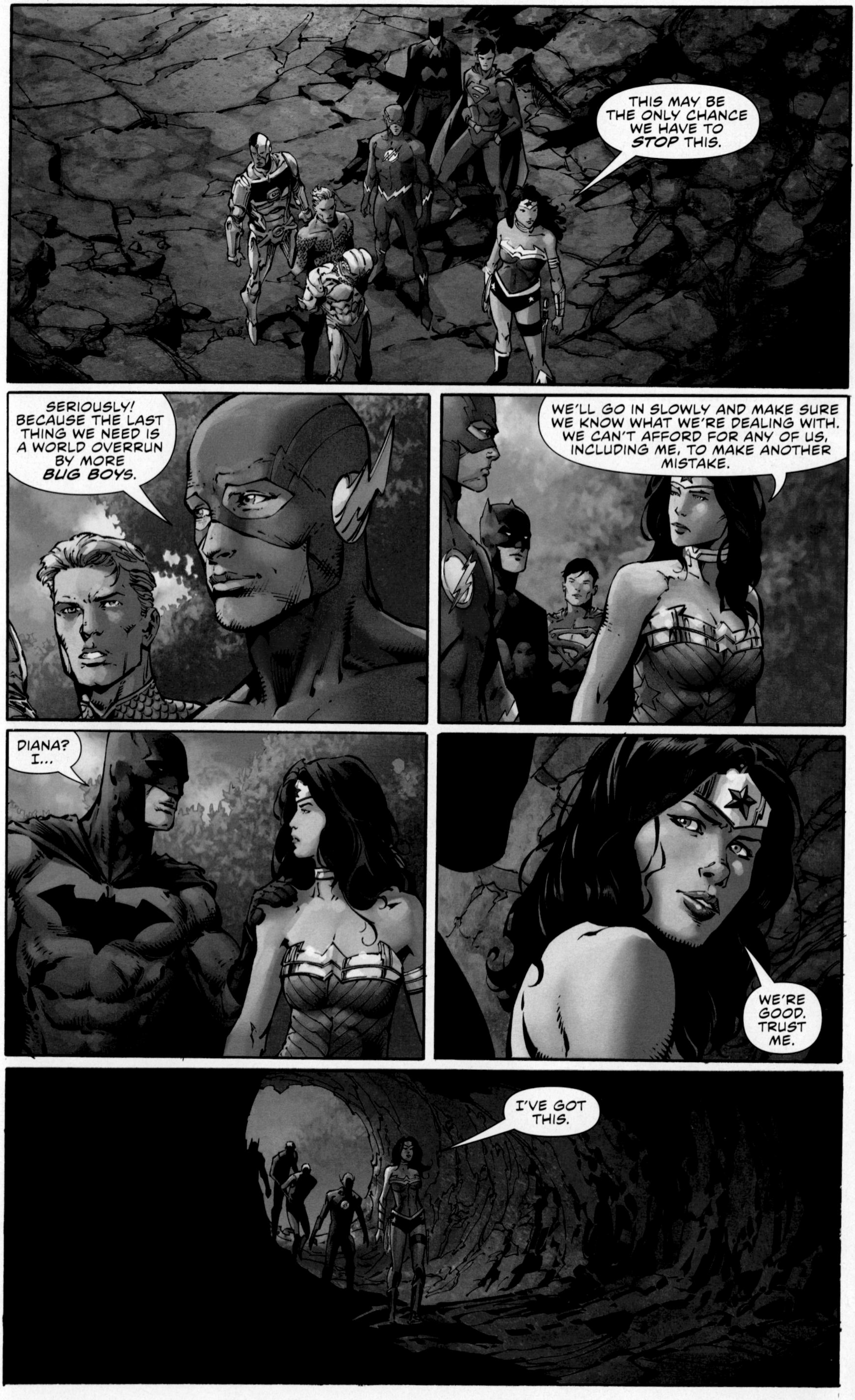
THIS MAY BE THE ONLY CHANCE WE HAVE TO STOP THIS.
SERIOUSLY! BECAUSE THE LAST THING WE NEED IS A WORLD OVERRUN BY MORE BUG BOYS.
WE'LL GO IN SLOWLY AND MAKE SURE WE KNOW WHAT WE'RE DEALING WITH. WE CAN'T AFFORD FOR ANY OF US, INCLUDING ME, TO MAKE ANOTHER MISTAKE.
DIANA? I...
WE'RE GOOD. TRUST ME.
I'VE GOT THIS.

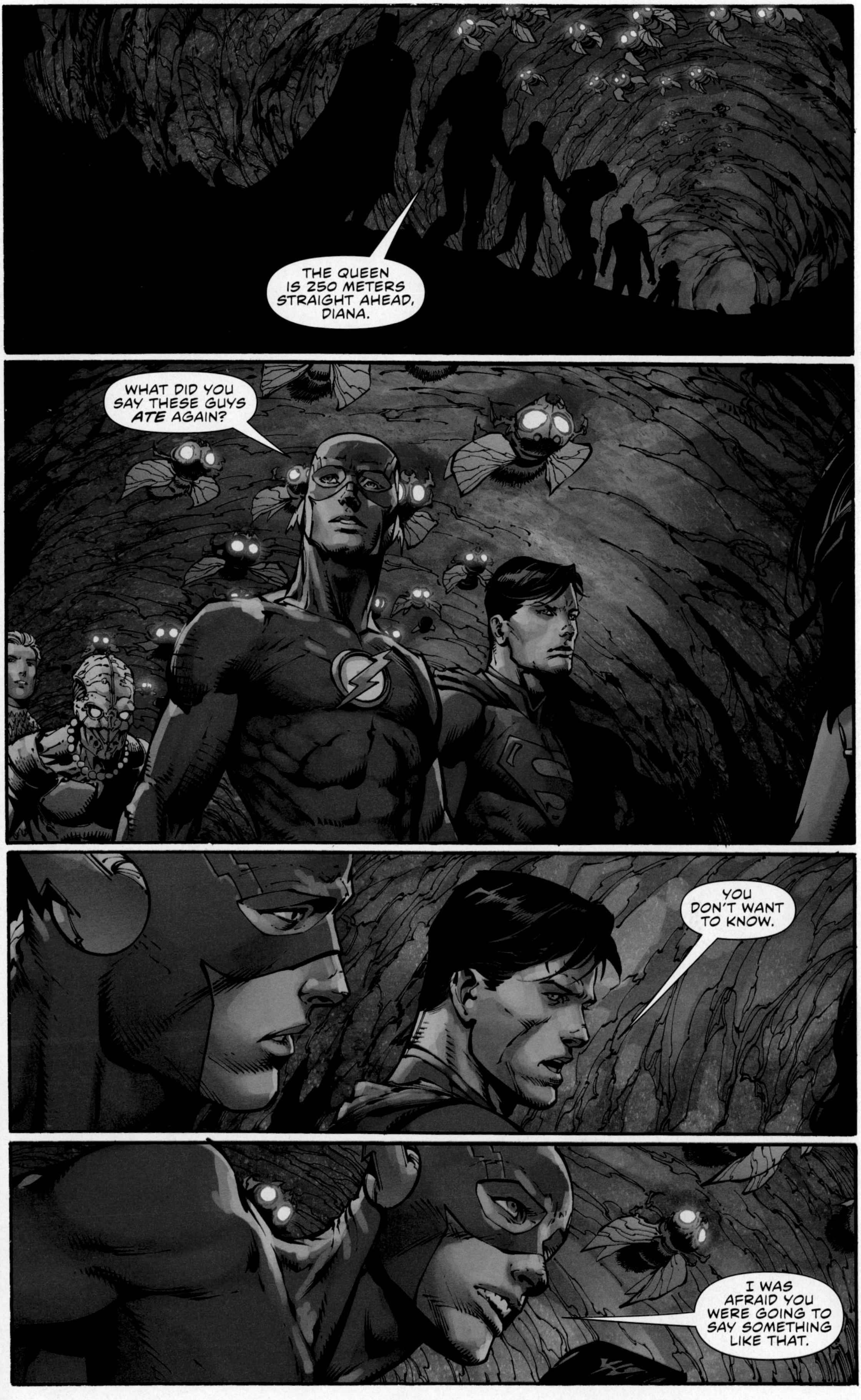
THE QUEEN IS 250 METERS STRAIGHT AHEAD, DIANA.
WHAT DID YOU SAY THESE GUYS *ATE* AGAIN?
YOU DON'T WANT TO KNOW.
I WAS AFRAID YOU WERE GOING TO SAY SOMETHING LIKE THAT.

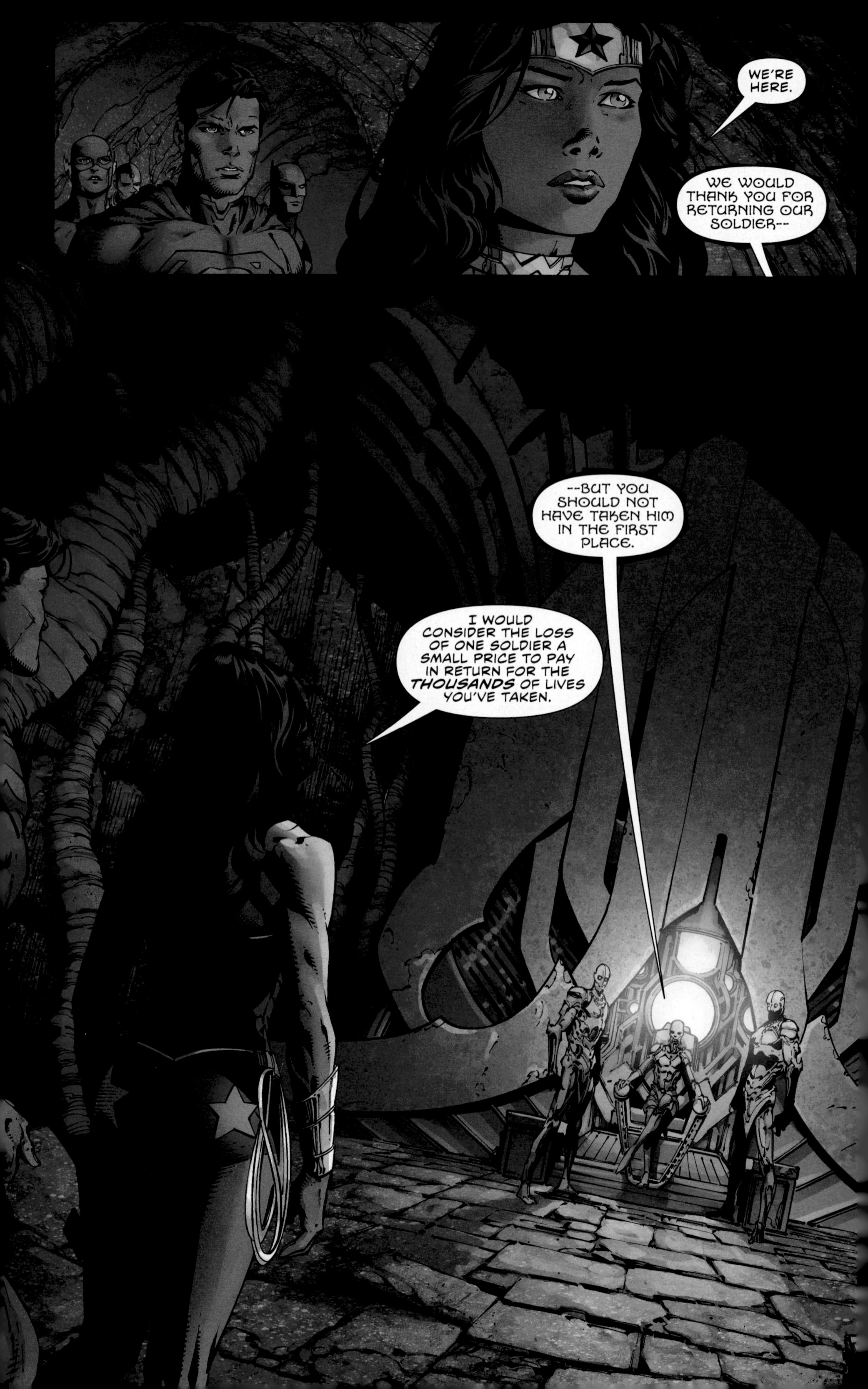
WE'RE HERE.
WE WOULD THANK YOU FOR RETURNING OUR SOLDIER--
--BUT YOU SHOULD NOT HAVE TAKEN HIM IN THE FIRST PLACE.
I WOULD CONSIDER THE LOSS OF ONE SOLDIER A SMALL PRICE TO PAY IN RETURN FOR THE *THOUSANDS* OF LIVES YOU'VE TAKEN.

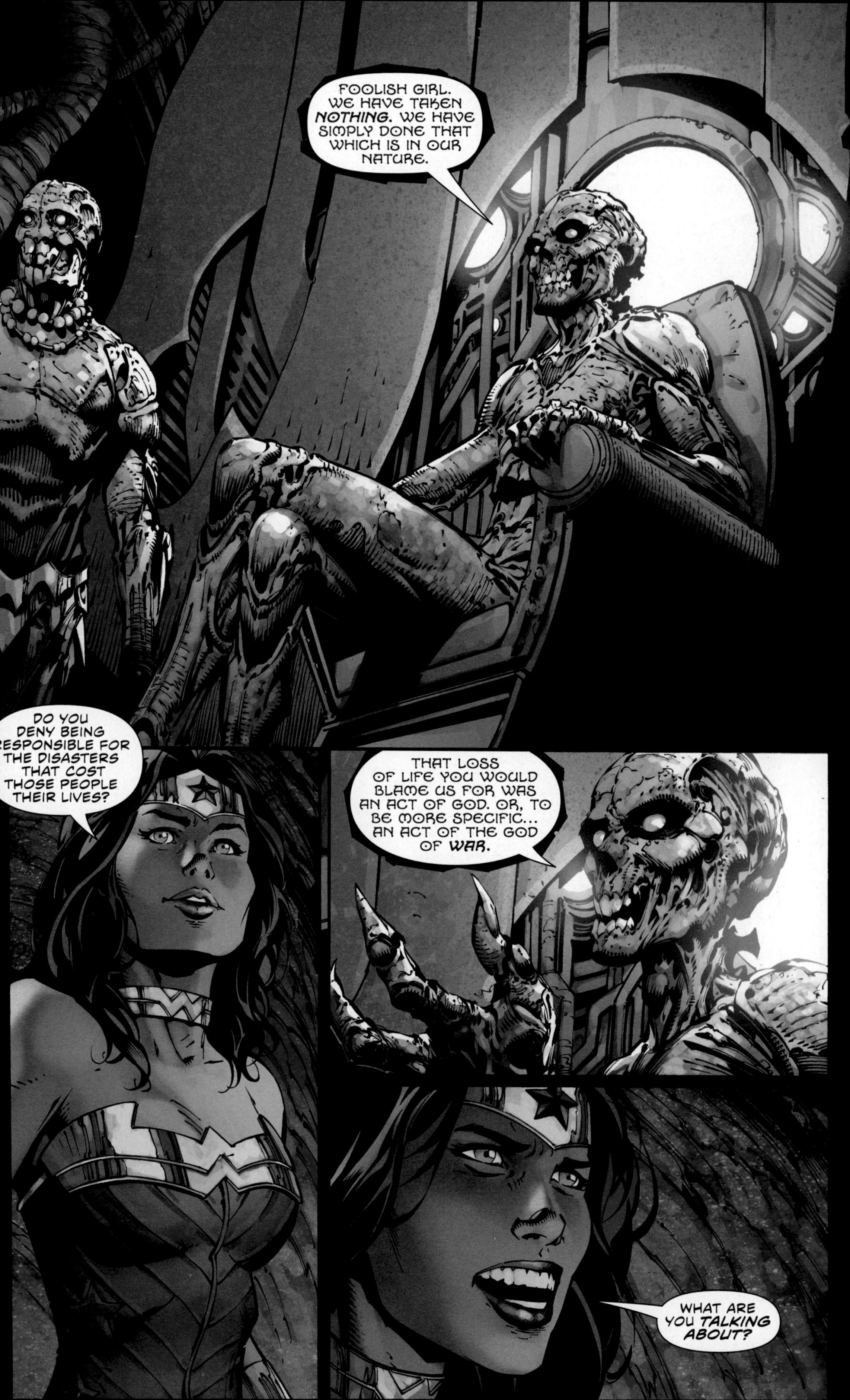
FOOLISH GIRL. WE HAVE TAKEN NOTHING. WE HAVE SIMPLY DONE THAT WHICH IS IN OUR NATURE.
DO YOU DENY BEING RESPONSIBLE FOR THE DISASTERS THAT COST THOSE PEOPLE THEIR LIVES?
THAT LOSS OF LIFE YOU WOULD BLAME US FOR WAS AN ACT OF GOD. OR, TO BE MORE SPECIFIC... AN ACT OF THE GOD OF WAR.
WHAT ARE YOU TALKING ABOUT?

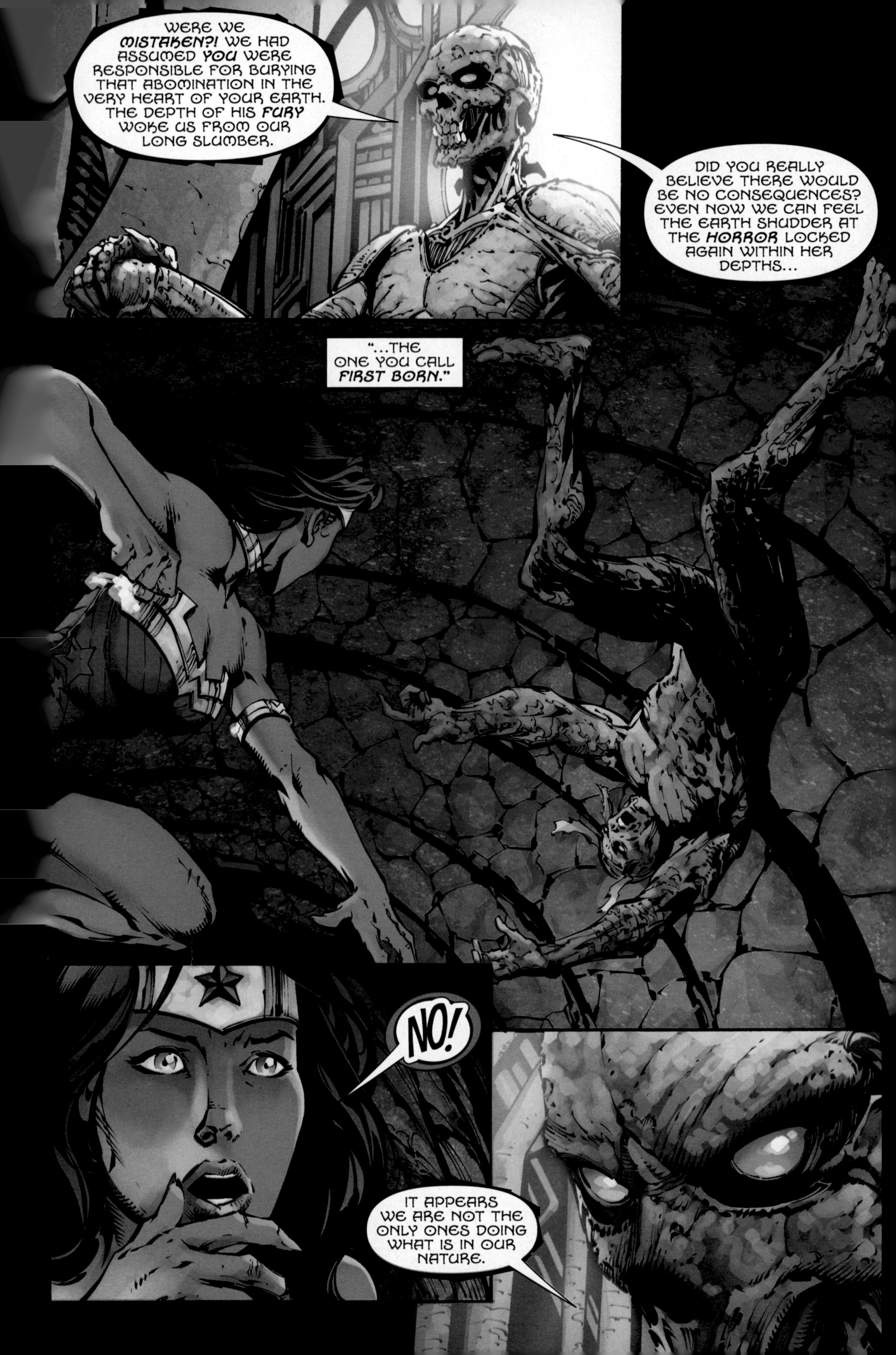
WERE WE MISTAKEN?! WE HAD ASSUMED YOU WERE RESPONSIBLE FOR BURYING THAT ABOMINATION IN THE VERY HEART OF YOUR EARTH. THE DEPTH OF HIS FURY WOKE US FROM OUR LONG SLUMBER.
DID YOU REALLY BELIEVE THERE WOULD BE NO CONSEQUENCES? EVEN NOW WE CAN FEEL THE EARTH SHUDDER AT THE HORROR LOCKED AGAIN WITHIN HER DEPTHS...
"...THE ONE YOU CALL FIRST BORN."
NO!
IT APPEARS WE ARE NOT THE ONLY ONES DOING WHAT IS IN OUR NATURE.

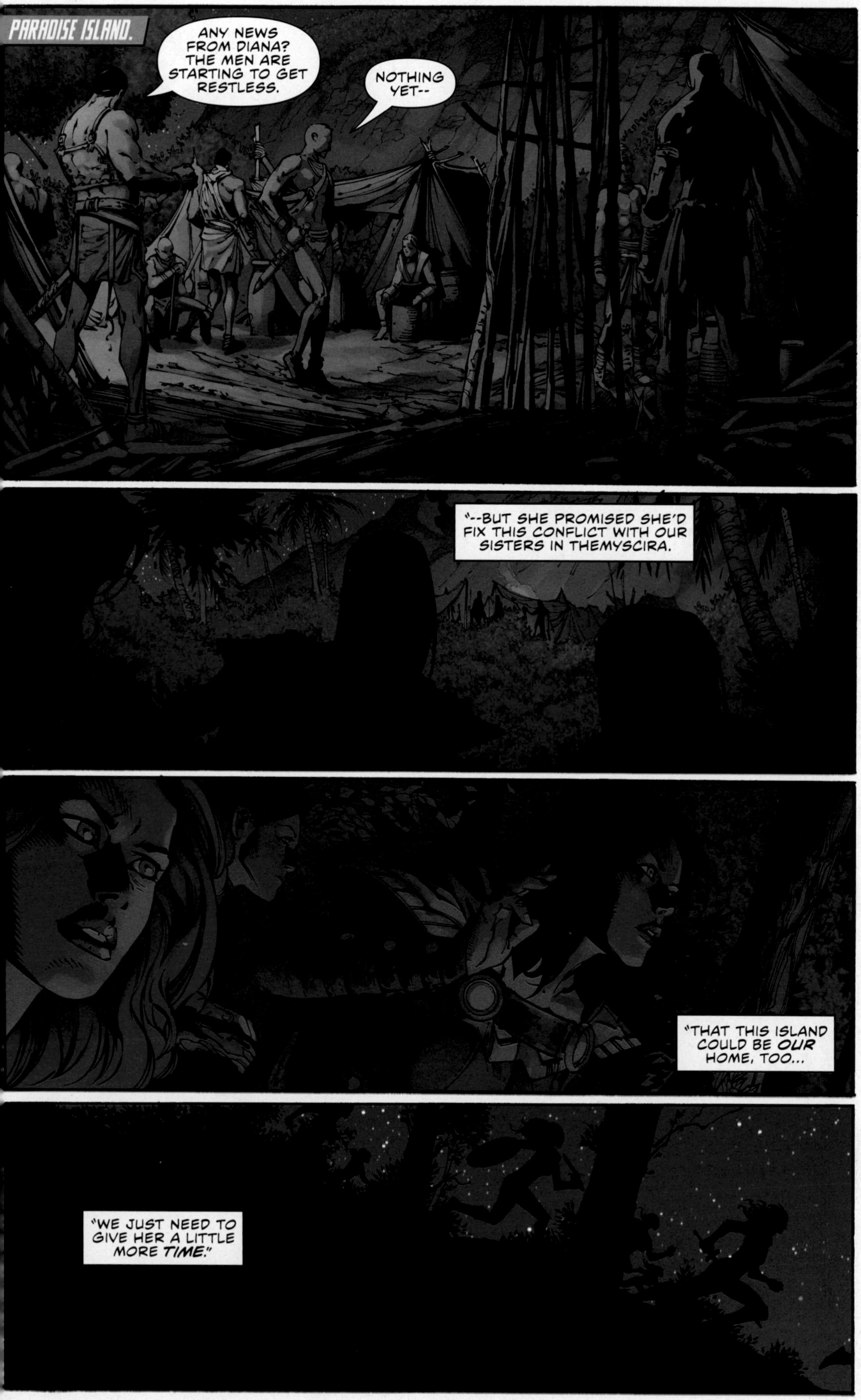
PARADISE ISLAND.
ANY NEWS FROM DIANA? THE MEN ARE STARTING TO GET RESTLESS.
NOTHING YET--
"--BUT SHE PROMISED SHE'D FIX THIS CONFLICT WITH OUR SISTERS IN THEMYSCIRA.
"THAT THIS ISLAND COULD BE OUR HOME, TOO...
"WE JUST NEED TO GIVE HER A LITTLE MORE TIME."

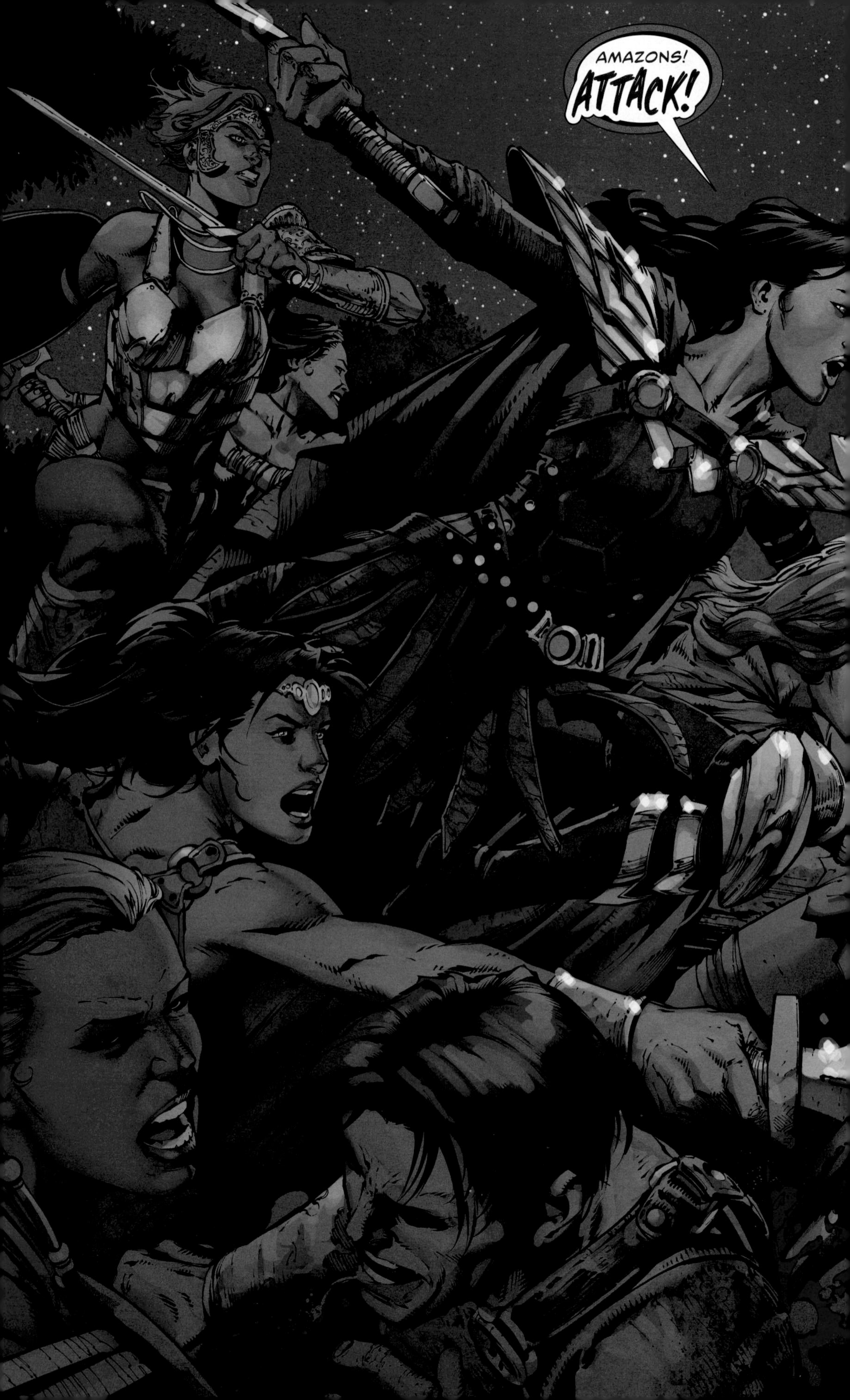
AMAZONS! ATTACK!

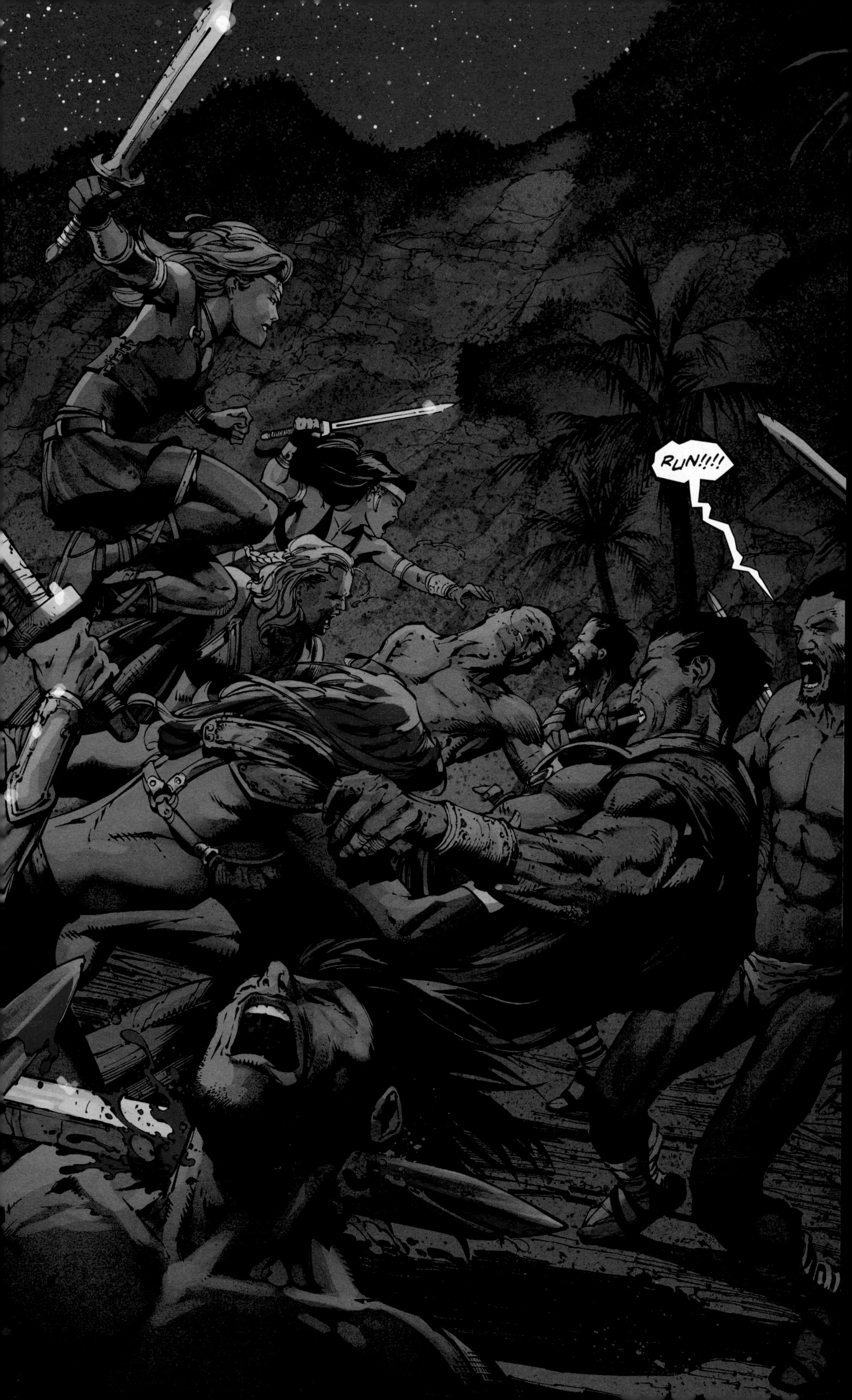
RUN!!!!

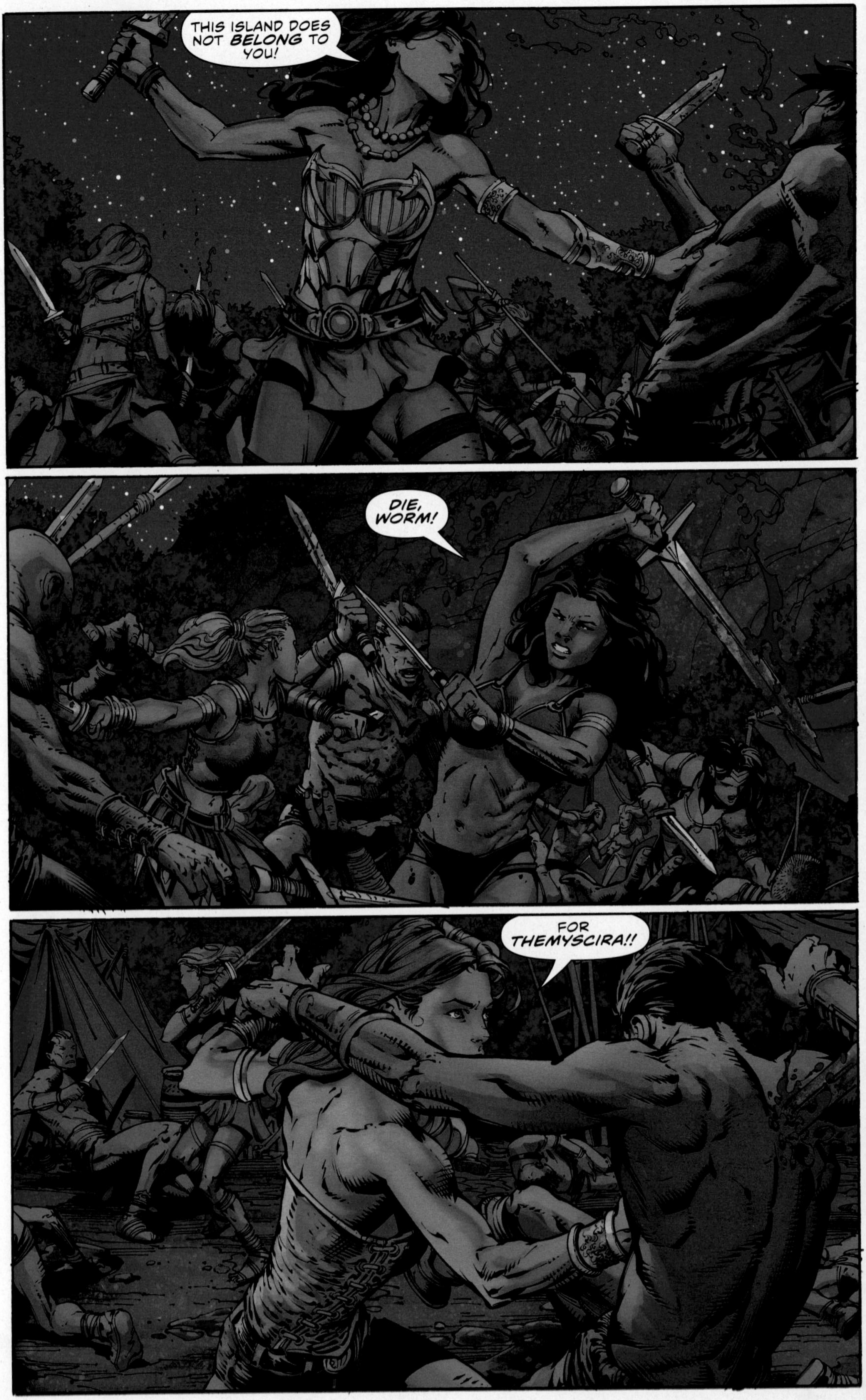
THIS ISLAND DOES NOT BELONG TO YOU!
DIE, WORM!
FOR THEMYSCIRA!!

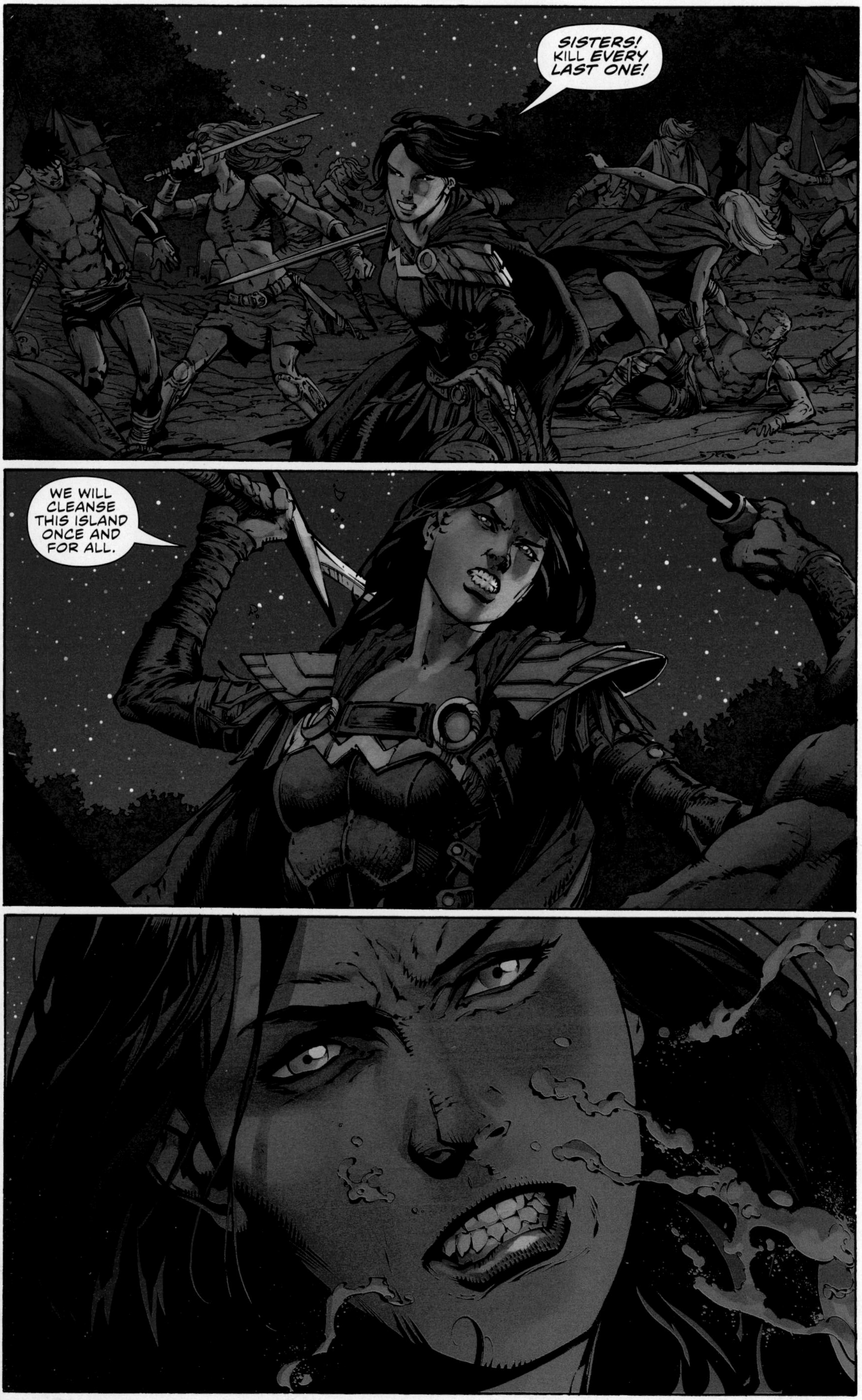
SISTERS! KILL EVERY LAST ONE!
WE WILL CLEANSE THIS ISLAND ONCE AND FOR ALL.

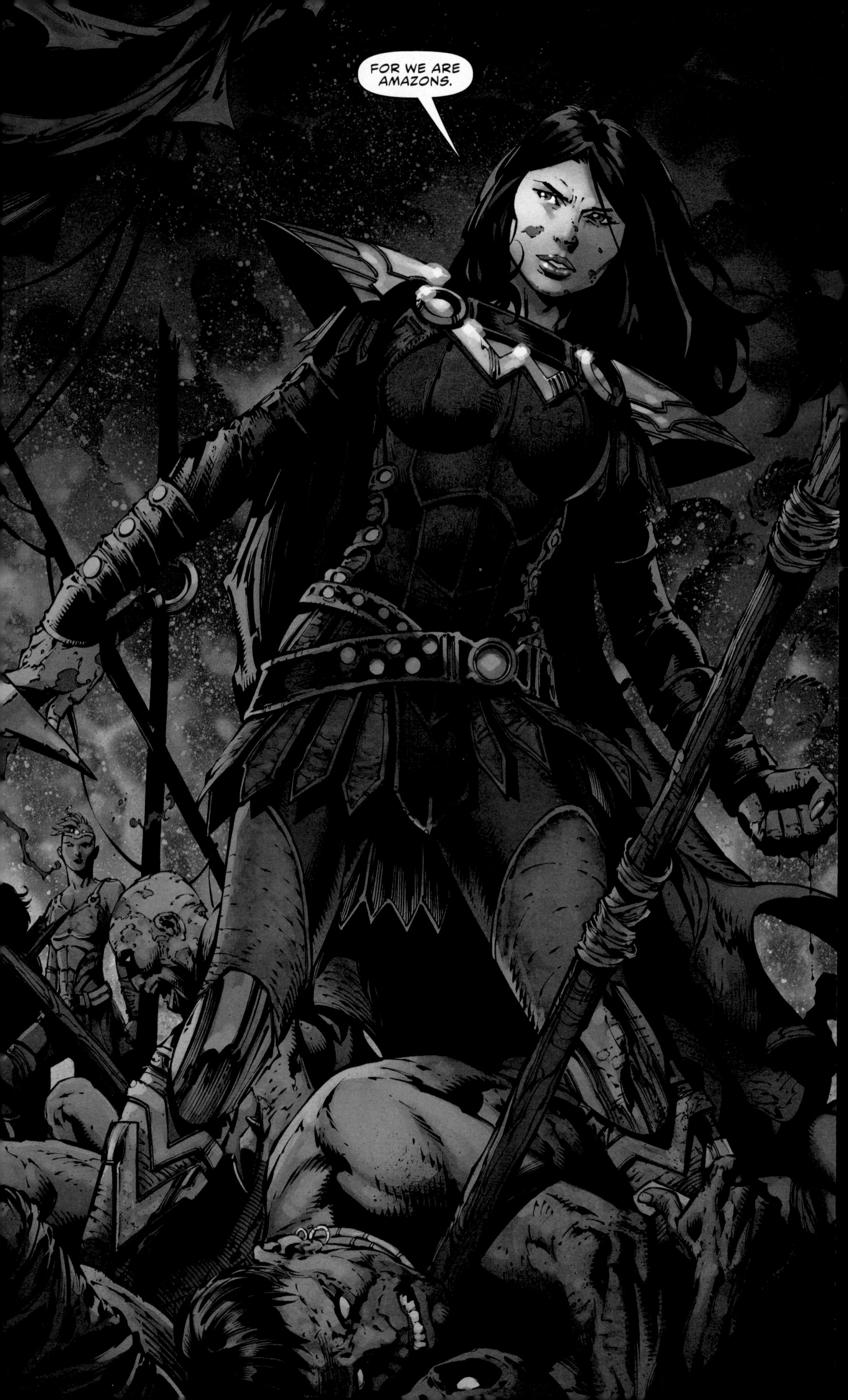
FOR WE ARE AMAZONS.

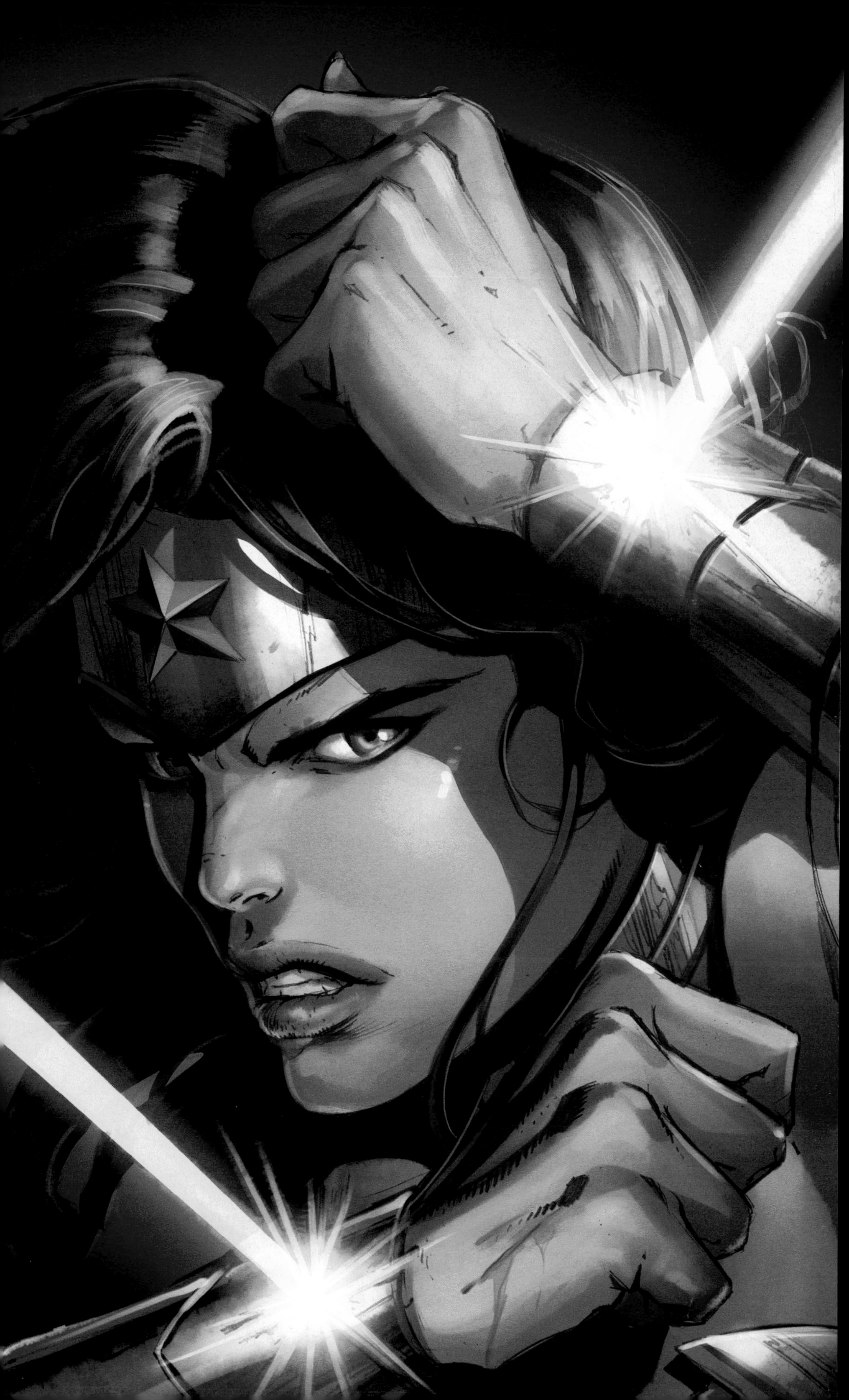

WAR-TORN FINAL CHAPTER

MEREDITH FINCH writer **DAVID FINCH** penciller **JONATHAN GLAPION JOHNNY DESJARDINS** inkers **BRAD ANDERSON** colorist **ROB LEIGH** letterer cover by **FINCH and OBACK**

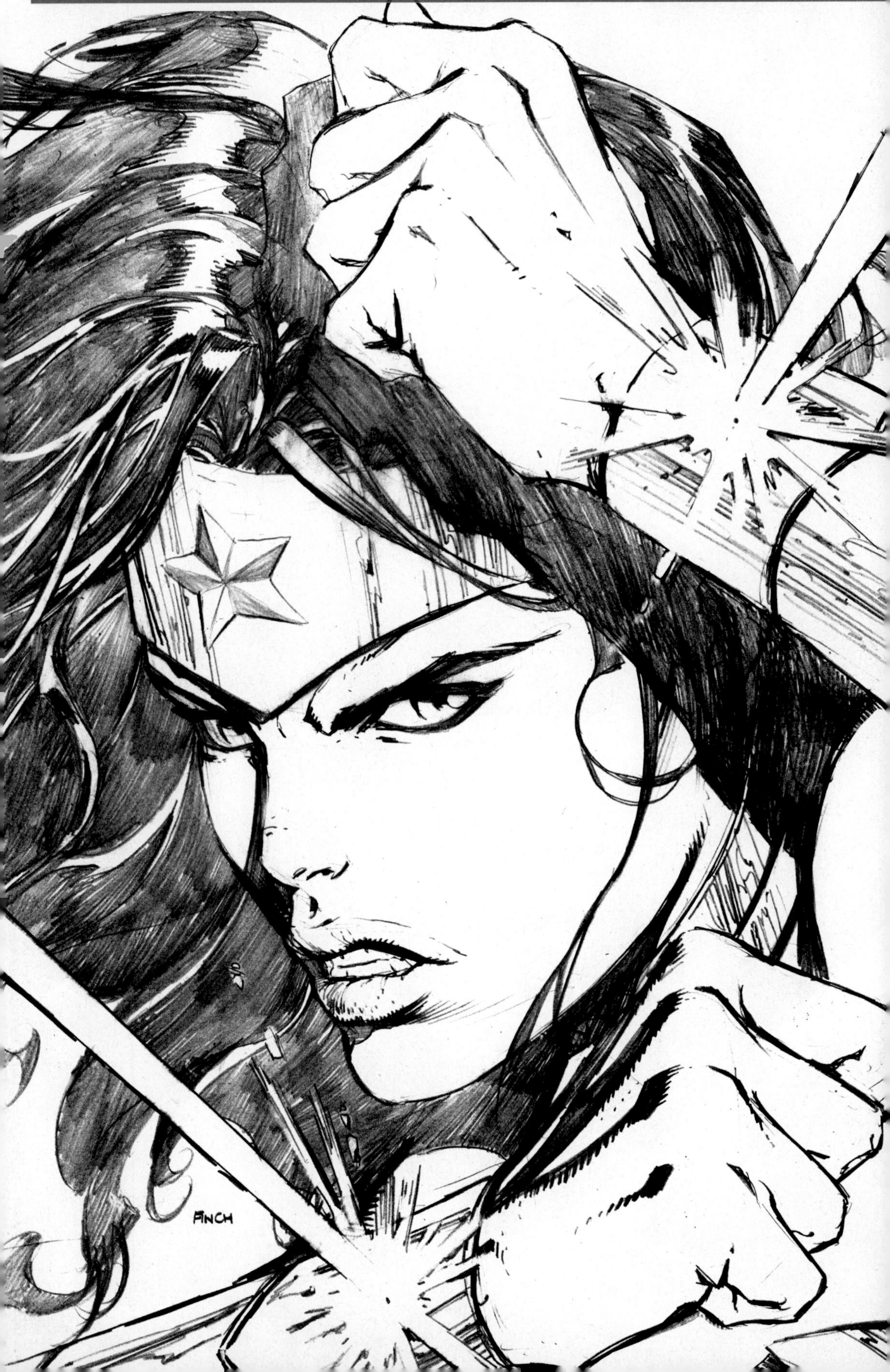
FINCH

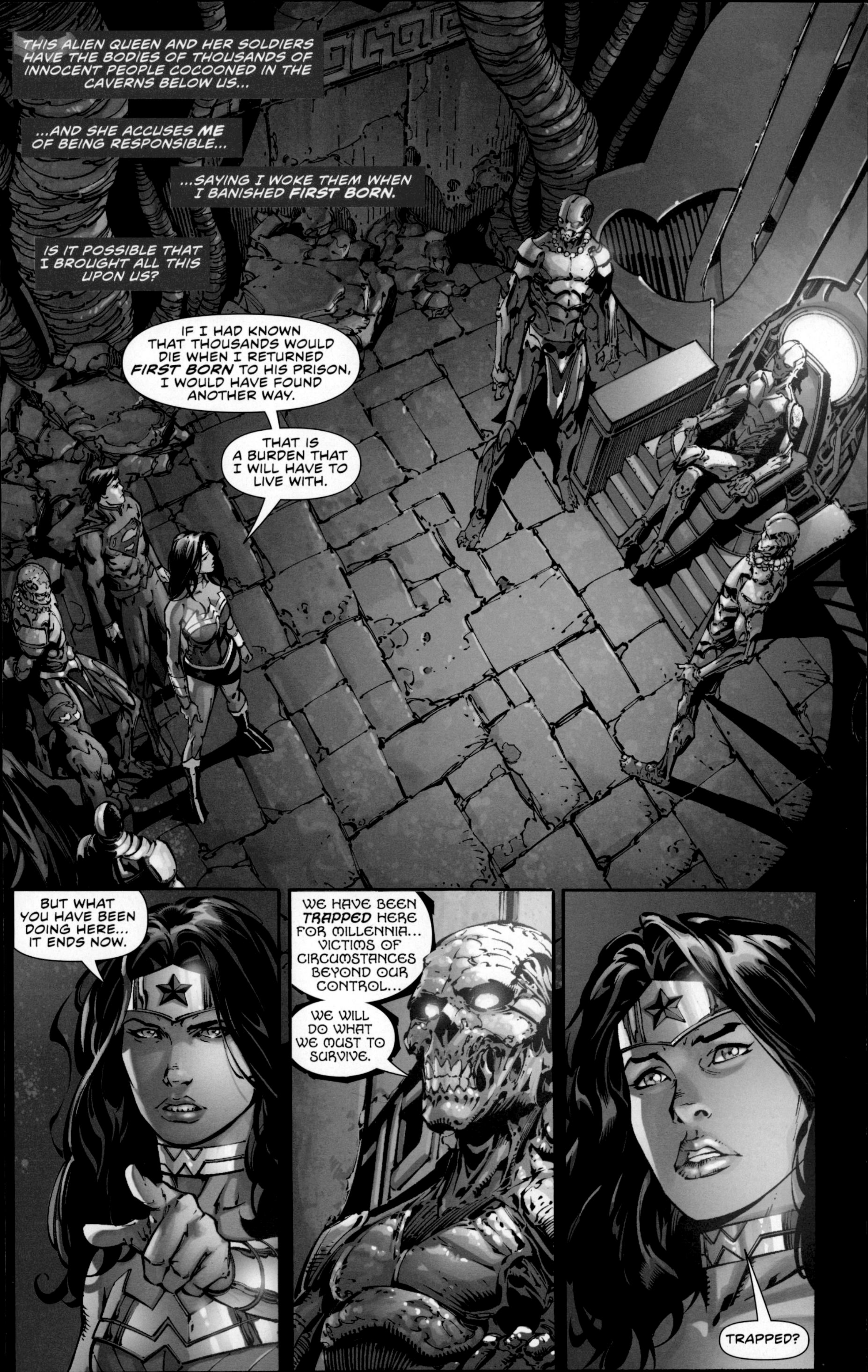
THIS ALIEN QUEEN AND HER SOLDIERS HAVE THE BODIES OF THOUSANDS OF INNOCENT PEOPLE COCOONED IN THE CAVERNS BELOW US...
...AND SHE ACCUSES ME OF BEING RESPONSIBLE...
...SAYING I WOKE THEM WHEN I BANISHED FIRST BORN.
IS IT POSSIBLE THAT I BROUGHT ALL THIS UPON US?
IF I HAD KNOWN THAT THOUSANDS WOULD DIE WHEN I RETURNED FIRST BORN TO HIS PRISON, I WOULD HAVE FOUND ANOTHER WAY.
THAT IS A BURDEN THAT I WILL HAVE TO LIVE WITH.
BUT WHAT YOU HAVE BEEN DOING HERE... IT ENDS NOW.
WE HAVE BEEN TRAPPED HERE FOR MILLENNIA... VICTIMS OF CIRCUMSTANCES BEYOND OUR CONTROL...
WE WILL DO WHAT WE MUST TO SURVIVE.
TRAPPED?

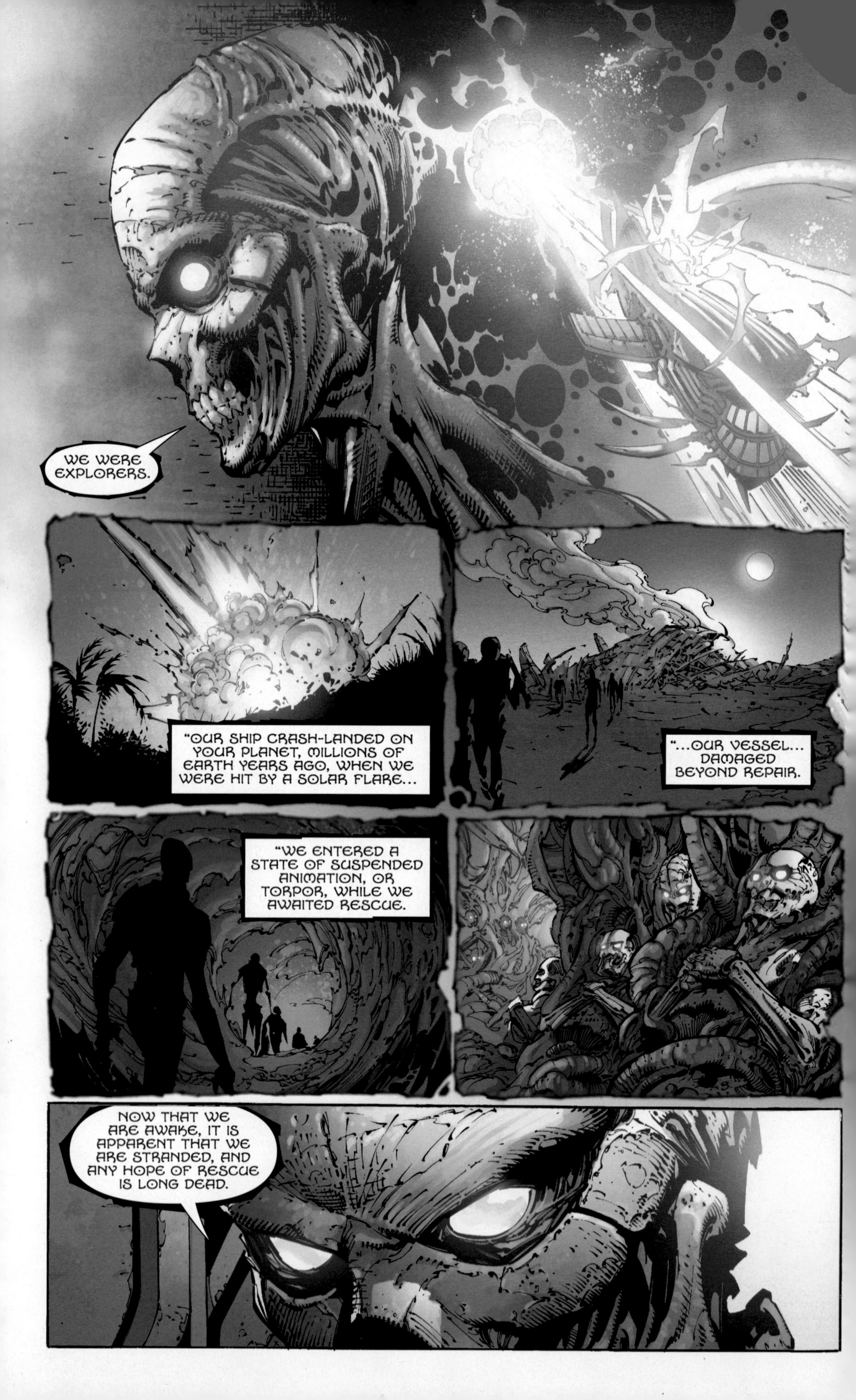
WE WERE EXPLORERS.
"OUR SHIP CRASH-LANDED ON YOUR PLANET, MILLIONS OF EARTH YEARS AGO, WHEN WE WERE HIT BY A SOLAR FLARE...
"...OUR VESSEL... DAMAGED BEYOND REPAIR.
"WE ENTERED A STATE OF SUSPENDED ANIMATION, OR TORPOR, WHILE WE AWAITED RESCUE.
NOW THAT WE ARE AWAKE, IT IS APPARENT THAT WE ARE STRANDED, AND ANY HOPE OF RESCUE IS LONG DEAD.

THAT DOESN'T EXCUSE WHAT YOU HAVE DONE.

YOU ARE MISTAKEN IF YOU THINK WE WILL NOW SIT BACK AND WATCH OUR PEOPLE DIE. WE WILL DO *WHATEVER* IS NECESSARY.

WHAT IF IT *WASN'T* NECESSARY? WHAT IF YOU COULD GO HOME AGAIN? WOULD YOU EVEN WANT TO?

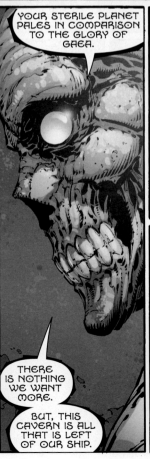

YOUR STERILE PLANET PALES IN COMPARISON TO THE GLORY OF GAEA.

THERE IS NOTHING WE WANT MORE.

BUT, THIS CAVERN IS ALL THAT IS LEFT OF OUR SHIP.

SO MUCH HAS CHANGED SINCE YOU CRASH-LANDED.

YOU ARE NOT THE ONLY ONE HERE FROM ANOTHER PLANET.

WHAT IF YOU *COULD* GO HOME AGAIN?

WE ARE LISTENING.

CYBORG, IS IT POSSIBLE?

IT'S WORTH A TRY, BUT I'LL NEED TO RUN A FEW SCANS OF THE SHIP FIRST TO KNOW FOR SURE.

THE ESSENTIAL COMPONENTS LIKE THE COMPUTERS AND NAVIGATION SYSTEM ARE ALL STILL INTACT...

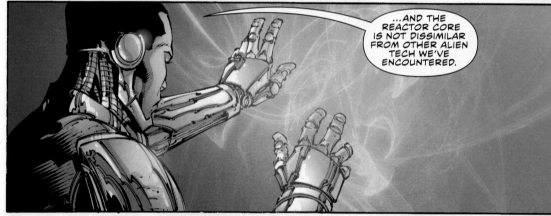

...AND THE REACTOR CORE IS NOT DISSIMILAR FROM OTHER ALIEN TECH WE'VE ENCOUNTERED.

IT WILL TAKE SOME TIME-- BUT IT CAN BE DONE.

WELL?

WE DID NOT DARE TO HOPE THAT IT COULD BE POSSIBLE... TO GO HOME AGAIN.

THANK YOU.

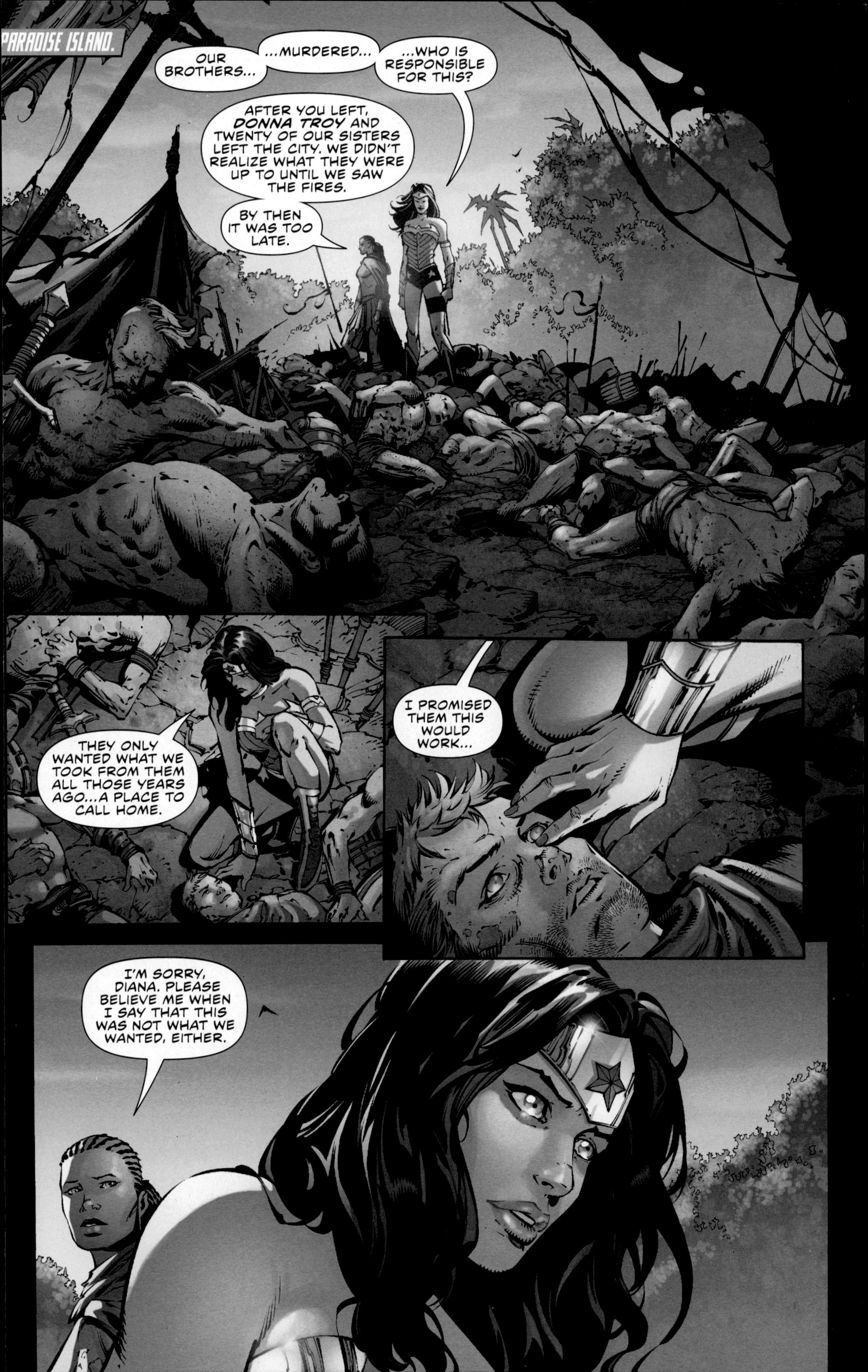
PARADISE ISLAND.
OUR BROTHERS...
...MURDERED...
...WHO IS RESPONSIBLE FOR THIS?
AFTER YOU LEFT, DONNA TROY AND TWENTY OF OUR SISTERS LEFT THE CITY. WE DIDN'T REALIZE WHAT THEY WERE UP TO UNTIL WE SAW THE FIRES.
BY THEN IT WAS TOO LATE.
THEY ONLY WANTED WHAT WE TOOK FROM THEM ALL THOSE YEARS AGO...A PLACE TO CALL HOME.
I PROMISED THEM THIS WOULD WORK...
I'M SORRY, DIANA. PLEASE BELIEVE ME WHEN I SAY THAT THIS WAS NOT WHAT WE WANTED, EITHER.

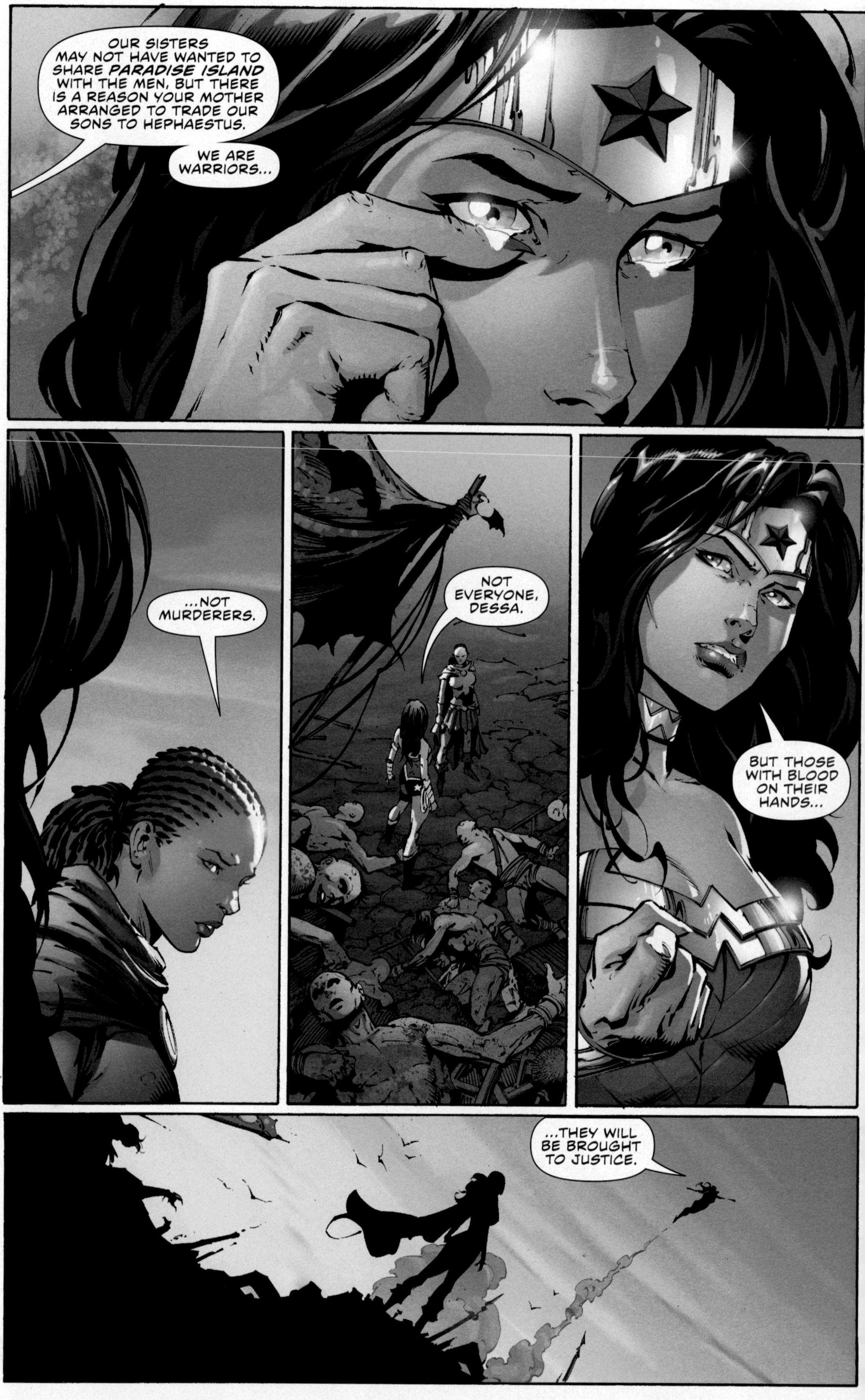
OUR SISTERS MAY NOT HAVE WANTED TO SHARE *PARADISE ISLAND* WITH THE MEN, BUT THERE IS A REASON YOUR MOTHER ARRANGED TO TRADE OUR SONS TO HEPHAESTUS.
WE ARE WARRIORS...
...NOT MURDERERS.
NOT EVERYONE, DESSA.
BUT THOSE WITH BLOOD ON THEIR HANDS...
...THEY WILL BE BROUGHT TO JUSTICE.

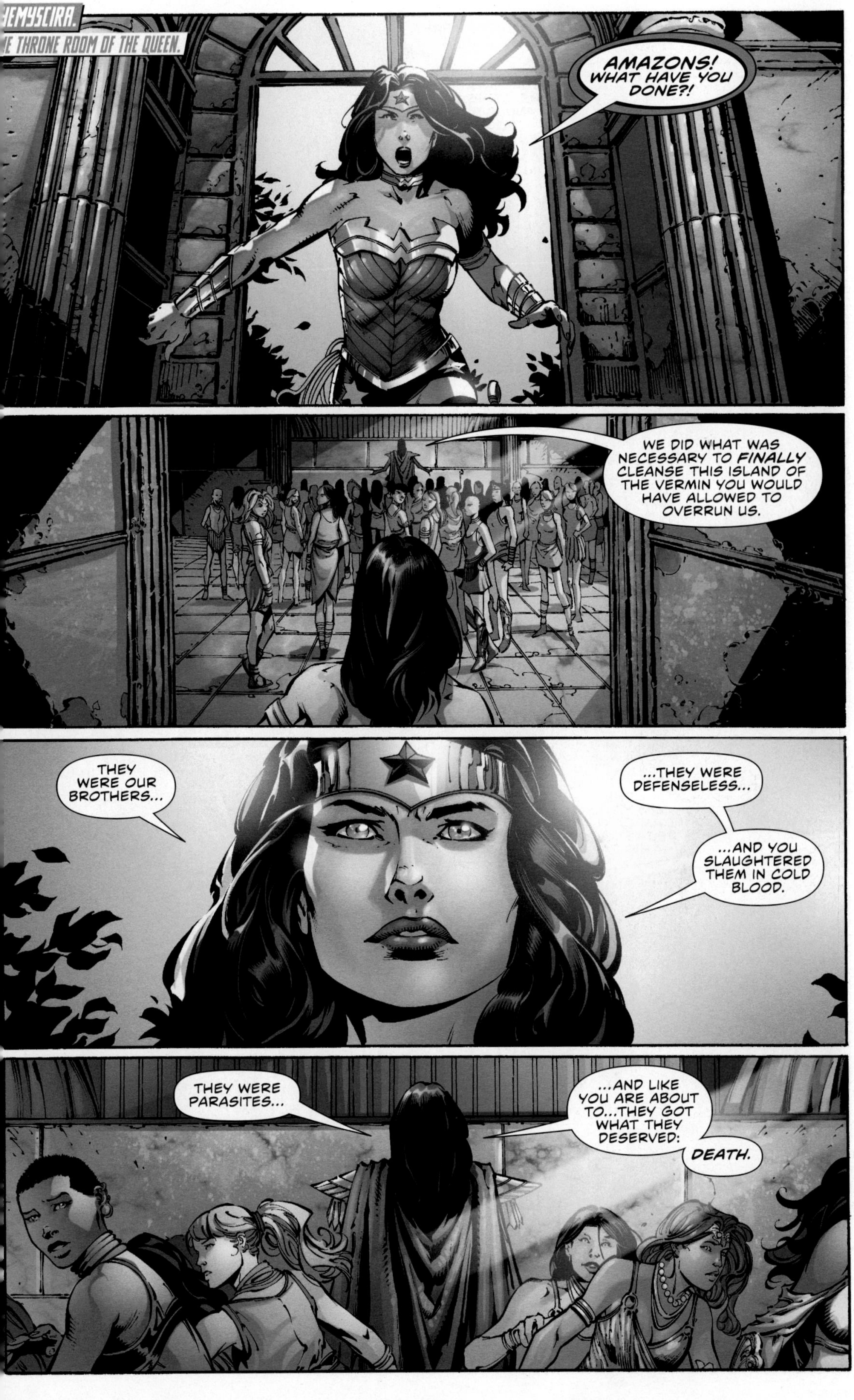
HEMYSCIRA.
E THRONE ROOM OF THE QUEEN.
AMAZONS! WHAT HAVE YOU DONE?!
WE DID WHAT WAS NECESSARY TO FINALLY CLEANSE THIS ISLAND OF THE VERMIN YOU WOULD HAVE ALLOWED TO OVERRUN US.
THEY WERE OUR BROTHERS...
...THEY WERE DEFENSELESS...
...AND YOU SLAUGHTERED THEM IN COLD BLOOD.
THEY WERE PARASITES...
...AND LIKE YOU ARE ABOUT TO...THEY GOT WHAT THEY DESERVED:
DEATH.

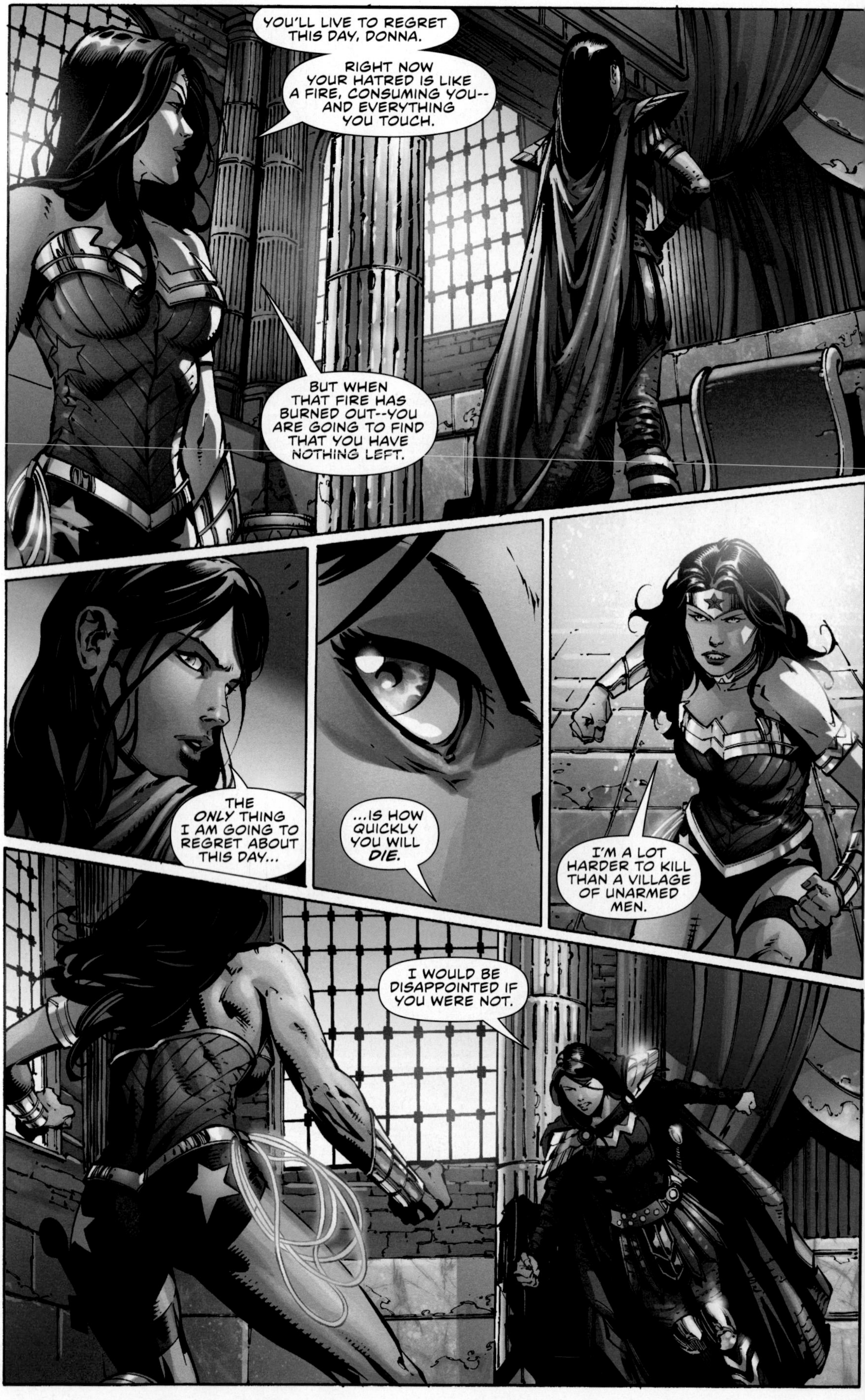
YOU'LL LIVE TO REGRET THIS DAY, DONNA.
RIGHT NOW YOUR HATRED IS LIKE A FIRE, CONSUMING YOU-- AND EVERYTHING YOU TOUCH.
BUT WHEN THAT FIRE HAS BURNED OUT--YOU ARE GOING TO FIND THAT YOU HAVE NOTHING LEFT.
THE ONLY THING I AM GOING TO REGRET ABOUT THIS DAY...
...IS HOW QUICKLY YOU WILL DIE.
I'M A LOT HARDER TO KILL THAN A VILLAGE OF UNARMED MEN.
I WOULD BE DISAPPOINTED IF YOU WERE NOT.

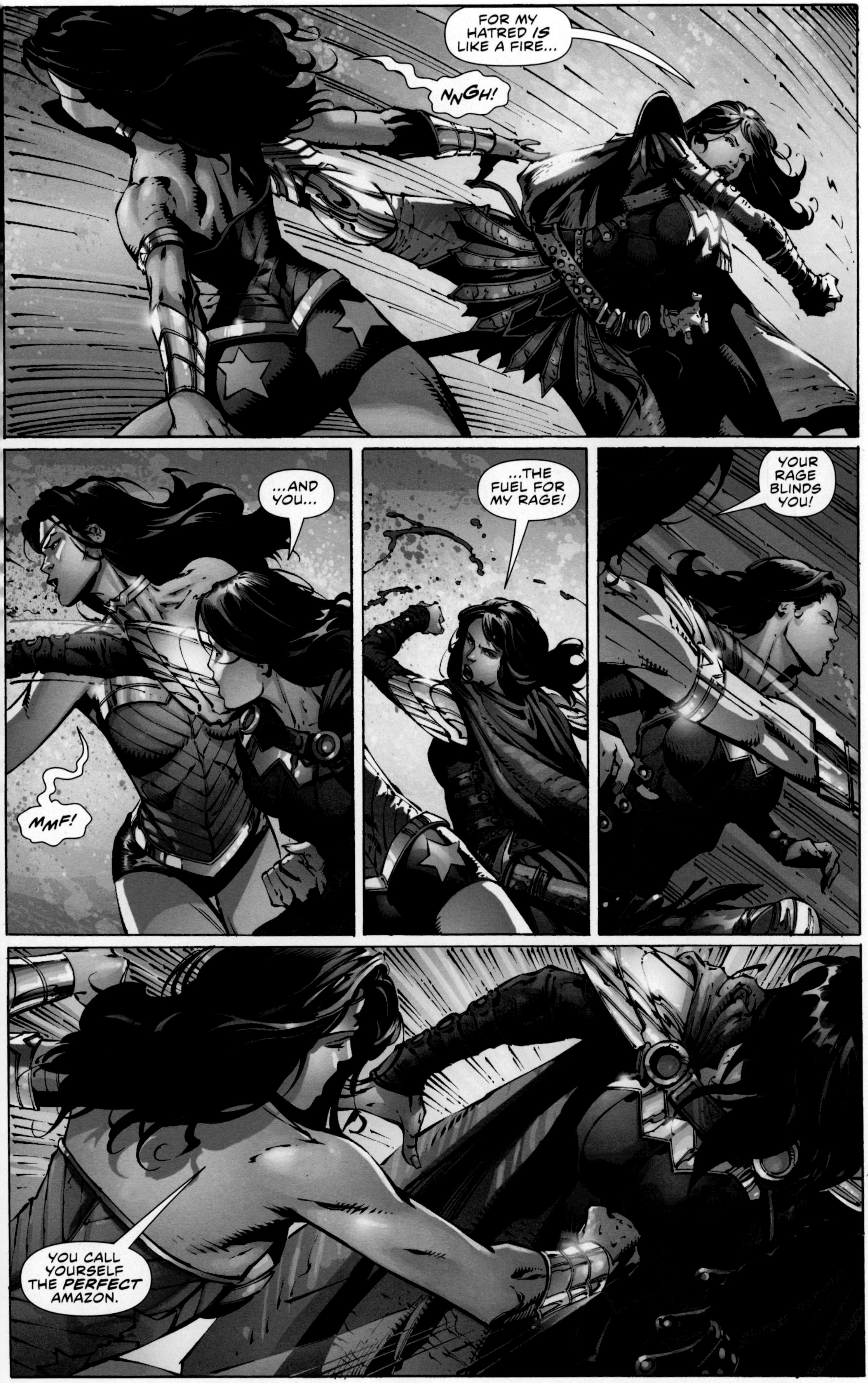
FOR MY HATRED *IS* LIKE A FIRE...
NNGH!
...AND YOU...
MMF!
...THE FUEL FOR MY RAGE!
YOUR RAGE BLINDS YOU!
YOU CALL YOURSELF THE *PERFECT* AMAZON.

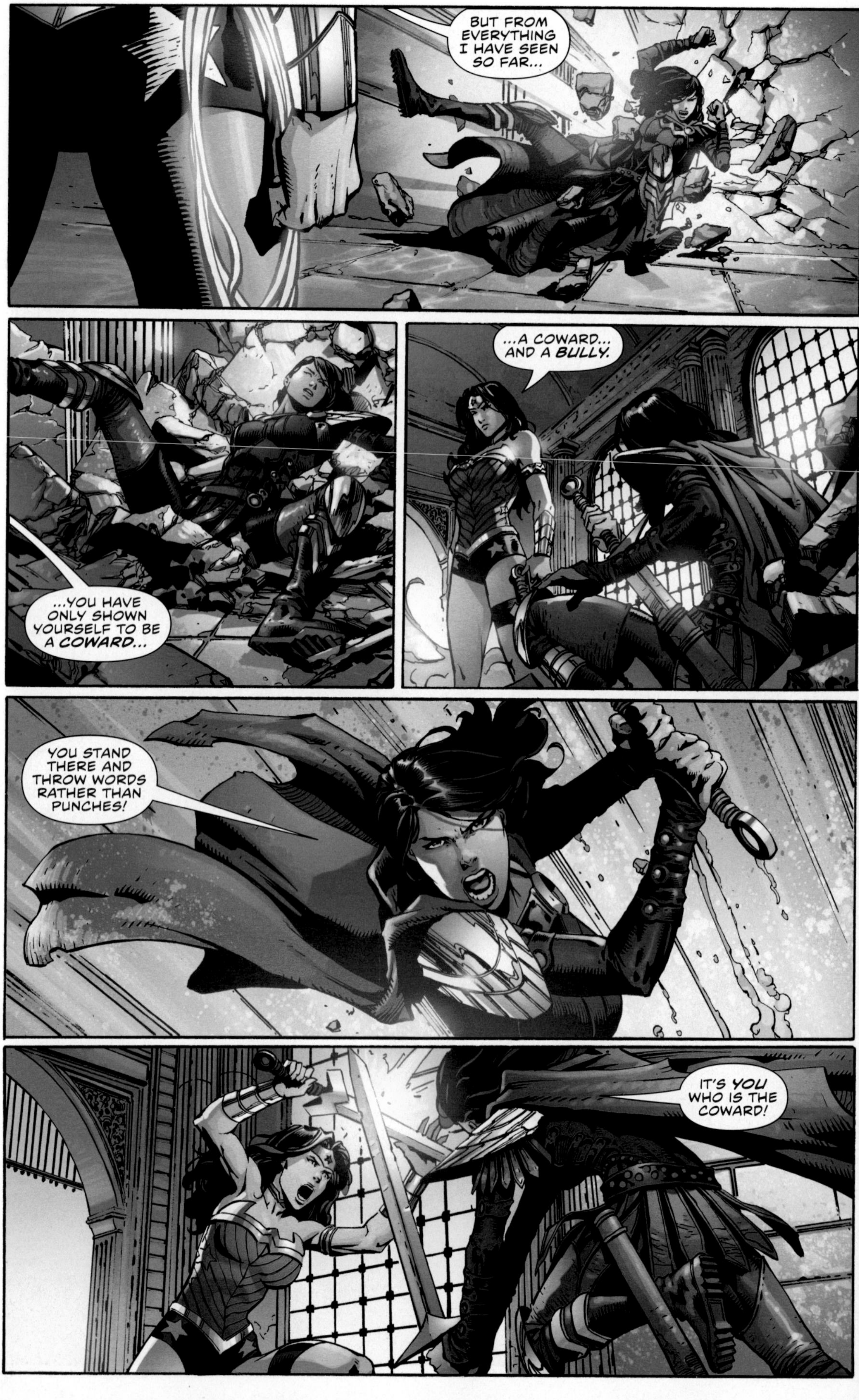
BUT FROM EVERYTHING I HAVE SEEN SO FAR...
...YOU HAVE ONLY SHOWN YOURSELF TO BE A COWARD...
...A COWARD... AND A BULLY.
YOU STAND THERE AND THROW WORDS RATHER THAN PUNCHES!
IT'S YOU WHO IS THE COWARD!

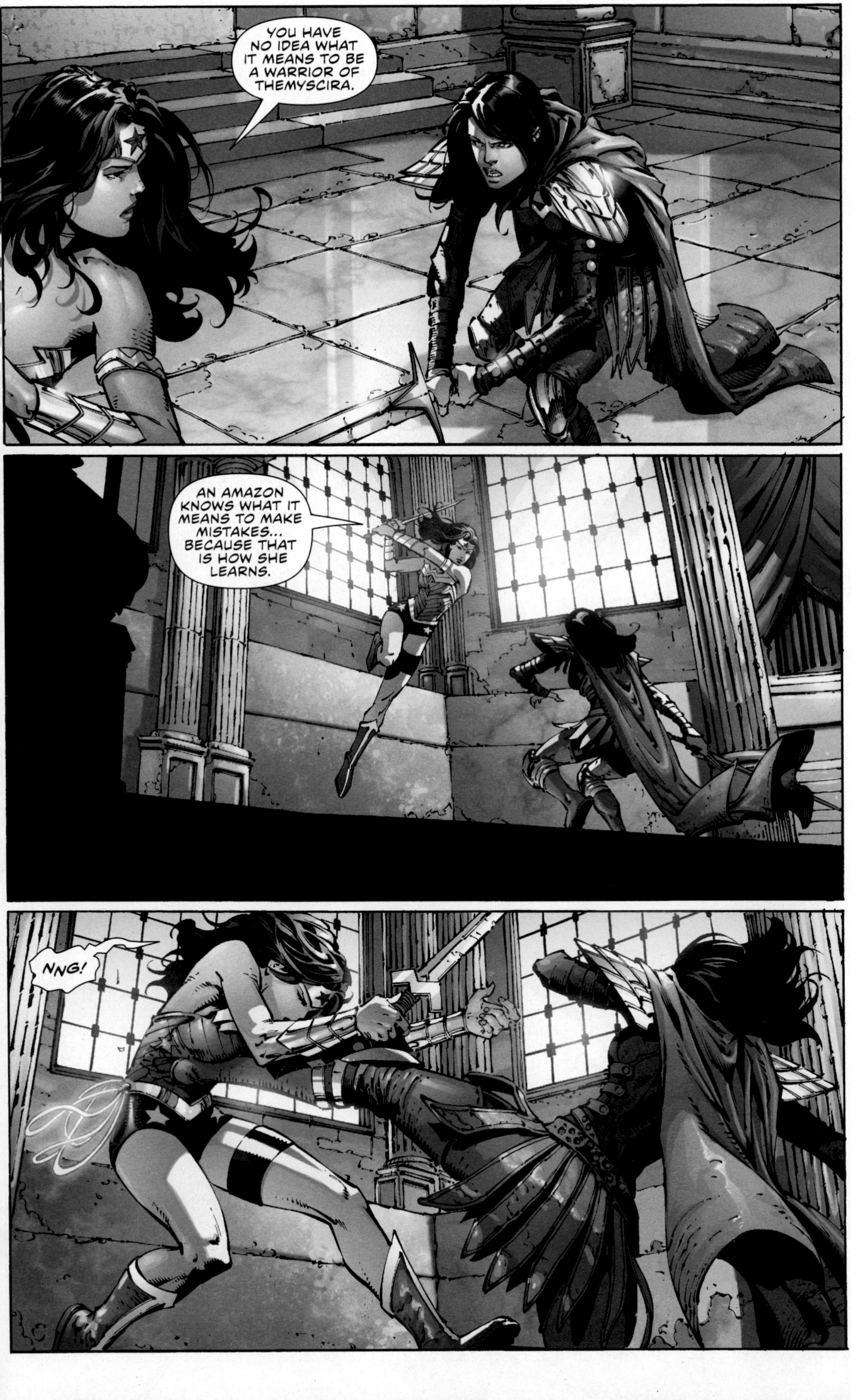
YOU HAVE NO IDEA WHAT IT MEANS TO BE A WARRIOR OF THEMYSCIRA.
AN AMAZON KNOWS WHAT IT MEANS TO MAKE MISTAKES... BECAUSE THAT IS HOW SHE LEARNS.
NNG!

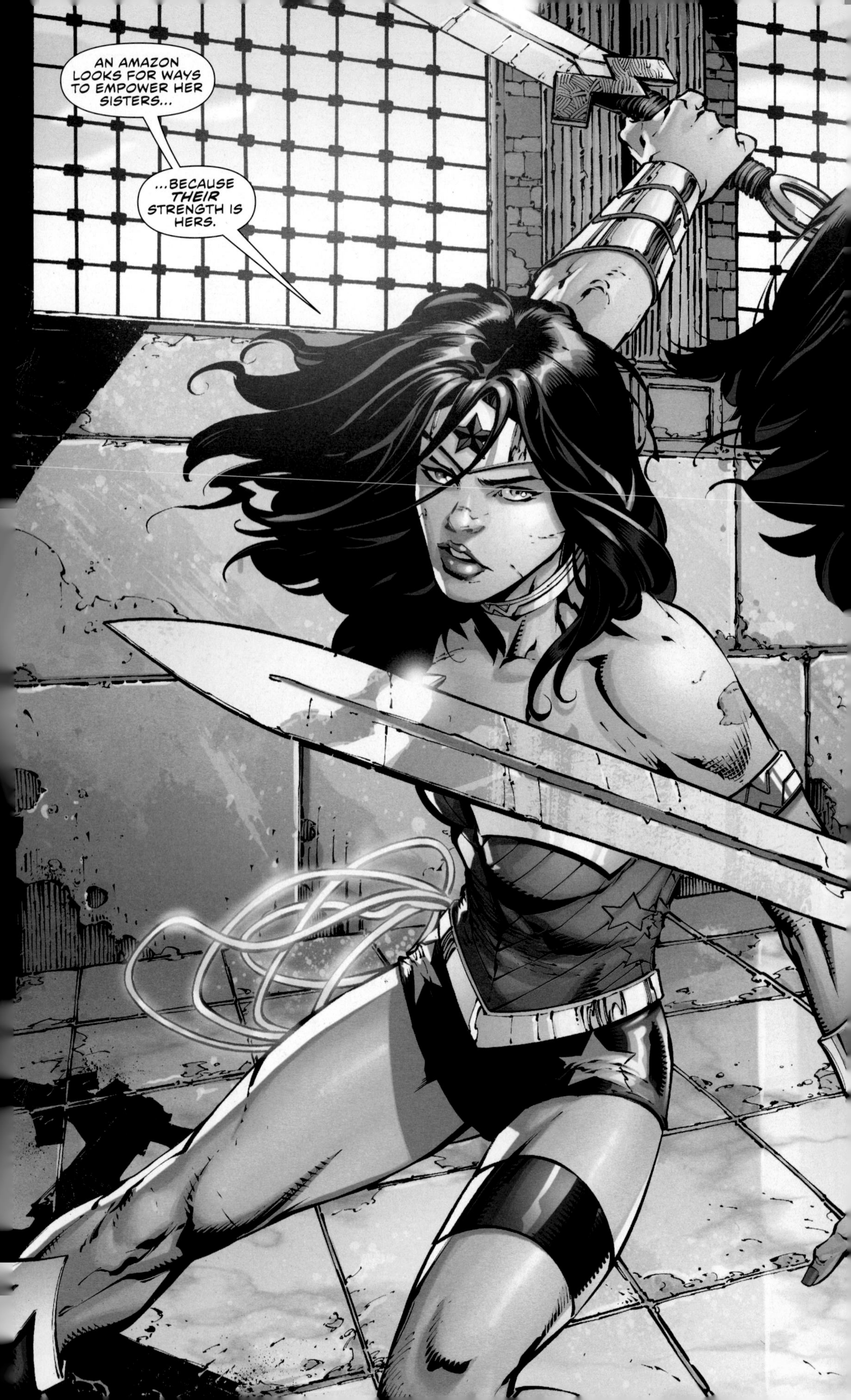
AN AMAZON LOOKS FOR WAYS TO EMPOWER HER SISTERS...
...BECAUSE *THEIR* STRENGTH IS HERS.

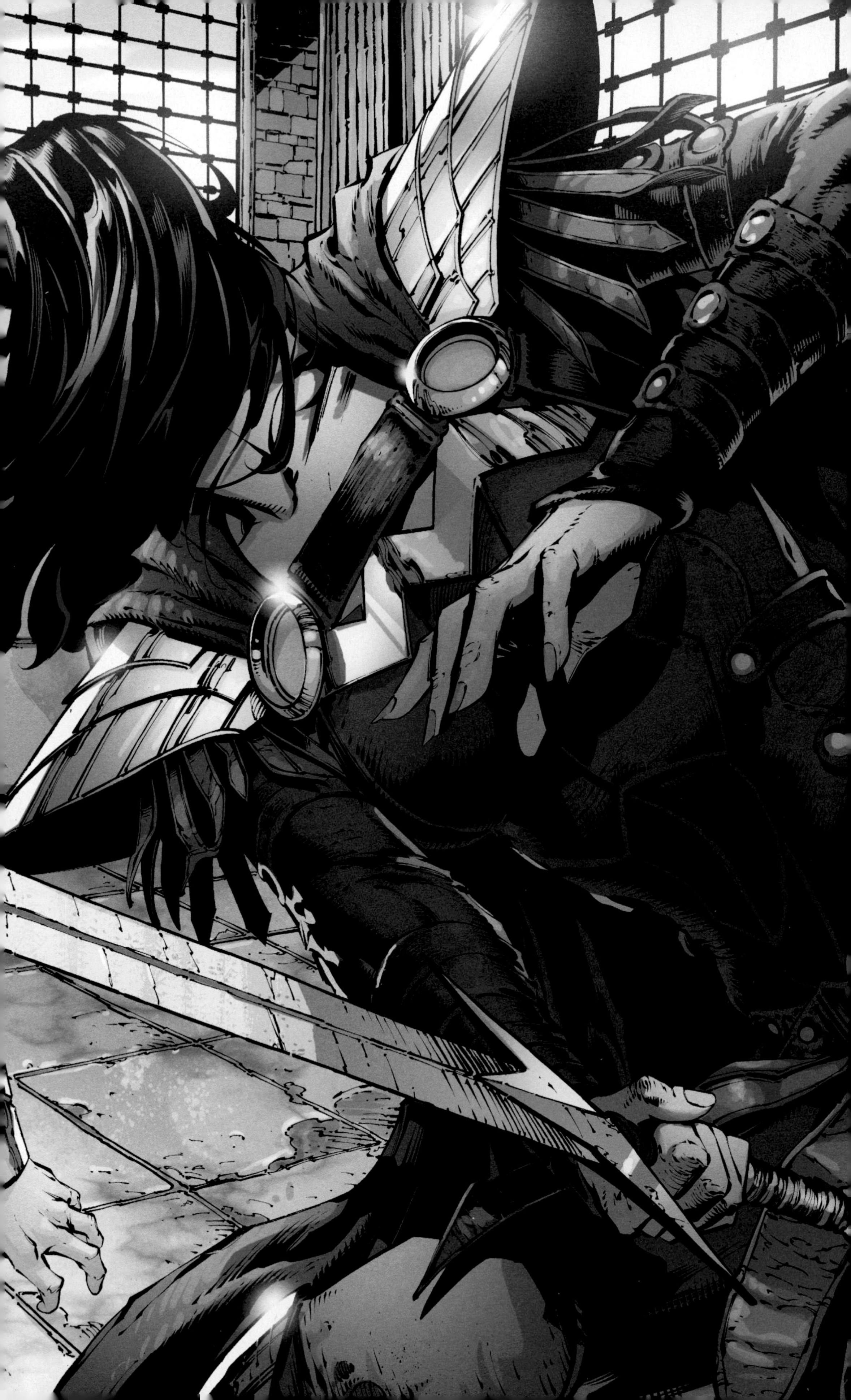

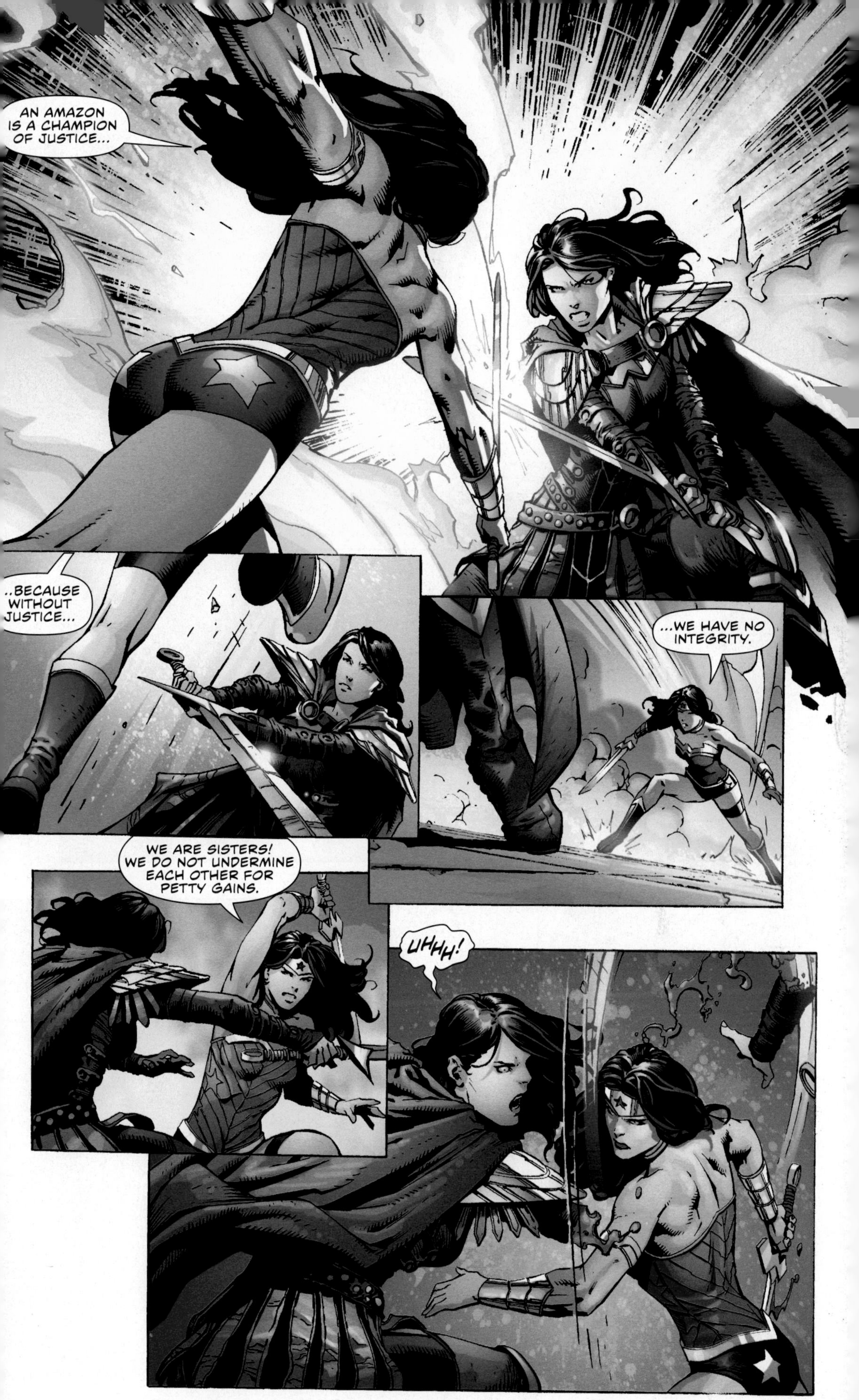
AN AMAZON IS A CHAMPION OF JUSTICE...
..BECAUSE WITHOUT JUSTICE...
...WE HAVE NO INTEGRITY.
WE ARE SISTERS! WE DO NOT UNDERMINE EACH OTHER FOR PETTY GAINS.
UHHH!

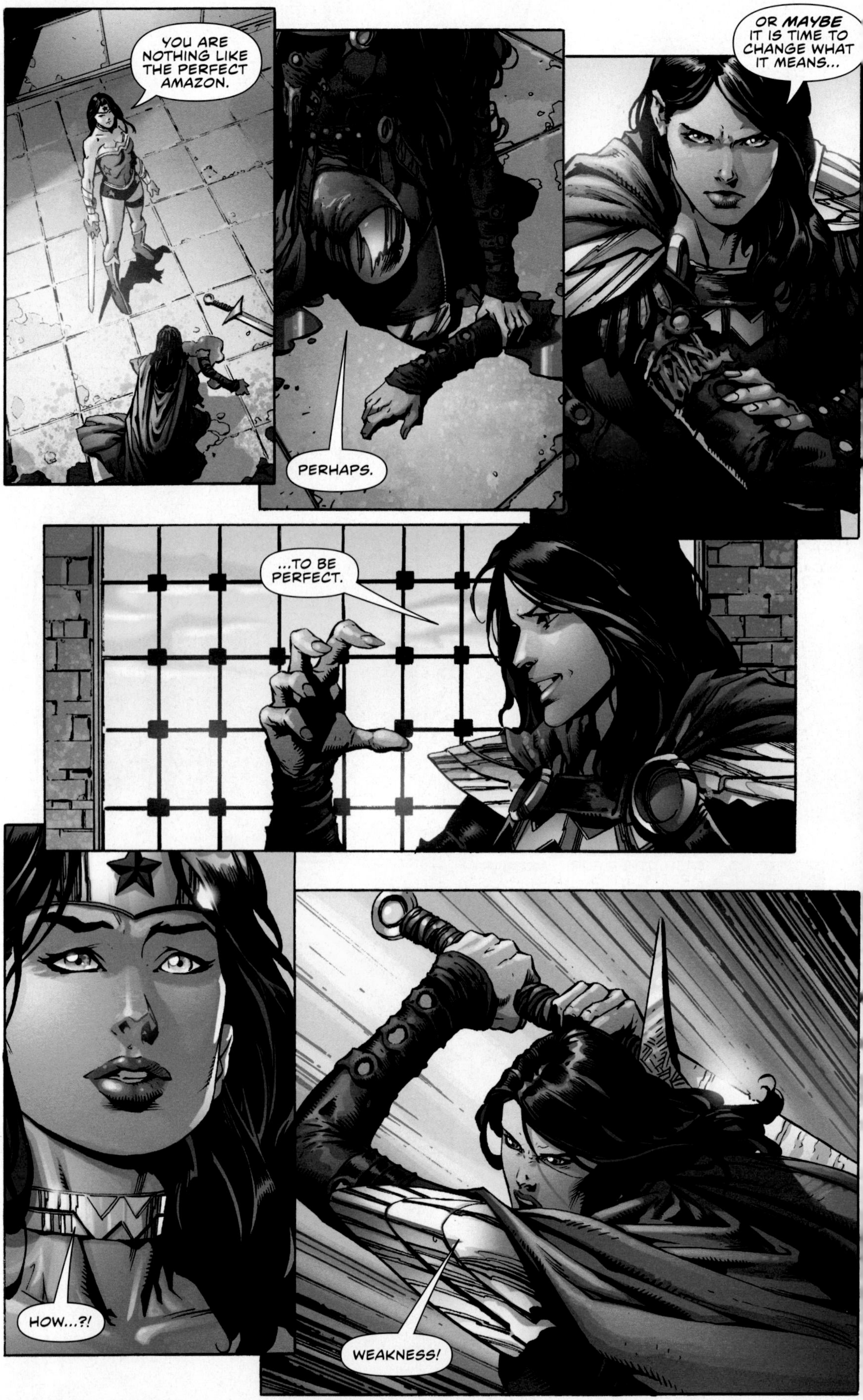
YOU ARE NOTHING LIKE THE PERFECT AMAZON.
PERHAPS.
OR MAYBE IT IS TIME TO CHANGE WHAT IT MEANS...
...TO BE PERFECT.
HOW...?!
WEAKNESS!

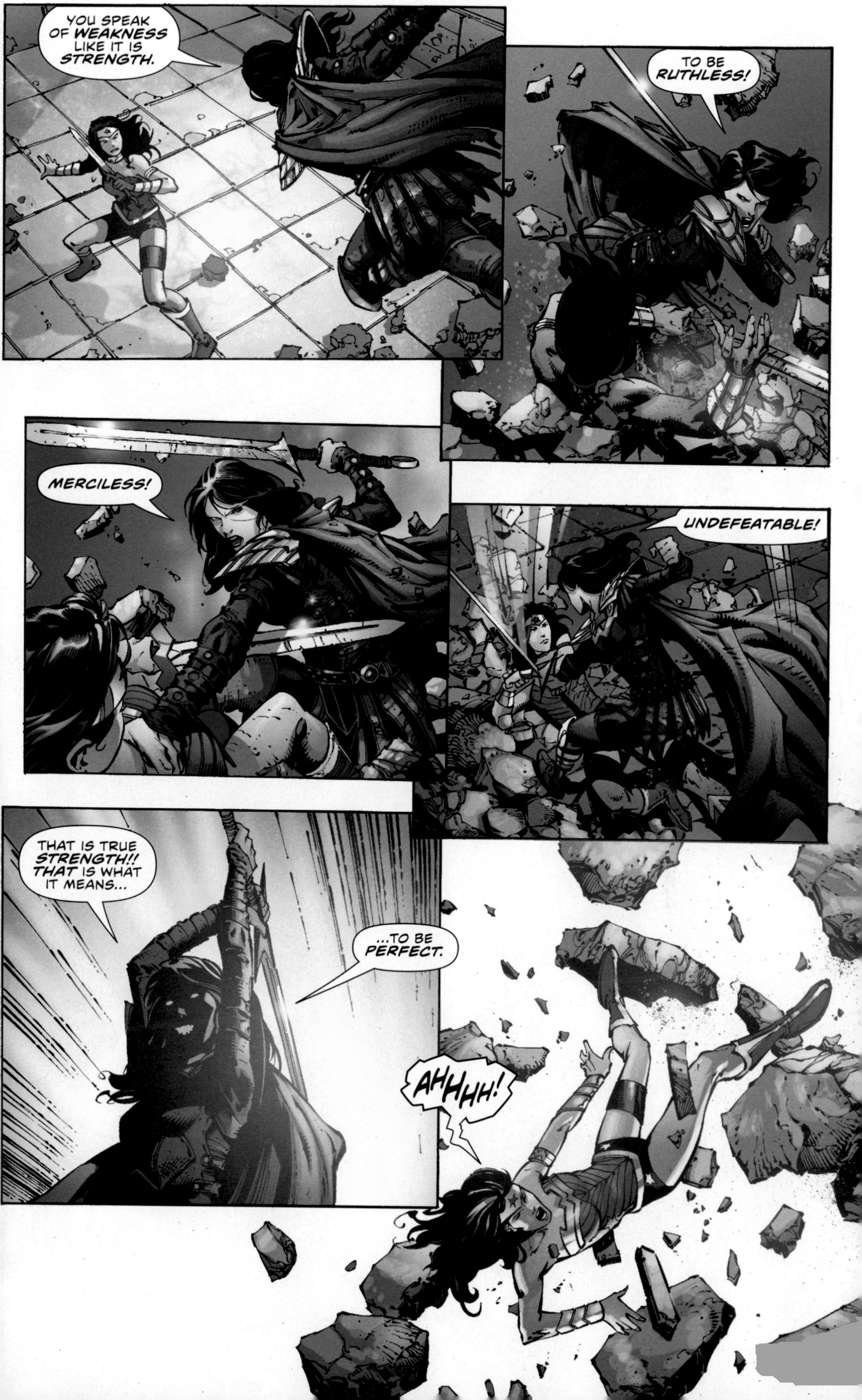
YOU SPEAK OF WEAKNESS LIKE IT IS STRENGTH.
TO BE RUTHLESS!
MERCILESS!
UNDEFEATABLE!
THAT IS TRUE STRENGTH!! THAT IS WHAT IT MEANS...
...TO BE PERFECT.
AHHHH!

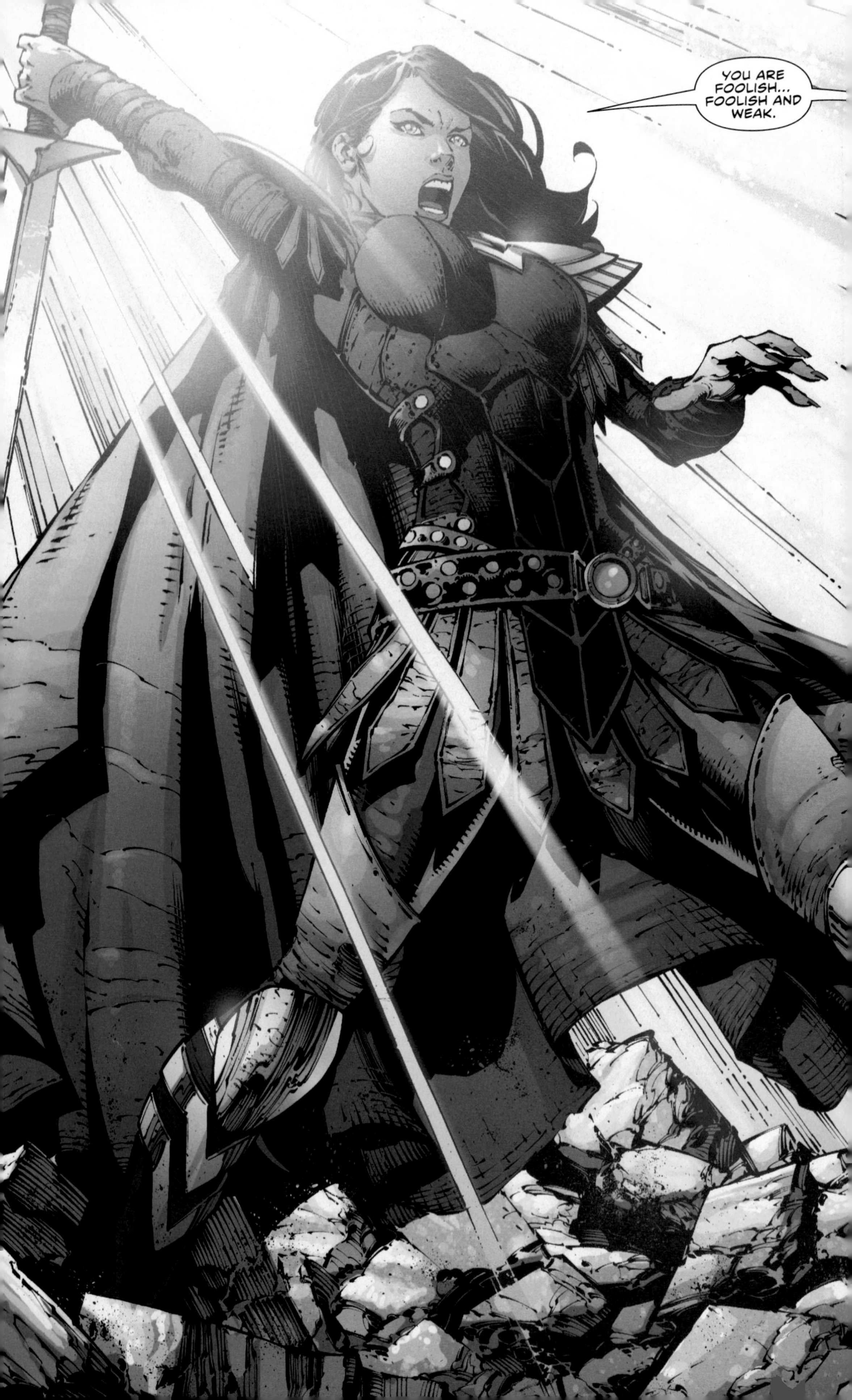
YOU ARE FOOLISH... FOOLISH AND WEAK.

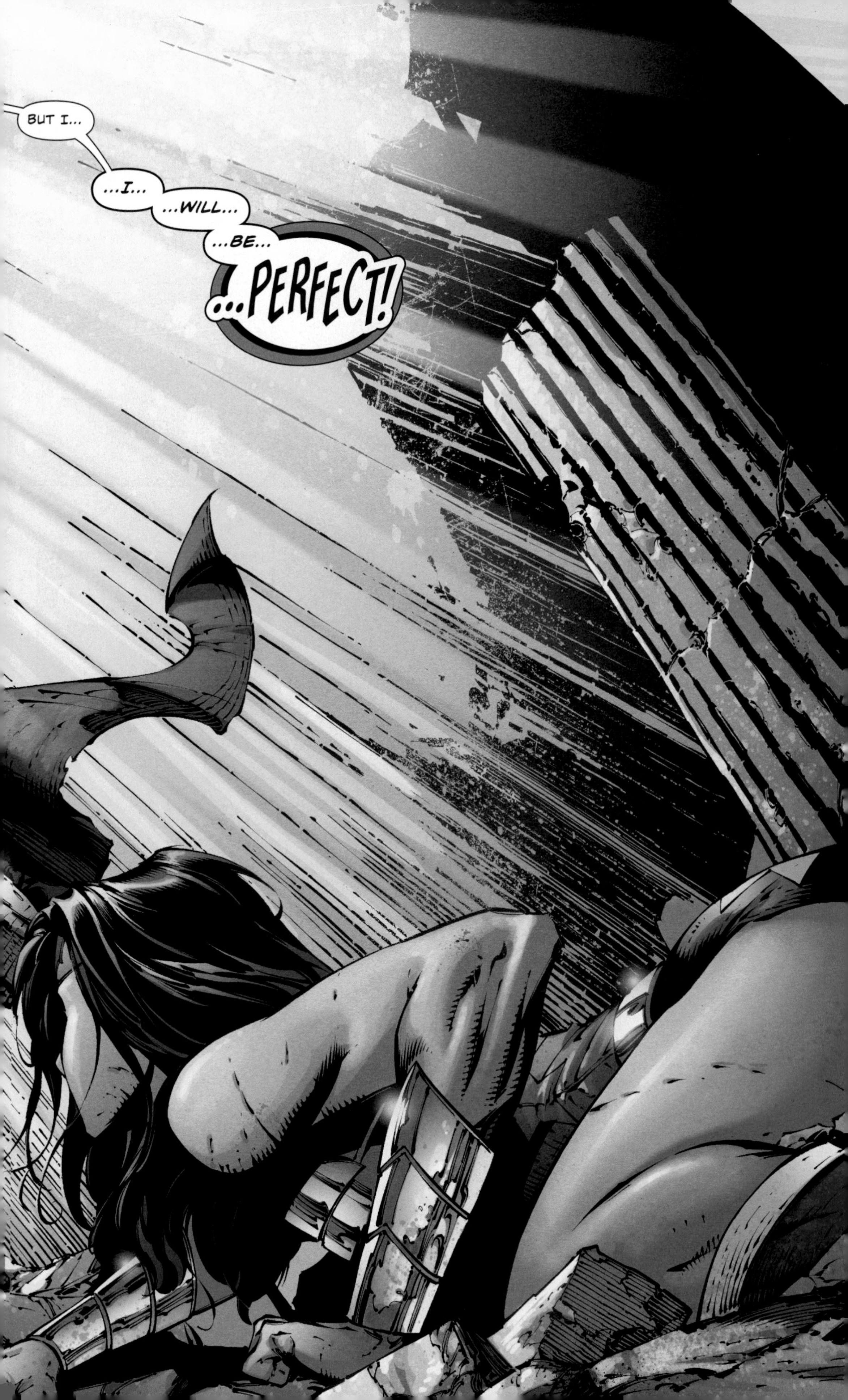
BUT I...
...I...
...WILL...
...BE...
...PERFECT!

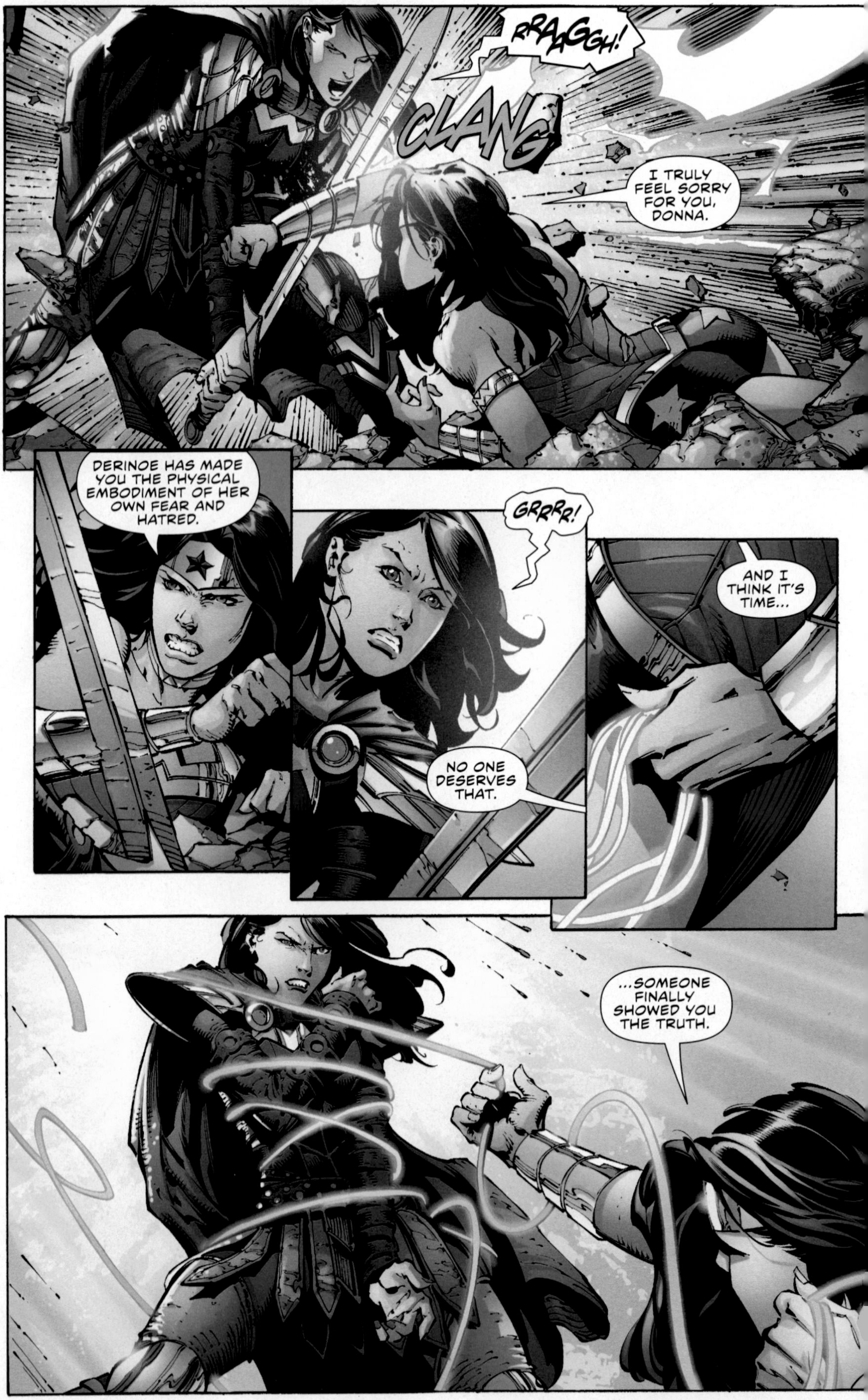

RRAAGGH!
CLANG
I TRULY FEEL SORRY FOR YOU, DONNA.
DERINOE HAS MADE YOU THE PHYSICAL EMBODIMENT OF HER OWN FEAR AND HATRED.
GRRRR!
NO ONE DESERVES THAT.
AND I THINK IT'S TIME...
...SOMEONE FINALLY SHOWED YOU THE TRUTH.

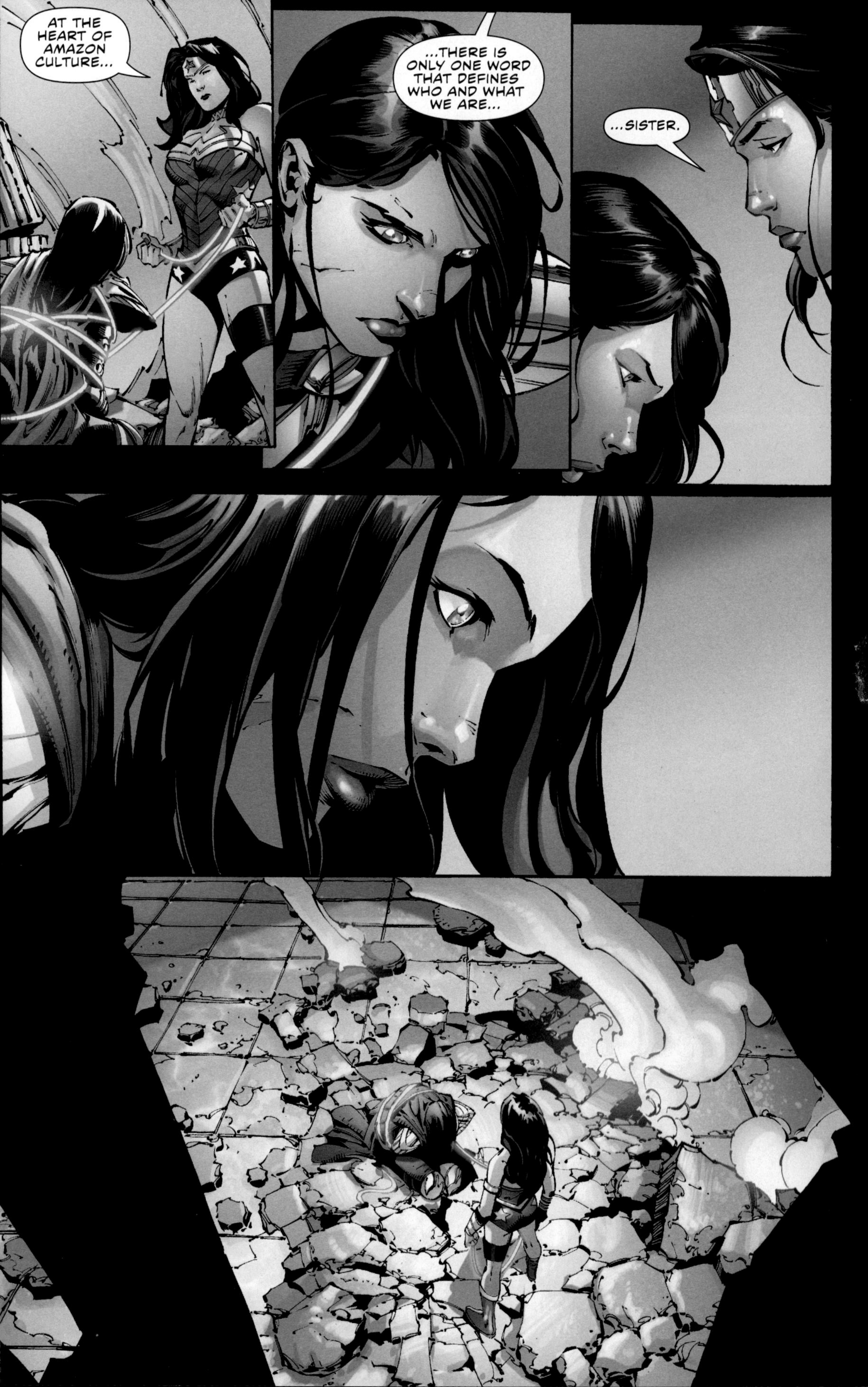
AT THE HEART OF AMAZON CULTURE...
...THERE IS ONLY ONE WORD THAT DEFINES WHO AND WHAT WE ARE...
...SISTER.

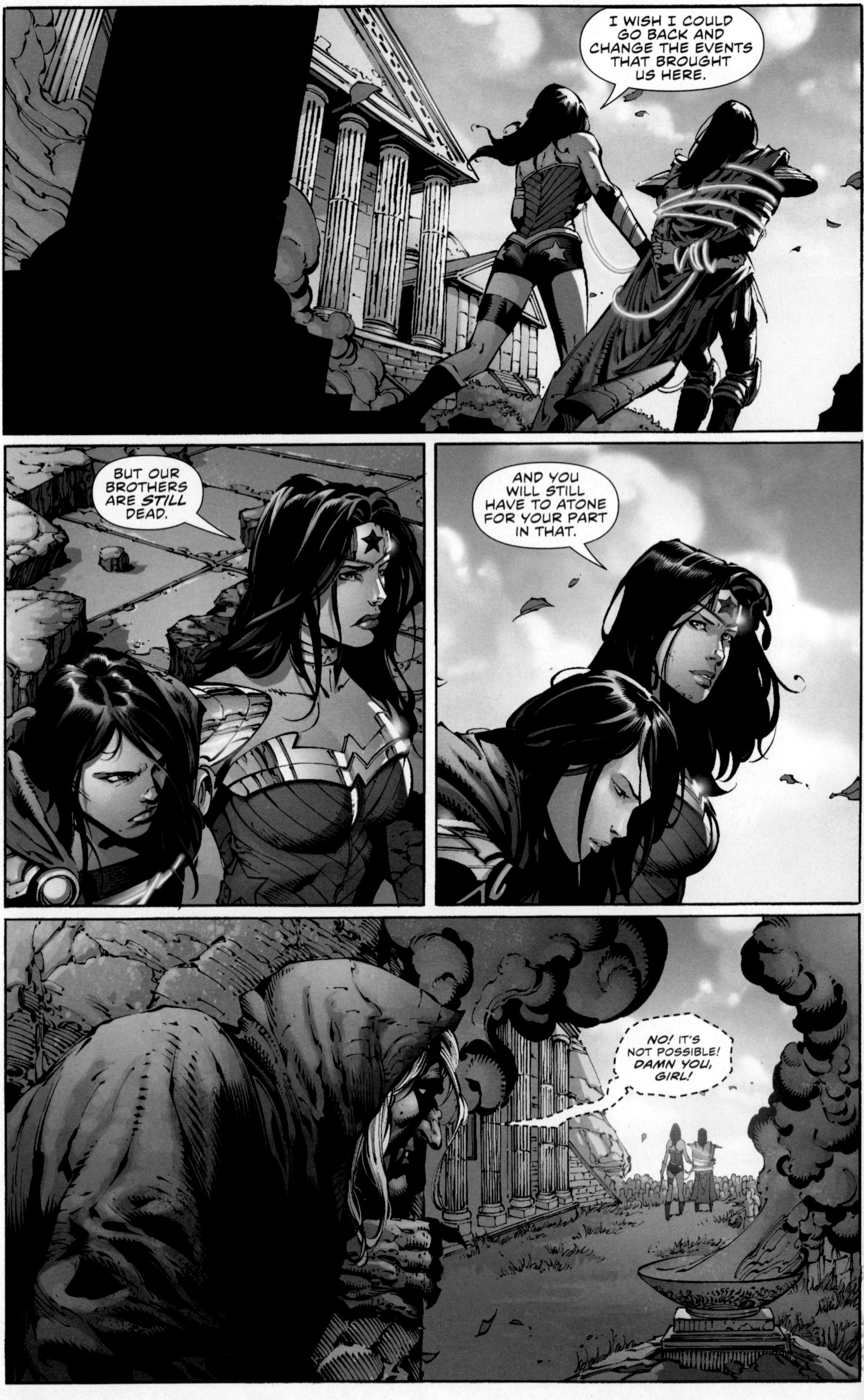
I WISH I COULD GO BACK AND CHANGE THE EVENTS THAT BROUGHT US HERE.
BUT OUR BROTHERS ARE STILL DEAD.
AND YOU WILL STILL HAVE TO ATONE FOR YOUR PART IN THAT.
NO! IT'S NOT POSSIBLE! DAMN YOU, GIRL!

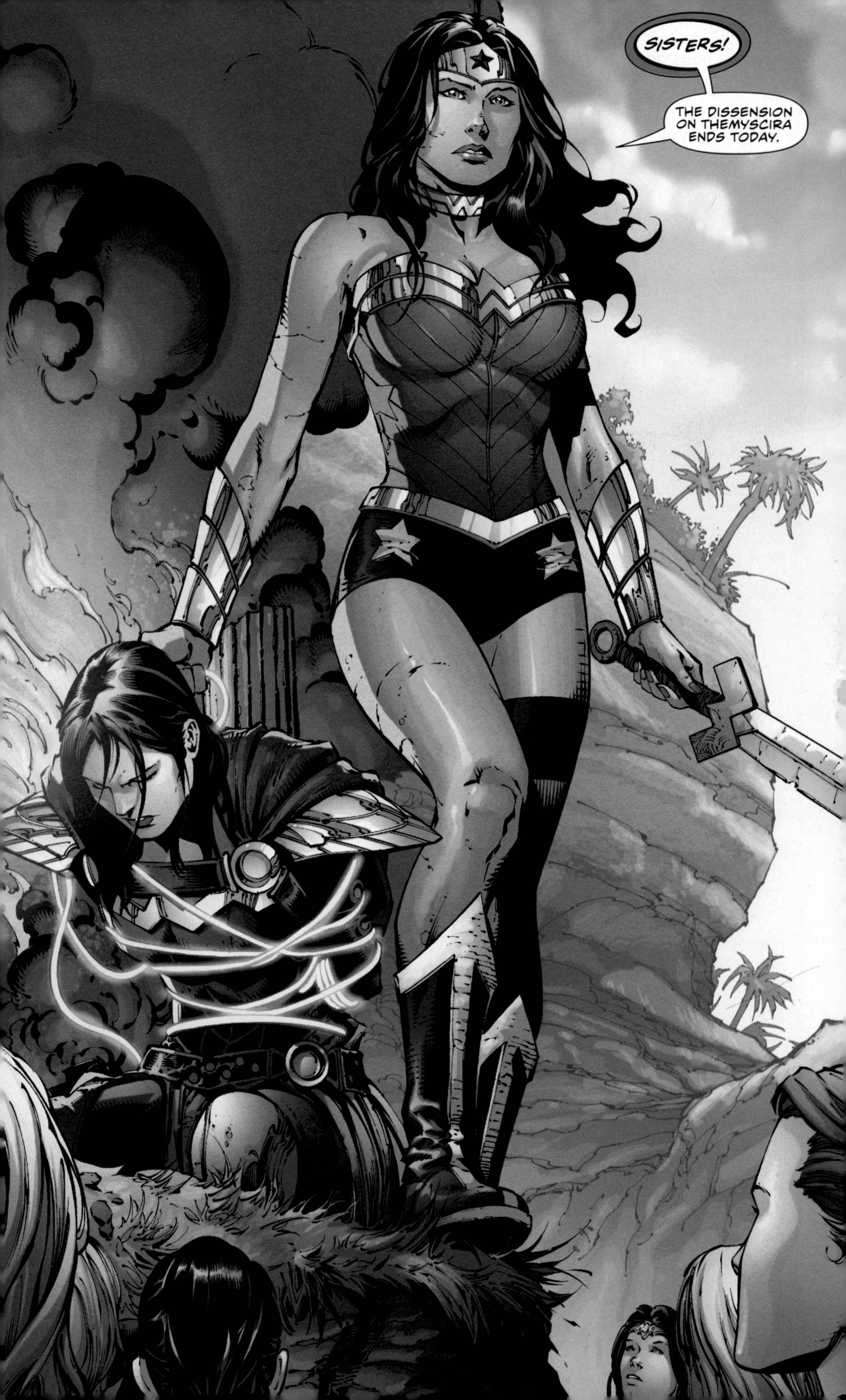
SISTERS!
THE DISSENSION ON THEMYSCIRA ENDS TODAY.

THOSE OF YOU WHO PARTICIPATED IN THE RAID ON THE MEN'S VILLAGE WILL BE BROUGHT TO JUSTICE.

WE HAVE FORGOTTEN *WHO* AND *WHAT* WE ARE.

AN AMAZON OF THEMYSCIRA IS MORE THAN JUST A WARRIOR.

SHE IS A SISTER...

...A MOTHER...

...A LOVER...

...A FRIEND.

SHE DOES NOT RUN FROM HER FEARS...

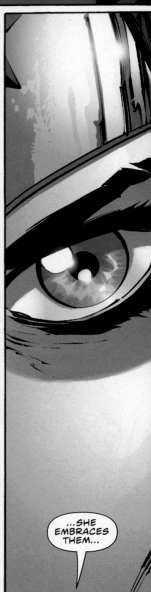

...SHE EMBRACES THEM...

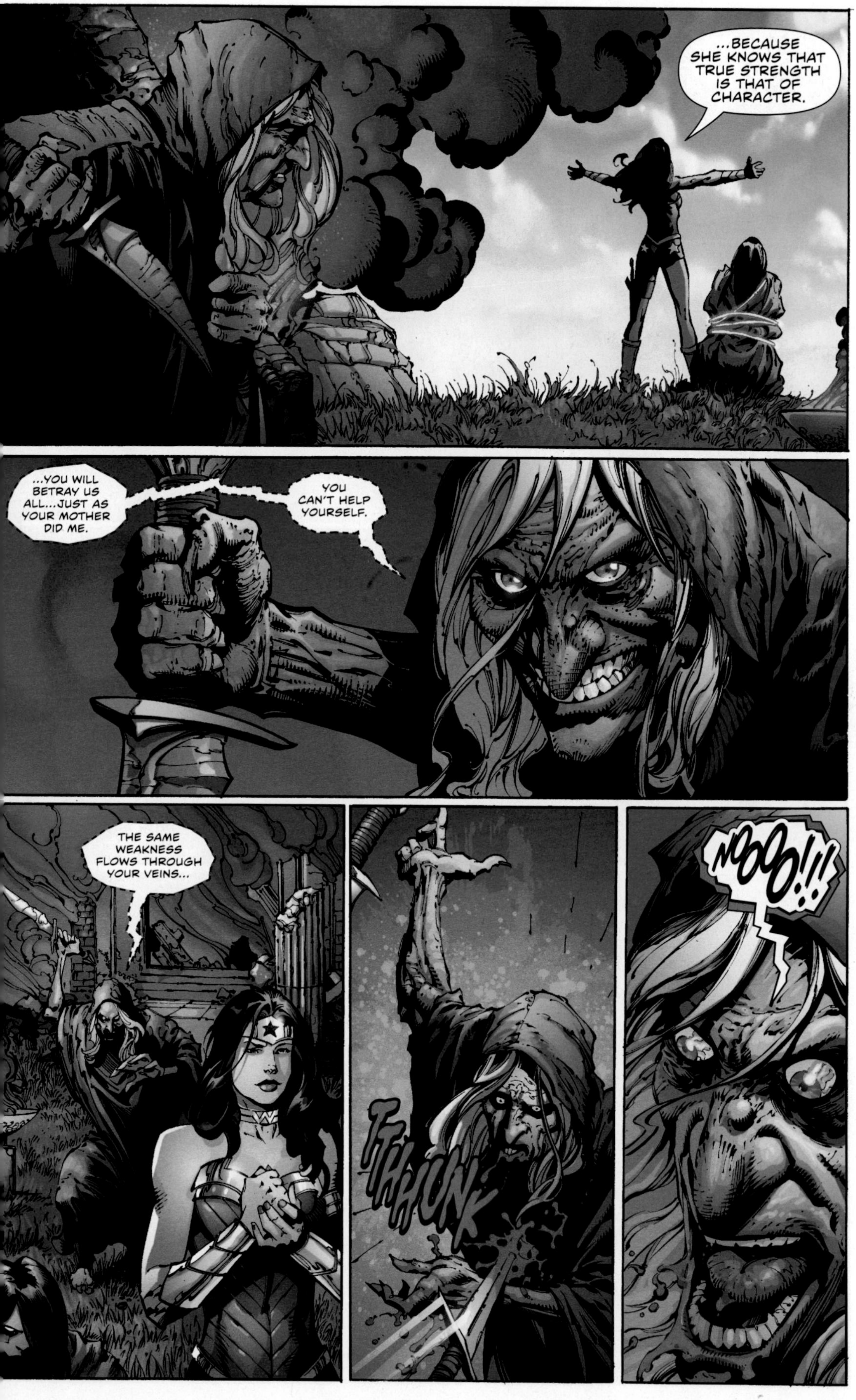
...BECAUSE SHE KNOWS THAT TRUE STRENGTH IS THAT OF CHARACTER.
...YOU WILL BETRAY US ALL...JUST AS YOUR MOTHER DID ME.
YOU CAN'T HELP YOURSELF.
THE SAME WEAKNESS FLOWS THROUGH YOUR VEINS...
TTHHUNK
NOOOO!!!

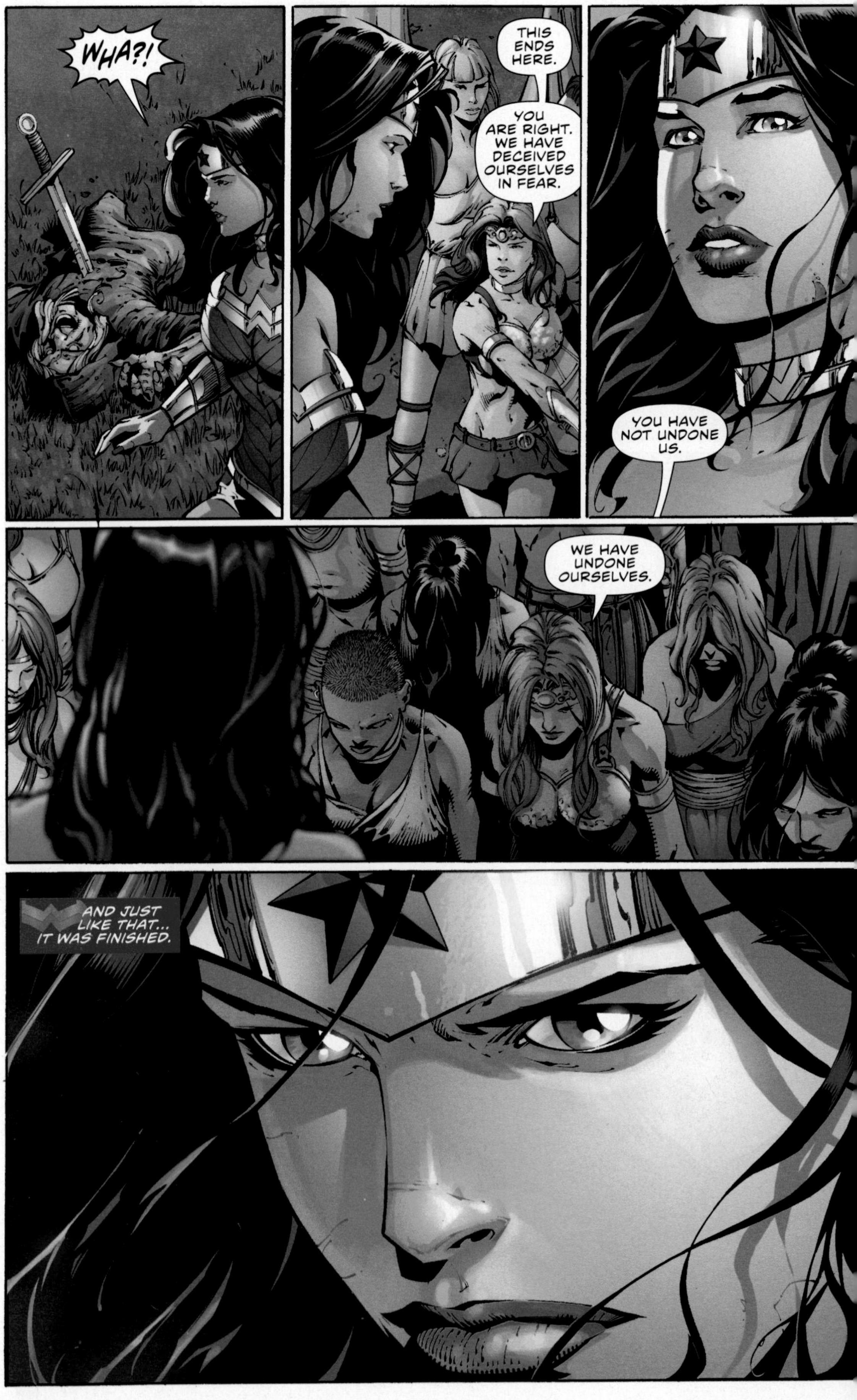
WHA?!
THIS ENDS HERE.
YOU ARE RIGHT. WE HAVE DECEIVED OURSELVES IN FEAR.
YOU HAVE NOT UNDONE US.
WE HAVE UNDONE OURSELVES.
AND JUST LIKE THAT... IT WAS FINISHED.

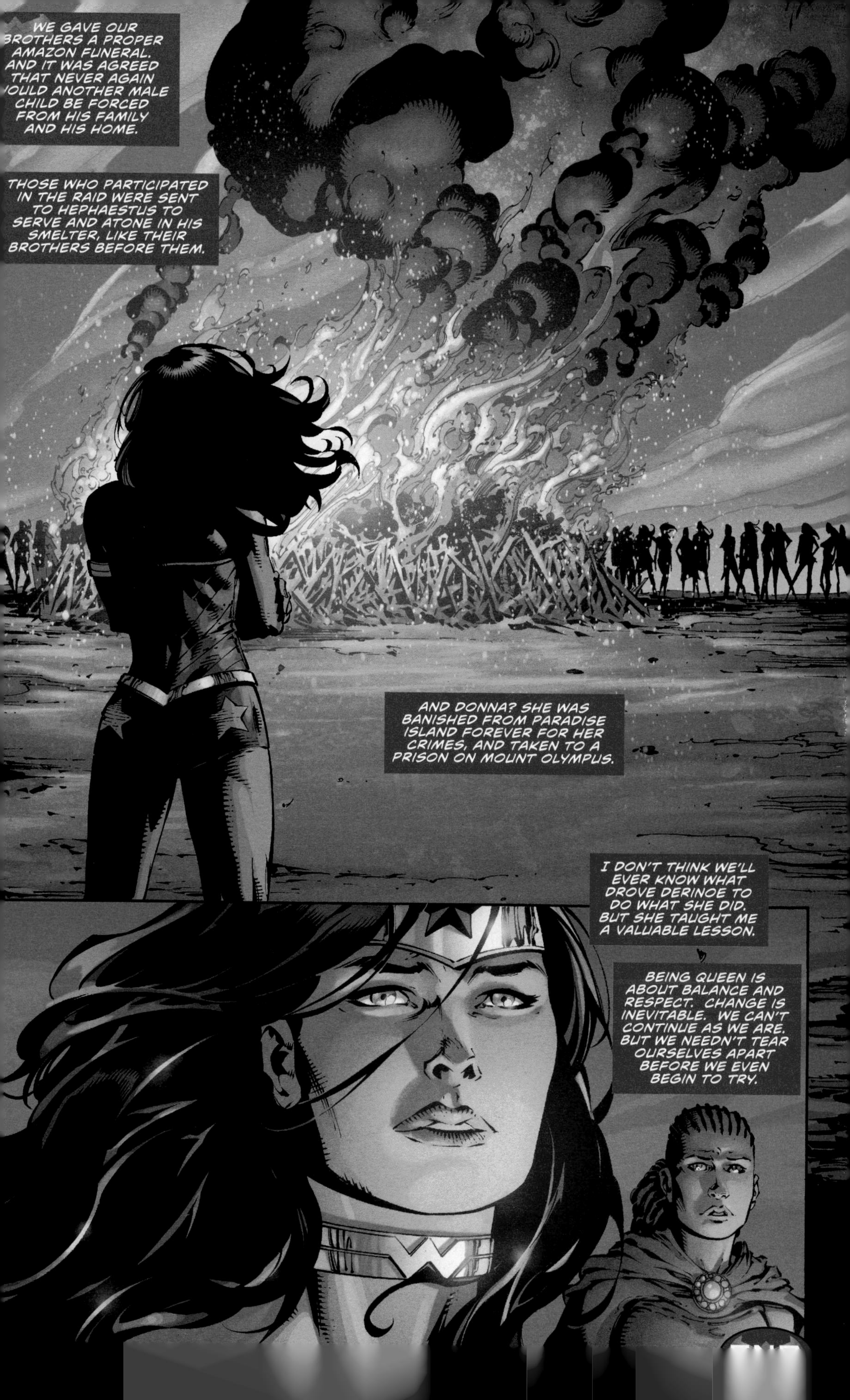
WE GAVE OUR BROTHERS A PROPER AMAZON FUNERAL. AND IT WAS AGREED THAT NEVER AGAIN WOULD ANOTHER MALE CHILD BE FORCED FROM HIS FAMILY AND HIS HOME.
THOSE WHO PARTICIPATED IN THE RAID WERE SENT TO HEPHAESTUS TO SERVE AND ATONE IN HIS SMELTER, LIKE THEIR BROTHERS BEFORE THEM.
AND DONNA? SHE WAS BANISHED FROM PARADISE ISLAND FOREVER FOR HER CRIMES, AND TAKEN TO A PRISON ON MOUNT OLYMPUS.
I DON'T THINK WE'LL EVER KNOW WHAT DROVE DERINOE TO DO WHAT SHE DID. BUT SHE TAUGHT ME A VALUABLE LESSON.
BEING QUEEN IS ABOUT BALANCE AND RESPECT. CHANGE IS INEVITABLE. WE CAN'T CONTINUE AS WE ARE. BUT WE NEEDN'T TEAR OURSELVES APART BEFORE WE EVEN BEGIN TO TRY.

FOR THE LOVE OF A QUEEN

MEREDITH FINCH writer **GORAN SUDŽUKA** artist **IVE SVORCINA** colorist **TOM NAPOLITANO** letterer

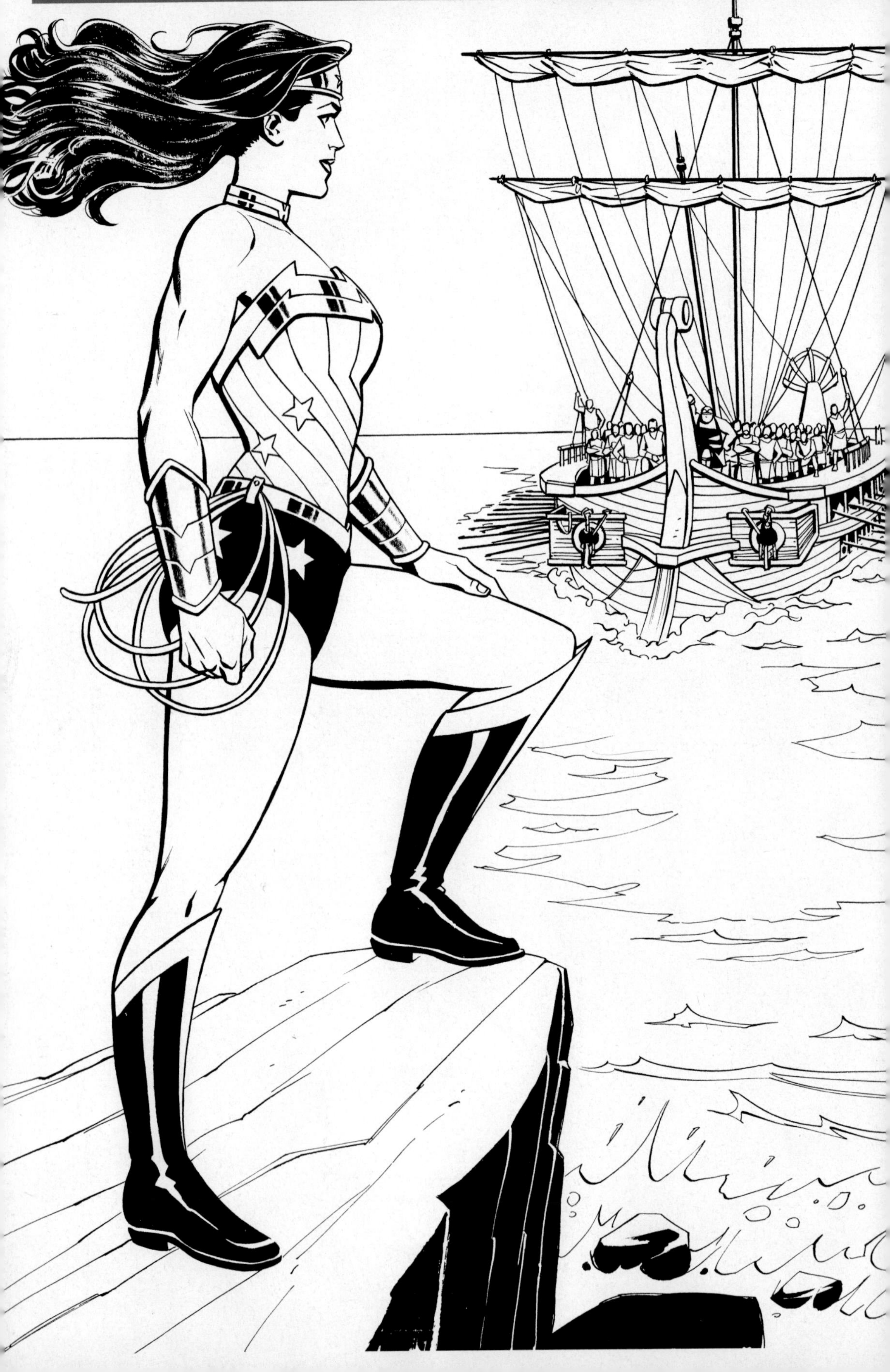

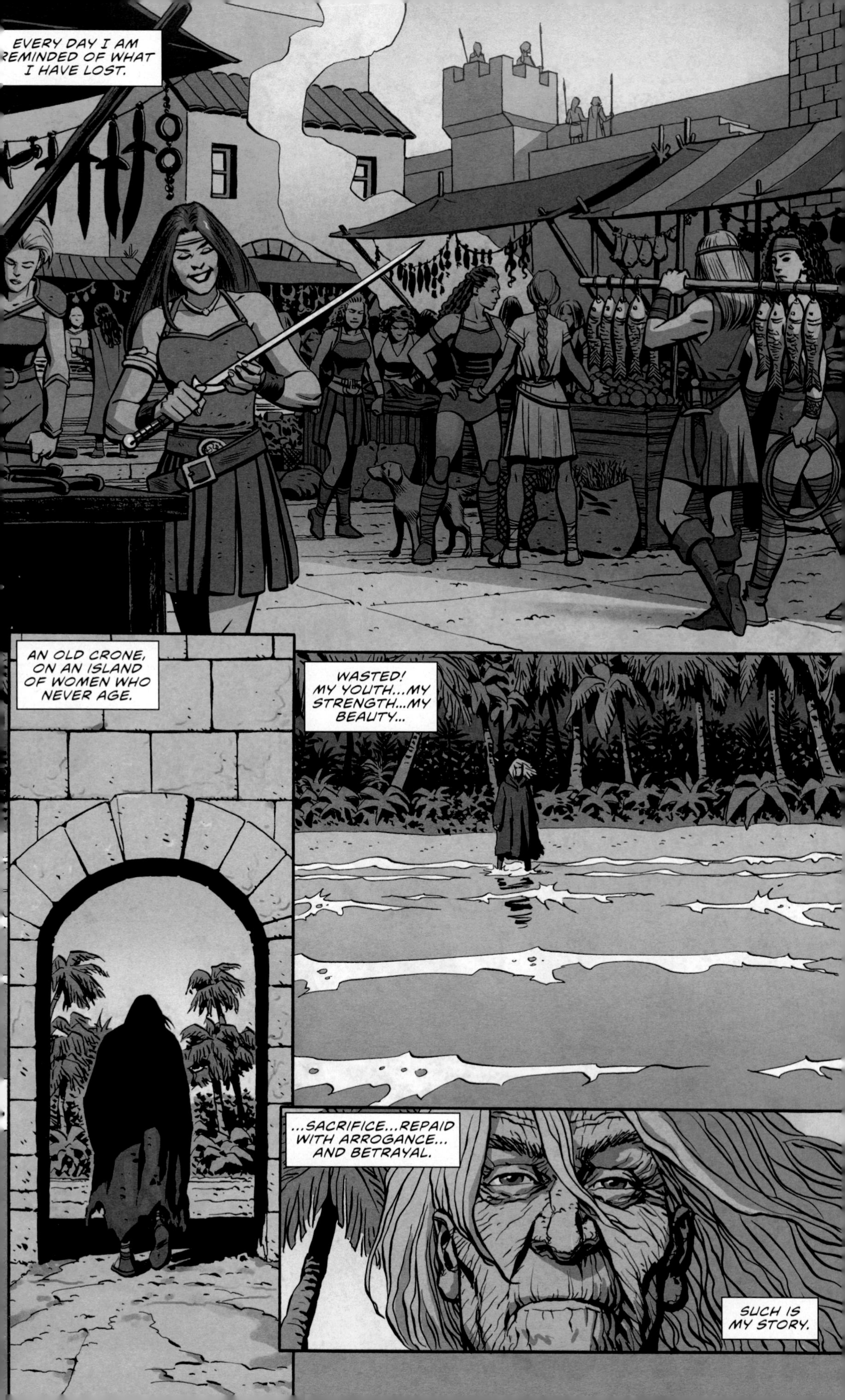
EVERY DAY I AM REMINDED OF WHAT I HAVE LOST.
AN OLD CRONE, ON AN ISLAND OF WOMEN WHO NEVER AGE.
WASTED! MY YOUTH...MY STRENGTH...MY BEAUTY...
...SACRIFICE...REPAID WITH ARROGANCE... AND BETRAYAL.
SUCH IS MY STORY.

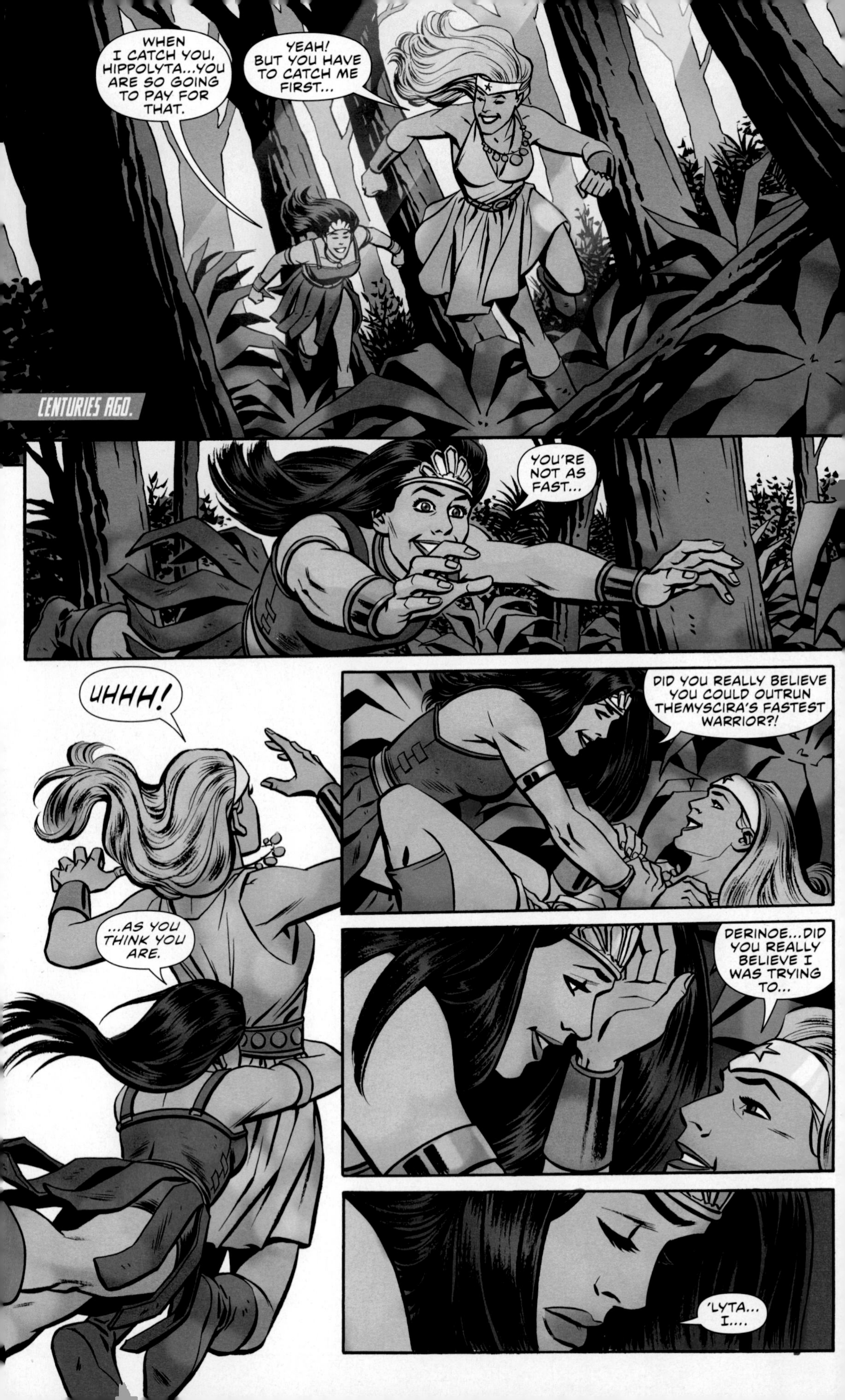
WHEN I CATCH YOU, HIPPOLYTA...YOU ARE SO GOING TO PAY FOR THAT.
YEAH! BUT YOU HAVE TO CATCH ME FIRST...
CENTURIES AGO.
YOU'RE NOT AS FAST...
UHHH!
...AS YOU THINK YOU ARE.
DID YOU REALLY BELIEVE YOU COULD OUTRUN THEMYSCIRA'S FASTEST WARRIOR?!
DERINOE...DID YOU REALLY BELIEVE I WAS TRYING TO...
'LYTA... I....

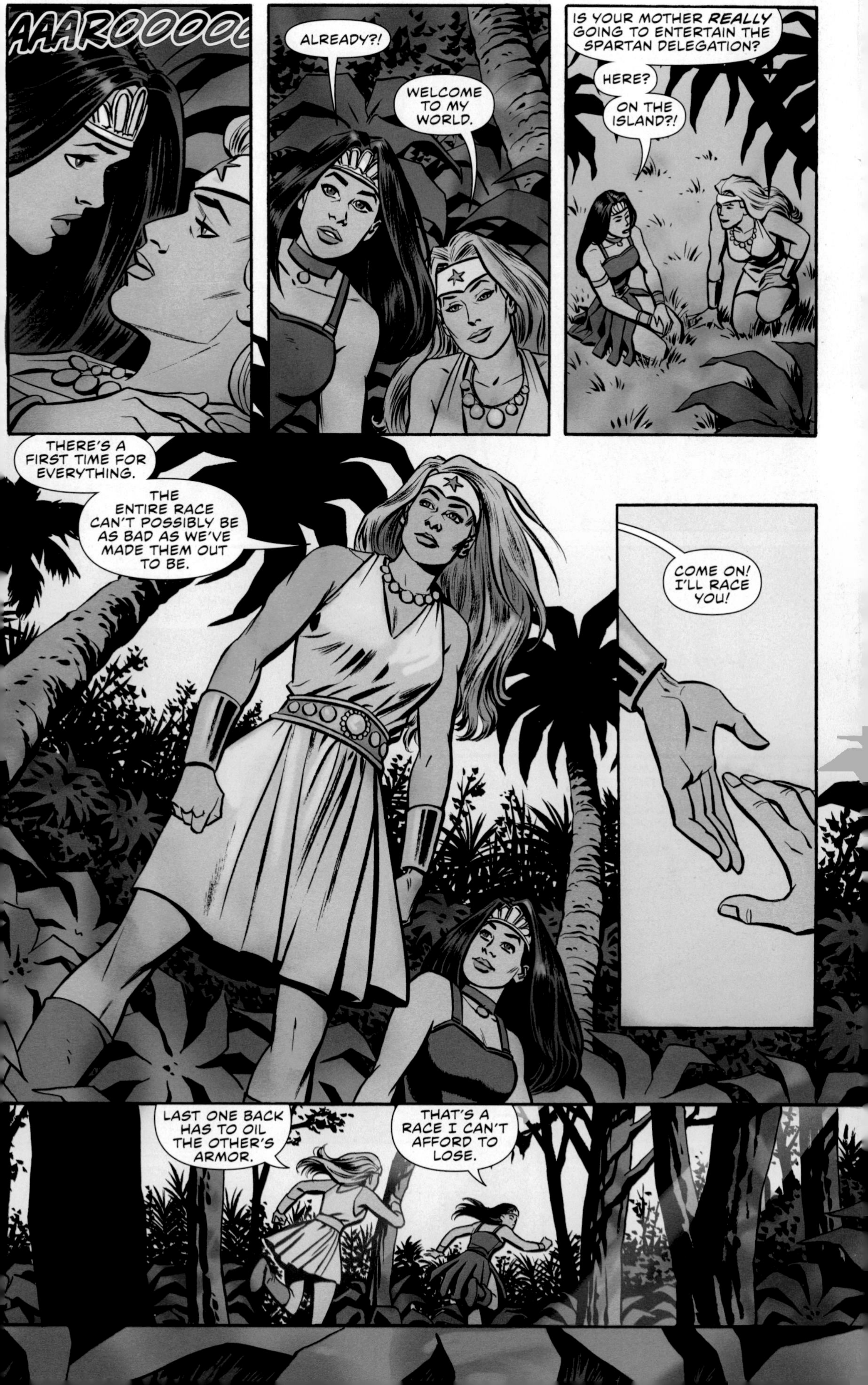
AAAROOOOO
ALREADY?!
WELCOME TO MY WORLD.
IS YOUR MOTHER REALLY GOING TO ENTERTAIN THE SPARTAN DELEGATION?
HERE?
ON THE ISLAND?!
THERE'S A FIRST TIME FOR EVERYTHING.
THE ENTIRE RACE CAN'T POSSIBLY BE AS BAD AS WE'VE MADE THEM OUT TO BE.
COME ON! I'LL RACE YOU!
LAST ONE BACK HAS TO OIL THE OTHER'S ARMOR.
THAT'S A RACE I CAN'T AFFORD TO LOSE.

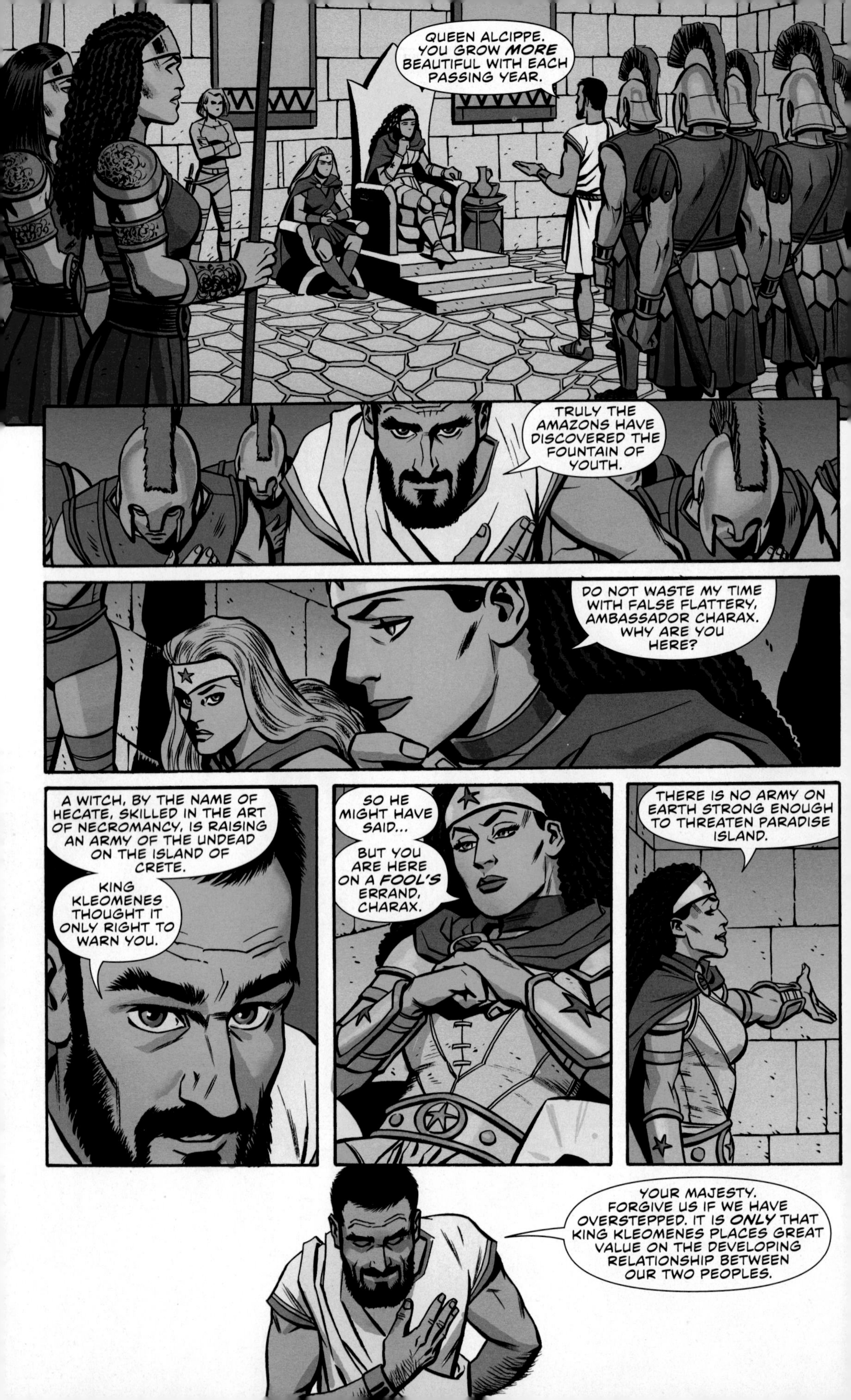
QUEEN ALCIPPE. YOU GROW MORE BEAUTIFUL WITH EACH PASSING YEAR.
TRULY THE AMAZONS HAVE DISCOVERED THE FOUNTAIN OF YOUTH.
DO NOT WASTE MY TIME WITH FALSE FLATTERY, AMBASSADOR CHARAX. WHY ARE YOU HERE?
A WITCH, BY THE NAME OF HECATE, SKILLED IN THE ART OF NECROMANCY, IS RAISING AN ARMY OF THE UNDEAD ON THE ISLAND OF CRETE.
KING KLEOMENES THOUGHT IT ONLY RIGHT TO WARN YOU.
SO HE MIGHT HAVE SAID...
BUT YOU ARE HERE ON A FOOL'S ERRAND, CHARAX.
THERE IS NO ARMY ON EARTH STRONG ENOUGH TO THREATEN PARADISE ISLAND.
YOUR MAJESTY. FORGIVE US IF WE HAVE OVERSTEPPED. IT IS ONLY THAT KING KLEOMENES PLACES GREAT VALUE ON THE DEVELOPING RELATIONSHIP BETWEEN OUR TWO PEOPLES.

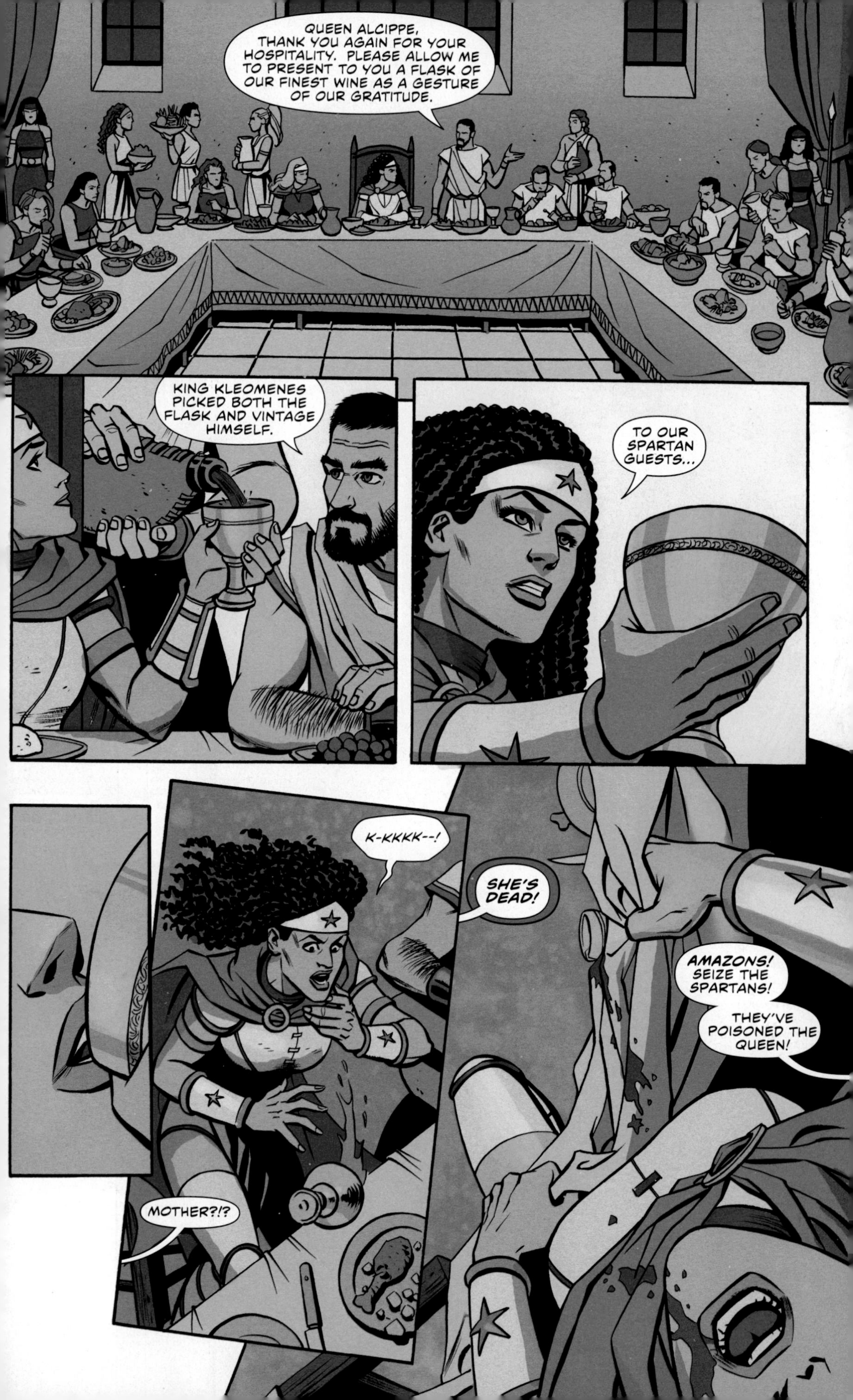
QUEEN ALCIPPE, THANK YOU AGAIN FOR YOUR HOSPITALITY. PLEASE ALLOW ME TO PRESENT TO YOU A FLASK OF OUR FINEST WINE AS A GESTURE OF OUR GRATITUDE.
KING KLEOMENES PICKED BOTH THE FLASK AND VINTAGE HIMSELF.
TO OUR SPARTAN GUESTS...
K-KKKK--!
MOTHER?!?
SHE'S DEAD!
AMAZONS! SEIZE THE SPARTANS!
THEY'VE POISONED THE QUEEN!

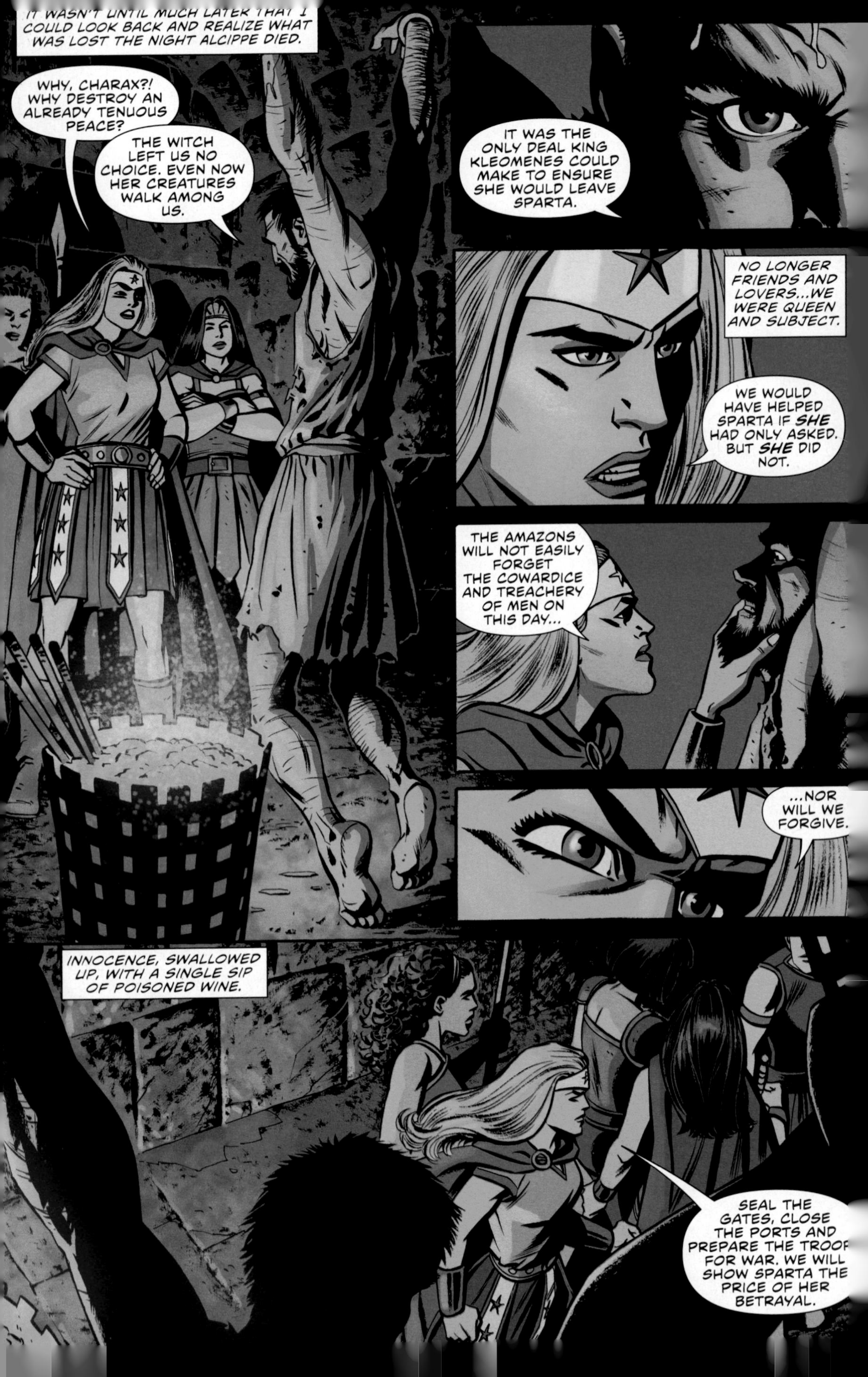
IT WASN'T UNTIL MUCH LATER THAT I COULD LOOK BACK AND REALIZE WHAT WAS LOST THE NIGHT ALCIPPE DIED.
WHY, CHARAX?! WHY DESTROY AN ALREADY TENUOUS PEACE?
THE WITCH LEFT US NO CHOICE. EVEN NOW HER CREATURES WALK AMONG US.
IT WAS THE ONLY DEAL KING KLEOMENES COULD MAKE TO ENSURE SHE WOULD LEAVE SPARTA.
NO LONGER FRIENDS AND LOVERS...WE WERE QUEEN AND SUBJECT.
WE WOULD HAVE HELPED SPARTA IF SHE HAD ONLY ASKED. BUT SHE DID NOT.
THE AMAZONS WILL NOT EASILY FORGET THE COWARDICE AND TREACHERY OF MEN ON THIS DAY...
...NOR WILL WE FORGIVE.
INNOCENCE, SWALLOWED UP, WITH A SINGLE SIP OF POISONED WINE.
SEAL THE GATES, CLOSE THE PORTS AND PREPARE THE TROOP FOR WAR. WE WILL SHOW SPARTA THE PRICE OF HER BETRAYAL.

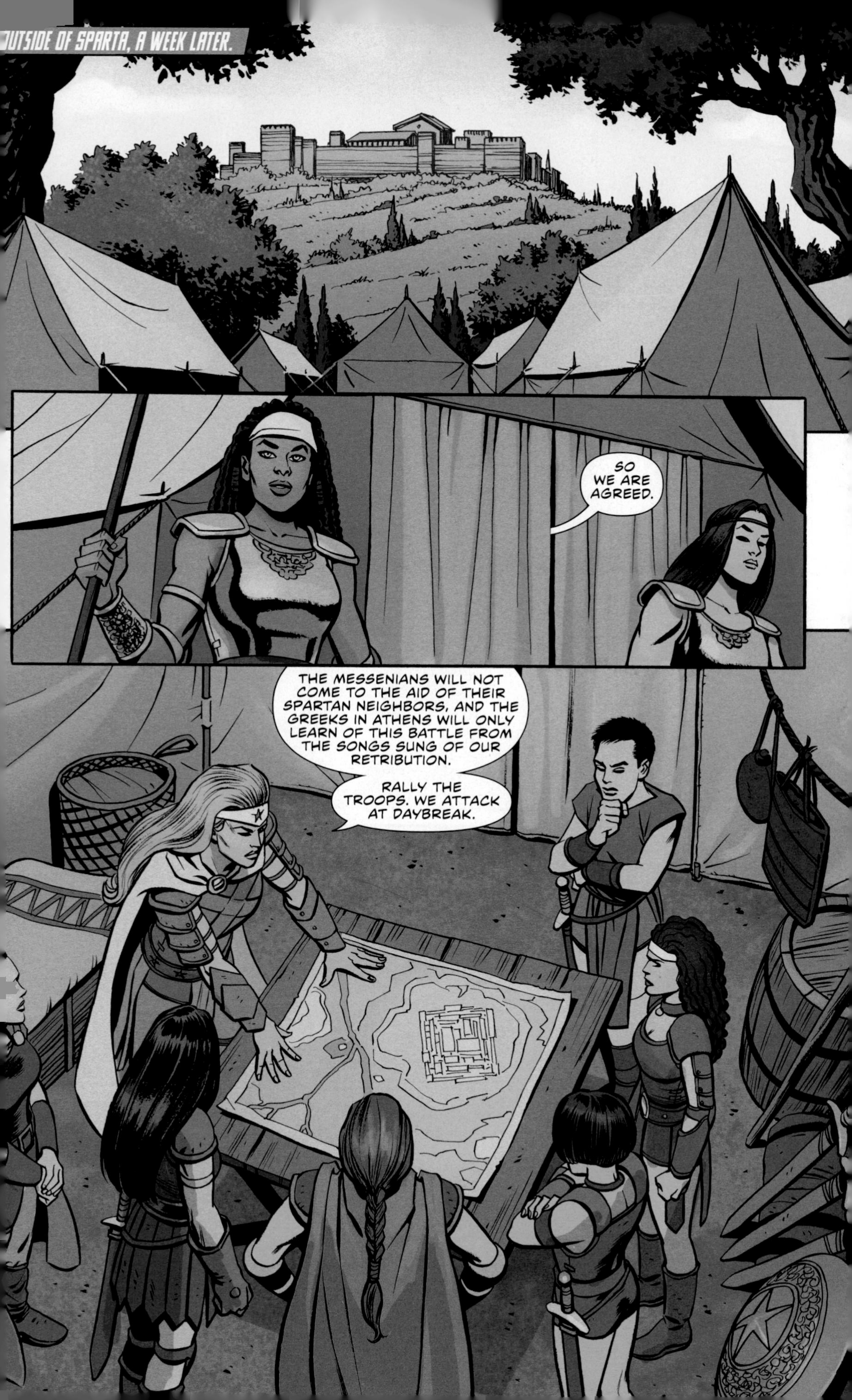

OUTSIDE OF SPARTA, A WEEK LATER.
SO WE ARE AGREED.
THE MESSENIANS WILL NOT COME TO THE AID OF THEIR SPARTAN NEIGHBORS, AND THE GREEKS IN ATHENS WILL ONLY LEARN OF THIS BATTLE FROM THE SONGS SUNG OF OUR RETRIBUTION.
RALLY THE TROOPS. WE ATTACK AT DAYBREAK.

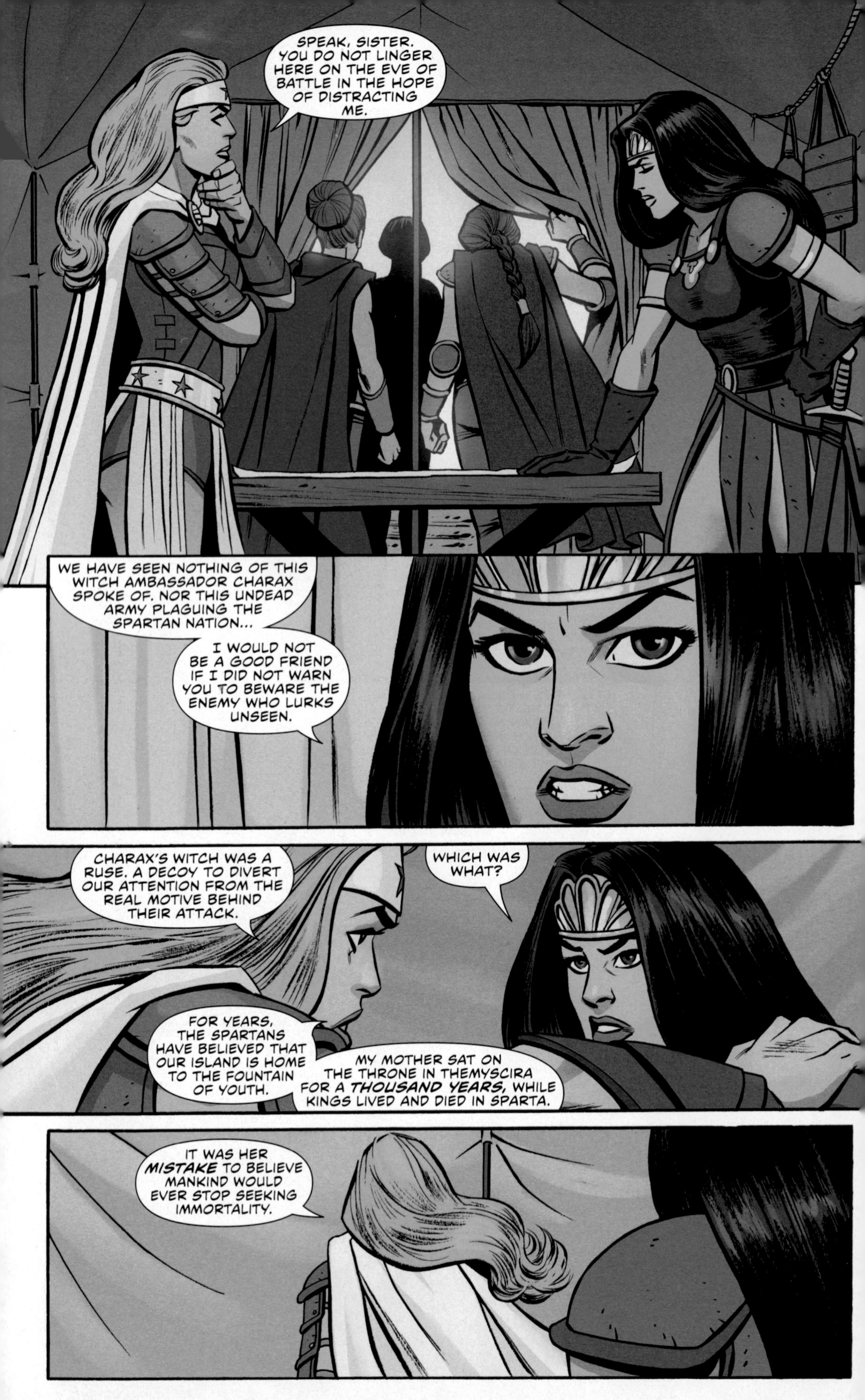
SPEAK, SISTER. YOU DO NOT LINGER HERE ON THE EVE OF BATTLE IN THE HOPE OF DISTRACTING ME.
WE HAVE SEEN NOTHING OF THIS WITCH AMBASSADOR CHARAX SPOKE OF. NOR THIS UNDEAD ARMY PLAGUING THE SPARTAN NATION...
I WOULD NOT BE A GOOD FRIEND IF I DID NOT WARN YOU TO BEWARE THE ENEMY WHO LURKS UNSEEN.
CHARAX'S WITCH WAS A RUSE. A DECOY TO DIVERT OUR ATTENTION FROM THE REAL MOTIVE BEHIND THEIR ATTACK.
WHICH WAS WHAT?
FOR YEARS, THE SPARTANS HAVE BELIEVED THAT OUR ISLAND IS HOME TO THE FOUNTAIN OF YOUTH.
MY MOTHER SAT ON THE THRONE IN THEMYSCIRA FOR A *THOUSAND YEARS,* WHILE KINGS LIVED AND DIED IN SPARTA.
IT WAS HER *MISTAKE* TO BELIEVE MANKIND WOULD EVER STOP SEEKING IMMORTALITY.

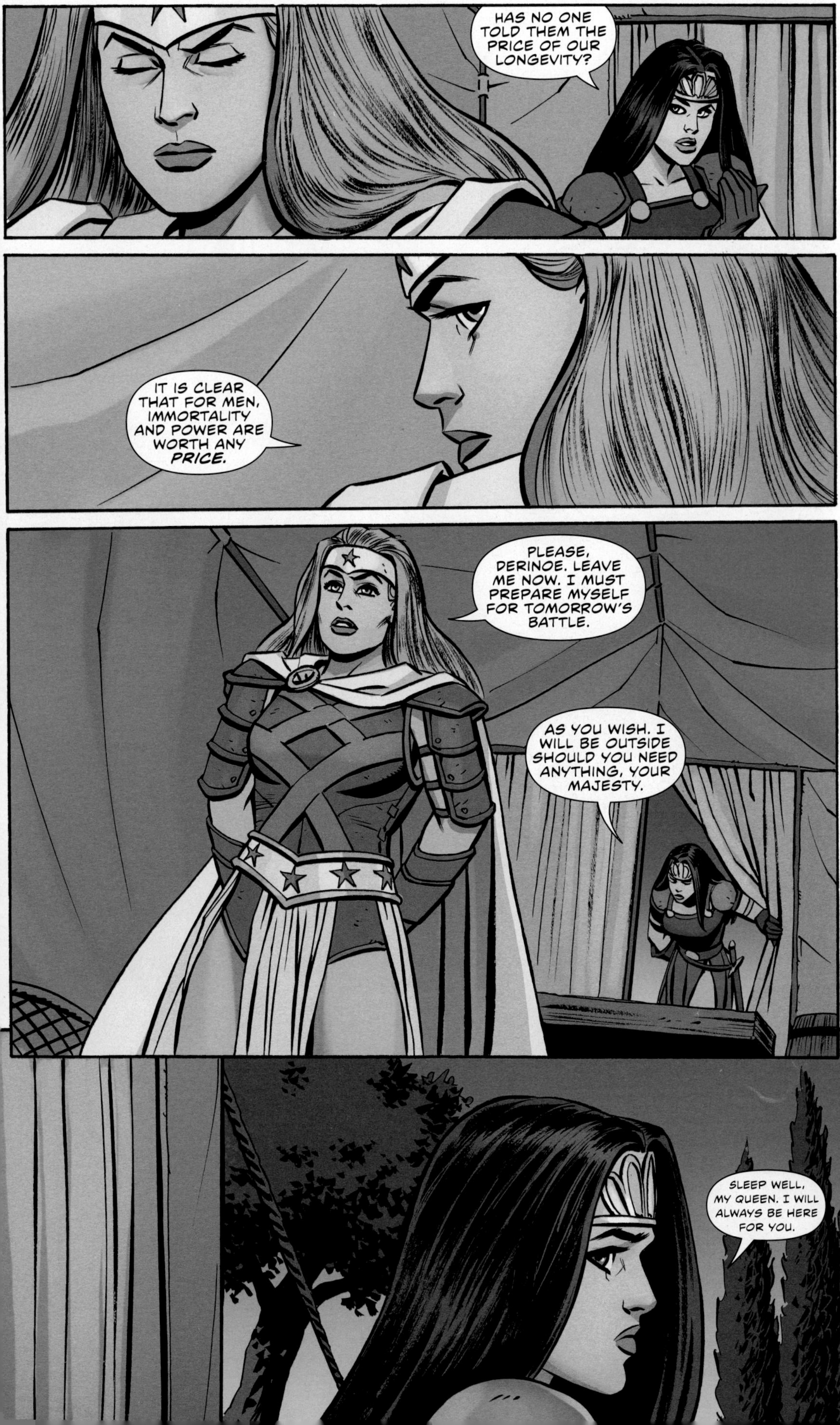
HAS NO ONE TOLD THEM THE PRICE OF OUR LONGEVITY?
IT IS CLEAR THAT FOR MEN, IMMORTALITY AND POWER ARE WORTH ANY *PRICE*.
PLEASE, DERINOE. LEAVE ME NOW. I MUST PREPARE MYSELF FOR TOMORROW'S BATTLE.
AS YOU WISH. I WILL BE OUTSIDE SHOULD YOU NEED ANYTHING, YOUR MAJESTY.
SLEEP WELL, MY QUEEN. I WILL ALWAYS BE HERE FOR YOU.

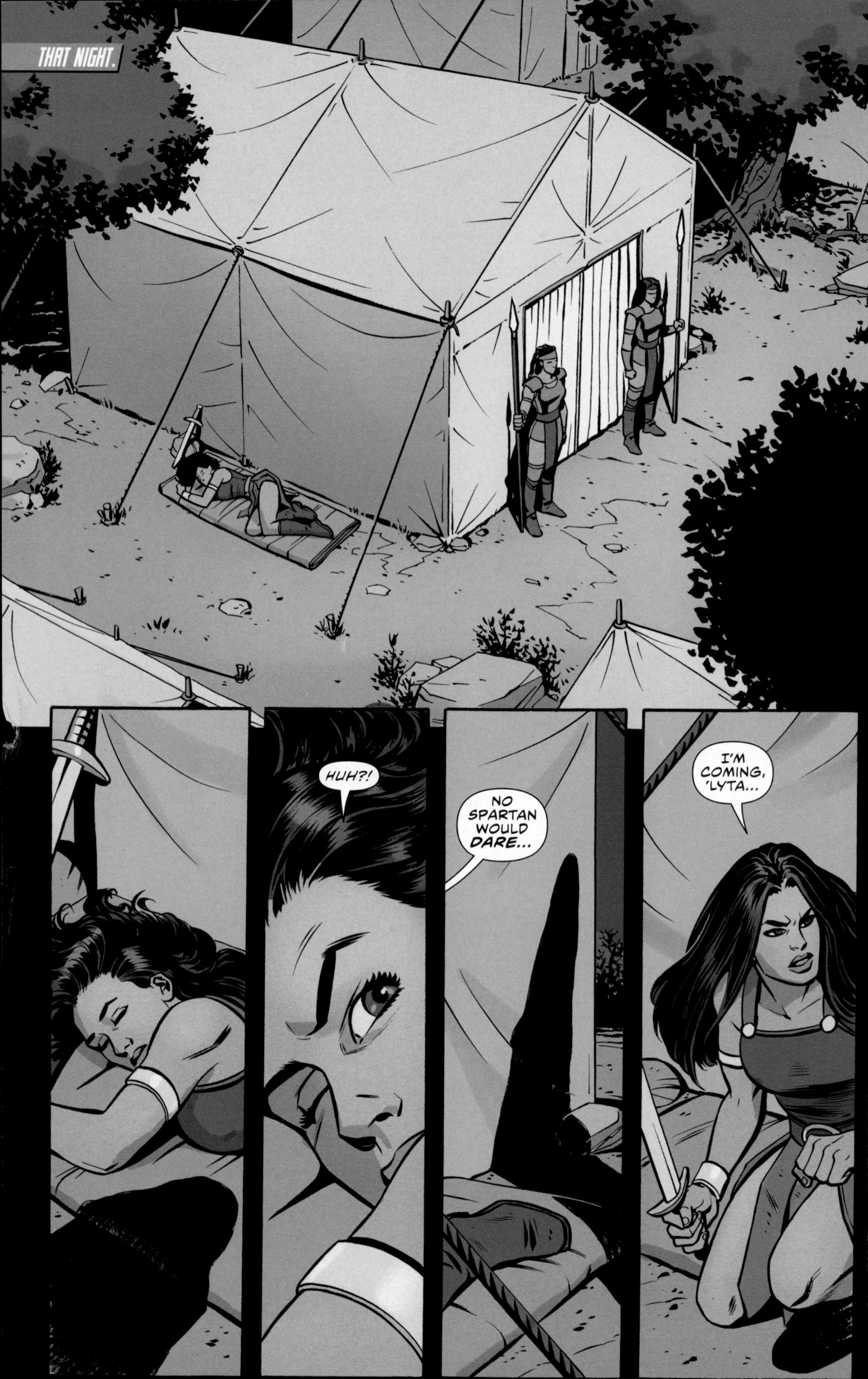
THAT NIGHT.
HUH?!
NO SPARTAN WOULD DARE...
I'M COMING, 'LYTA...

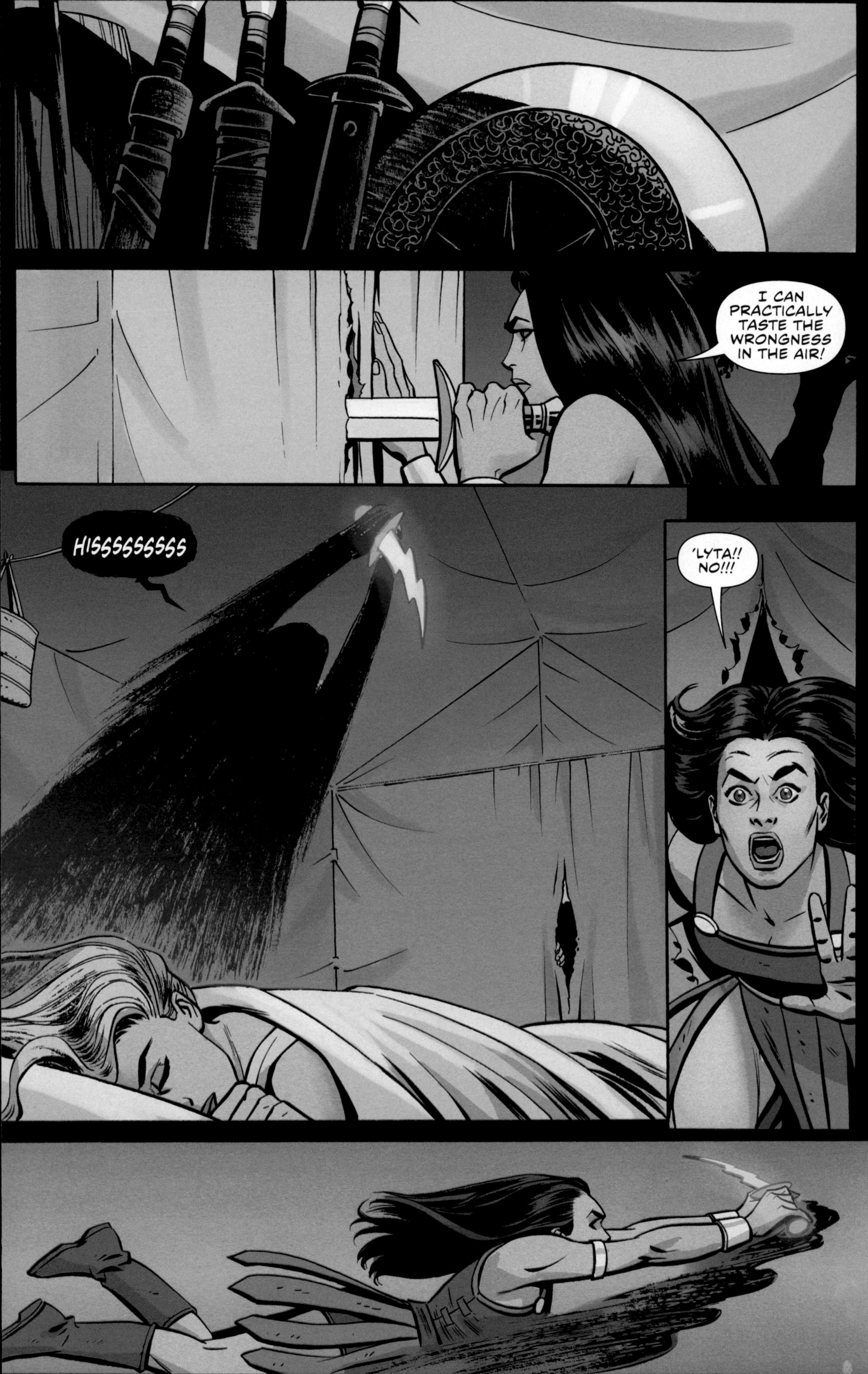
I CAN PRACTICALLY TASTE THE WRONGNESS IN THE AIR!
HISSSSSSSSS
'LYTA!! NO!!!

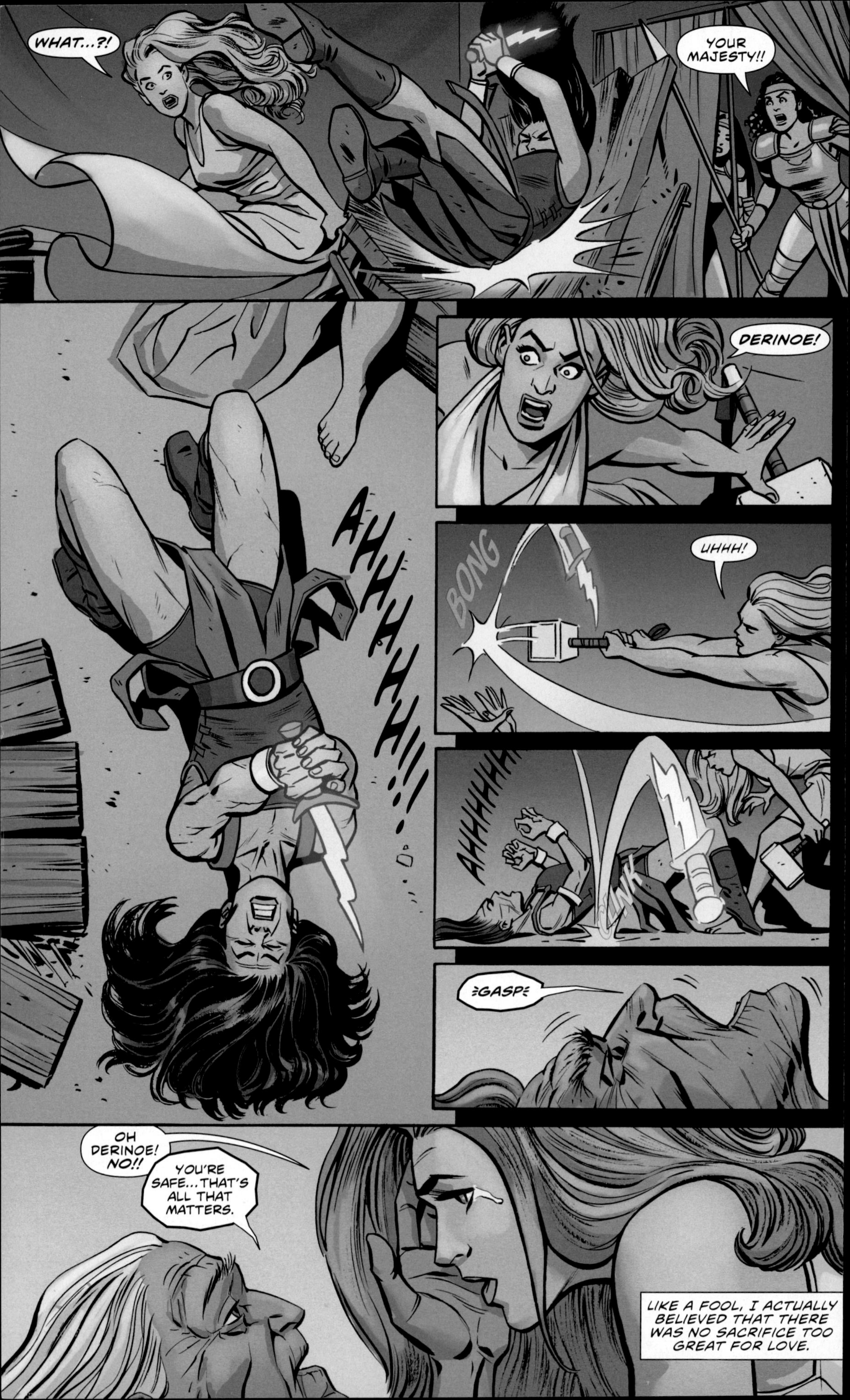

WHAT...?!
YOUR MAJESTY!!
AHHHHH!!!
DERINOE!
BONG
UHHH!
AHHHHHH
CLINK
GASP
OH DERINOE! NO!!
YOU'RE SAFE...THAT'S ALL THAT MATTERS.
LIKE A FOOL, I ACTUALLY BELIEVED THAT THERE WAS NO SACRIFICE TOO GREAT FOR LOVE.

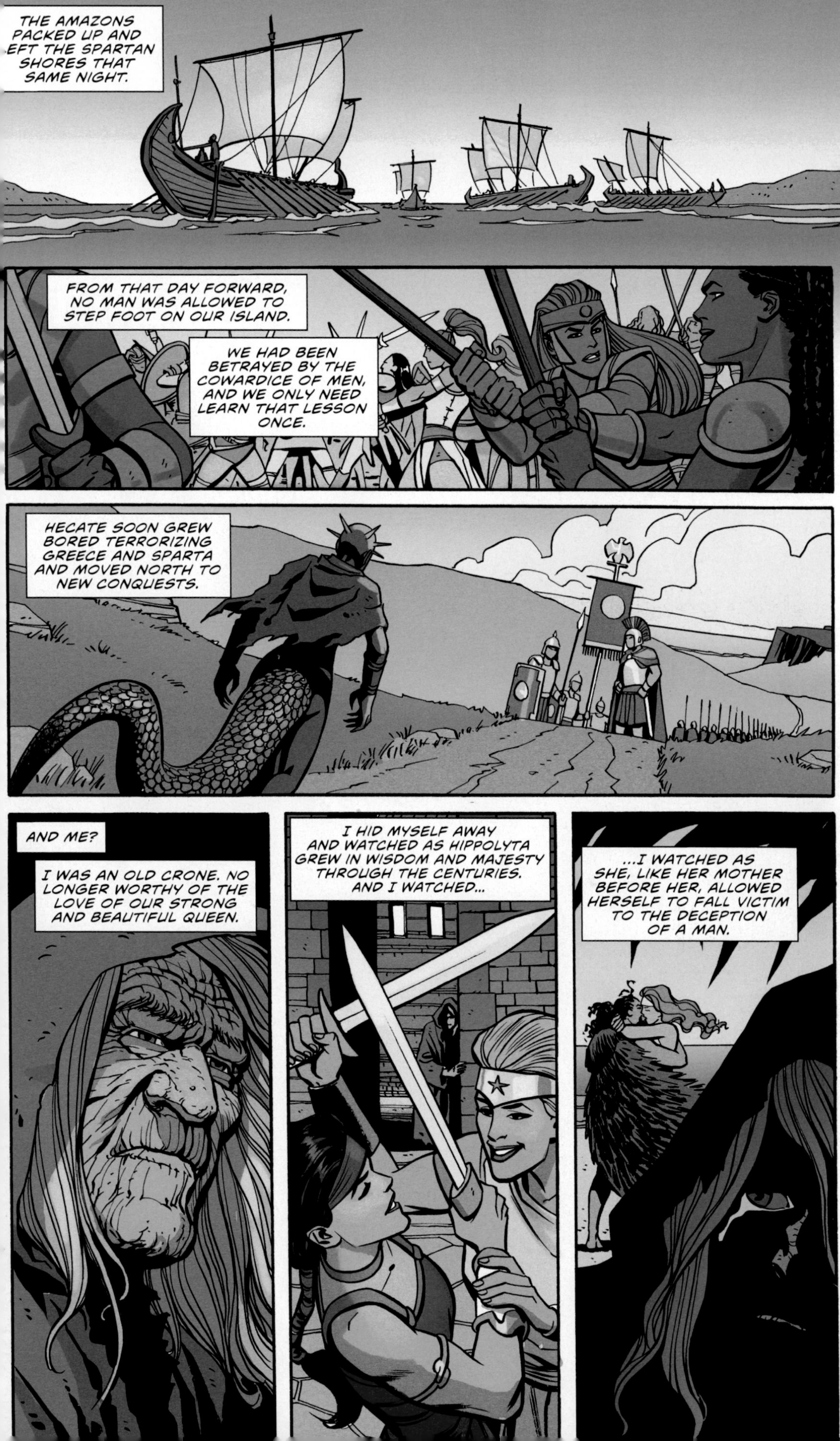
THE AMAZONS PACKED UP AND EFT THE SPARTAN SHORES THAT SAME NIGHT.
FROM THAT DAY FORWARD, NO MAN WAS ALLOWED TO STEP FOOT ON OUR ISLAND.
WE HAD BEEN BETRAYED BY THE COWARDICE OF MEN, AND WE ONLY NEED LEARN THAT LESSON ONCE.
HECATE SOON GREW BORED TERRORIZING GREECE AND SPARTA AND MOVED NORTH TO NEW CONQUESTS.
AND ME?
I WAS AN OLD CRONE. NO LONGER WORTHY OF THE LOVE OF OUR STRONG AND BEAUTIFUL QUEEN.
I HID MYSELF AWAY AND WATCHED AS HIPPOLYTA GREW IN WISDOM AND MAJESTY THROUGH THE CENTURIES. AND I WATCHED...
...I WATCHED AS SHE, LIKE HER MOTHER BEFORE HER, ALLOWED HERSELF TO FALL VICTIM TO THE DECEPTION OF A MAN.

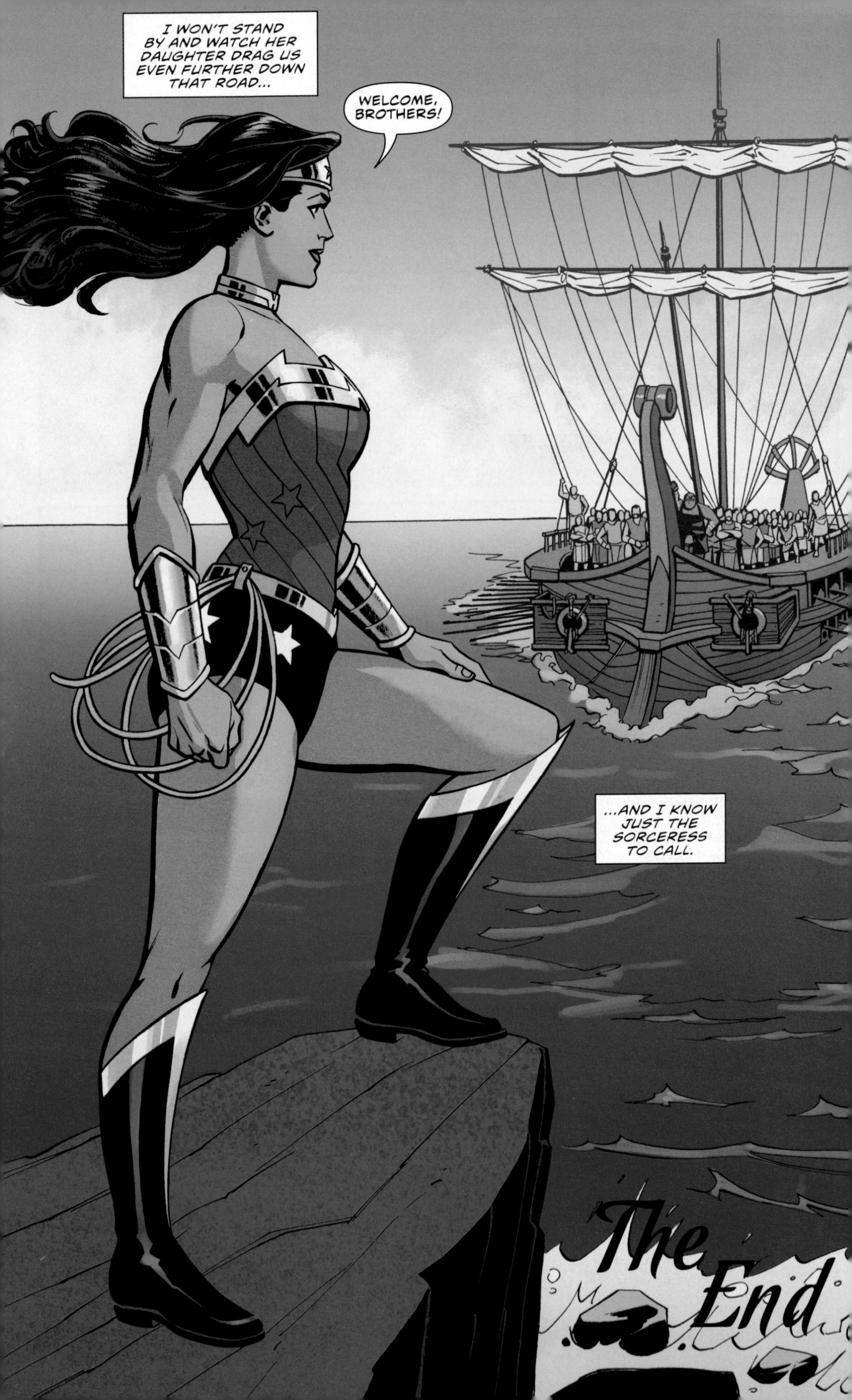
I WON'T STAND BY AND WATCH HER DAUGHTER DRAG US EVEN FURTHER DOWN THAT ROAD...
WELCOME, BROTHERS!
...AND I KNOW JUST THE SORCERESS TO CALL.
The End

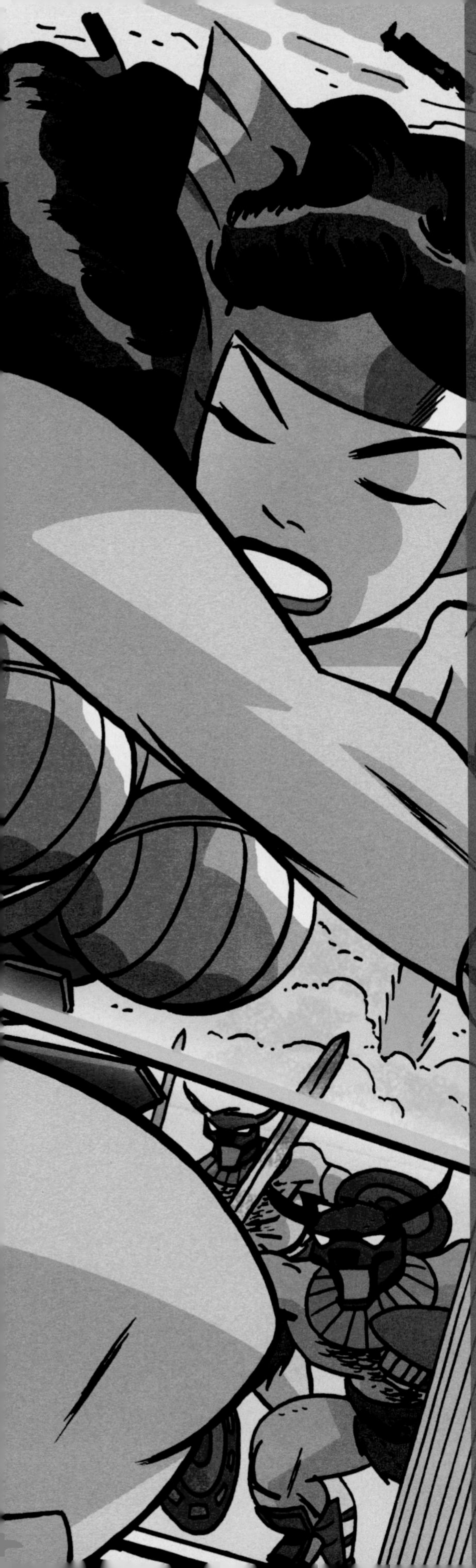

VARIANT COVER GALLERY

WONDER WOMAN #36
VARIANT COVER BY
DAVID FINCH, RICHARD FRIEND
AND SONIA OBACK

WONDER WOMAN #36
LEGO VARIANT COVER

WONDER WOMAN #37
VARIANT COVER BY
DAVID FINCH, BATT
AND SONIA OBACK

WONDER WOMAN #37
VARIANT COVER BY
DARWYN COOKE

WONDER WOMAN #38
VARIANT COVER BY
DAVID FINCH, BATT
AND JUNE CHUNG

WONDER WOMAN #38
FLASH 75TH ANNIVERSARY COVER BY
TERRY AND RACHEL DODSON,
AFTER ROSS ANDRU AND MIKE ESPOSITO

WONDER WOMAN #39
VARIANT COVER BY
EMANUELA LUPACCHINO
AND TOMEU MOREY

WONDER WOMAN #39
HARLEY QUINN COVER BY
PHIL JIMENEZ AND HI-FI,
AFTER RICH BUCKLER

WONDER WOMAN #40
VARIANT COVER BY
JAE LEE AND JUNE CHUNG

WONDER WOMAN #40
MOVIE POSTER COVER BY
BILL SIENKIEWICZ

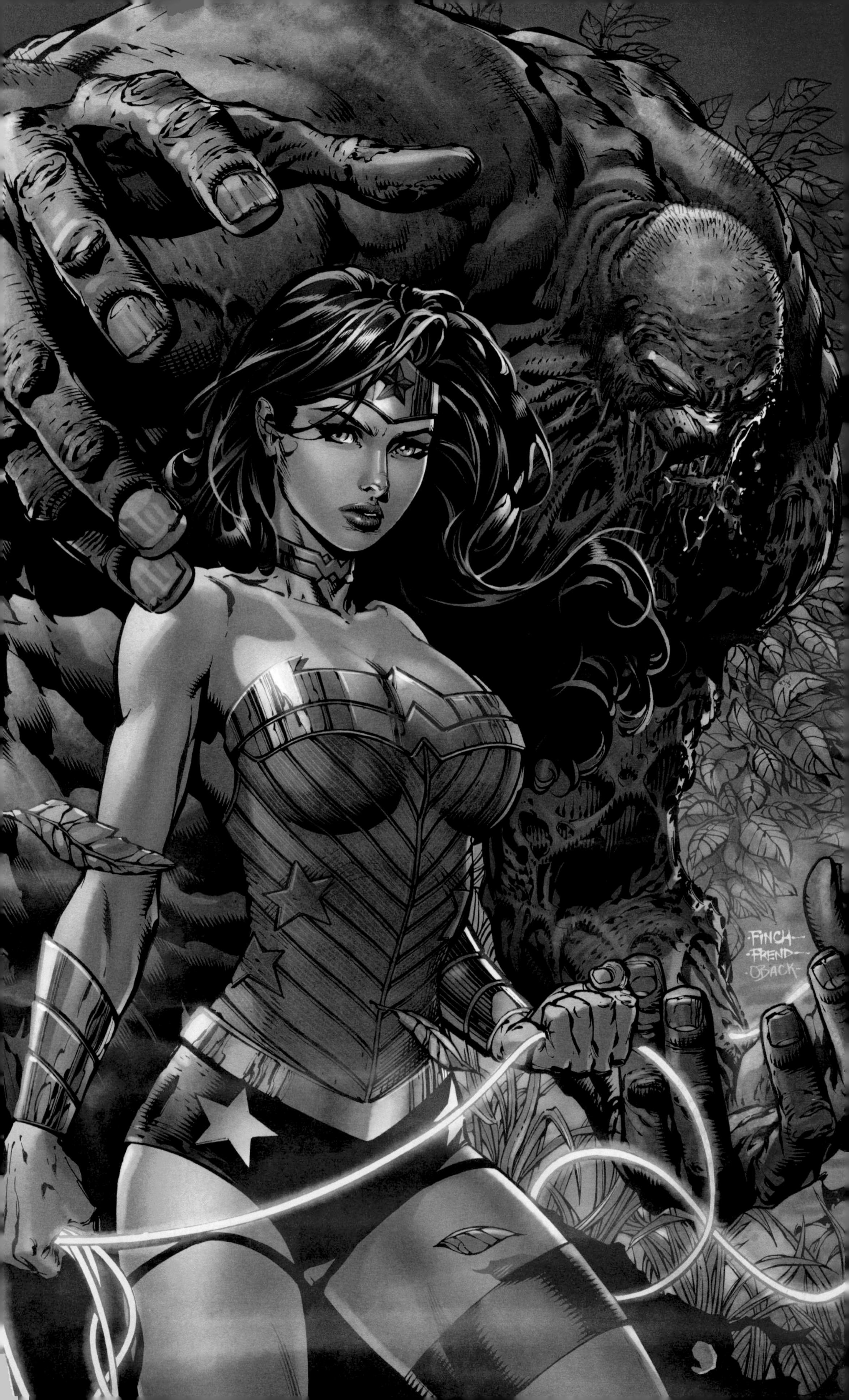
FINCH
FREND
OBACK

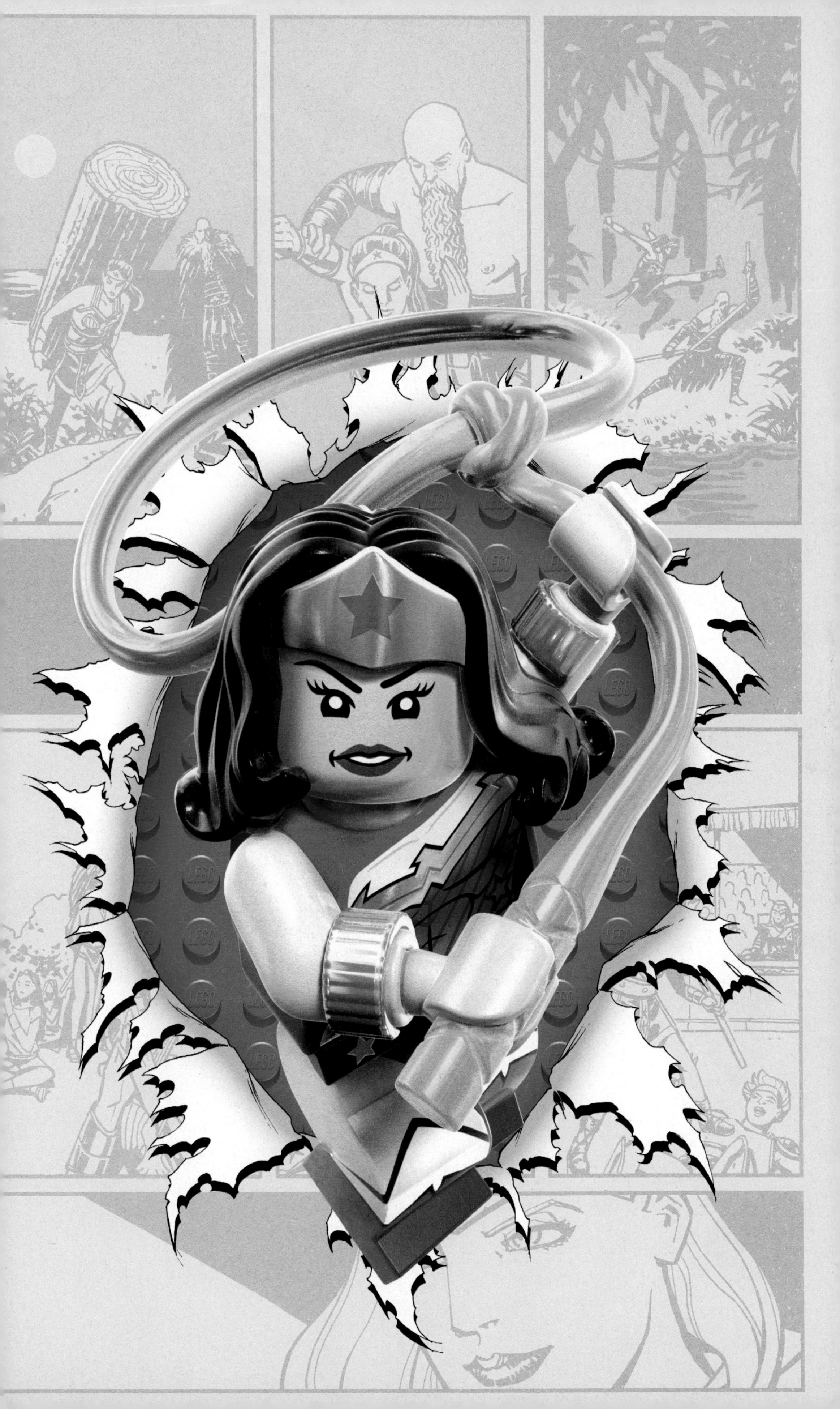

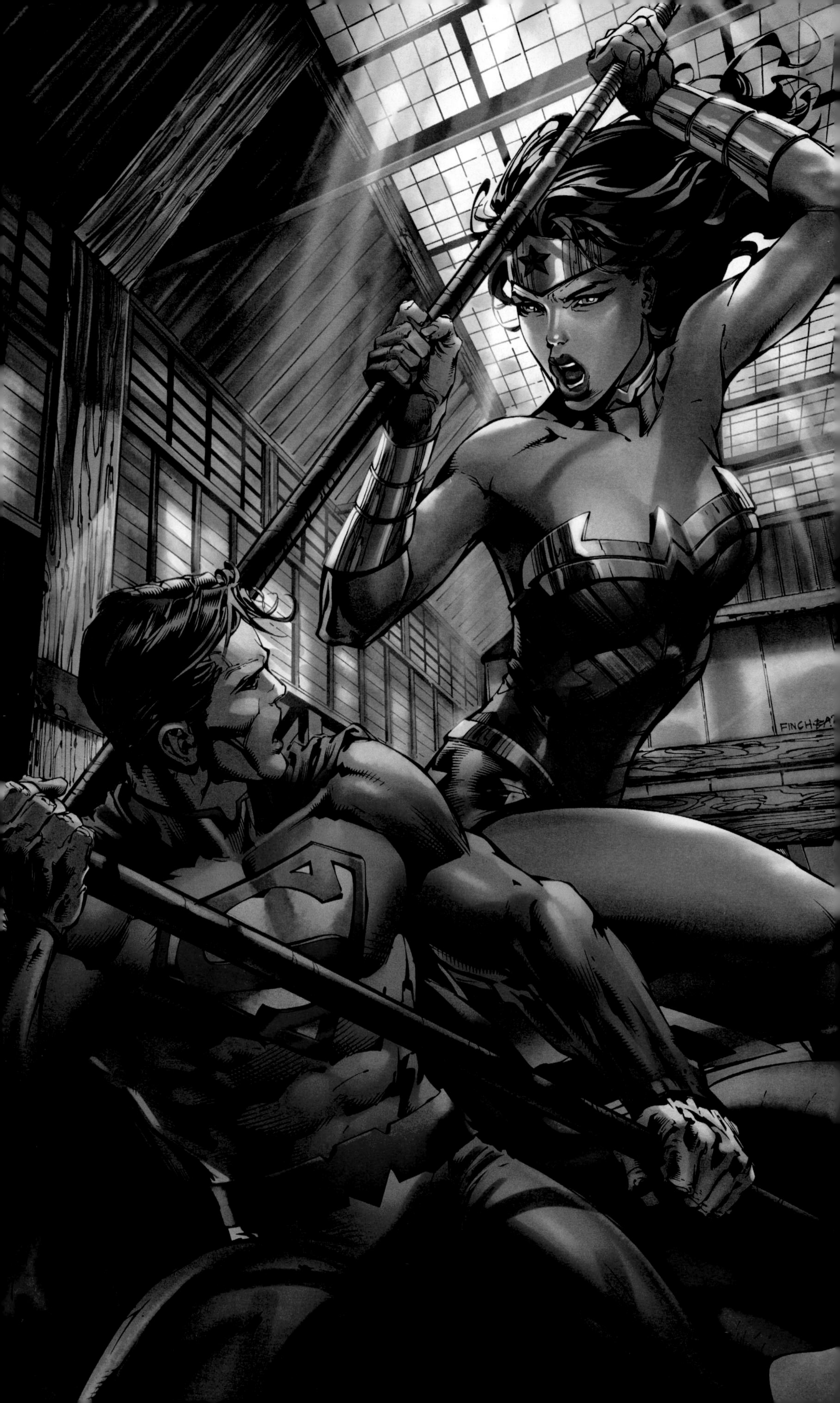
FINCH

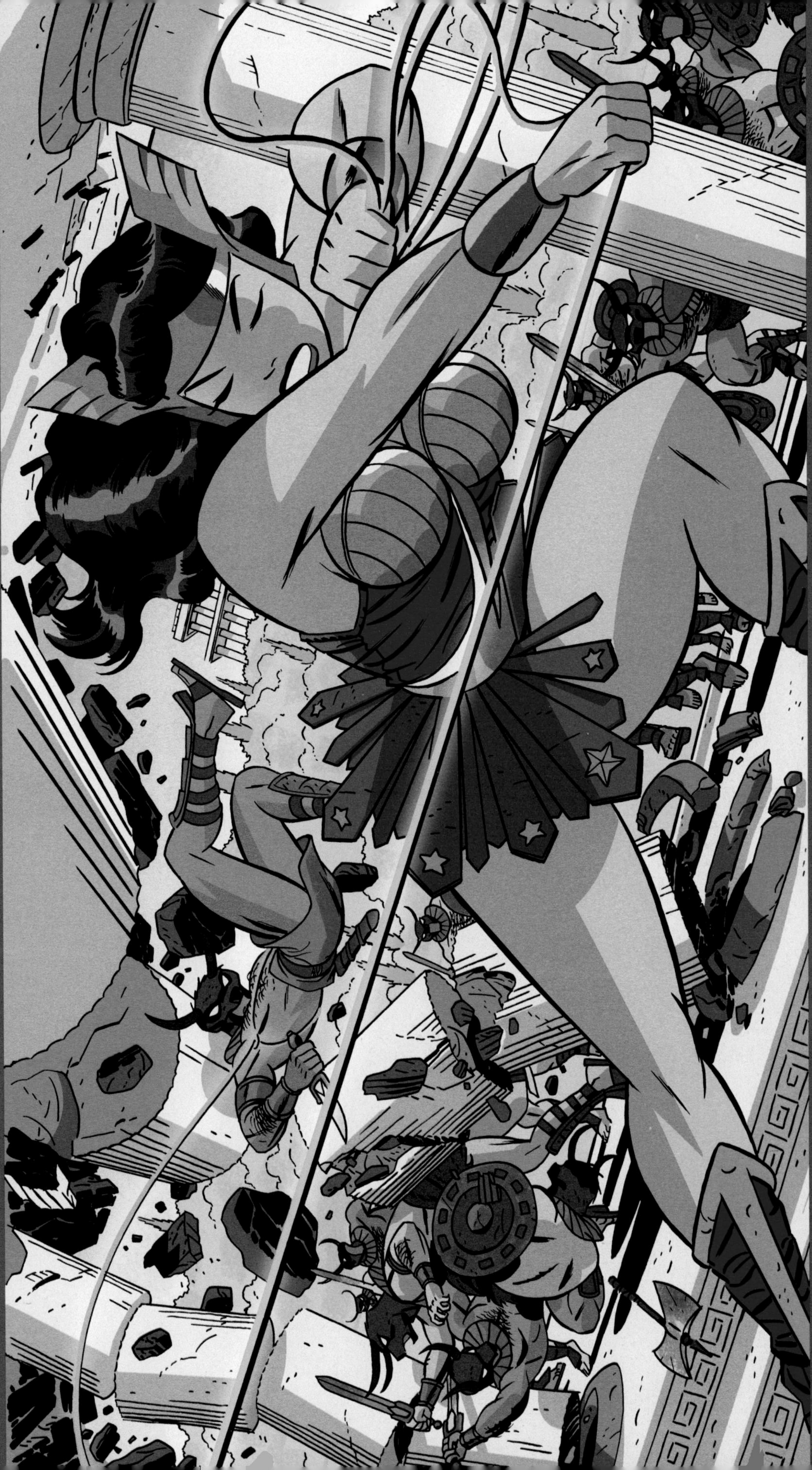

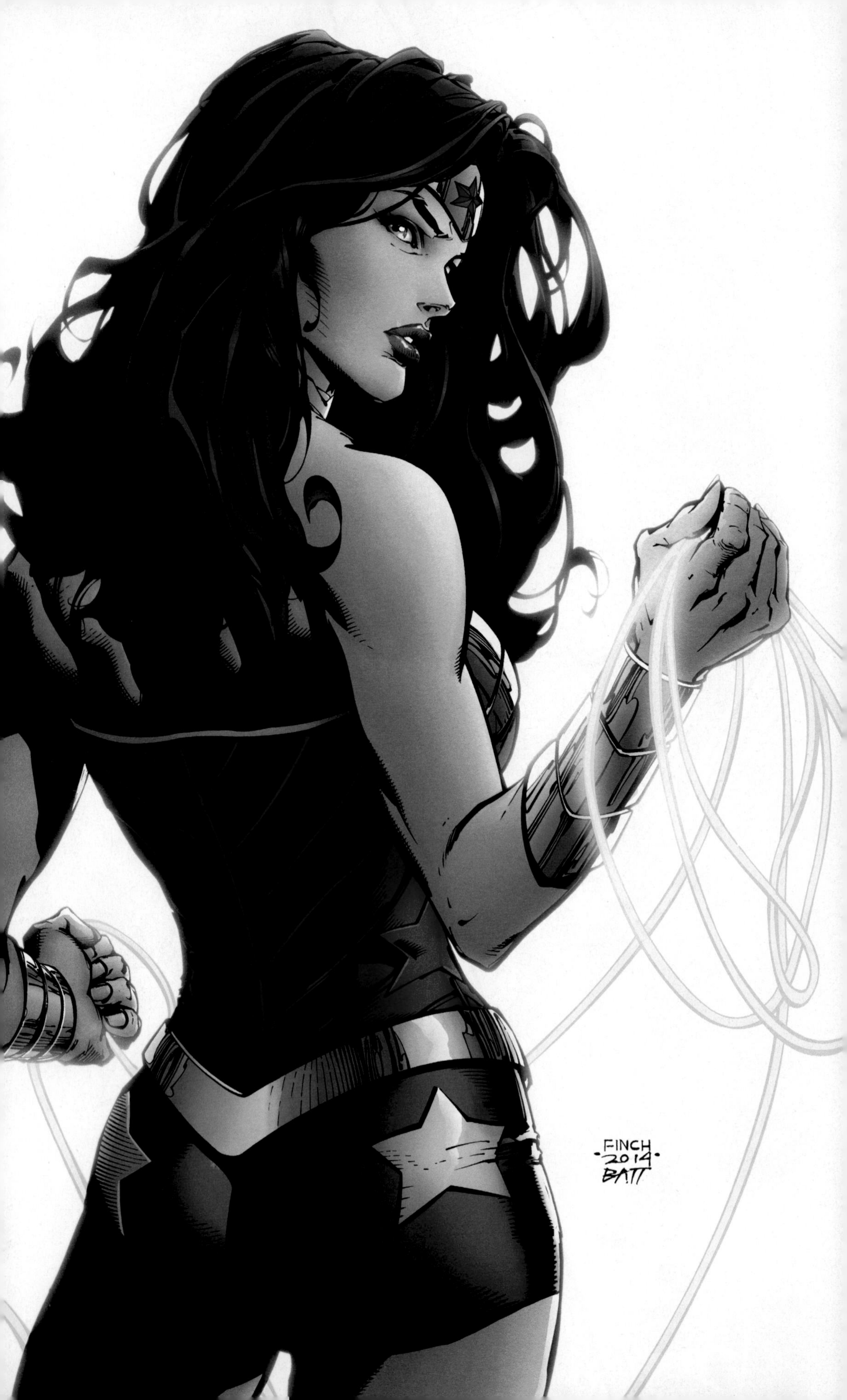
FINCH
2014
BATT

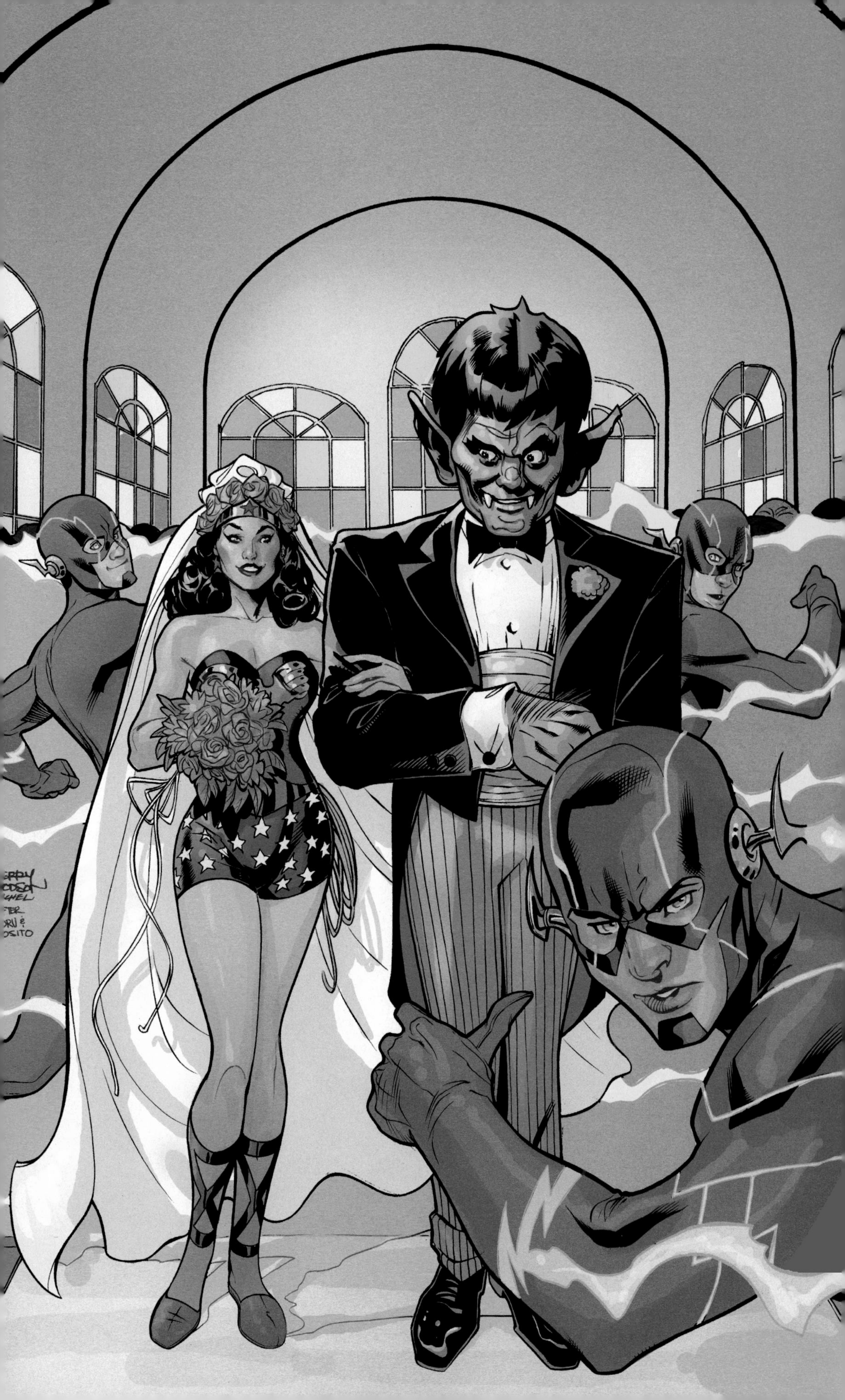

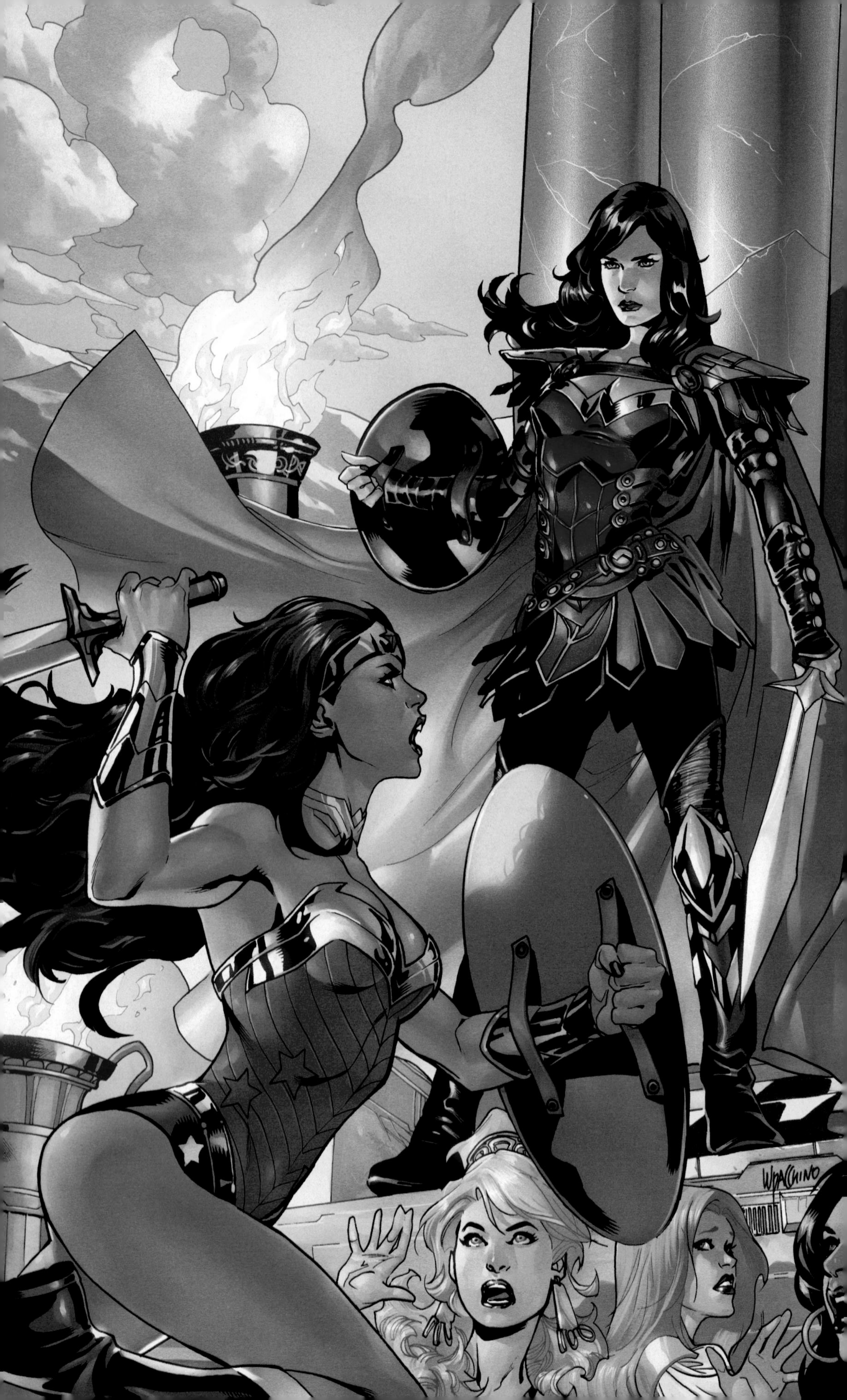

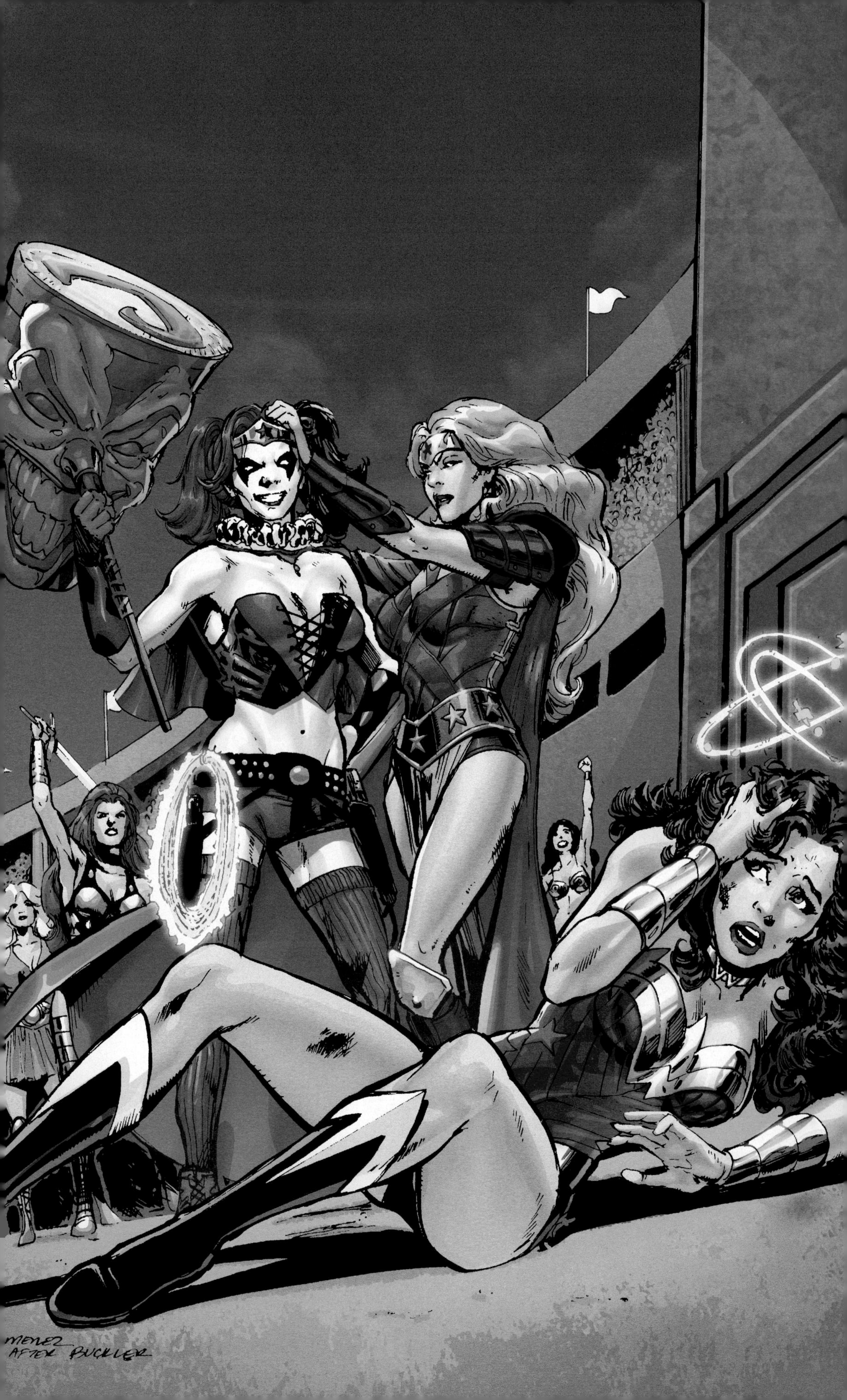
AFTER BUCKLER

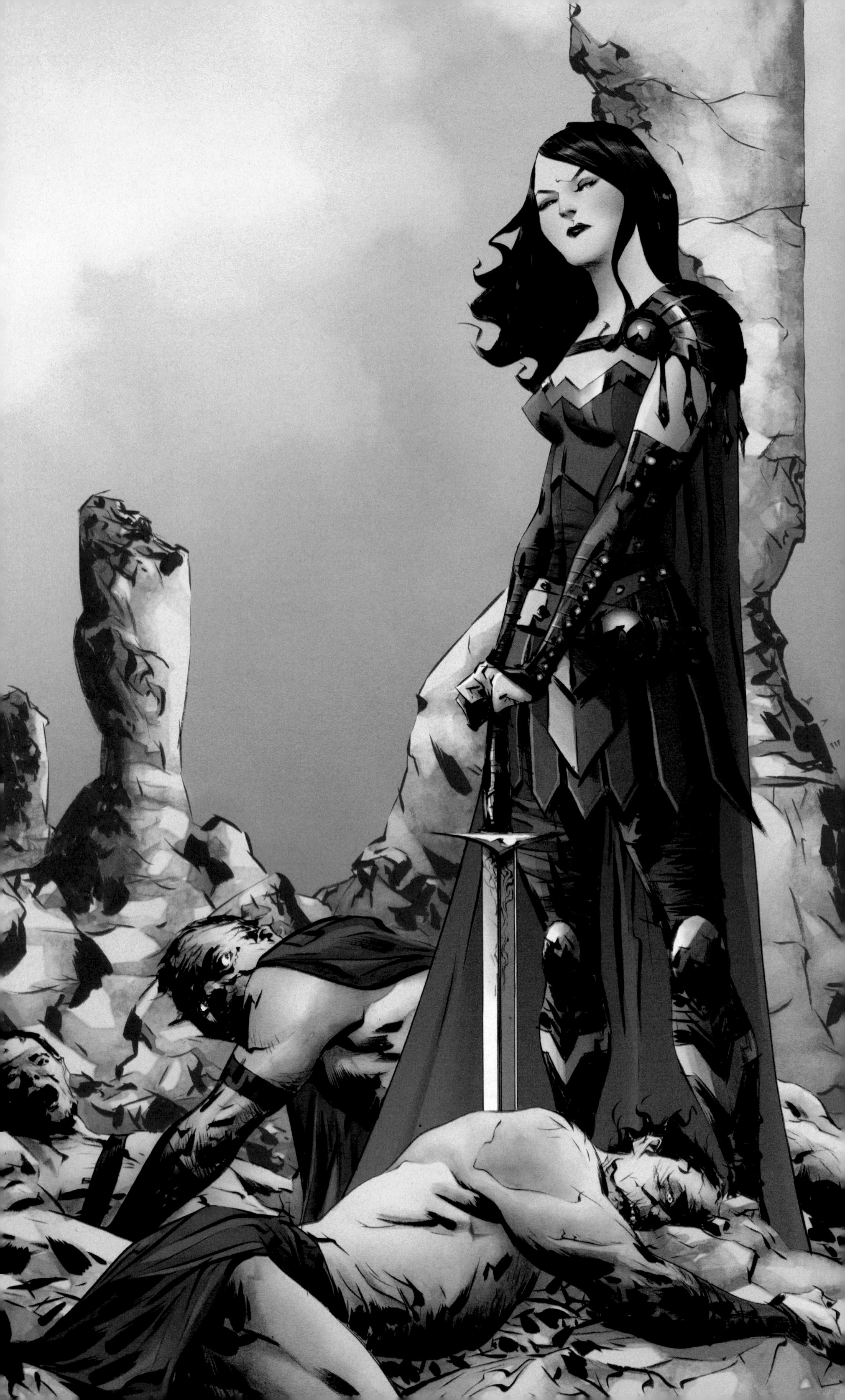

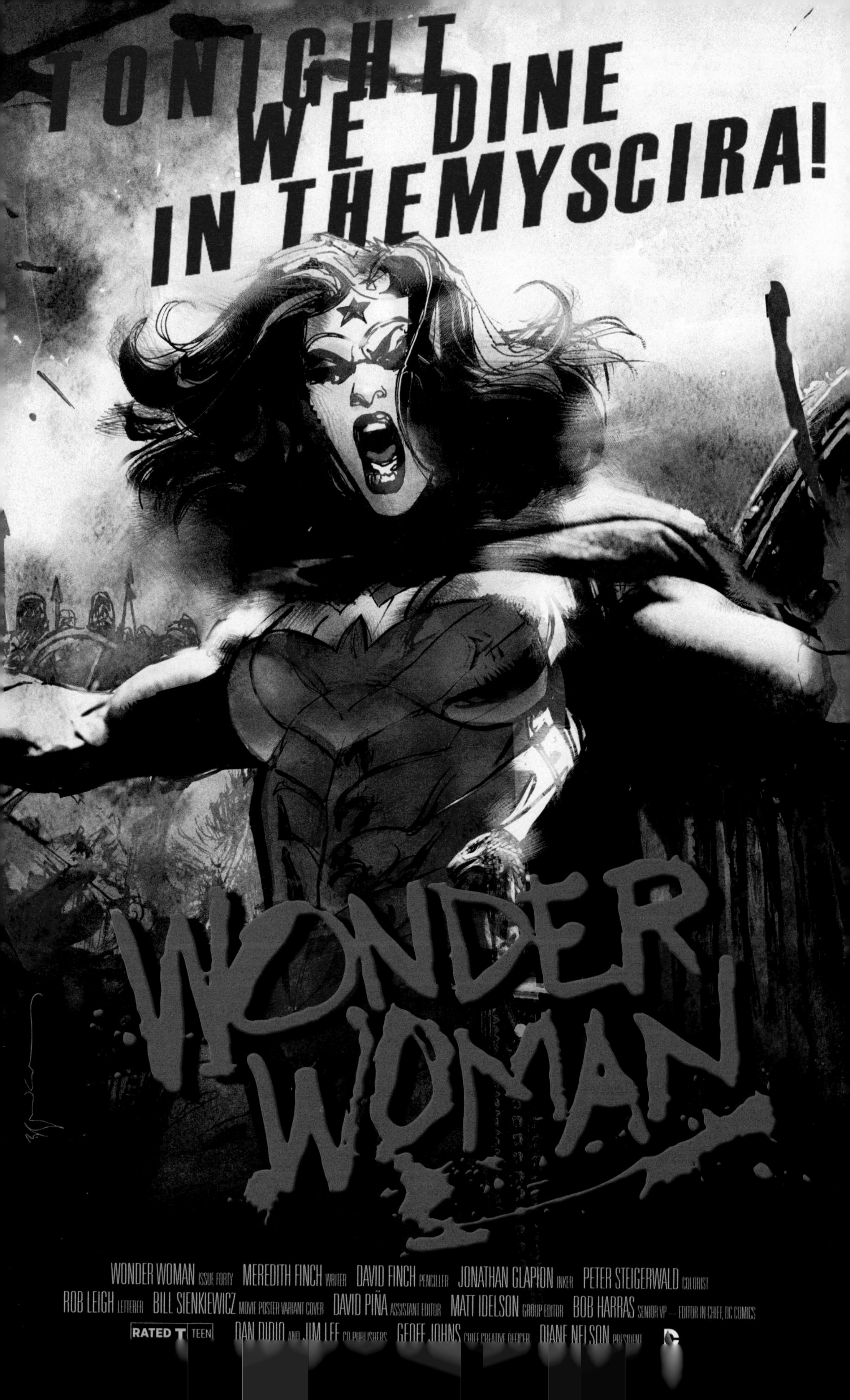
TONIGHT WE DINE IN THEMYSCIRA!
WONDER WOMAN
WONDER WOMAN ISSUE FORTY MEREDITH FINCH WRITER DAVID FINCH PENCILLER JONATHAN GLAPION INKER PETER STEIGERWALD COLORIST
ROB LEIGH LETTERER BILL SIENKIEWICZ MOVIE POSTER VARIANT COVER DAVID PIÑA ASSISTANT EDITOR MATT IDELSON GROUP EDITOR BOB HARRAS SENIOR VP — EDITOR-IN-CHIEF, DC COMICS
RATED T TEEN
DAN DIDIO AND JIM LEE CO-PUBLISHERS GEOFF JOHNS CHIEF CREATIVE OFFICER DIANE NELSON PRESIDENT

COVER SKETCHES BY DAVID FINCH
WONDER WOMAN #36

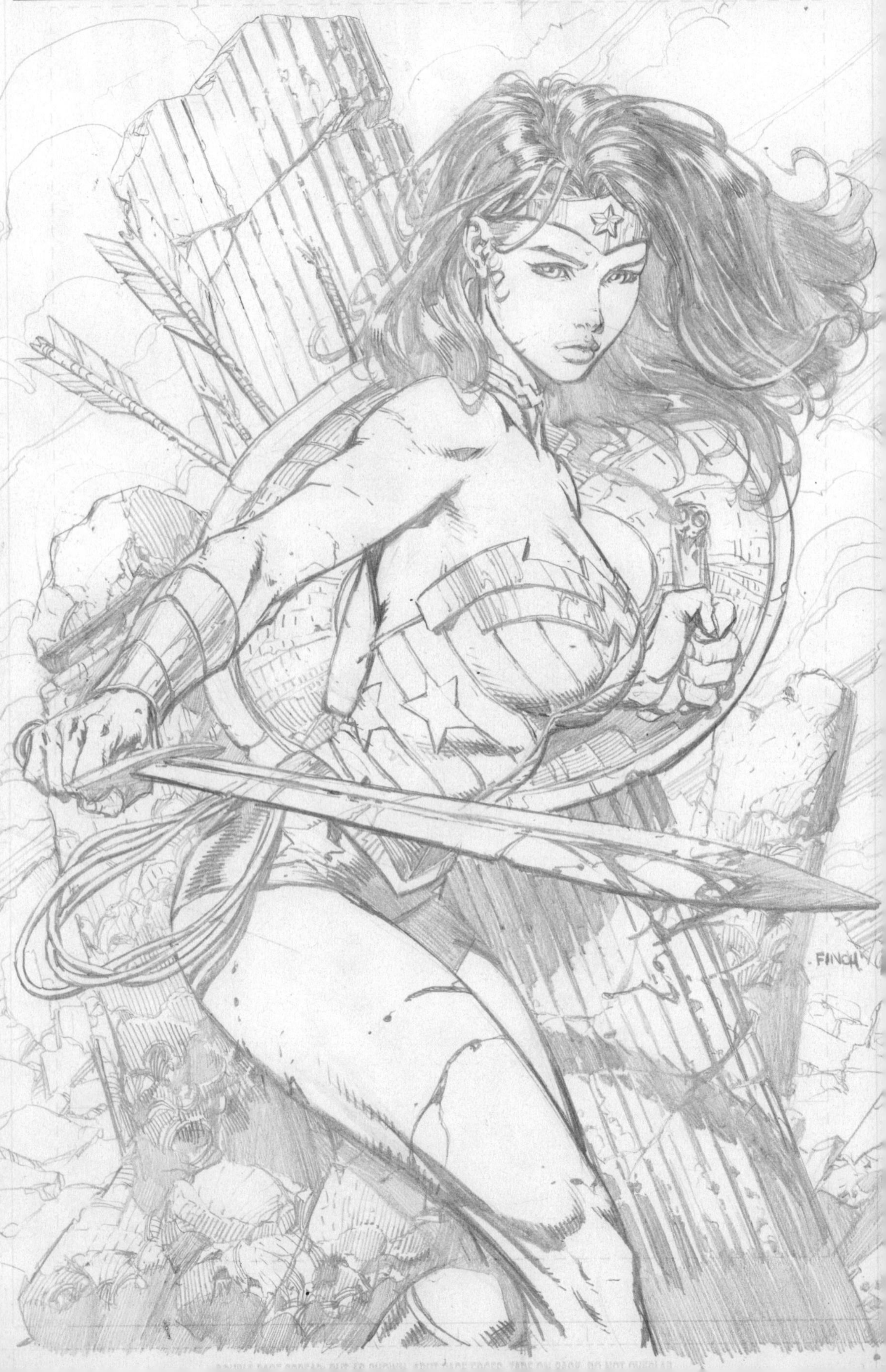

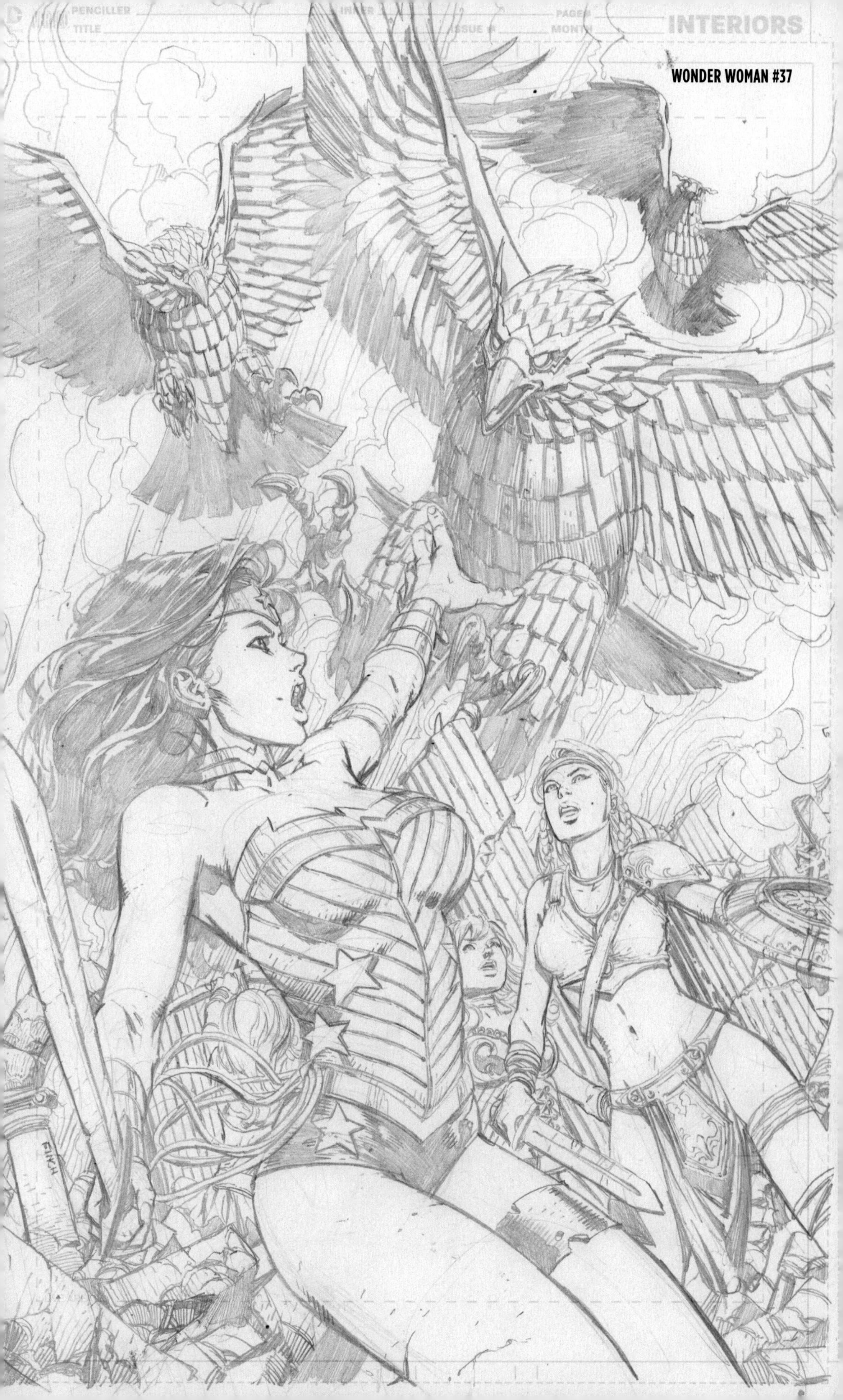
PENCILLER
TITLE
INKER
ISSUE #
PAGES
MONTH
INTERIORS
WONDER WOMAN #37

WONDER WOMAN #38

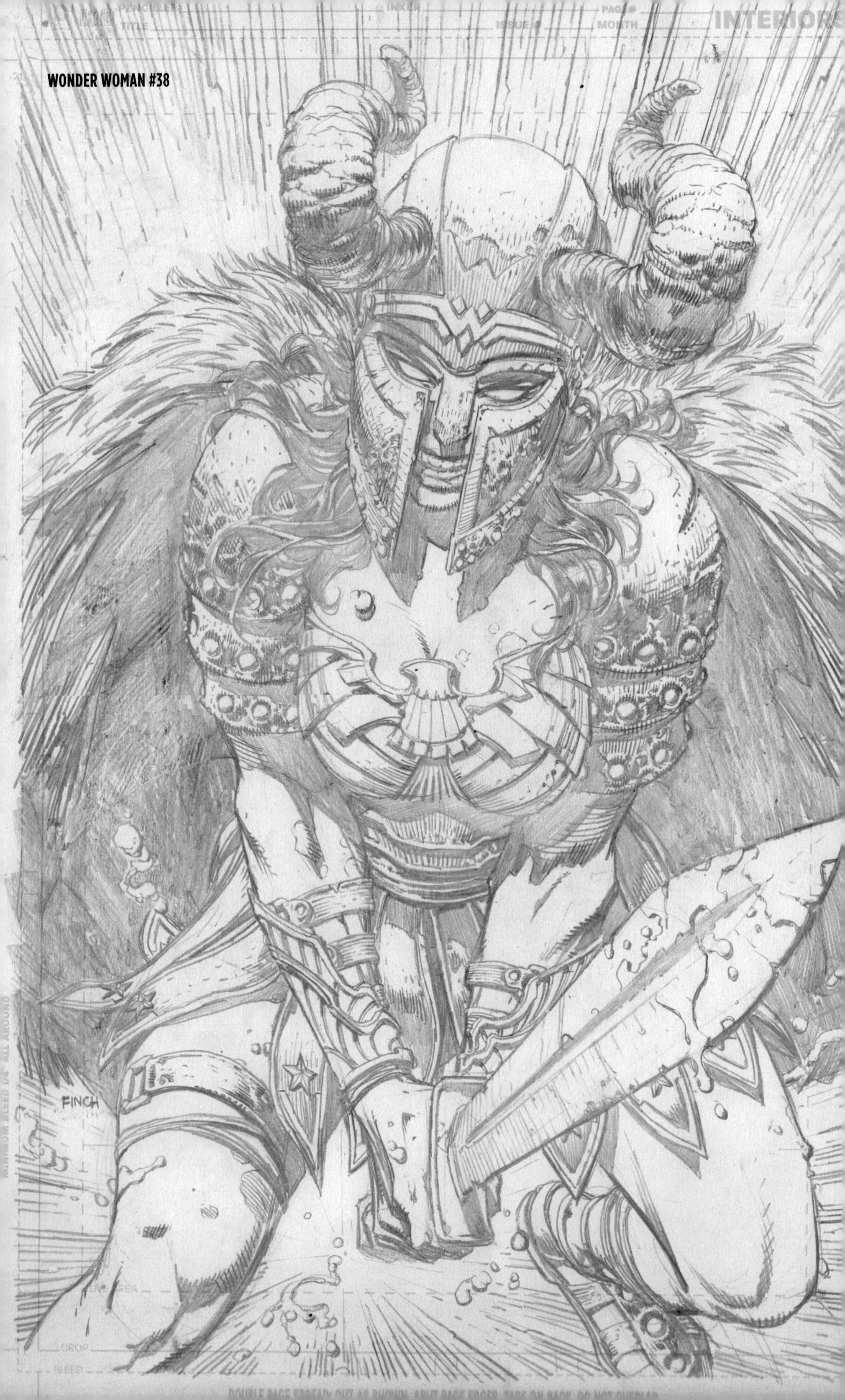
INTERIORS
FINCH

WONDER WOMAN #39

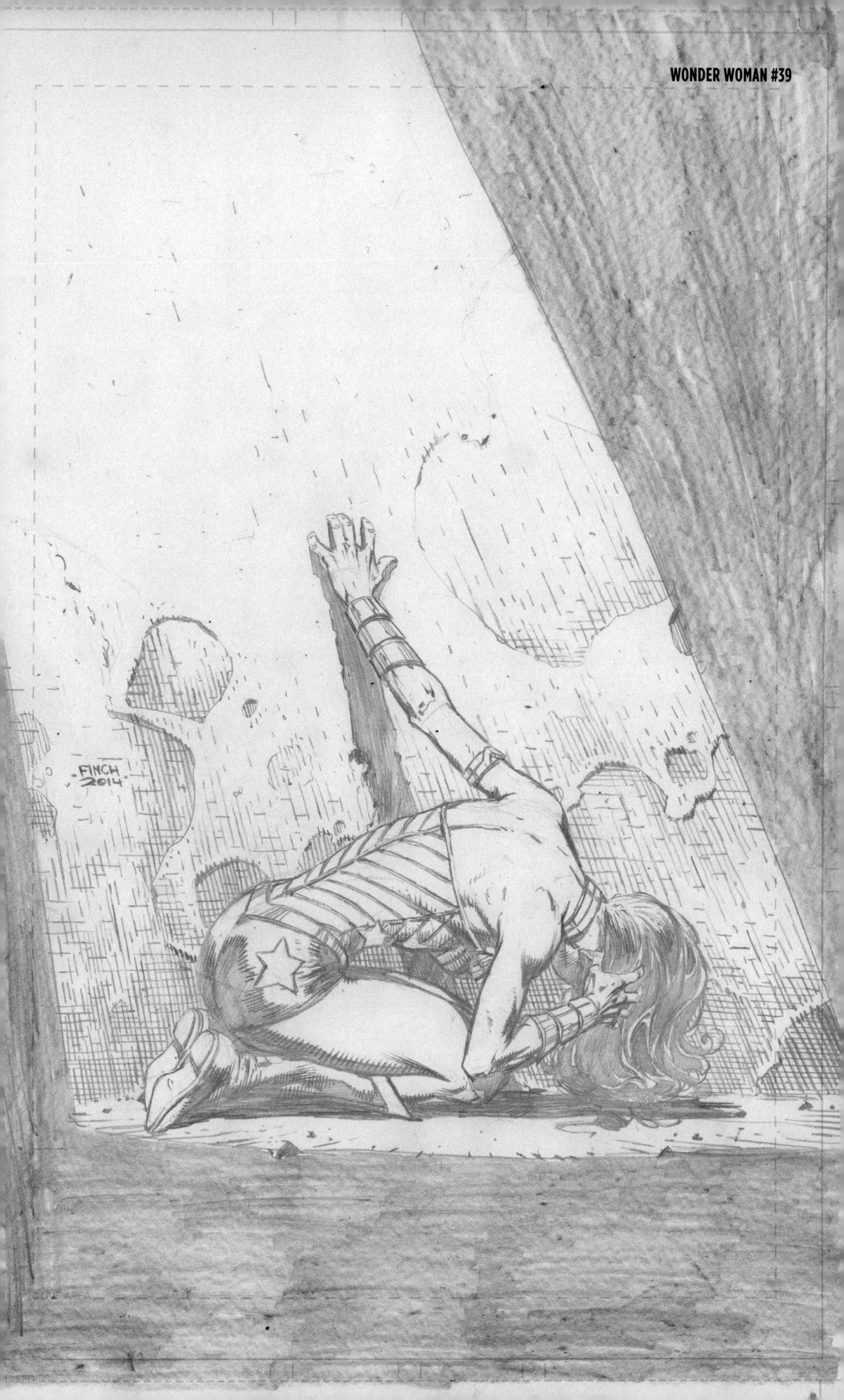
FINCH
2014

WONDER WOMAN #40

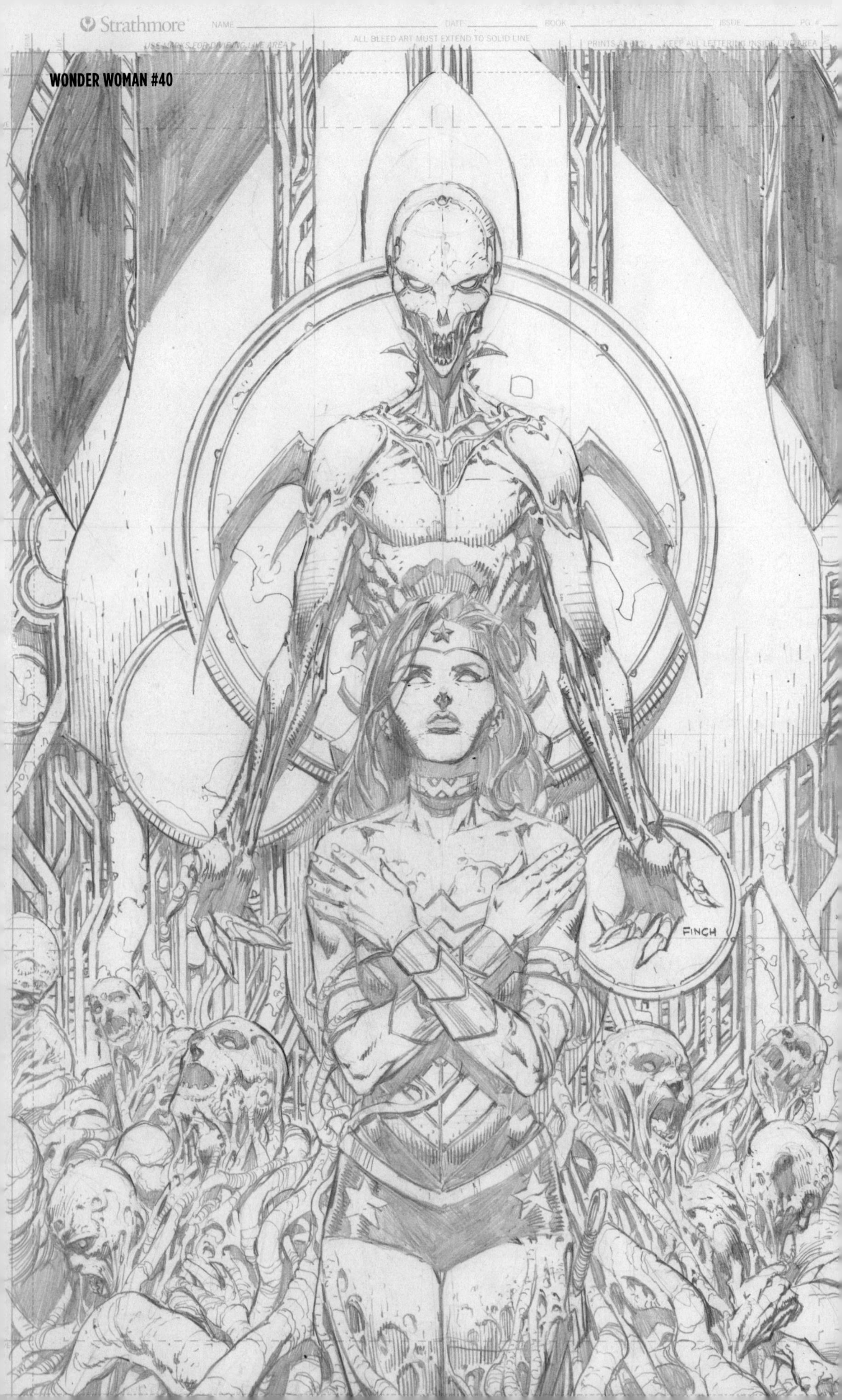
Strathmore
ALL BLEED ART MUST EXTEND TO SOLID LINE
FINCH

"Clear storytelling at its best. It's an intriguing concept and easy to grasp."—THE NEW YORK TIMES

"Azzarello is rebuilding the mythology of Wonder Woman."
—CRAVE ONLINE

START AT THE BEGINNING!

WONDER WOMAN VOLUME 1: BLOOD

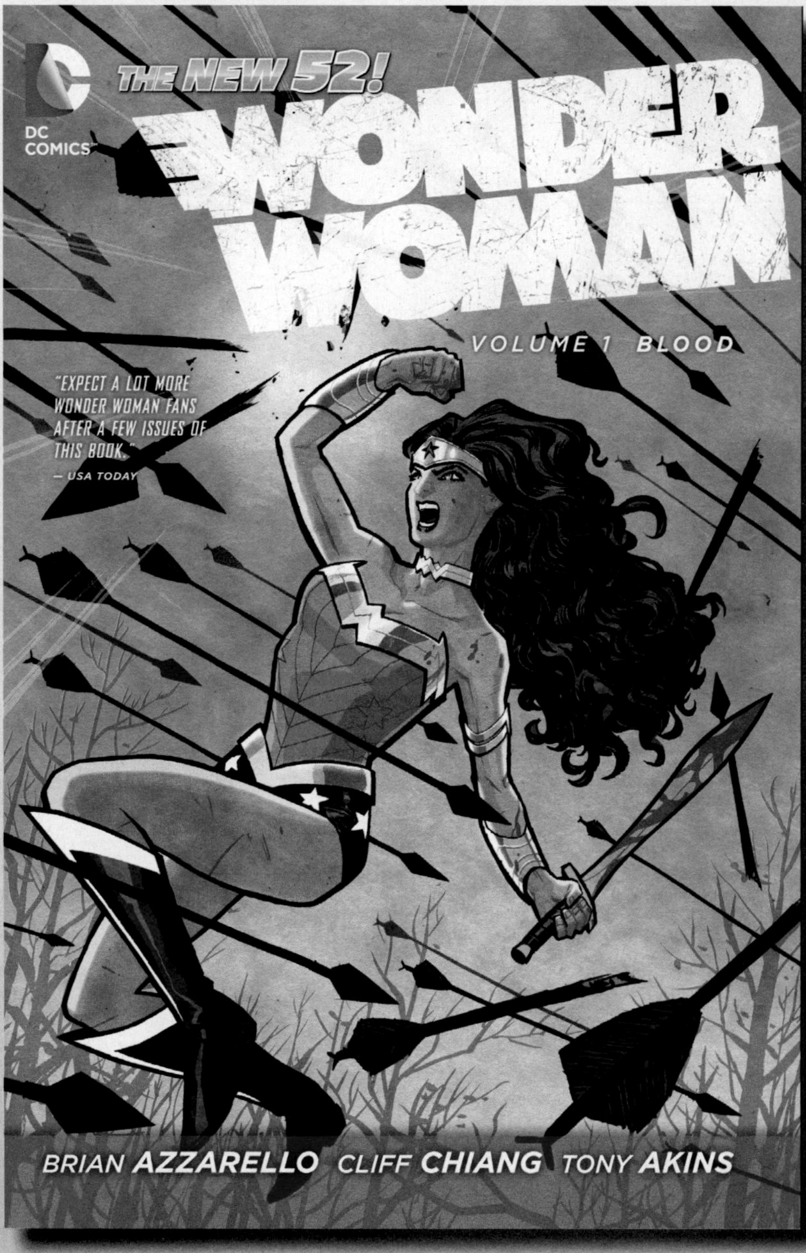

DC COMICS
THE NEW 52!
WONDER WOMAN
VOLUME 1 BLOOD
"EXPECT A LOT MORE WONDER WOMAN FANS AFTER A FEW ISSUES OF THIS BOOK."
— USA TODAY
BRIAN AZZARELLO CLIFF CHIANG TONY AKINS

WONDER WOMAN VOL. 2: GUTS

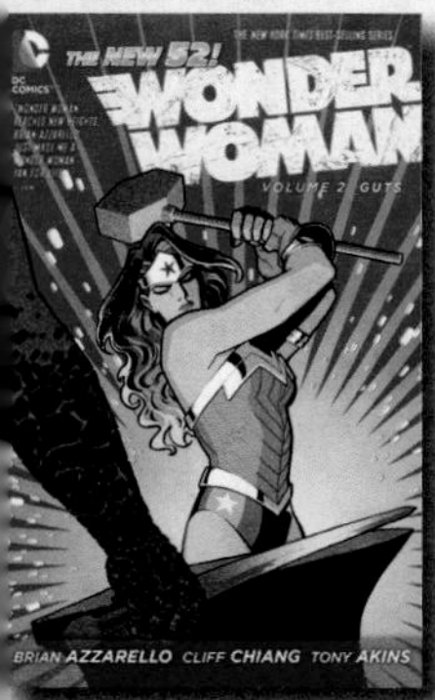

THE NEW 52!
WONDER WOMAN
BRIAN AZZARELLO CLIFF CHIANG TONY AKINS

by BRIAN AZZARELLO and CLIFF CHIANG

WONDER WOMAN VOL. 3: IRON

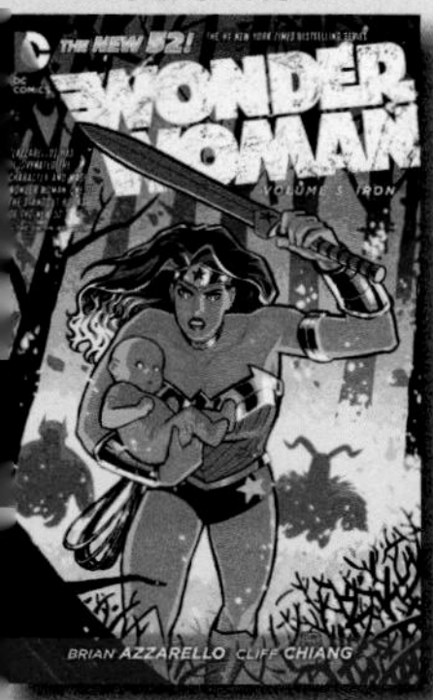

THE NEW 52!
WONDER WOMAN
BRIAN AZZARELLO CLIFF CHIANG

by BRIAN AZZARELLO and CLIFF CHIANG

SUPERGIRL VOL. 1: LAST DAUGHTER OF KRYPTON

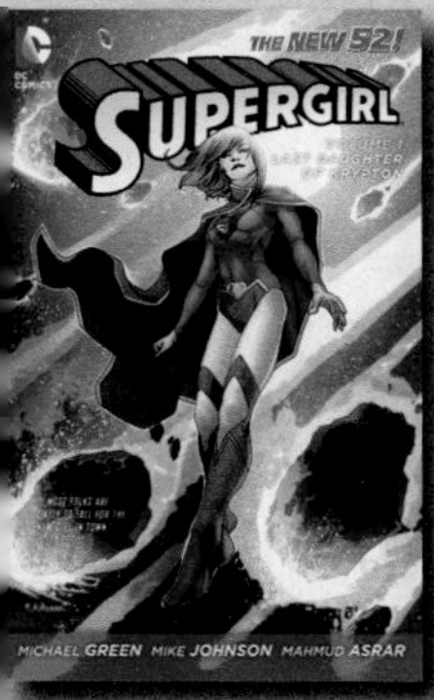

THE NEW 52!
SUPERGIRL
MICHAEL GREEN MIKE JOHNSON MAHMUD ASRAR

DC COMICS™

"Writer Geoff Johns and artist Jim Lee toss you–and the
heroes–into the action from the very start and don't put o
the brakes. DC's über-creative team craft an inviting world fo
those who are trying out a comic for the first time. Lee's art i
stunning."—USA TODA

"A fun ride."—IG

START AT THE BEGINNING!

JUSTICE LEAGUE
VOLUME 1: ORIGIN
GEOFF JOHNS and JIM LEE

JUSTICE LEAGUE
VOL. 2: THE VILLAIN'S
JOURNEY

JUSTICE LEAGUE
VOL. 3: THRONE OF
ATLANTIS

JUSTICE LEAGUE
OF AMERICA VOL. 1:
WORLD'S MOST
DANGEROUS

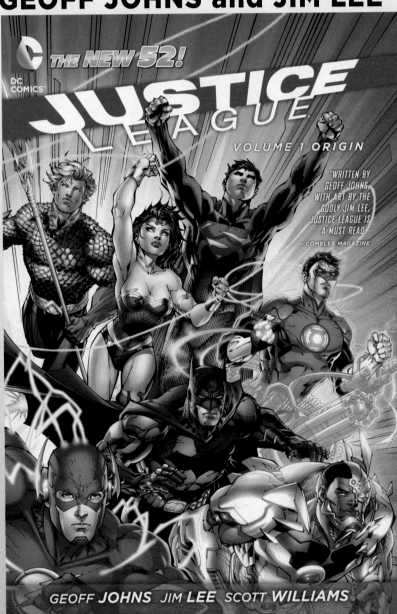

DC COMICS™

THE NEW 52!

JUSTICE LEAGUE

VOLUME 1 ORIGIN

"WRITTEN BY
GEOFF JOHNS,
WITH ART BY THE
GODLY JIM LEE,
JUSTICE LEAGUE IS
A MUST READ."
— COMPLEX MAGAZINE

GEOFF JOHNS JIM LEE SCOTT WILLIAMS